THE EUROPEAN HANDBOOK OF MANAGEMENT CONSULTANCY

The EUROPEAN HANDBOOK *of* MANAGEMENT CONSULTANCY

Strategic Innovation —
A European Approach to
Management Consultancy

EUROPEAN INNOVATION PROGRAMME
(PROJECT RA340 TER)

Oak Tree Press
Dublin

*Strategic Innovation — A European Approach
to Management Consultancy*
Supported by Directorate General XIII-D of the European
Commission. Project RA 340 Ter of the EC Innovation Programme
relates to the publication and dissemination of a manual on strategic
innovation consultancy and the methodology involved throughout
Member States of the European Union.

ISBN 1-86076-010-4 (hbk.)

Printed in Ireland by Colour Books Ltd.

Publisher's Note

To avoid the inappropriate usage of "he" as a general pronoun, as
well as the awkward usage of "he/she" and "his/her" phrasing, this
book follows the convention of using the neutral plural pronoun to
include both men and women as recommended by *Collins Concise
English Dictionary*, e.g., "the analysis will have to be done by the
consultant, since they will have to follow up later."

CONTENTS

I.
OVERALL ORIENTATION

II.
DIAGNOSTIC PHASE

III.
STRATEGIES AND ACTION PLANS

V.
GENERAL TOPICS

FOREWORD

We are living in a global economy and there is ever-increasing pressure on SMEs (small and medium-sized enterprises) to continuously monitor and improve their competitiveness in the context of the international commercial arena.

Although there is a large body of knowledge available in universities, research institutions, development agencies and consultancy firms, nevertheless SMEs often find it difficult to access this knowledge base to enable them to run their businesses using a more structured and planned developmental approach.

In Norway, we succeeded in assisting SMEs in the achievement of their commercial objectives using the BUNT project as a vehicle for change. We organised a joint project organising financial bodies, research institutions, trade associations and consultancy firms including political support from Government. The essence of the project lay in bridging the gap between the external environment and a company's internal operations to harness available knowledge and stimulate SMEs to run their businesses in a more creative way. The main objective was clear:

> To provide long-term profit for SMEs encountering serious competition at home and abroad by improving their competitiveness by using new technology in a strategic and structured way.

In this context the role of consultants as "agents of change" was both pivotal and vital. The best consultants and methodology experts in a variety of organisations were selected with a combination of interpersonal, theoretical and practical skills. They were given the task of keeping and compiling "state-of-the-art" material to initiate effective assignments in companies. In parallel, a comprehensive training programme was put in place to upgrade the consultancy skills profile. The conduct of the training programme was integral to the overall success of the project. The objective was to provide a pool of trained consultants with increased flexibility and professionalism.

In addition, extensive promotion and marketing of the project to SMEs was carried out, along with tight follow-up of assignments and external evaluation of the project impact using independent evaluation personnel.

Solutions were customised for individual companies in terms of the company's business and commercial objectives, rather than the brilliance of the solutions or options proposed.

Can this feat be repeated? My answer is undoubtedly, yes. This project can be repeated in member states throughout the European Union with even better results. The change process can be accelerated and the level of professionalism increased. The real challenge is to locate and identify the people and organisations who are skilled and willing to pull together in the same direction.

I wish you well in reading this book as a reference manual of "best practice".

More importantly, I wish you every success in the implementation of future assignments and trust that these will have the required impact on the improvement of SMEs' competitiveness in your own country.

Erik Skaug
Director, Industry and Energy of
the Research Council of Norway

PREFACE

CONSULTANTS AS AGENTS OF CHANGE

This handbook, as the name suggests, is aimed at management consultants in Europe. A central theme of this manual is the concept of "strategic innovation" — the use of consultants by SMEs to assist them to *innovate* and to change on an ongoing basis.

Thus, the manual asserts the importance for consultants to be able to stimulate improvements in the companies that are their clients. Improvements should include new methods of working, the introduction of new systems, new equipment and organisational changes. Consultants must impress upon their clients the importance of innovation and change on an ongoing basis — those companies that are not developing will ultimately not survive. In today's competitive environment, a company must be continually progressing forward. If it is not, it will automatically be in a state of decline — it is not possible to stand still.

When carrying out consultancy assignments, consultants must gain an understanding of the company's overall situation so that any recommendations made are done with reference to the commercial realities. Thus, this manual proposes the following general method for conducting consultancy assignments in SMEs:

- **Step 1:** Carry out a general strategic analysis of the company to arrive at the main issues that are of prime concern to the company.

- **Step 2:** Follow on with more detailed work on devising a strategy and action plans in relation to the areas identified during the general strategic analysis.

- **Step 3:** Implementation of measures and evaluation of results. The responsibility for implementation should primarily rest with the client.

The above methodology closely mirrors that of the Norwegian BUNT (Business Development using New Technology) programme. BUNT, however, concentrated on identifying areas in which *technology* could be used to support and complement the company's overall business strategy. In this handbook, the emphasis is on *innovation by all means*. The use of technology is just one method, albeit an extremely important one, through which innovation can be introduced.

A competent consultant will always seek to understand all aspects of a client company's situation (whether the client offers the information readily or not). In this sense, the competent consultant will use many of the techniques and methods presented in this manual as a matter of course, and will not confine their investigations exclusively to a given problem area for which they may have been hired to solve. This book, however, attempts to bring the relevant techniques together into a structured unit to assist the consultant in executing the consultancy assignment more efficiently.

OBJECTIVES

The specific objectives of this manual or "toolkit" are as follows:

1. To produce a comprehensive handbook in which consultants can find guidance on most topics relevant to management consultancy in SMEs.

2. The handbook is based on the Norwegian BUNT concept and methodology combined with the experience and methodology of the Irish NTAP (National Technology Audit Programme). Contributions from RKW in Germany and from DTI in Denmark are also included.

3. The manual can be used as an aid for training management consultants, both public and private, with particular emphasis on strategic innovation.

STRUCTURE

Following an introduction, this handbook is presented in five sections:

Introduction

This gives an account of the background to the material that was used in compiling the manual. A brief description of the BUNT programme in Norway and of the National Technology Audit Programme in Ireland is included. The objectives of the manual are presented.

Section 1: Overall Orientation

This section presents some general concepts that are considered to be relevant to all consultancy assignments today. Topics covered include strategic management, new management concepts, the management of change, and process consultancy.

Sections 2 – 4: Consultancy Phases

These sections give practical notes which are aimed at assisting the consultant at carrying out assignments. Each of these three deals with a different phase of the consultancy work:

Section 2: Diagnostic Phase

Section 3: Strategy and Action Plan

Section 4: Implementation and Evaluation

The division of the consultancy work into three phases is done for analytical convenience — in practice, the three phases will overlap and consultants will find themselves backtracking from time to time. This is essential so as to take new factors, new ideas or new opportunities into account as they arise and as projects develop.

Section 5: General Topics

This section is made up of a body of reference material which the consultant should find useful when more detailed information on a specific topic is required. The intention is that consultants will select those sections within this part of the handbook that are relevant to a given assignment at any time.

INTRODUCTION

This handbook has been assembled from material prepared in Norway, Ireland, Germany and Denmark.

- The bulk of the Norwegian contribution is made up of a series of *"Theme Booklets"* and *"Technique Notes"* which were written for the BUNT (Business Development Using New Technology) programme in that country.

- The bulk of the Irish contribution is made up of a series of lecture notes prepared by Forbairt (formerly EOLAS, The Irish Science and Technology Agency) for a training programme carried out during 1992 in Greece. The objective of the training was to introduce the methodology of the NTAP (National Technology Audit Programme), which has been running in Ireland since 1989, into Greece.

- The German contribution comes from RKW (Rationalisierungs-kuratorium der Deutschen Wirtschaft) and includes papers dealing with the concepts of Lean Production.

- The Danish contribution comes from DTI (Danish Technological Institute) and includes papers on matters relating to human resources.

THE BUNT PROGRAMME IN NORWAY

The BUNT programme was carried out in Norway between 1989 and 1992. It was funded by the Royal Norwegian Council for Scientific and Industrial Research (NTNF).

The idea behind the BUNT programme was to link the use of new technology with strategic planning. Accordingly, a sub-programme administered by Teknologisk Institutt — Strategic Business Development (SBD) — formed part of the BUNT programme. As part of this sub-programme, a group of experienced Norwegian consultants were trained to disseminate strategic thinking to the participating companies. The training was quite extensive. In all, the consultants were in training for ten days spread over three gatherings. The courses gave those attending an introduction to strategic planning, some information on new technology as a development factor, and a little about how they were to contribute to company-internal development processes.

Practical BUNT assignments were carried out in participating companies in three phases:

- First, a general strategic analysis was carried out. This phase, referred to as the BUNT "pilot project", involved between 3 and 5 days of the consultant's time. The report from this phase formed the basis of deciding whether to proceed with a main project and if so what were the areas which were to be worked on.

- The second phase, involving the remaining 15 to 17 days of the consultant's time, looked at areas identified in the pilot project in greater detail. It involved carrying out further analyses and arriving at a list of prioritised measures.

- The third phase involved implementation of the measures adopted. Implementation was the responsibility of the companies themselves.

The target group was industrial production companies facing competition, with over twenty employees. In all, there are about 1,200 such companies in Norway of which 327 entered the SBD programme. The programme was extensively subsidised, with only 25 per cent of consultancy costs being financed by the companies themselves.

The analyses carried out were based on the strategic thinking of the Harvard school. This American model emphasises that for each product/market combination a company has, it must choose whether it wishes to focus most on price, quality, customisation or other aspects. Then the company must draw up action plans with measures (technological, financial, organisational etc.) which support the strategy. A clear distinction between planning and implementation is also assumed.

In addition to the strategic analyses in individual companies, a number of individual projects were carried out. The aim of these projects was to *encourage strategic alliances between companies*. These projects can be categorised as follows:

- Projects with the aim of solving specific, limited technical problems in individual companies.

- Projects oriented towards the transfer of new technology to specific groups of companies.

- Projects that focused on the various production phases of a product with the aim of optimising value creation in a production chain running through several companies.

It was also an important strategy to integrate the thinking in BUNT with other ongoing programmes for technology transfer or business development. The basic idea was that the companies would emerge strengthened from a unified, concentrated application of resources.

BUNT was also active on the European scene. As early as the initial phases it was clear that the EC programme SPRINT was interested in the models on which BUNT was based. Over a period of two years a co-operative arrangement was developed on the use of BUNT in Europe. This effort was given the name EURO-BUNT. Through this activity BUNT was also linked with recent progress in business development programmes in the EC. The new MINT (Managing the Integration of New Technology) programme can to a great extent be viewed as a large-scale application of central models from BUNT.

During the course of the BUNT programme a group of researchers were associated with the programme so they could continuously monitor all the activities. They reported regularly to the programme management on the progress and results of the programme. This activity, which is called *formative evaluation*, was meant to generate data and analyses which would be useful in the work of the programme management.

USE OF CONSULTANTS

Consultant Training

The SBD part of the BUNT programme trained its own consultants to conduct strategic analyses in companies. A "toolkit" was created, consisting of about 50 Technique Notes and 11 Theme Booklets. The aim was to give consultants a specialised background for implementing strategic analyses in the companies. The course material was drawn up by two central consultancy firms (ISI and Habberstad), the National Institute of Technology, SINTEF and NTNF.

The courses were very popular. For the first course, the BUNT programme received 250 applications for 20 places. Of those who participated, 80 per cent were engineering or economics graduates with industrial experience.

Gradually this training attracted great attention to the point where many people from the *resource apparatus*, i.e. public agencies supporting businesses with knowledge or funding, expressed a wish to participate in the training without any ambition to practice as consultants. A shorter BUNT course was therefore developed, lasting seven days. Thus the BUNT thinking has been widely dispersed throughout the resource apparatus and it is felt that the programme has helped to define a professional standard for consultants accordingly.

Furthermore, BUNT assignments carried out by the private consultancy sector have helped to develop the professional position of the consultancy firms involved. Analysis of the programme shows that the BUNT resources triggered off an extensive effort oriented towards the consultants' own competence development.

QUALITY ASSURANCE

In the BUNT programme there was a strong focus on quality assurance. The first phase of the quality assurance process related to a review of the pilot project reports by the BUNT management team. This gave the programme management the opportunity to evaluate the quality of the consultants' work and also to assess whether the company should continue with a main project. In all, 22 per cent of projects were stopped after completion of the pilot project. This demonstrates the level of importance the programme management attached to quality rather than quantity.

The second phase of quality assurance work involved a systematic review by the management of the BUNT programme of the report on the main project. The companies themselves generally assessed the work of the consultants as having been most valuable. Most of the consultants were considered very able, and the amount of negative feedback was very small.

THE STRATEGY PERSPECTIVE

Results in the SBD Companies

The participating companies that completed a BUNT main project have become better equipped for adaptation and development measures. This also includes an improved ability to use external consultants. These improvements in strategic competence and capacity for development work are quite clearly due to BUNT.

The companies' ability to implement prioritised measures, however, still needs to be more strongly developed if good measures are not to be given too low a priority. The companies implemented a third of all the planned tasks in the course of a few months after the completion of the project. The progressive drive contributed by the project and the consultant gradually faded out, and many tasks were given excessively low priority. The rationale of having the programme assist with planning and having the companies themselves take care of the implementation was challenged in many companies.

BUNT has, on the other hand, made a clear contribution to improved competence in strategic planning, and the companies have increased their capacity for this kind of work, particularly through reorganisations.

STRATEGIC ANALYSES AS A MEANS

In 23 per cent of the companies that participated in the programme, BUNT did not initiate the most important technological solutions that were in fact implemented. The implication from this is that companies may have changed their strategy, their internal analyses and their orientation in the technology market, *independently* of the specific recommendations of the main project report. This would indicate that the companies engaged in strategic work where planning was not as strictly separated from implementation as required in the course material for the BUNT consultants. This indicates that BUNT contributed to a Norwegian-style strategy process which combined the best of the Harvard school with the best of the Mintzberg tradition, which places more emphasis on strategy and which does not make as clear a distinction between planning and implementation.

STRATEGIC ALLIANCES

None of the projects exhibit examples of companies succeeding during the planned project period in achieving vertical integration of the production chain among two or more co-operating companies. The conclusion is that there is no sign of any substantial progress in the interplay between the companies.

From Technological Push to Technological Pull

In BUNT, the implementation of the strategic analyses makes technology a subordinate issue. Insofar as technology can provide solutions to the problems of the company, the company will place its technological wishes in an overall, financially profitable context. The company has thus become a demander of new technology (pull logic). Traditionally, public agencies have tried to get businesses which were aware of new technologies to adapt and use those technologies (push logic). The BUNT programme shows that the companies' need for new technology is great and that the vast majority of companies have in fact implemented new technology.

The advantage of the pull logic is that the companies place the use of new technology in an overall framework, and that the risk of mistaken investments and over-investment in new technology becomes substantially less than has often been the case when a push logic is used.

PROGRAMME MANAGEMENT

The BUNT programme has had a management culture which has many features in common with good corporate management.

Other programmes could learn from this to their advantage. The following factors should be considered in this regard:

- BUNT systematically developed the programme on the basis of the experience gained along the way. The development of the programme was based on the personal experience gained by the programme management's open, receptive attitude to the users of the programme — mainly the companies — and by their reflection on the discussion of input from the evaluation team.

- The BUNT programme entered into several strategic alliances at the programme level. This has meant that thinking and experience from the BUNT programme quickly spread to other relevant environments.

- The BUNT courses held for other interested parties (Norwegian Regional Development Fund, The Norwegian Industrial Fund, the ministries and the NTNF) meant that the basic BUNT model for business development was communicated to all the central Norwegian players in the field of management consultancy.

- The BUNT programme included seminars to which consultants, people in the resource apparatus and the evaluation team could meet for discussions. BUNT, therefore, opened up a forum for dialogue between all of the parties involved in consultancy in Norway.

- The BUNT programme brought new experience of formative evaluation to those in the public sector who were involved in managing the programme. A formative evaluation is conducted for the programme management while the programme is in progress. The formative evaluation thus ensured that the BUNT programmes took on the character of a *learning organisation*.

LESSONS LEARNED FROM BUNT

The eight points that follow represent the central elements in what was learnt about the contribution of BUNT to the total Norwegian resource apparatus:

The Companies

1. Strategic thinking as in the BUNT programme model can function as an important tool for making technological investments within a wider economic framework. In this way, investments in technology must always be commercially justified.

2. It is important to link the drawing-up of a strategic plan more with the implementation of measures that are identified. This way one can ensure that the company becomes a continuously learning organisation.

The Consultants

3. If consultants are to play a central role in a national innovation system, then the consultancy sector must be provided with competence that will make it professionally capable of performing its functions. In addition, it is important to ensure that their work is subject to quality assurance by establishing standards of good work and systems to make sure that quality standards are maintained.

4. The work of consultants should help to solve the short-term problems of companies; but the consultants must also be able to work such that the companies themselves learn something. To achieve this, consultants must not only have an adequate specialised background, but must also be aware of theories, methods and techniques which ensure that the employees of the company learn and develop as a result of the work of the consultant.

5. In a situation where the management in many companies is up to its ears in everyday chores, an external agent can have a positive effect by drawing attention to project implementation.

Thus consultants can become the driving force behind implementation of measures.

Programme Level

6. Publicly-subsidised programmes for business development must have a different management culture from that of the administration. It is of fundamental importance that programmes for business development are viewed as learning organisations where continuous, genuine monitoring of developments contribute directly to a learning process that means that the programme can be adapted in the light of new experience gained. A programme for business development must have a management which thinks strategically and tactically.

7. The formative model for evaluation which has been used in BUNT can form a pattern for, amongst other things, the activities of the SPRINT programme. A great deal of effort has been spent in Norway on developing this evaluation model, and it is important to develop it further.

8. New programmes for business development should become part of the infrastructure of the public support system, even if the programmes are successful. It is important to think of programmes as systematic efforts to find new and better ways of providing support for the development of companies. The activities in a programme must also be such that systematic experimentation and evaluation are carried out.

THE NATIONAL TECHNOLOGY AUDIT PROGRAMME IN IRELAND

The National Technology Audit Programme (NTAP) was launched in Ireland in 1989. The Programme is co-funded by the European Regional Development Fund and is administered by Forbairt (formerly EOLAS, The Irish Science and Technology Agency).

A Technology Audit is an assessment of the current status of technology employed in a company in relation to products, human and material resources. It recommends how existing technology can be improved to increase profitability. Technology cannot be examined in isolation and finance, marketing, product quality and management, where they impact on production, will influence the recommendations made.

The NTAP is presently carried out in two phases. The initial audit (phase I) was augmented in 1990 by the introduction of an Implementation Programme (phase II) which was designed to support and assist companies in the implementation of recommendations and strategies made in phase I.

The output from phase I — the initial audit — is a detailed report identifying opportunities which form the basis for the company's future manufacturing and/or business strategy. Phase II represents the implementation of the developmental strategy identified in the initial audit.

The number of projects completed by mid-1995 was as follows:

Phase I audits	630
Phase II implementation projects	250

The NTAP is designed to reduce costs and to improve profits. Participating companies are provided with an action plan containing recommendations on:

- Improved manufacturing techniques including purchase of capital equipment on a cost/benefit basis.

- Opportunities for cost reduction and/or productivity improvement.

- Improved product quality, reduction of inventory and minimisation of waste.

- Long-term company development.

The emphasis is on appropriate technology, realisable by client companies.

The NTAP is targeted primarily at small to medium-sized indigenous manufacturing enterprises (SMEs) employing less than 50 people and with an annual turnover of less than IR£3 million.

METHODOLOGY

The programme is executed by an experienced team of engineering and business consultants, with extensive "hands-on" experience in manufacturing and/or commercial management. The core team may be augmented by other specialist consultants, depending on the nature of the assignment.

Each audit involves:

- Interviews with key company personnel, normally for about half a day

- On-site assessment of methods and procedures, lasting two to five days

- Investigations off-site and preparation of a detailed report lasting five to seven days

- A follow-up visit usually about six to twelve months after completion of the initial audit.

RESULTS TO DATE

The initial phase I audit is in effect a "snapshot" of the business and it identifies potential opportunities for enhancing the operational efficiency of SMEs by reducing costs, increasing efficiency, improving productivity and customer service. All of these opportunities enable the companies to grow with a consequent impact on wealth and added value in the Irish economy and on employment. Typically, the phase I audit attracts SMEs into the use of external expertise, where before companies either did not identify the need or could not afford the cost.

Phase II assignments are longer term, more in-depth and of a more strategic nature. In effect, they assist companies to continue to exploit the opportunities identified in phase I and to structure specific strategic projects harnessing expertise not normally within, or identified by, the company.

Audits have been carried out across all sectors of Irish manufacturing industry. The table in Figure 1 gives a breakdown by industry sector of phase I audits carried out during 1993:

Figure 1: Audits by Industry Sector

Sector	No. of companies	%
Engineering	31	34
Chemical/pharmaceuticals	8	9
Furniture/timber processing	6	7
Food processing	7	8
Plastics	5	5
Electronics	10	11
Clothing/textiles	12	13
Paper processing	9	10
Other	3	3

Recommendations arising from phase I audits vary from company to company. The table in Figure 2 gives a breakdown of recommendations made during 1993 by category.

Figure 2: Phase I Recommendations by Category

Category	% of Total Recommendations
Management information systems	17
Investment in equipment	14
Manufacturing methods	13
Manufacturing systems	12
Quality systems	11
Layout and material flow	11
Cost control	10
Management structure	8
New products	4

A brief description of recommendation categories is given below:

- **Management information systems.** Advice on improving management information systems. This includes methods to improve production planning and control, inventory control, maintenance management and marketing.

- **Investment in equipment.** Advice on investment in new machinery. Details are given on the type of machine to purchase and the capital costs. In many cases, a cost/benefit analysis is carried out on the equipment recommended.

- **Manufacturing methods.** Advice on improving methods of manufacture by reducing production costs, improving quality and increasing production output.

- **Manufacturing systems.** Advice on improving systems of manufacturing to achieve optimum productivity.

- **Quality systems.** Advice on the installation of Total Quality Management systems, normally with a view to achieving registration to ISO 9000.

- **Layout and material flow.** Advice on improving factory layout and material flow to enable the achievement of more effective utilisation of space and improved handling systems.

- **Cost control.** Advice on cost control to enable the standardisation of initial product costing and thereafter ensure effective control of all costs.

- **Management structure.** Advice on management structure to ensure that effective reporting functions were identified and put in place.

- **New products.** Advice relating to diversification of product range into new complimentary products.

An important finding of the programme over the past five years is that the over-riding need of Irish small industry lies in the general area of organisation. Most small industries have a working knowledge of their individual technologies but seem to have difficulty in bringing to bear the necessary disciplines and procedures to make their companies smooth running and efficient.

The audits point to significant weaknesses and scope for improvement in manufacturing efficiency, productivity improvement and cost reduction with a resultant impact on enhanced profitability. It is also noted that the level of product and process innovation is low.

PROGRAMME IMPACT

A database has been used since the early years of the programme to assess its impact. Information extracted from this database shows that on average 50 per cent of recommendations are adopted and implemented by participating companies. This figure relates to the number of recommendations either started or completed at the time of the return visit which is carried out between 6 and 12 months after the initial audit. The database also reveals that companies plan to implement a further 25 per cent of recommendations, thus leaving only 25 per cent of all recommendations that are discarded by participating companies.

When performance data for participating companies is analysed, results show that companies on average have improved between the time of the audit and the return visit as follows:

Employment	+ 5.4 %
Turnover/employee	+ 12.3 %
Turnover	+ 18.4 %
Profit	+ 41.3 %

In summary, the following points can be made:

1. The level of receptivity to both phases of the programme in the market-place continues to be high. Phase II, the implementation phase, is consistently attracting greater interest since it was introduced in 1990.

2. The performance of companies that have accessed the programme is considerably better than average in terms of employment creation, turnover increase and profit generation.

3. The value of the programme in the context of industrial development has been demonstrated and closer links will continue to be forged with other development agencies, to more fully exploit the potential of the programme and to ensure its integration with the company development process.

4. The programme is cost-effective and represents "value for money" for the State.

PART I

OVERALL ORIENTATION

STRATEGIC MANAGEMENT

INTRODUCTION

This chapter deals with how a company should work on strategic management, what analyses should be carried out, and how a business strategy should be formulated.

The concept of strategic management includes both the *formulation* and *implementation* of the business strategy. In this chapter, however, the emphasis is on the formulation of the strategy, rather than on implementation. This emphasis does not mean that implementation is in any way less important — in fact, quite the contrary is true. The reason for emphasising strategy formulation at this point is that a large number of techniques and tools are available to assist with the formulation of a business strategy, whereas implementation on the whole follows the same pattern as other processes of transformation.

Strategy today is very much a matter of beating competitors in over-saturated markets. Business is often likened to a kind of warfare. Hans Werthén, Chairman of Electrolux, has said: "Unlike the military, industry is always at war. In peacetime, this is called 'cartels' and as we know this is illegal."

In this chapter, strategic management is looked at under the following headings:

- The Concept of Strategy and Strategic Management

- The Strategy Process

- Assessment of External Factors

- Assessment of Internal Factors in the Company

- Assessment of Strengths and Weaknesses against Opportunities and Threats

- Formulation of Strategy
- Technology Strategies
- Implementation of the Strategy.

THE CONCEPT OF STRATEGY AND STRATEGIC MANAGEMENT

At present there is no unambiguous, generally accepted definition of the concept of business strategy. It is important, therefore, to clarify what is meant by strategy in this case. The definition that will be used here is:

> "A strategy is a general plan for the way the company will deploy its competence and resources in order to achieve its overall goals."

A strategy states how the company will deploy its competence and resources to meet market needs such that it will earn money. It is therefore important to define what the company can do and what it cannot do, and the means at its command. These impose constraints on its potential for development. The company's competence and resources must be assessed against the demands made by the market, and against the competence and resources of competitors.

Strategy involves positioning relative to markets and competitors in a way that gives the company competitive advantage. The important thing is to give customers increased satisfaction of their needs, and/or to create this customer perception of value more effectively than the competitors.

The main goal in business is to increase the value of the company to the owners. In most cases this can be expressed in the form of return on capital investment. Return on investment is in turn a function of the earnings created by the company compared with the capital employed to achieve this. Return on investment is therefore affected both by earnings and capital utilisation.

In a strategy one also wants to set oneself certain subgoals that state how the company will achieve its main goal. The subgoals are more operational in nature and are tied to the "functions" (i.e. units) of the company. One subgoal, for example, could be to become the market leader. Becoming the market leader is not a goal in itself, but is likely to give the company a position that means it will create more value relative to its competitors, and will thus have a better return on investment than is usual in the industry. In other words, subgoals are means of achieving the main goals.

That a strategy is a general plan means that it should state the general direction in which the company is to move. The plan is also a rough statement of how the company is to move in the required general direction.

Often there will be several possible general directions and thus several ways of reaching the goal. This means that a strategy is a deliberate choice. Strategy is, in other words, not something that comes by itself, but something that management takes an active decision on. So it is dependent on the way management perceives and defines its activities and its surroundings. The plan is a guiding framework for all the decisions that are necessary to determine the nature, direction and rate of development of the enterprise.

A strategy will in general have a long-term perspective. Companies will nevertheless change strategy at regular intervals as the need arises.

Strategic management involves the drawing up and implementation of a strategy. The task itself therefore becomes a process. In drawing up a strategy it is important to have a good methodology for analyses and discussion in the management group. When it comes to the initiation of the strategy, it is important to arrange the process so that it creates commitment and follow-up in the organisation. The strategy must be detailed for each of the functional units of the company in the form of measures and budgets. So that the company will know whether it is moving in the right direction, routines for following up on the plan must be established. Deviations from the plan must be analysed, and the strategy must be adjusted if the assumptions on which the plan is based change radically.

THE STRATEGY PROCESS

Every company must have customers. In a competitive situation it needs to offer products and services that are more attractive than those of the competition, and must at the same time do this more effectively than the competition, so that the company will earn money. The problem is that both the market and the competitors are in constant flux, so the company must constantly think ahead. The "strategic triangle" shown in Figure 1.1 expresses the essence of business activity.

Figure 1.1: The Strategy Triangle

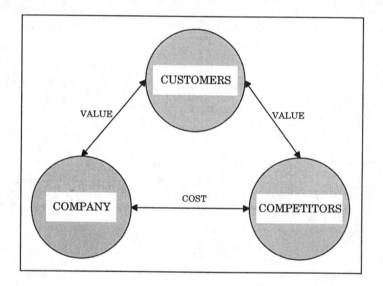

An important point of departure for a strategy is that the company has a map of the territory in which it competes. This means that it will know its own and its competitors' positions in the market. In addition, the company must understand the driving forces behind developments in the competitive situation, and the positions that competitors and the market are likely to have in a few years. This analysis of the company's environment reveals *opportunities* and *threats*.

Another important starting point is the fact that the company knows its own *strengths* and *weaknesses*. In the strategy context, these are the strengths and weaknesses that are significant in terms of the environment — which are interesting and important. Analysis of strengths and weaknesses compared with opportunities and threats is important for the company's strategy formulation. Such an analysis is often called a "SWOT analysis" (Strengths, Weaknesses, Opportunities, Threats). It can provide an answer to how the company should use its strong points to exploit the opportunities, and can consciously improve its weak points to reduce the threats from the environment.

In the work of formulating a strategy, the management will often discover a need for further analysis. So it is important to start the work of actual formulation early and to work in parallel with the collection of data and analyses. Figure 1.2 outlines a model for use when drawing up a business strategy.

Figure 1.2: Strategy Model

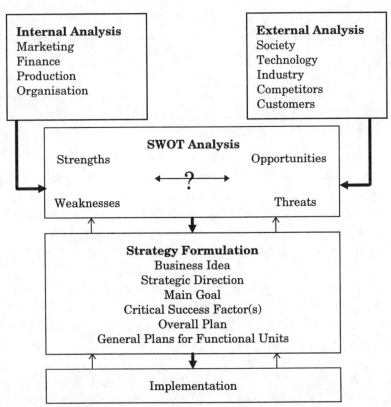

ASSESSMENT OF EXTERNAL FACTORS

Society

The external framework formed by the society in which the company operates imposes clear limitations and will be a crucial determinant of the company's business activities. These external factors cannot normally be influenced by the individual company. The external environment can be described in terms of political, economic and social factors:

- Direction and stability in *political* factors are very important for the development of the company. Policy-makers define laws and regulations with which the company must at all times comply. These factors not only have a direct effect on the company, but also have an indirect effect through their effects on suppliers, customers and competitors. Taxes and duties, price and income regulations and pollution laws are examples of political factors.

- *Economic* considerations depend on the situation and development of the economy in general. Since consumer patterns are affected by the economic situation, the company must understand which socio-economic factors are important. Interest rates, inflation, personal taxation and unemployment are examples of factors with a direct influence on consumer patterns.

- *Social* considerations include important social changes that affect the company directly or indirectly. One of the most important changes in recent times is the growing number of working women. Women have not only gained better positions in working life, but the social transformation has created a need for a whole range of new products and services (for example, kindergartens, fast food and microwave ovens). Two-job households are better off economically and are willing to pay more for homes, furnishings, eating out and holidays. Other examples of social factors are changes in age mix, marital status, religion, culture and lifestyle.

Technology

An understanding of technological trends is important if the company is to "catch on to the right technology at the right time". The creative use of technology can lead to new or substantially altered products, new manufacturing processes and better management and control.

For the company, it is important to survey technological development, to understand what will happen in the course of the next few years, to know the kind of applications new technology will have, and what effect this technology can or will have on the market in which the company competes.

Industry

Competition within a market, in terms of both type and intensity, depends on five main forces as illustrated in Figure 1.3.

To take the "offensive" in relation to these forces, it is important to be thoroughly familiar with the ones prevalent in the industry in which the company competes. It is also important to predict how these forces will affect the company during the next few years. With such an understanding the company can adapt better, and can also exploit the potential offered by the competitive situation.

In relation to the company, for example, customers are strongly placed if there are few of them, or if individual orders are large. Losing a single customer or a single big order will then have great negative consequences for the company, which will then be the weaker party in a bargaining situation. This is the case for many SMEs.

Correspondingly, the bargaining power of suppliers is great if they supply a product part on which the company is completely dependent in its own business activities, and if there is a lack of alternative suppliers.

Figure 1.3: Forces of Competition

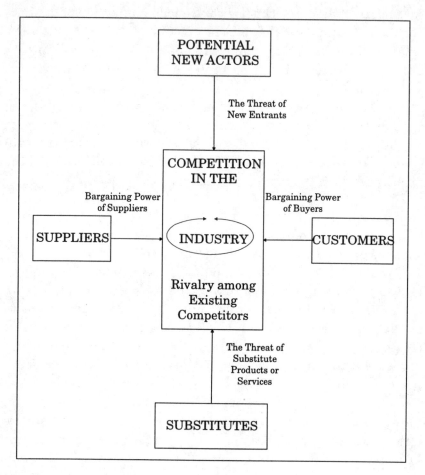

During analysis of the industry, the following key questions should be addressed:

1. What is the company's industry? Can it be divided up geo-graphically (districts, countries, continents etc.), demographi-cally (population groups, age groups etc.), in business terms (companies of a certain size, in certain industries etc.) or in other ways?

2. What kind of rivalry between existing competitors is there within the industry today and what tendencies are there for the years to come? Are there:

- Many equally large competitors?

- Low growth in the industry?

- Little differentiation ("standard products") and stiff price competition?

- High costs involved in "getting out" (high tied investments)?

3. What is the bargaining position of the suppliers and customers, and what tendencies are there for the years ahead? Are there:

- Few suppliers? Few customers, each of whom buys a substantial percentage of the company's products?

- Suppliers with unique products? Customers with many potential suppliers other than the company?

- Suppliers for whom the company's industry is a relatively insignificant market? Customers with small margins who are squeezing the company's prices?

- Suppliers/customers who could conceivably take over the function of the company (by integrating forwards/backwards)?

4. How great is the threat of there being new entrants with capacity to break into the industry — i.e. how high are the entry barriers in the industry?

- Are there high margins in the industry, making it attractive to break in?

- Does it take a lot of capital to start up in the industry?

- Is it expensive/difficult for the customer to change suppliers in the industry?

- Does one need access to an extensive distribution network controlled by the existing competitors in the industry?

- Are there official regulations that prevent new entrants from breaking in or make it difficult for them?

5. What substitute products could meet the same customer needs as the company's products?

- Is it very profitable to operate in the industry, so that big actors with plenty of capital will develop new products/technologies and out-compete the company's products/services?

- Could new technologies make the existing products/services in the industry obsolete and wholly or partially replace them with new ones?

6. What political, socio-economic, social and technological trends are of greatest importance for the competitive situation in the industry, and how does the company intend to exploit/protect itself against these?

Competitors

In the strategy context we analyse competitors for two reasons:

1. To find out what their plans are

2. To find out how they will react to our measures, and what consequences this will have for us.

Of course we cannot obtain this information directly. Instead we must interpret data and impressions that we have collected. The methodology is in many respects like detective work. On the basis of many small clues the detective can eliminate the suspects until there is only one left. We do not know the truth, but can infer what it is likely to be.

By analysing the competitors systematically, we can come a long way without any kind of espionage. By simply collating the items of information one can find in annual reports, interviews, articles and the like, we can elicit very clear pictures of what we are actually looking for. Often a systematic arrangement of what the company itself already knows will be just what we need.

When we analyse the measures or anticipated countermeasures of competitors, it may be useful to think through the:

- Probability

- Risks

- Timing

of such measures.

During our work on strategy, we often come up with several alternative plans for approaches to competition. By systematically reviewing the countermeasures with which competitors are likely to meet potential plans, we will often discover which strategies are best. If the competitors do not react to our measures, and at the same time we manage to take a substantial market share while maintaining profitability, then we have identified a successful strategy. As the strategist Sun Tzu (500 BC) is supposed to have said:

> "A good general (strategist) has the wisdom and strength to manoeuvre so his own forces can exploit the advantages of the terrain while the enemy is forced to fight in unfavourable terrain. The general chooses the battlefield with care, lures the enemy into meeting him there, and wages battle on his own terms."

Customers

The starting point for all business activity is the existence of customers who buy the company's products and services. So it is quite fundamental to strategy that we understand the customers' problems and needs, both now and in future. It is not the technical quality of the products as such that determines whether the customers buy them, but the way the customers perceive this quality. This means that to understand buyer behaviour we must also understand the psychology behind it.

The first requirement is that the company knows who the customers of today are, and who the potential customers are. Once the company has a systematic description of its present and potential customers, it can be useful to ask the following question:

> "Why do we have the customers we have?"

The next question concerns buying criteria — that is, what the customers attach importance to in the buying situation, and what they will attach importance to in future. The customers will of course vary in what they emphasise, but very often there will be clear tendencies.

For example, there is a clear tendency for most people to assign great importance to travelling time in the choice of means of transport to and from work. The cost of transport today comes far down their list of priorities. Thus, if a public transport company is to compete with private cars, it should first and foremost work on transport time, since it is most people's perception that the car is much better suited by this criterion. If the public transport company manages to reduce travelling time, this will lead to a much better return than a reduction in fares.

Segmentation has become a key concept in modern marketing. The company has to find a segment or niche where it enjoys competitive advantage. A good example of this is the buying criteria for beer. Most people buy the beer that is in the shop, and preferably the cheapest: "beer is beer". In a market like this, efficient exploitation of distribution and production are the most important competitive parameters. But nothing is static (fortunately) and in the last few years a market for quality beers has developed. This segment places greatest emphasis on taste and quality image, and develops clear brand preferences. It is also willing to pay a higher price and accepts that it must seek out the shops that distribute the beer it is looking for. This requires a quite different type of competitive effort, where promotional profiling is probably the most important factor.

How the customers perceive one company (or product or service) compared with the competitors is important. In the first place, the market must know of the company's products, and the product must be available where the market wants to buy it. In today's over-saturated markets this can be a considerable problem in itself. But it is not enough to be known and accessible. The customers must also prefer the company's products and services. In a situation of choice it must argue — and if necessary document — that its products are better than those of the competition in the areas that are important. So it is important to know how the market assesses the company's products compared to those of the competition in terms of the buying criteria that are most meaningful to the customers.

In situations where long-term customer relations have been established, it is important to keep this clientele. It is easier to sell to existing customers than to new ones, and satisfied customers are the company's best advertisement. A list of high-priority customer problems gives the company useful information in its strategy work.

ASSESSMENT OF INTERNAL FACTORS IN THE COMPANY

Marketing

An important starting point for the analysis of the company's marketing is to gain a true picture of the profitability of product and customer groups. It is important to emphasise profitability, not just turnover. By profitability we mean the contribution of the product group or customer group after separate costs (investment) have as accurately as possible been distributed over the products. The important questions that arise then are:

"Where does the company earn its money (which customers, products and sales outlets)?"

"Does the company achieve its goals?"

The results obtained by the company are directly dependent on how effectively it works on marketing. Important questions are which target groups the company must reach, the availability of the company's products to these groups, how competitive they are compared with those of the competitors, and whether the company is pursuing the right pricing policy.

Effectiveness and results in sales and marketing are in turn linked with the company's systems for managing this functional area. So it can be useful to check whether the reporting routines and controls established provide support for the overall goals of the company and whether they provide feedback in the form of operational information.

In addition to analysing current profitability and efficiency, the company must assess its future efficiency and profitability as regards the products and markets with which it works. The companies must therefore constantly work on product and market development. Central questions here are:

"Will current products and markets also give us the desired profitability in future?"

"Is the company working rationally with the development of new markets and products?"

Finances

In the strategy work, financial aspects are important in several ways. The most important ones are:

- Financial scope
- Profitability
- Control systems.

It is important to know how much *financial scope* the company has to invest in new areas. One can see this in the first instance from the balance sheet, which shows how much equity capital the company has compared with its debts. Another criterion is liquid assets — first and foremost money in the bank. If you have money in the bank you can act quickly if something interesting turns up; and you have the "backbone" to stand a period of relative decline. The ability to finance new projects is partly a matter of the company's financial situation, but is also very dependent on the company itself. The ability to raise funding is crucial.

Profitability is another central topic in connection with strategy. A survey of the areas in the company that are doing well and those that are doing badly forms a starting point for any strategic discussion. Figures like these should be studied over time, and you should try to estimate the direction further development will take. It is important to find out why profitability is the way it is. Are there problems with productivity in the company, or does the explanation lie in inadequate turnover and poor pricing?

The company's *control and monitoring* of earnings, costs, receivables and stocks gives important indications of its competence in these functions. Important questions here are what management's control parameters are, and whether management is getting the right information at the right time for making decisions.

Production
One of the most important indicators of the competitiveness of the company is the development of productivity. In the first place, it is important to compare productivity figures to corresponding figures for the competitors. Secondly, it is important to study the development of productivity over time and to analyse the reasons for the current level.

Flexibility or the ability to adapt production can be an important competitive parameter on some markets.

New technology can make companies more competitive — by reducing unit costs among other ways. The problem for the company is that new technology costs money, and production volumes may be too low for the efficient utilisation of the technology. In the analytical work one often includes an analysis of the technological level compared with competitors and with existing possibilities.

Efficient production is directly dependent on control systems and good demand forecasts. Bad forecasting means overstocking if the forecasts are too high, and extra costs in the form of overtime and poor customer service if they are too low.

Organisational Structure
The motivation of personnel and their attitude to their own work is probably one of the most critical success factors in a company. Motivated employees work more and work better. Motivated, positive employees are also important image assets in their surroundings, and this can in turn be important for the company's recruiting and sales.

Those factors that affect employee motivation on a day-to-day basis can be referred to as environmental factors. The extent to which one is satisfied or dissatisfied with these factors determines much of the sense of well-being in the company. Examples of these factors are job assignments, relations with one's immediate superior, job security, the pay system and belief in the company and its products.

Knowledge of and attitudes to the general strategy of the company and management philosophy also affect motivation and staff attitudes to their own work. First, employees must feel confident that the management is doing the right things. Secondly, one must understand how the general strategy affects the individual, and what demands it makes on them.

The company not only needs motivated employees, it also needs people with the right competence. You can obtain an indication of the level of competence by looking at the level of wages and salaries. Another indication of low competence is a high staff turnover rate. When an employee stops working for the company, they take away knowledge of the company and its work which it often takes a long time to build up again.

ASSESSMENT OF STRENGTHS AND WEAKNESSES AGAINST OPPORTUNITIES AND THREATS

The point of the so-called SWOT analysis is to compare threats and opportunities in the environment of the company to the company's ability to handle the problems and to exploit the opportunities. So it is the actual comparison of the elements in the internal and external analysis that is important. A constantly recurring key question is:

"What does this mean for our company?"

There are many systematic approaches to this work. Figure 1.4 shows one simple, but very useful, arrangement of the factors.

The point of the table is to identify critical or important changes in the background conditions of the company. The external analysis has reviewed the areas of society, technology, industry, competitors and customers, and has identified the events which on the face of it seem to have some significance. At this stage one tries to analyse these events in more detail. First we must have a time perspective on what we are assessing. A change in technology that will only have consequences in fifteen years' time is of little importance in this context.

Figure 1.4: Assessment of Threats and Opportunities

<------------------------------>
Consequences

Threats and Opportunities	Event	Time	Prob-ability	Buying Criteria	New Actors	Profit-ability
Society						
Technology						
Industry						
Competitors						
Customers						

Nor are all events equally certain. So it may be wise to include a probability assessment. For example, OPEC could conceivably agree on production ceilings that would take oil prices up to $35 a barrel. Such a rise in oil prices would mean a lot to the rest of the economy, and would thus affect most companies. But when we assess the probability of OPEC reaching an agreement and observing this agreement, most people would conclude that it is a small one.

The interesting thing is to assess the consequences of the various events, and of course in particular those that affect the company. Important questions are:

"Will anything happen to change the buying criteria on the market?"

"Will anything happen that will cause new actors (competitors, suppliers, customers etc.) to appear on the scene, or that will make current actors more active on the market?"

"Will anything happen that will radically change the level of profitability in the industry in general and for our company in particular?"

Once the most important events have been identified and analysed, it is important to compare these with the company's ability to handle them. What are the company's strengths and weaknesses in relation to what can happen? The table in Figure 1.5 can be useful to run through.

Figure 1.5: Assessment of Critical Events

Consequences for the Company

$\longleftarrow \cdots\cdots\cdots\cdots\cdots\cdots\cdots\cdots\cdots\cdots\cdots\cdots\cdots\cdots\cdots \longrightarrow$

Critical Events	Marketing	Finance	Production	Organisation
1. _____				
2. _____				
3. _____				
4. _____				
5. _____				

The analysis of internal and external factors, and the comparisons made in the SWOT analysis, identify the most important threats and opportunities for the company. When we then compare these with the company's strengths and weaknesses, we identify a number of factors that it will be important to tackle in the future. The main question is how the company can exploit its strengths to overcome its weaknesses. The aim is to arrive at a list of critical factors (without priorities). Gradually, as the final strategy is established, these factors will become clearer, and it will be possible to assign priorities to the most critical ones.

The result of the SWOT analysis should be the identification of:

• The major threats

• The major opportunities

• How the company should exploit its strengths to overcome its weaknesses

• A list (without priorities) of the critical success factors.

FORMULATION OF STRATEGY

Business Idea

A business idea describes the product, market and technology areas in which the company is involved. A business idea should also expresses values and priorities. A good business idea must be so simple that it is easy to communicate to others, and gives directional signals to the personnel in the various functions. Fundamental questions one asks in this context are:

"What is our branch of industry?"

"What customer needs does the product meet?"

"What alternative products (substitutes) can the customer buy to meet these needs?"

"Which customer groups buy the product?"

"What competitors does the company have?"

After these questions have been reviewed, the needs are grouped so that certain main areas emerge. These main areas form the company's strategic business units — now defined in terms of needs. The aim of defining the product areas in terms of need or function is to bring out a simpler, more operational matrix for product areas oriented towards customer groups (a product/market matrix).

In the strategy work it is important to analyse the various product/market areas and to assign priorities to those that are most important for the company. This way resources are channelled in directions that are likely to lead to the best returns. The primary criterion for assigning priorities will always be anticipated profitability.

In the work of defining what the company is actually doing, it is important not to be too short-sighted. In other words, it is a matter of extrapolating a general formula which will not be tied too much to the company's current products.

One of the better examples of this was Nobel's business idea of "breaking rocks". Its old business idea was "to produce dynamite".

This imposed quite clear limitations on the opportunities it saw for further development. With the new definition it initiated quite new applications of other technologies — for example, chemical expansion.

Other examples of how a business idea could be reviewed are given in the table in Figure 1.6.

Figure 1.6: The Business Idea

Company	From	To
Gillette	Aerosol Deodorants	Underarm Products
Xerox	Copy Machines	Office Automation Systems
Helly Hansen	Rainwear	Waterproof Garments
Bang & Olufsen	Radios	Home Entertainment

Main Goal

The main goal in business is to increase the value of the company to the owners. In most cases this can be expressed in the form of return on capital. But the owners may also have non-financial goals with the company. An entrepreneur may, for example, be more interested in creating a business and realising their own ambitions than in earning money. On the other hand, the company has to be run at a profit or it will not survive. So in this context we will focus on aspects relating to business economy. In the context of strategy formulation, the setting of main goals concerns the following:

- Profitability

- Productivity

- Competitive position

- Corporate culture, and

- Technological initiative.

All too often, one sees management setting itself goals that are fine and proper as far as they go, but the organisation does not work to achieve them. It is, of course, difficult to set oneself good goals, but the following criteria are worth checking:

- Will the goals be accepted?

- Are they measurable?

- Do they motivate personnel?

Goals, therefore, must be ambitious (but achievable), specific and relevant. To satisfy each of these criteria, the main goals must be broken down into subgoals in a coherent goal hierarchy.

Strategy

One result of the analysis is that the general strategic directions the company can take begin to emerge. The main question is:

"Where does the company want to be in five years?"

Strategic positioning involves exploiting the strong points of the company and the opportunities in its environment, so the company will earn more money than it would have done otherwise. The company must identify and develop its competitive advantage. The company can develop in two general strategic directions:

- Cost leadership

- Differentiation.

Within each of these two general directions the company can choose different approaches.

There is no recipe for the right strategy. However, studies of the strategic choices companies have made show that there are certain tendencies. Such an overview is shown in the table in Figure 1.7.

The companies in the first quadrant — those in a strong position in a high-growth market — are in an excellent situation. These companies should exploit the situation as much as they can. It is also natural for these companies to experiment with other products and markets close to their core activities. If the company has resources, it may also be relevant to invest profits in the expansion of activities oriented towards supplier links or distribution/dealer links. This is often called "vertical integration". Control of the whole manufacturing chain from crude oil to distribution has, for example, been the main strategy of the major oil companies. A company that is doing well in a growth market should also think about the fact that such prosperity does not last for ever. So for many companies it is natural to invest part of their surplus in another business with a quite different risk profile ("risk spreading").

Figure 1.7: Examples of Strategy Alternatives

Market Growth	Competitive Position			
	Strong		*Weak*	
Fast	1. Concentration 2. Vertical Integration 3. Risk Spreading	I	1. Repositioning 2. Horizontal Integration 3. Sales	II
Slow	1. Risk Spreading 2. Co-operation	IV	1. Turnaround 2. Risk Spreading 3. Sales	III

Companies in the second quadrant — those in a weak position in a growth market — should make a thorough analysis of the way they are working on this market. They must find out why their present strategy does not work, and whether the company on the whole has the ability to compete effectively. The most natural course for the company is to reposition itself by concentrating on what it can really achieve, and to phase out or give a lower priority to what it cannot manage. Another alternative is to "integrate horizontally" — that is, to co-operate, merge with or buy out competitors. This is a matter of finding natural partners to obtain a synergetic effect. The last resort is to sell the company. Since the market is a growing one, this may be the most profitable course for the owners.

Companies in the third quadrant — those in a weak position on a low-growth market — will probably first try to adapt company size to earnings. A "turnaround" operation with firm cost cuts, new management and concentration on profitable parts of the business will probably often be the right course. As an alternative, or in combination with the former course, the company may seek to move its resources to markets with better prospects, where the company has good qualifications ("risk spreading"). Here too there is the option of selling or winding down the business. If the prospects of earning money are close to zero, the company should probably try to sell. If this is not possible, it should be wound down.

Companies in the fourth quadrant — those with a strong position in a slow-growing market — will probably limit their investments in this business area to a minimum to maintain competitiveness. The investments must go into market areas with better prospects ("risk spreading"). Another natural strategy in this situation may be co-operation with other companies to achieve efficiency benefits.

Critical Success Factors

The identification of critical success factors is based on an assessment of the company's strengths and weaknesses, and the threats and opportunities posed and offered by the environment (both in the immediate market and in the industry as a whole).

It is always difficult to identify the right factors. One way of arriving at the critical success factors is to analyse why the company is what it is today, given the situation it was in between three and five years ago, and to make similar analyses of competitors. Three key questions are:

"What distinguishes the companies on the market who succeed from those who do not?"

"What is it that makes the big difference in competition?"

"Where in our value creation do we have the greatest potential?"

It is important that the main goals set up in the strategy reflect the critical success factors. The main goals must guide the organisation so that, as far as possible, the most important things are given the highest priority.

In the business plan, the critical success factors are related to operations so they become specific and measurable. If the most critical success factor for the company, for instance, is a strong position in the distribution channel, the business plan could include a specific target for a delivery reliability percentage of 97 per cent.

General Plan and Plans for Individual Functions

Even when the general strategy, main goals and critical success factors have been defined, the job is far from over. The task of implementing and monitoring still remains.

A plan in the strategy context is a set of measures. Some of the measures will be of a general nature and will apply to the whole business (for example, buying Company X, co-operating with Supplier Y). Other measures will be related to the individual functional areas in the company (for example, a new computer system for financial management). In other words, the plans are a kind of specification of what the general strategy actually means. The question is:

> "If we succeed at the general level, what will be the consequences for the individual functions (e.g. marketing, logistics, production, finance, research and development)?"

TECHNOLOGY STRATEGIES

In general, there is considerable scope for innovation through the use of new technology. This may be relevant for three main types of application:

- Products

- Production process

- Management/control.

There is no point in new technology if it does not improve the company's profitability in the short or long term. Technology can primarily lead to better profitability by:

- Creating value in the company more efficiently, and

- Increasing the "value" of the products or services from the customer's point of view.

Remember:

> The goal is not to have the world's best product at the lowest price, but to be just so much better than the competition that the company gets the sales and the customer is satisfied.

Product

The point of departure for evaluating new technology in relation to the product or service the company sells is the buying criteria of the market. It is particularly important to focus on important changes that will happen to these in the course of the next few years. For example, developments in research and new technology may lead to radical changes. Electronic data processing is a good example of the way new inventions and discoveries cause fundamental changes in the requirements and wishes of the market. A comparison of the ten biggest printer manufacturers on the European market showed that only two of those on the list in 1986 were still there in 1988. The company must constantly seek to be better than the competitors in terms of the criteria that *determine* customer choices, and to be good enough in terms of the others.

When we evaluate technology in relation to products, we have to think about the total product the customer buys. The way the product is delivered (time and place) may, for example, be just as important a criterion as features of the product itself. For instance, several companies have invested in terminals for their customers to make ordering routines simpler and more manageable — while at the same time this "locks" the customer into the supplier's system.

Important questions here are:

> "Can new technology substantially increase the value of the products to the customers?"

> "Can new technology in delivery substantially increase the value of our services?"

"What plans do the competitors have for new product or de-livery technology?"

"What new technology can become important in our industry in the next few years? What will happen?"

Production Process

New technology in the actual production process may aim:

- At more efficient resource deployment, or

- To increase the value of the product.

Here too the starting point is the company's general business strategy. Technology is only relevant to the extent that it can im-prove the company's profitability through improved competitive-ness.

Technology alone rarely lies at the root of the problem. Human factors — knowledge, motivation and management — are often at least as important. And it is often combinations of solutions that produce results. In the table in Figure 1.8, we show some exam-ples of the kind of measures that the general goals of the business strategy can lead to in the actual manufacturing process. As we can see, the measures are in varying degrees dependent on tech-nology. The technology-related measures that the company finally chooses to implement are in other words solidly grounded in a business assessment of the company's competitive situation and strategic position.

Management and Control

New technology for controlling company finances and various other functions is a matter of managing information. Information technology is therefore crucial in this context.

Investments in new technology in connection with control sys-tems will almost always have the basic aim of making value crea-tion in the company more efficient. Some relevant investments in technology for controlling the functions in the company are shown in the table in Figure 1.9.

Figure 1.8: Manufacturing Consequences of Strategy Goals

Business Strategy	Consequences for Manufacturing
Achieve Cost Leadership	Longer production series Few product changes More special equipment More specialised units
Achieve Quality Leadership	More quality assurance More accurate equipment Higher competence
Better Customer Service	More employees in service divisions Higher competence in service divisions More stocks of spare parts Quicker response to customer enquiries
Better Delivery Service	Better co-ordination with sales Stock automation Decentralised stores

Figure 1.9: Technology Investment in Control Systems

Functional Unit	Technological Control System
Sales and marketing	Stock and distribution Budget control Market information Sales planning and follow-up Formulation of quotes/tenders Ordering/cancelling Dealer support
Production	Production planning Production control Quality control Computer-aided production Supplier control
Product development	Computer-aided design Production-integrated systems Component databases Knowledge databases
Administration	Invoicing systems Payroll and accounting systems Budgeting Cost control Project planning and management Office automation

IMPLEMENTATION OF THE STRATEGY

After the analysis has been done and the strategy formulated, the job of relating the strategy to the company's operations begins. Companies have different ways of going about this part of the strategy work. In general, however, there now exists a higher degree of interaction between top management and other levels in the organisation during the actual drawing-up and implementation of the strategy than before. The working procedure can thus be regarded as an iterative process. Some of the advantages of such an approach are:

- Because the staff are involved, they are also motivated and can see the benefits of the strategic planning.

- The total knowledge and insight of the organisation is exploited more efficiently. More relevant problems emerge, and more constructive, realistic solutions may be seen.

- Employees are as a rule more concerned with the overall goal of the company — improved profitability — so productivity tends to rise.

- Power and role conflicts are often clarified in such a process.

- General resistance to change is reduced.

Studies from the USA show that companies which work with strategic planning have clear profitability advantages, and that those which work iteratively on implementation also achieve better profitability in the longer term.

The new strategy can also have consequences for the structure, management and corporate culture of the company. A structural transformation may involve reorganisation of management and of individual divisions. In certain situations this means that some employees will become redundant or must be transferred. Of course this is a difficult and unpleasant task, both for those who have to implement the changes and those they affect.

If the company is to make radical changes it may often be necessary to replace all or part of top management. In the first place, the personal qualities of managerial staff may mean that they are unsuited to the new strategy. Some people are typical "growth managers", while others are best at "consolidation" or "restructuring". In the second place, the social links of managers with staff may make it difficult for them to carry out the necessary measures.

Corporate culture is concerned with the values and norms according to which the organisation functions. We often describe organisations as "bureaucratic", "dynamic", "profit-oriented", "market-oriented" and so on. Changing the corporate culture of the company from, for instance, "bureaucratic" to "market-oriented" often involves the use of a number of symbols. An example of this are the measures Janne Carlsson introduced to turn the corporate culture around in SAS. The first symbol was a new leader who was "people-oriented". One does not talk about "Mr. Carlsson" but about "Janne". He also sent all the staff on a "smile course" and gave customer service pride of place. Another measure was painting all the planes white.

2

NEW MANAGEMENT CONCEPTS

INTRODUCTION

In this chapter, a selection of some of the most popular "new" management concepts are presented. It is not within the scope of this handbook to give a thorough description of each concept, but the intention is to present the reader with an overview of each that can be followed up by further reading of the source material listed at the end of the chapter if so desired. The different concepts are compared to each other with a view to identifying aspects that are common to them all.

A brief overview of nine different management concepts is given followed by a more detailed account of two of these: Total Quality Management and Lean Production.

How the various concepts deal with the change processes that must take place for an organisation to move from its old ways to adaptation of a new management style is also discussed.

The material in this chapter is presented under the following headings:

- Common Aspects of Modern Management Ideas

- Overview of Different Management Concepts

- Using Modern Management Ideas

- Total Quality Management

- Lean Production.

COMMON ASPECTS OF MODERN MANAGEMENT IDEAS

The various approaches to organisational development and change presented below may be thought of as concepts. A concept consists of two major parts: The ideas and the methods.

> Concept = Idea + Methods

- The ideas represent certain goals that the concepts are aiming for: customer focus, quality, continuous learning and improvement, participation, etc. The goals illustrate a philosophy, a set of values or basic assumptions about how to create a profitable and developing business organisation.

- The methods are the ways in which goals are to be achieved: Kanban, zero inventory, documentation, routines, information technology, etc.

All the management concepts presented below have a few basic ideas in common, even if the methods differ. The most prominent is that they see *the organisation as an integrated whole*.

The resources available to the organisation — the people, the technology, the product, the customers, the suppliers, and the routines and systems — need to work as a unified whole in order to maximise profitability and flexibility. Optimising only one part of the organisation — individual skills, information systems, inventories or customer relations — leads to sub-optimisation, which is not competitive in the long run. This idea is very clear in concepts like Total Quality Management, Lean Production, Learning Organisation, and Business Process Re-engineering.

Other ideas that are common to all or most of the concepts are:

- Basic "truths" in traditional management thinking need to be re-thought. Examples of such truths are: Minimise stoppage time in manufacturing; organise by function in hierarchies; optimise the technology; and centralise decisions, information and learning. These worked fine in stable environments, with growing markets and mass production. In today's turbulent markets, what is needed is flexibility, low capital costs, variety, service, and co-operation.

- Organisations need to change, and to keep on changing. Learning must be continuous.

- In an organisation in which knowledge, customer service, quality, continuous improvement, and interpersonal skills are important, employees in manufacturing need competence and freedom to be flexible and creative.

- Continuous learning, flexibility and creativity implies employee participation. In some way or another, all concepts have ideas about employee involvement or participation in decision-making, at least within a defined manufacturing area.

- The need for integration implies that it is necessary to close the gap between different professional worlds (engineering, management, accounting and economy).

OVERVIEW OF DIFFERENT MANAGEMENT CONCEPTS

Total Quality Management (TQM)

As the name indicates, TQM takes a holistic approach. TQM assumes that quality is something that is embedded in all activities that take place within an organisation. It is significant to note that management is part of the title. Quality is accordingly a matter of importance for management. Furthermore, quality is something that should be managed in a conscious way.

TQM views an organisation as an open system. The transformation must be co-ordinated and linked to both suppliers and customers. The raw materials and the parts entering the organisation must have the right quality, as must the products delivered to customers. The quality requirements must be met every time, be it from suppliers or in the products delivered to customers. Internally, the main focus is on how value is added to the products. The organisation must be geared to handle continual improvements, and every single employee is responsible for working out the expected and agreed upon level of quality. Continual improvement is seen as a core issue, and it has to be built into every action. Furthermore, the production system is considered as a totality, in which each element is linked to others forming the complex whole production system.

Lean Production

Lean Production is another westernisation of Japanese manufacturing and business philosophies, aiming at low costs. A "lean" organisation is one in which all unnecessary costs have been cut out, and in this regard the idea is the same as Just-in-Time Manufacturing. The difference between the two, however, is that Lean Production encompasses the whole business. It includes manufacturing, the supply chain, product development, customer relations, and the "total lean enterprise".

Womack et al. (1990) coined the phrase "lean production" in a study of the Japanese and American automobile industries. It is seen as a contrast to mass production. Lean Production involves using less of everything in comparison to mass production: man-hours, space, tools, investments, engineering time, and inventory. It also involves having fewer defects and a greater and growing variety of products. The techniques and methods for doing this are roughly the same as for Just-in-Time: A "pull" method of production, very quick tool changes, a different thinking about quality etc. The difference is that it applies to the company in general, and that broader ideas on the competence of workers, careers, team work, organisation and management are taken into consideration.

Other concepts related to Japanese industries, and focusing on roughly the same issues, are: *The Toyota System* (Shingo, 1981), *Theory Z* (Ouchi, 1981), *Optimised Production Technology (OPT)* (Goldratt and Cos, 1984) and *World Class Manufacturing* (Schonberger, 1982).

Kanban

Kanban is a technique for reducing inventories and batch sizes in manufacturing. When Kanban techniques are being used, a company decides that inventory levels will be kept at a specific, very low level. No part is produced unless that part is virtually out of stock (specifically, a location on a rack or shelf being empty). The consequence is that the company uses a "pull" production method. No part is produced until it is needed. In this way, the cost of capital is reduced. The extreme result may be that unless parts are needed for assembly, there is no production. This is in contrast to the concept of mass production in which machines are kept going no matter what.

In order to simplify this system, a special card or shelf, usually with a number or colour coding, is used for each different part.

Only a limited number of cards or shelves exist in production. Once a given quantity of parts (specified on the card) has been used in assembly, the card or empty shelf is used to signal to production, so that the manufacture of that particular part is initiated. In this way, it is easy to get an overview of production, and inventories are kept at a specified low level.

There are of course organisational and business aspects to this technique as well. Relations with both customers and suppliers are affected, for example. Minimum inventories requires market "pull" and frequent deliveries.

Just-in-Time

The main idea in Just-in-Time (JIT) Manufacturing is to remove all unnecessary costs in manufacturing. The main principles for achieving this are:

- Use of the market pull principle in production control

- A levelling of manufacturing through small batch production and through avoiding production peaks

- Continuous flow in the manufacturing process.

The goals of JIT manufacturing are zero faults, zero time to change or adjust tools and equipment, zero inventory, zero materials handling, zero stops in production, zero production flow time, and a manufacturing batch size of one.

Just-in-Time is one of the oldest of the Japanese management theories promoted in Western countries. It was first developed in the Toyota company, as were many of the other concepts. It is difficult to clearly distinguish between the various concepts inspired by Japan. Much of this is because different authors develop their own sets of concepts, theories and techniques, differing more in name than in content. It is however common to see JIT as the part of Lean Production that focuses on the technical side of the manufacturing process, whereas Lean Production is more concerned with organisation and management. Kanban is a method which is used within the JIT approach to achieve zero inventories.

ISO 9000

The International Standardisation Organisation (ISO) has developed a standard for how to achieve a certificate assuring that a company follows certain procedures in quality assurance. The main idea is to provide a structure within which companies describe and analyse the main elements of their production system. Obtaining certification according to the ISO 9000 standard implies that all production and quality systems are documented and comply with the standards set by ISO. This identifies that the documentation is according to standards and also that the routines documented are followed. The ISO standard in itself leaves important issues to be decided by the actual company.

If a company merely views ISO 9000 as being a series of mandatory requirements which document the routines that take place in conjunction with the writing of a quality manual, the actual implementation of the standard will have little impact on the day-to-day operation of the company. In such a case, the ISO certificate will be effective only in marketing relations, and of less importance in supporting a change process in the organisation.

If, on the other hand, the company approaches the issue of ISO standardisation by letting the employees themselves do the work, then considerable benefits can be realised. The idea is that the standardisation procedure will support a process whereby problems in the production system are identified by those responsible for running the operation on a daily basis. In this way the identification of problems will be followed by immediate actions to meet the challenge. Such an approach to ISO standardisation will result in big improvements but with less focus on the documentation standards.

Business Process Re-engineering (BPR)

Business Process Re-engineering is currently the most fashionable of the organisational change concepts. BPR's proponents would argue that it is something more than, or different to, quality. It is a revolutionary approach to restructuring the value-creating processes in the organisation. The idea is to gain significant benefits in productivity, profitability, service and quality through maximising the potential of individuals and teams. That it is revolutionary means that instead of trying to improve on al-

ready existing processes and organisational forms, it suggests
that it is better to throw it all away and start from scratch. However, the goals and methods for re-engineering the organisation
are well-known from many other approaches during the last decades.

BPR has the customer as a starting point. It aims to develop
organisations which will provide value, service and quality to all
customers, external and internal. Focusing on the business processes is the same as focusing on the activities in the organisation
which turn input into output by adding value. The aim is to fundamentally question and change the way this is done in the organisation. This includes both looking at how people work in the
organisation and what technology they use.

The move away from functional specialisation and towards
teams is important within BPR. The idea is to be customer-
focused, by letting a small sub-part of the organisation handle one
customer instead of having a huge number of people perform the
various functions. Other important aspects are technology to support the team-based, customer-focused organisation (especially
information technology), a reduction of the hierarchy, rewards systems, strategy and culture.

A related concept, which is less radical in its approach, is
Business Process Redesign (also BPR). Instead of focusing on the
total process in the organisation, it rather focuses on key sub-
processes.

Anthropocentric Production Systems

The term Anthropocentric Production Systems originated in
Germany and was developed through the EU FAST Programme.
In this respect it reflects a European tradition in focusing on the
employee as being a major resource for the organisation. It is
thus in line with the socio-technical tradition by identifying that a
production system can be more effective only if it is designed so
that human resources and technology are mutually designed to fit
each other.

The main focus in the Anthropocentric Production System is to
take advantage of workers' skills. The governing principle is to
design technology and thus production systems in such a way that
this human orientation ensures a situation in which workers can

use their skills both to operate and to innovate the production system. The management principle focuses also on how a participative approach creates a collaborative organisation where management and workers co-determine important decisions. The idea is further based on utilisation of highly advanced technology. In this respect the Anthropocentric Production System combines the use of advanced technology with highly participative approaches demanding skilful workers.

High Involvement Management

This concept was developed by Professor Ed Lawler and associates at the Centre for Effective Organisations at the University of Southern California. The main focus of that research group was to investigate the impact of *participation* on the working environment. From the work carried out it was clear that employee participation was an important factor with regard to effectiveness, flexibility, quality of output, quality of decisions and skill development. The main idea within this frame of thinking is to increase the employees' opportunities of having a say in the day-to-day running of the firm.

Participation of employees creates the possibility for improving almost every aspect of an organisation's performance. The arguments for promoting participation are drawn from "quality circles", which are understood as a way of using the workers' manual and intellectual skills to enhance continual improvement at the shop floor level. It is argued that further job enrichment will have the same effects, since work-teams help to increase an organisation's potential to be competitive.

High-involvement management is based on increasing the employees' control over their own working conditions. The management principle is closely associated with a concept of employees being people who can be trusted to make important decisions.

Employees have the opportunity to learn and thereby develop their skills, and trusting workers to make decisions will automatically result in improved overall effectiveness of the organisation. The resulting organisational structure will have few layers, and the numbers in management will be low. The new organisational structure will be based on gain-sharing plans as reward systems. The leadership style will be very different from the traditional pattern. Four aspects of high-involvement management are:

- Build trust and openness

- Provide a vision and communicate it

- Move decisions to the proper locations

- Empower others.

One of the final conclusions is that a leader must preach and practice openness as well as moving decisions to where relevant expertise is found.

Learning Organisations

Learning Organisations refers to a systems approach to developing organisations that are able to adapt to (or learn from) changing markets and environments. The concept may be related to the idea of "organisational learning", which has been a part of organisation theory and development for years. However, the term "learning organisations" refers specifically to the approach of Peter Senge, in which he combines contemporary systems theory with various management approaches.

Learning Organisations excel in five disciplines:

- Personal mastery

- Mental models

- Building shared vision

- Team learning

- Systems thinking ("the fifth discipline").

Obviously the concept takes various ideas that have dominated management thinking over a number of decades and integrates them through systems thinking. The idea is that it is not enough to be good at one of these disciplines. The true Learning Organisation is good at each of them and at combining them into a whole.

USING MODERN MANAGEMENT IDEAS

Books, academicians and consultants have promoted various methods for using the modern management ideas already presented to bring about change and improvements in organisations. The problem, however, is that once you start changing an organisation through the use of techniques, you very often end up with an organisation similar to the one you were trying to get away from. For example, if ISO 9000 when implemented is viewed as being merely a set of handbooks and routines, implemented by a consultant, and evaluated through strict control measures, then the whole benefit is gone. Similarly, you don't get "lean" or "learning" organisations by Kanban, teamwork or new IT programs alone.

A method or technique is in itself sub-optimising. It usually leads to a set of rules, roles, control mechanisms and management practices which are not really much different from the machine-like bureaucracies of the mass production period. It is based on the idea that one solution will fix all problems, that the expert or manager should develop this solution, and that hierarchical control is necessary in order to make the organisation work.

> Paradoxically, the methods and techniques for change are reflections of what we are trying to change away from, and not of what we want to achieve.

A major obstacle in organisational design is the separation of the *ideas* on which the desired operational characteristics of the organisation are based, from the *methods* for changing the organisation. For instance, it is hard to see how participative management can be created unless the organisational design process is participative. High involvement can never be mandated, but has to be developed through the change process in itself.

Most modern management ideas are based on concepts of resource integration (technology, human resources and economy) and on participation in every layer of the organisation. The successful organisation is clearly identified as the one that promotes flexibility and creativity through high involvement. In this regard, the aim is easily understandable.

The road to reaching the desired organisation and management style, however, *is seldom articulated in the vision related to the new management principle*. Often, changing an organisation will at best be identified as applying a set of techniques over a limited period of time. At the end of the period, the organisation will have obtained the results, once and for all. A common approach will be to hire consultants to do the job. When the contracting period is over, one expects the new organisation to be installed. Consultants can be very important in supporting innovations in organisations, but they can be used in much smarter ways than described above.

The main obstacle in this approach to organisational change is the uncommunicated model of how to design an organisation. The underlying idea is that a new organisational design can be installed once and for all. But issuing a new organisational chart, quality handbooks or IT accounting systems does not immediately create a new organisation. People have ways of working, personal relationships, experiences, knowledge and feelings that all together determine how people relate to each other. The way they relate and solve tasks based on interpersonal routines creates the organisation and management. Basically, an organisation is created and recreated through the way the employees do their daily work. If this is true, real organisational change can only take place if the change process is integrated in everyday organisational life.

> Thus, if the desired goal is to create participative management, it can only be achieved through participative change processes.

The main challenge in modern management principles is to utilise every employee's manual and intellectual capacities, integrated into an overall attempt to make the best possible use of the total available resources. This can only be done by creating a process in which each member of the organisation can have a say both in daily work and in changing the organisation. From what is said above, everyday work and work on changing the organisation cannot really be separated. The participation of all employees makes the working organisation.

TOTAL QUALITY MANAGEMENT

Quality is a powerful competitive strategy. The Japanese in particular have demonstrated this to the Western world by conquering large market shares on the basis of "superior" quality, in the auto and electronics industries for example. Among European SMEs there are also good examples of what can be achieved by focusing on quality.

What is Quality?

A customer who buys a product has certain expectations. Here the intended use plays an important role, but so do other factors like appearance and useful life. Expectations depend on the supplier's reputation and the price too. Higher prices mean higher expectations.

When the product fulfils these expectations in use the customer is usually pleased and assesses the quality as high. Otherwise the quality is regarded as low.

> We can therefore define quality as the product's capacity to fulfil the customer's expectations.

There are two dimensions to the quality concept (illustrated in Figure 2.1):

• The specifications must fulfil the customer's expectations

• The products must have no deficiencies or faults.

Figure 2.1: The Two Dimensions of Quality

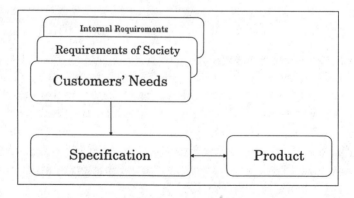

It is important to distinguish between both dimensions. The specifications are established by studying the needs of the market and during product development. Deficiencies and faults usually arise in production and in the use of the products.

Products can be either goods or services. In both cases requirements and expectations must be specified as thoroughly as possible, even though this can be difficult, especially for services.

The quality concept must be adapted to the individual company. For an industrial manufacturer, for example, a number of product features may be relevant, such as:

- The basic functions of the product

- Additional functions

- Reliability

- Lifetime

- Ease of servicing

- Appearance

- Reputation.

In service businesses other factors may be central. For a transport company, for example, punctuality, safety and undamaged goods are crucial quality parameters.

Details of contact with the company staff, for example, how agreements are honoured and the personal service given, may be crucial for the impression the customer is left with. The "soft qualities" may be more important than the "hard" ones. A positive attitude from the individual employee is necessary to create quality. And in all cases, process quality to avoid deficiencies and faults is of great importance.

The quality concept does not only apply in relation to the company's customers. Its internal divisions too have their "customers" with their own expectations. The quality concept must gradually spread through the whole organisation.

For a consultant, the discussion of the quality concept with the company is of crucial importance. The discussion should be tied to the discussion of buying criteria. Only when the company has arrived at the buying criteria which are important in *its industry* is it possible to set specific goals for quality, and to take measures to improve its status.

Strategies in the Work with Quality

Some major features of international development in the quality area are shown in Figure 2.2.

Figure 2.2: Quality Strategies

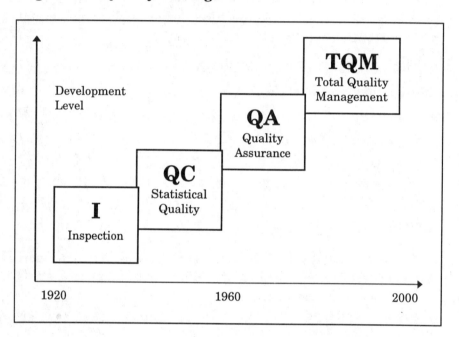

The diagram illustrates that back in the 1920s quality meant simple "quality control", where inspection and testing were used as the basis for acceptance or rejection of products. Gradually, statistical quality control was introduced, i.e. statistical methods were used to make the inspection work more efficient. Samples were used instead of 100 per cent inspection.

In the 1960s quality assurance was developed as a system for controlling one's own company, with great emphasis on documentation and internal procedures. The systems followed a standardised plan.

In the last ten years, a much wider quality strategy has gained a foothold in the USA and Europe based on the Japanese model.

Internationally it is often called Total Quality Management (TQM) or simply Quality Management. Experience from many countries has shown that this is the most powerful strategy for creating better quality.

Quality Management is a flexible, goal-oriented management strategy. One of its major ideas is to initiate an improvement process in which many of the employees participate. Quality improvement is described in a special section below.

Quality Management ranges over a far wider spectrum of methods and techniques than previous quality strategies. The strategy runs deeper and is more demanding, both for the company and for the consultant, but the results provide an extraordinarily good reward for the effort put in. In companies which focus on quality management there is a change in the attitude to quality, prompted by the priorities of management.

What advice should consultants give their client companies? The answer depends on the situation of the company.

Do the authorities, customers or others make special demands on the documentation of quality? Then quality assurance is the right strategy from the start. But quality must be brought into focus, so that the system does not become an end in itself. Later the work can go on to become a strategy for quality management.

If the company has serious quality problems, or is in a weaker situation than important competitors, it must focus on determined quality development. Then quality management is the right strategy. The planning of a development programme is described in a later section.

As for those companies which have not yet established any special strategy for quality — and that means most of them! — it is high time to bring up the issue. Once one lags behind in competition it may be too late.

The basis of the consultant's advice must be an understanding of the organisational structure of the company.

Principles of Control

Whichever quality strategy is selected, the principles of control are basic. Control consists of deliberate measures aimed at fulfilling specified goals, for example products supplied in accordance with a contract.

The basic control loop is shown in Figure 2.3, with an example from a production company. The goals reflect not only the customer's needs, but also society's needs (e.g. its health, safety and environmental needs) and the company's internal requirements (e.g. resource husbandry and economy).

Figure 2.3: Basic Control Model

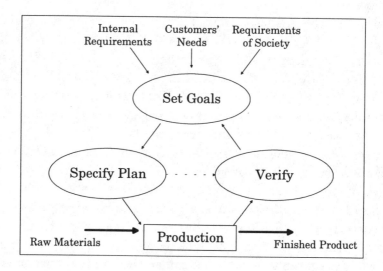

Production itself consists of processing raw materials into finished products. The technical specifications must be met in the production process. Reports from production are compared with the technical specifications in a verification process. If the specifications have been met, agreement with them can be confirmed; if not, deviations must be reported. The deviations are dealt with in a new round of the control loop, so that all finished products conform to the requirements.

Running in parallel with production there are also testing, inspection and other forms of direct "control", as illustrated in Figure 2.4. The control report is also part of the basis of verification, and is meant to confirm that the specifications have been met.

Every company has systems, developed to varying degrees, which are meant to perform the functions described above. In standards for quality assurance, as described in the next section, there are requirements for such systems.

Figure 2.4: Control Model with Monitoring and Inspection

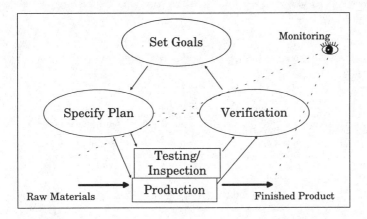

In addition to the company's own systems there may be external monitoring, as illustrated by the eye in Figure 2.4. This may be from the authorities themselves, a body authorised by the authorities, a customer granted insight into the company or the company's own quality division. Such monitoring often takes the form of a *quality audit*, which is a systematic and independent examination of the quality activities.

In a company there are many such processes, each with its own control loop. They are all interlinked in a system of customer-supplier relations as shown in Figure 2.5. While the products move forward in the process, information on the customers' needs is fed back.

Figure 2.5: Relationships between Processes

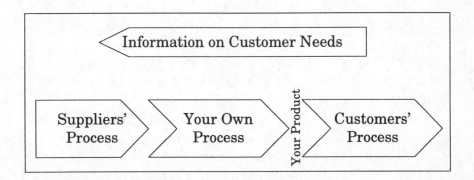

A simplified network showing the processes in an industrial company, with links to customers and suppliers, is shown in Figure 2.6.

Figure 2.6: Customer-Supplier Relations in an Industrial Company

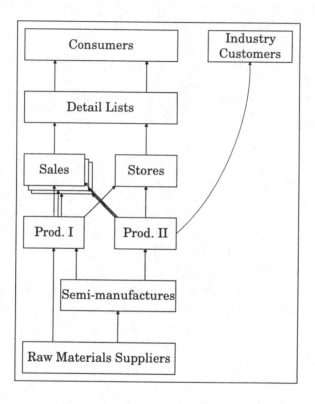

Introduction of Quality Assurance

Many companies have quality assurance as the main strategy for their quality work, and have introduced systems based on ISO 9001/02/03. Quality assurance emphasises the establishment of systems for controlling one's own company, and documenting this to clients and authorities.

Properly used, quality assurance is an effective, appropriate system for control and monitoring, ensuring that customers, authorities and the companies themselves can feel confident that deliveries conform to specifications and requirements. Quality assurance, and not least certification of the systems, is also an effective way of making your quality work visible. Certification of quality assurance systems may be demanded, for example, in connection with the EU Single Market.

But quality assurance also has disadvantages. The development of systems is time-consuming, documentation requirements are extensive, and costs can grow with the volume of paper and data.

A consultant who has to assist a company in introducing quality assurance should exercise caution. Without previous experience of such work, expert help, for example, from a specialist consultant or a certification institution, should be obtained once the first few items below have been introduced. The following is presented as a working draft:

1. The main job must be done by the company's own staff. The consultant should support and motivate, but company commitment, especially from management, is absolutely essential.

2. Start by specifying the company's buying criteria for quality. "What does quality mean to us?"

3. Review the company as a control system:

   • Who are the customers?

   • What are the products?

   • What processes are centrally placed?

   • How are these processes controlled? Are the control loops "closed"? Do they also match up across organisational boundaries?

   • How is responsibility distributed? Is there a clear job specification for management? Do all important processes have a responsible manager/supervisor?

   • How is the information system set up? Are quality results reported, including deviations? Does documentation conform to contractual requirements, official rules and regulations, and does it meet the company's own needs?

4. What requirements must the quality assurance system meet? Usually one refers to one of the international standards ISO 9001 or 9002. Important customers may have their own requirements. The company must familiarise itself thoroughly with the requirements which are to be met, and should not forget its own needs.

5. Describe the company's quality system. Use a form adapted to the company's own systems and existing documentation. Write briefly and succinctly, and only about what the company itself needs, and what is a direct requirement from customers and authorities. Keep an overview of all items where changes in the company's normal practice are necessary.

6. Implement the system in the organisation. Give special emphasis to the points that involve changes in relation to previous practice. Make sure line management follows up.

7. Have a quality audit or audits done by an experienced auditor or by a certification institution. The aim is to find out (a) whether the system conforms to the established requirements and (b) whether the system is observed in practice.

Quality Improvement

Continuous quality improvement is the most important tool in the work for better quality. The aim is to reduce quality costs — which are the costs of *poor* quality. Examples are control costs, and the cost of rejections and reprocessing, complaints and guarantees.

The difference between quality improvement and the control of quality described above is illustrated in Figure 2.7. The figure shows how a process is controlled in principle within a zone with quality costs corresponding to 20-25 per cent of turnover. This is a common level in industry. We can also see how deviations sometimes result in a steep temporary increase in costs. Such deviations are often corrected by "fire-extinguishing" actions. A good quality assurance system reduces the risk of such deviations considerably.

The aim of quality improvement measures is to improve the whole process, so that the quality costs are substantially reduced — in the example down to 3-5 per cent of turnover. There are many examples of savings of this order being achieved.

Figure 2.7: Quality Control and Quality Improvement

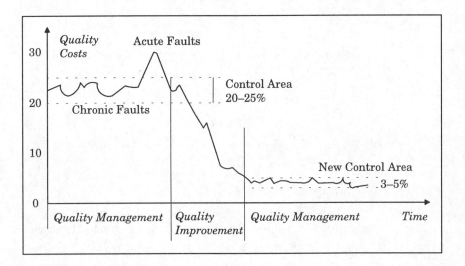

Quality improvement of this type is done by means of project-oriented problem-solving. Quality problems must be mapped out and assigned priorities. Then they can be solved one by one with goal-oriented improvement measures at all levels of the company.

If quality improvement is to be permanent, the problems must be solved by removing the cause. It is not enough to attack the symptoms. Project-oriented problem-solving thus has two main elements as illustrated in Figure 2.8:

- From symptom to cause, and

- From cause to remedy.

When one starts up a quality improvement programme in the company, the first projects must be chosen with care so that the likelihood of success is high. Use the following criteria when selecting a project:

- The problem should be chronic and well known
- Significant savings must result if it is solved
- The possibility of a successful solution should be good
- Results must be measurable.

Figure 2.8: Outline for Problem-Solving

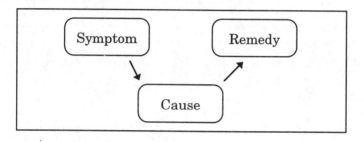

Quality Development Programme

Companies which want to use quality measures to enhance their competitiveness focus on a spectrum of tools adapted to the company itself and the industry in which it works. Such a development programme will last several years, and will typically have a structure of the type shown in Figure 2.9.

Figure 2.9: Main Elements of a Quality Development Programme

Start the development programme with a one to two-day management meeting on quality. Here are some central issues for discussion at the meeting:

- What is quality in our business?

- How does our quality rate compare with the competition?

- What are the demands of our customers?

- What are the demands of the authorities?

- What are our three most serious quality problems, and what are their causes?

- What is the goal of our quality work?

A pilot project should be established in connection with the management meeting. The aims of the pilot project are:

- Motivation to make an effort

- Setting goals for the work

- Planning the measures.

Some relevant measures in the pilot project are:

- A survey of the status of quality work, for example using quality audits

- A review of control and distribution of responsibility

- Identification of problem areas

- Development and prioritising of quality goals

- Survey of quality costs.

It is the task of management to set goals, organise the work, deal with training and later to follow up on results. It is the staff who have to "bear the load", but support from above is crucial to success.

An important aspect of quality development is customer information. In planning for quality, the needs of the customer must be considered and converted into product features. Figure 2.10 illustrates the main elements in the process of customer-oriented planning for quality.

Training plays an important role in all successful quality development programmes. Training is necessary at all the three levels as illustrated in Figure 2.9:

- For management, a two to three days' course is recommended. This gives them a broad overview of the quality area and of how the various methods and techniques should be applied. Such courses may be external or company-internal.

- Specialist training is necessary in a number of areas, e.g. production, purchasing, product development, quality control and assurance. In this case, external courses are most relevant.

- For large groups of employees, internal training is preferable for practical and economic reasons. There are now complete training programmes for this purpose. Organisers of the internal training must be specially trained.

Figure 2.10: Planning Quality

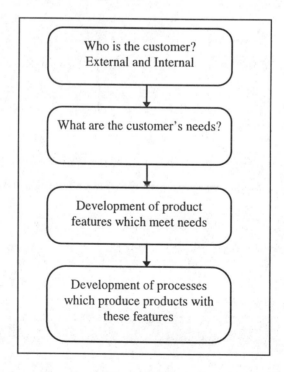

Experience has shown that a number of conditions must be met if quality development is to be successful. We can sum up some success criteria here:

- **Management commitment**: Management must actively participate in the work, from the top down. This is the most important single factor for achieving results.

- **Participation**: The whole organisation must gradually be involved in the quality work.

- **Training**: Training is a precondition of the ability to do the job correctly.

- **The quality work must penetrate into daily operations:** Quality development is not a task for quality experts, but part of the day-to-day activities of the firm. The attitude to quality must be influenced throughout the organisation.

- **Results must be followed up:** "What gets measured gets done", says Anders Scharp, General Director of Electrolux. Active follow-up of important quality parameters in itself contributes to quality improvement.

- **Annual quality plans:** After the first period of enthusiasm, the work can easily fizzle out. To maintain attention to quality the quality work must be planned and followed up.

The Rewards Can Be Great
The work for better quality requires a determined effort over an extended period. Nevertheless, those who have seriously made the effort have found that the rewards are great compared with the effort. The results are evident in many areas:

- **Stronger market position:** Competitive quality is a condition of the survival of the firm. Satisfied — or enthusiastic — customers are the best basis for positive development.

- **Reduced costs:** Quality costs often make up 20 – 30 per cent of turnover in production companies. In service industries the percentage can be over 50 per cent. Halving these costs within three years is a realistic goal and will have a strong impact on the financial results of the company.

- **Laws and other requirements are observed:** Quality requirements and quality assurance requirements are becoming an increasingly important part of the inspection function of the authorities. The establishment of the EC Single Market will make new demands on many industries. Stricter laws and legal practice in matters of product liability are becoming more and more central issues, not only in the USA, but also in Europe.

- **Satisfied staff:** The work for better quality means commitment among the staff, as there will be fewer "fire-extinguishing" actions, a tidier structure for responsibility and working relationships, and room for personal development. The staff will appreciate this.

European Foundation for Quality Management (EFQM)

The European Foundation for Quality Management developed a European model for self-appraisal to assist companies to clearly identify their strengths and the areas in which improvements can be made. Essentially, self-appraisal involves the regular and systematic review of the organisation's activities and results. The model provides a framework for self-appraisal that is applicable to virtually every business organisation.

The model presents nine elements that can be used to appraise the organisation's progress towards TQM. The nine elements are broken down into *Enablers* and *Results* and are as follows:

Enablers:

1. **Leadership:** the behaviour of all managers in driving the organisation towards Total Quality.

2. **Policy and Strategy:** the organisation's values, vision and strategic direction and the ways in which the organisation achieves them.

3. **People Management:** the management of the organisation's people.

4. **Resources:** the management, utilisation and preservation of resources.

5. **Processes:** the management of the value-adding activities within the organisation.

Results:

6. **Customer Satisfaction:** what the perception of external customers, direct and indirect, is of the organisation and of its products and services.

7. **People Satisfaction:** what the people's feelings are about their organisation.

8. **Impact on Society:** what the perception of the organisation is among society at large. This includes views of the organisation's approach to quality of life, the environment and to the preservation of global resources.

9. **Business Results:** what the organisation is achieving in relation to its planned business performance.

Malcolm Baldridge Award

The table given in Figure 2.11 shows the main points used in the Malcolm Baldridge award and is presented to assist companies in assessing where they stand with regard to quality.

Figure 2.11: Main Points in the Malcolm Baldridge Award

Where Do You Stand in Quality Work? (Test your own business in the areas below.)		Weighting
1. Management	Has management succeeded in building up a positive attitude to quality?	100
2. Information and data analysis	How good is the system for reporting and analysing data on quality and quality improvement?	70
3. Strategic planning of quality	Is quality part of the company's strategic planning?	60
4. Use of human resources	To what extent is the potential of employees used in the work for quality?	150
5. System for quality assurance and improvement	How well is the system developed and implemented in the organisation?	140
6. Quality achieved	What results has the company achieved in the work for better quality?	180
7. Satisfied customers	How does the company know the customers' wishes and the capacity of the products to fulfil these wishes?	300
Total		1,000

LEAN PRODUCTION

Overview

Today's markets are customer-oriented and are no longer vendor-oriented, as they have been for decades. Only those enterprises whose products, production and services are in line with customers' demands will succeed in holding on to market share. Flexible production means reacting quickly to customers' demands, by producing the right product in the right quality, offering it at the right time and supplying it to the right place.

Competition is a permanent, never-ending process which presents a continuous challenge to companies in today's market. Thus innovation must become a normal and natural component of the way in which companies do business — all efforts must be focused on satisfying customers' requirements.

In this situation of customer-orientation, business structures with regard to organisation and product can be in conflict with market requirements, because in many cases the structures correspond to the requirements of a vendor-oriented market. There are above all three characteristics of traditional structures that give cause for concern:

1. The ratio of direct to indirect activities in the organisational structures is poor. These structures have given rise to excessive indirect costs and low productivity.

2. Production is based on the division of labour and is organised according to performance production arrangements. As a consequence, throughput times are too long (over 90 per cent is taken up with the product waiting between successive operations), so that levels of work-in-progress are too high.

3. The ability of companies to bring about fast and consistent innovation of products and processes is poor because the structures of the organisation are based on the division of labour, so that various activities are carried out to some degree in isolation. This is not conducive to bringing about improvements in products or processes.

Many organisations and operational processes in manufacturing enterprises are characterised by the division of labour, by each function thinking only within the limits of their own functional area, and by hierarchical structures. Thinking and acting are focused on the control of single *functions* and not on the control of constant and efficient *processes* in design, construction, production planning and manufacturing.

Concept of Lean Production

The starting-point for Lean Production can be understood through combining the advantages of both craft type and mass production systems, whilst avoiding the disadvantages of each. Models of each type of enterprise are given in the table in Figure 2.12.

Figure 2.12: Three Business Models

Characteristics	Typical example
Model 1: The small, entrepreneurial enterprise • Specialising in market niches or specific products • Very close to the market • Short throughput times and simple decision making • Compact organisational structure • Reasonable overheads	Craft industry
Model 2: The big, bureaucratic enterprise • Focused on volume • Not very close to the market • Long throughput times and complex decision making • Many levels to the organisation structure • High overheads	Large industrial corporations
Model 3: The flexible, market-oriented enterprise • Focused on relation between product and market • Fast reaction to the market • Performance is measured in terms of time • Flat organisation structure • Reduced overheads	Lean enterprise

Lean Production is "lean" because it uses less resources than mass production: half of the personnel in the factory, half of the factory space, half of the investment in tools and half of the development time for new products. It needs less than half of the inventories, makes fewer mistakes and can make products of greater variety than the enterprise that uses traditional ways of manufacturing.

Lean Production has the overall objective of (a) improving quality, (b) reducing throughput times and (c) reducing costs. This is done by achieving:

- No waste of value-adding resources

- Effective material flow instead of large stocks

- Prevention of mistakes instead of expensive rework

- Working competently, responsibly and autonomously.

Effects and Characteristics of Lean Production

The essential requirement of Lean Production is to perfect the process of productivity and to eliminate activities that incur indirect costs. Productive activities form whole integrated functional areas: from product development via production, assembly and co-ordination of supplies to distribution and customer service.

The effects of Lean Production are listed in the table in Figure 2.13.

The two main principles of Lean Production are:

1. Self-co-ordinating teams consisting of highly qualified personnel focus on continuously improving the productive activities assigned to them. These teams take the place of hierarchical structures which were based on a division of work and a distinct separation of direct and indirect areas.

2. Suppliers are not considered as being either external to the process or as being easily changed, but instead they are regarded as being members of the organisation. Consequently, they are integrated into the process of productivity.

The characteristics of Lean Production are given in the table in Figure 2.14.

Figure 2.13: Effects of Lean Production

- Reduction of quality problems experienced by the customer to zero
- Reduction of defects occurring during the production process to zero
- Development time for new products halved
- Throughput times reduced by half
- Inventory levels reduced by half
- Production of smaller batches with more diversity at same cost
- Reduction in investment in tool and equipment
- Reduction in manufacturing floor space
- Reducing number of personnel required in all processes.

Target: Today's efficiency to be doubled !

Figure 2.14: Characteristics of Lean Production

- Competition-oriented, adaptable with a well thought out business strategy which has been translated into action plans
- Simultaneous product and process engineering involving both customers and suppliers
- Permanent co-operation with customers and suppliers based on partnership
- Production uncompromisingly focused on: zero defects, zero inventories, endless production variety
- Use of interdisciplinary teams made up of multifunctional workers — consequent rejection of Taylorism
- Creativity and experience of employees used through their participation in teams
- Good quality performance at all levels — focus on product quality.

FURTHER READING

Crosby, Philip B. (1979) *Quality is Free*, New York: McGraw-Hill. A classic. Describes the "zero-fault" philosophy and Crosby's 14-point improvement programme.

Feigenbaum, A.V. (1986) *Total Quality Control*, New York: McGraw-Hill.

Floor, R.L. (1993) *Beyond TQM*, Chichester: John Wiley & Sons.

Goldratt, E.M. and Fox, J. (1984) *The Goal: A Process of Ongoing Improvement*, Aldershot: Gower.

Hammer, M. (1990) "Re-engineering Work: Don't Automate, Obliterate", *Harvard Business Review*, July-August.

Harrington, H. (1991) *Business Process Improvement*, New York: McGraw Hill.

Juran, J.M. (1989) *Juran on Leadership for Quality*, New York: The Free Press. A modern handbook with the main emphasis on the role of management, written by a world-famous authority.

Lawler, E.E. (1986) *High Involvement Management*, San Francisco: Jossey Bass.

Mohrman et al. (1989) *Large Scale Organisational Change*, San Francisco: Jossey Bass.

Nørby, M. (1992) *Just-in-Time: Visioner og Erfaringer*, København: Samfundslitteratur.

Ouchi, W. (1981) *Theory Z: How American Business Can Meet the Japanese Challenge*, Reading, MA: Addison-Wesley.

Schonberger, R.J. (1982) *Japanese Manufacturing Techniques: Nine Hidden Lessons in Simplicity*, New York: Free Press.

Senge, P.E. (1990) *The Fifth Discipline, The Art & Practice of The Learning Organisation*, London: Century Business.

Shingo, S. (1981) *A Study of the Toyota Production System: From an Industrial Engineering Viewpoint*. Cambridge, MA: Productivity Press.

Wobbe, W. (1991) *Anthropocentric Production Systems: A Strategic Issue for Europe*, Bruxelles: APS working paper series.

Womack, J.P., Jones, D.T. and Roos, D. (1990) *The Machine that Changed the World*, New York: Maxwell Macmillan.

MANAGEMENT OF CHANGE

INTRODUCTION

This handbook aims to assist consultants in their work with SMEs. In almost all assignments, consultants will be involved in assisting the client company on how to cope with change. The aim of all consultancy assignments in this regard should be to:

Ensure long-term profitability by improving company competitiveness through improving the "development environment" within the client company.

The term "development environment" refers to the company's ability to learn how to tackle issues *on its own*. In working to improve the development environment, the consultant sets out to teach the company how to tackle issues by itself after the consultant has left, or in other words:

To improve the company's ability to manage its own development on an ongoing basis.

It is extremely important that companies should develop in-house *competence* on an ongoing basis. Companies have to relate to a world that is constantly changing. This has never been more so than during the 1990s. Companies must always keep improving, therefore, if profitability levels are to remain satisfactory.

Companies should have as a target that they are:

Better than yesterday, but worse than tomorrow.

All change within a company must be implemented by people. When changes are being implemented, employees are being expected to carry out their functions in a way that is different to before. If change is to be implemented successfully, it is vital that all those involved understand the reasons for the changes and that they approve of them in advance.

As the demands for change and innovation become more pressing, companies should be aware of how to plan and implement changes. Information, education and the joint commitment of management and staff all play an important role in the successful implementation of change.

The difficulties associated with the implementation of change are illustrated by the following comments that are typical of companies involved in change:

> "It would be easier to construct a large town than to change the standards in this company."

> "It all looked very well on paper. In reality, however, things turned out very differently."

> "We had to put a lot of effort into convincing employees that it was not all about squeezing more work out of them."

> "Many unforeseen factors delayed the project significantly."

> "We put a lot of effort into keeping everyone informed but it was all in vain — the message still didn't get through to people."

In this chapter, the management of change is looked at under the following headings:

- Forces that Influence Companies
- Resistance or Joint Commitment
- The Importance of Information
- Employee Expectations
- Development of Employee "Competence"
- The Importance of One's Own Thought Processes
- Important Aspects of Good Management
- Conclusion.

FORCES THAT INFLUENCE COMPANIES

Companies are influenced by many different internal and external forces which, in a situation of stability, tend to balance one another. The fact that a system is stable means that, for better or worse, the system always seeks to return to normal when exposed to outside influences. Thus, when pressure is applied from one direction, forces will act in the opposite direction so as to oppose it. This desirable capacity that is present in healthy organisations ensures that the company is not put off course by small irregularities or unexpected external influences.

When changes are being introduced, however, many of the internal forces will act as obstacles to change. The better the organisation is at analysing, understanding and influencing the forces at work within the system, the better are the prospects for the successful implementation of change.

The production system of most companies can cope with the many unforeseen factors that occur from day to day. For example, urgent "rush" orders, machine breakdowns, influenza epidemics, new environmental regulations, variation in exchange rates, fluctuating interest rates, must all be dealt with as they arise. Nevertheless, many projects that involve changes are planned as if none of the above unforeseen factors exist.

During a process of change, a company is more vulnerable to external influences. Even the most detailed of plans are easily upset and if the company is not able to quickly adjust to unforeseen influences, the risk of project failure is high.

> The only thing that is certain about unpredictable factors is that they certainly will occur.

It is important, therefore, to take the following factors into consideration when changes are being planned:

- The plan must take *all aspects* of the company's operations into account — it should not focus too narrowly on one aspect only.

- The plan should describe how employees that will be affected by the changes can be *involved* in the implementation of those changes.

- The plan must be as *flexible* as possible so as it can accommodate revisions and adjustments as the need arises without losing sight of the overall objective the changes seek to achieve.

It is important also to appreciate a company's culture and to have a detailed knowledge of the company's resources, strengths and weaknesses so as to be able to take advantage of the forces that are at work within the company and its environment.

A company's "culture" — that is, its way of working, its strengths and weaknesses, its formal and informal systems of management, its traditions, its attitudes to the traditions associated with professional craftsmen, etc. — is not easily changed. (In many cases, this is desirable, in that a company's culture has learned how to compensate for inherent weaknesses which cannot be overcome at short notice).

A summary of some of the more important elements that should be contained in a plan for the implementation of changes are as follows:

- An analysis of the company's culture, strengths and weaknesses, traditions, level of education of employees as well as employee commitment should be carried out prior to any changes being implemented.

- The overall objective of the change must be clear to all concerned.

- An analysis of forces, both favourable and unfavourable, that will affect the change should be carried out. The strategy employed to bring about the change should take these forces as well as employee expectations into account.

- The dissemination of information should be carefully planned, taking employee interests and needs into consideration. The plan should allow for revisions to be made on the basis of developments that may occur during the course implementation.

- An analysis of available resources and any education or training needs should be carried out. This should be done in conjunction with those who will have to implement the changes.

- Implementation with ongoing monitoring of results as they become evident.

- Finally, the effect of changes should be evaluated. The process used should also be evaluated. The impact on future developments should be considered.

RESISTANCE OR JOINT COMMITMENT

A project to implement changes may face resistance in that it may be perceived as being not in the best interests of those who will be affected by the changes.

This conflict of interests may be tangible, such as with changes concerning wage levels, work loading, time-honoured benefits or manning levels. Such conflicts can generally be resolved through negotiation and compromise. In all cases, clearly defined objectives will help clarify the issues and thus assist with agreement being reached.

In some cases, however, conflict can arise as a result of changes being perceived differently by different people. Every company employee, by virtue of their role in the company, their means of influence and experience, will have a different opinion as to what is achievable and what is desirable.

Whether employees are motivated to participate in a process of change will depend on the impact each individual employee thinks the changes will have on their own special area of interest. Given that employee interests vary from one level to another within an organisation, a project will have a greater chance of success if it is able to accommodate these interests across all levels.

The reasons behind resistance to change are not always apparent — some employee concerns are quite legitimate and can be expressed openly and addressed, whereas other concerns are kept hidden and can thus give rise to problems.

The most effective way to overcome resistance to change is to foster joint commitment among management and staff. It is important, therefore, to examine the conditions necessary to ensure that an invitation to employees to participate in a project will be worthwhile and to look at the possibility of improving those conditions.

1. The first condition is that the objectives of the changes be understood and accepted. This is brought about through clear definition of the objectives and thorough dissemination of information about the changes, through being willing to listen to other points of view and to be influenced by them, and to be willing to make concessions to satisfy other peoples' interests.

2. The second condition is that there be openness and credibility in all matters relating to the change. The best way to promote openness and credibility is to present one's demands as clearly and frankly as possible, to be open about uncertainties and to take employees' concerns into consideration.

3. The third condition is that all those involved in changes should have a thorough knowledge of the areas affected. There is little point in inviting employees to participate in areas they are not familiar with. Consequently, an offer to participate in a project may have to be accompanied by some training.

4. The fourth condition is that employees demonstrate their interest in and commitment to planned changes. This will depend to a certain degree on existing company traditions and employee expectations — if employees feel that changes will not affect themselves, or that their concerns will be ignored, they will not be motivated to participate in the process of change.

The interest in and competence to participate in the decision-making process will develop as employees are trained and by encouraging them to participate at every opportunity. Even though initial attempts may prove to be unsuccessful, they will help form a basis for projects to be successfully implemented at some point in the future.

THE IMPORTANCE OF INFORMATION

Information is central to the successful implementation of changes within an organisation. To whom should information be given? When and how should information be given out? These are both important considerations.

The dissemination of information often constitutes the most difficult part of the whole process of change and many companies have difficulties in this regard. Unfortunately, there is no simple unambiguous formula for the dissemination of information that will guarantee success — the releasing of the right information at the right time depends entirely on each individual case. Nevertheless, the following guidelines are offered to help with deciding how information is given out during a process of change:

1. Employees are entitled to be given information about planned changes that will affect them as early as possible.

2. The earlier and more comprehensive the information, the better the chances are of avoiding rumours and misunderstandings.

3. Once information is successfully given out and understood, there will be a better chance of involving employees and their capabilities to bring about a successful change.

4. The quality, quantity and clarity of information is always considered to be better by those who give it out than by those who receive it.

5. Due to different interests, backgrounds and levels of comprehension among employees, the content of information right down to the specific meaning of individual words will be perceived differently at different levels within an organisation.

6. Communication is brought about by more than words alone — *"actions speak louder than words"*. Thus information and actions must coincide.

7. The effect from information depends more on a person's ability to listen than on their ability to express themselves.

In some cases, information may be withheld in order to protect a company's competitiveness. In other cases, information given out too early can lead to insecurity and confusion and eventually give rise to conflict. In all cases, however, the benefits from withholding information should be evaluated and compared with the difficulties caused by not making the information freely available.

Written information has the advantage of being easy and quick to distribute and is proof that certain information has been given out. Written information on its own, however, is generally not sufficient in that there is scope for misinterpretation and in that written information tends to be impersonal.

In many cases, information is better given out at meetings in that this indicates a willingness to communicate and issues are discussed openly in the presence of all those involved. At meetings people can be invited to ask questions and misunderstandings can be promptly cleared up so that the information given out is fully understood.

The size of the meeting is a factor that should be taken into account, however. Large meetings can have limited application in that participants may feel insecure and will not tend to ask questions for fear of being made to appear stupid. In general, small meetings held in the workplace at which issues can be discussed in detail can prove to be most effective.

EMPLOYEE EXPECTATIONS

Every company has its own system of expectations, including expectations as to what is viable, what is right and just, what management are up to, the importance given to individual feelings and ideas, etc. These expectations are based on tradition and experience and play a decisive role in the way in which changes are accepted.

Employee expectations may be deeply rooted, and it is not possible to fulfil these expectations through explanations and information only. It is important to bear in mind that the results of planned changes and the way in which they are implemented will have an influence on how future expectations are formed.

If management and staff are to co-operate successfully, openness and mutual trust are essential. If employees have experienced that their openness has been used against them in the past, then it will be very difficult to get them to participate positively in future projects.

If the situation is such that plans are frequently presented but nothing gets implemented, then new initiatives will not be taken seriously. If employees are used to not being listened to, it is going to be difficult to convince them that they will in future have a say in how the company is run. In companies where requests for improvements have been continually met with resistance from management, employees who are asked to make suggestions and contribute to a process of change will respond with scepticism.

It is thus very difficult to cope with negative expectations in that they are generally deeply rooted and any information given out will be interpreted in the light of these negative expectations. The best way to overcome this is through implementing a number of small changes quickly — see to it that employee requests for minor changes are implemented promptly so that their expectations are exceeded.

Fortunately positive expectations exist also. Employee expectations that they are individuals, that their needs are taken into account, that they can influence the situation and that changes are carried out for the common good are all positive. Expectations that planned changes will open up interesting challenges and make the company into a better place to work can have powerful motivating influences.

DEVELOPMENT OF EMPLOYEE "COMPETENCE"

Competence can mean many things. Generally, the word is used to describe a person's potential and ability to carry out certain activities. Competence refers to more than just knowledge, in that it also takes other factors into consideration, such as:

- Skills

- Experience

- Personal contact network

- Attitudes.

Competence development, therefore, is brought about by reference to the above factors.

- *Knowledge and skills* can be developed through study, training, practical work, on-the-job training etc.

- One gains *experience* by learning from one's own mistakes and successes. It is important to get feedback between planned results and the actual results, either through reports or from management. This learning process is a precondition of gaining more experience.

- Often, a *personal contact network* can be a way of obtaining knowledge and experience. It is important to create organisational structures and methods of working that facilitate contact networks both within and outside the company.

- *Attitudes* can be defined as willingness and preparedness to share in and be receptive to basic views. They are greatly influenced by the nature of management.

IMPORTANCE OF ONE'S OWN THOUGHT PROCESSES

The competence of company personnel depends on the individual and on each person's own thought processes. Each individual must take responsibility for learning themselves. This does not mean that individuals are unaffected by other people's thoughts. However, if personnel are unable to analyse and digest what is going on around them, they can easily end up copying other people's actions uncritically.

We talk about competence when it has arisen from our own needs and emerges as the result of independent thinking. At the same time, competence has not been proven until it has been used to bring about specific actions.

For every company the goal should be to develop competence such that the organisation is able to meet present and future needs and demands. These are needs and demands pressing on the company from the external surroundings and from its own employees. Competence can be developed in many different areas including technological development, production, marketing, information, financing, material administration, and personal and organisational development.

The development of competence within a company must be controlled. First and foremost, the company itself must assume the responsibility for initiating the process. The aim is to create a corporate culture which enables employees to think and act on the basis of the company's own needs.

Dependence on internal resources and energy improves the chance of keeping competence within the limits of the company, thus making it a natural component of the company's culture and identity. The result is an improvement in the self-esteem and self-confidence of the company's managers through confirmation of their own strength and faith in themselves.

Factors that are important in initiating a competence development process are illustrated in Figure 3.1. These factors help to ensure that the process does not come to a halt, but that it brings about permanent changes within the company.

Figure 3.1: Initiating One's Own Competence Development Process

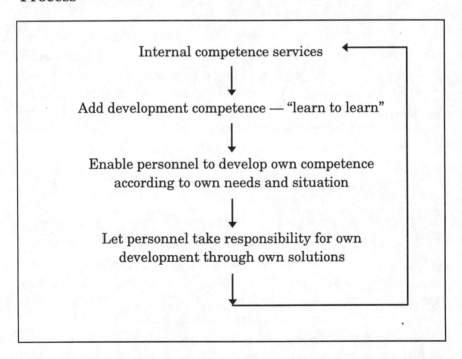

IMPORTANT ASPECTS OF GOOD MANAGEMENT

Competence produces its own rewards. All the same, most people also have a need to make their competence visible to the outside world. In an organisation this depends on management. Managers must acknowledge that such visibility is necessary and must take the attitude that the employees:

- Want to be competent

- Are capable of taking the correct course of action in a given situation

- Are productive.

One of management's tasks is to create an environment in which these basic attitudes to employees are expressed. Specifically, this should be brought about by:

- Making employees feel able and valuable

- Creating the right conditions for development of employees' competence.

To create a link between individual and collective competence, management must work to ensure that employees' individual commitment and creativity can be expressed collectively in the company. In this regard, management should take the following factors into consideration:

- Co-operation

- Commitment

- Creativity

The relationship between these three factors is illustrated in Figure 3.2. Co-operation is shown as a catalyst that triggers a series of processes which result in collective competence of company employees. Improved competence in turn triggers improved performance. The diagram indicates how both commitment and creativity are made possible by co-operation. Co-operation is crucial to commitment and increases the potential for creative solutions.

Figure 3.2: Important Aspects of Good Management

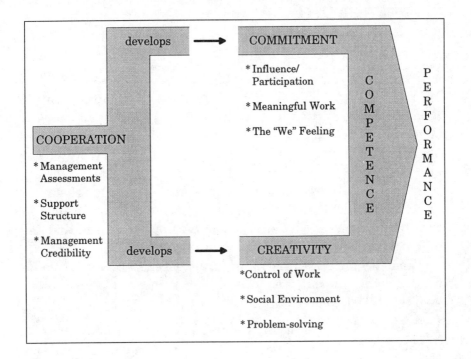

Co-operation

Co-operation is central to the development of competence within an organisation. When there is co-operation in a company, employees feel that they are helping to shape the company's development. Through co-operation employees get a clearer impression of their own areas of responsibility, and of what has to be done and how. Employees will understand the reasoning behind the specific guidelines that control their work because they have themselves been involved in discussing the different issues in an open process in which everyone has had to give and take. This open process demonstrates to employees that they have some degree of control over what happens in their own workplace.

It is the task of management to create the right conditions for genuine co-operation. The three most important factors in this regard are:

1. Management's value basis/view of the employees

2. Management's support structure

3. Management's credibility.

Management's Value Basis / View of Employees
Management's value basis/view of employees must incorporate a fundamental conviction that the work that employees are doing is of value to the company. Even if such a value basis is implicit, the message will be understood by employees, who will be personally and profoundly affected by it. The message in turn influences their ability to perform at their jobs and the potential for co-operation is further advanced. Management must acknowledge that employees seek and are capable of competence, and that the organisation and its employees are interdependent.

The following questions are normally asked to assess the value basis of management, and will show whether the organisation inspires staff to co-operate:

- **How are the people in the organisation valued?** Are employees respected as important people because they do jobs that are important to the company and themselves — or is their value only appreciated in terms of the functions they perform and the positions they have?

- **How does management view the competence of employees?** Does management hope for the best and rely on the employees to be willing and able to do their work properly — or does management doubt the employees' abilities and motives?

- **What types of systems of power and influence are characteristic of the organisation?** Is power shared with those who need it to do their work — or are there only a few people who can exercise power and make decisions?

The central factor in these questions is respect. When respect is evenly shared throughout the organisation, this forms the cornerstone of all co-operation. Respect for the individual is a precondition of both personal development and a productive attitude among company employees.

Support Structure

The extent to which management attempts to promote co-operation in an organisation quickly becomes evident from how the organisation is structured by management. Both the physical and the psychological structures of the organisation are important if meaningful co-operation between employees is to be achieved.

In order to bring about co-operation, the organisational structure must first and foremost reflect the need for management to be accessible. Employees must have easy access at all times to managers and colleagues with whom they need to co-operate. Information in the form of memoranda, reports, meetings or accounts must flow to those who need it and who can complement it with relevant information of their own. Prioritise between information that is "nice to know" and information that employees "need to know". Managers themselves must motivate employees to be active in the organisation by removing physical and psychological obstacles.

To establish whether the physical and psychological structure of the organisation is conducive to co-operation, the following questions should be considered:

- **How is the flow of information organised within the company?** Is the flow of information controlled by the needs of those who do the work, and does it go directly to them — or does it follow a chain of command that reflects rank or position?

- **How do managers treat views that are expressed frankly?** Do they encourage employees to express themselves and to speak their minds — or do they work against any attempts to do this by ignoring, making fun of or censoring suggestions received?

- **How are working relationships organised in the company?** Can employees contact colleagues and managers who have an effect on their work — or is the organisational structure such that it is difficult or impossible to discuss or exchange information?

These are questions relevant to the support structure. The answers to them show whether co-operation can be fully realised.

Credibility of Management

In order to be credible, management must consistently follow up on suggestions made on how co-operation can be improved. This can be done by setting up a simple feedback process which shows how action on specific suggestions is progressing so that the person who made the suggestion is kept informed on developments. When specific actions are taken in response to suggestions, the credibility of management increases.

The credibility of management can be assessed through considering the following questions:

- **What results do employees expect when they make suggestions and express views to management?** Do employees think that their suggestions are taken seriously — or does the suggestion fizzle out after a few half-hearted attempts at implementation?

- **How are rules and routines treated by management?** Can the principles be discussed and adapted by those who use them — or are they treated as though they are "cast in stone" so that it is impossible to modernise or simplify them?

- **How does management choose the "experts" who are responsible for planning and carrying out the work?** Is an expert a person who has a lot of experience of what has to be done; does the person have a theoretical background or is it someone with enough power to make decisions?

Commitment

Co-operation is an important prerequisite, but is no guarantee that employees will be committed to bringing about improvements.

Although most managers would like employees to be committed to realising the goals of the organisation, they often misunderstand what gives rise to commitment. Some managers see commitment as a product that can be bought with bonuses or special incentives. Others think is something that can be stimulated by holding competitions or giving pep talks about motivation.

It is naive of a manager to use such superficial measures. In the competence process the commitment of employees is more than an organisational asset. Commitment is the only source of vitality and energy at the workplace. The three most important factors influencing commitment are:

- Influence

- Meaningful work

- The "we" feeling.

Influence

The quickest way to destroy commitment is to let employees feel that in spite of good co-operation with one another and management, they still cannot make things happen.

It is a precondition of commitment that personal influence is guaranteed. For this guarantee to apply, management must make sure that those who have participated in planning the way work is to be done also have an influence on what happens later. They must have the opportunity to carry out the measures that management has asked them to make a decision on.

Experiments have shown that productivity is greatly affected when employees are given personal influence and when there is a reasonable balance between the responsibility and authority an employee has. Every time that employees are given a chance to influence their working situation, commitment increases.

The following questions can be used to measure the degree of employee influence in the company:

- **How much control do employees have over their own work priorities and their own working speed?** How much freedom do employees have to assess how much time is necessary to do the work? Are work rates and job priorities worked out in co-operation with those who have to carry out the work — or does management use external consultants or time and motion studies for each job, to establish a *"normal"* work rate?

- **How much control do employees have over routines and rules in their own part of the organisation?** Are the employees themselves involved in creating norms and routines for the organisation? Are they themselves involved in making the necessary decisions in their part of the organisation? Does this give them the opportunity to discuss with management how their department should be run?

In general, we can say that the more choice that employees have in a given situation, the more influence they will feel that they have.

Meaningful Work

Employee commitment can be maintained if employees feel that the jobs they are assigned are meaningful to them as well as compatible with the goals of the organisation. Relevant questions in this regard are:

- **Can employees exploit their skills and interests?** Is the work designed bearing in mind that employees have a need to feel that they have something unique and valuable to contribute towards realising the goals of the organisation — or is the work mainly based on narrow skills and objectives in exchange for a poor wage system?

- **How realistic and challenging are the goals that the employees are asked to aim for?** Can employees see the relationship between their jobs, their capacity and the organisation's needs, so that they feel that they are developing and being stimulated — or is this link missing, so that the work becomes uninteresting to do satisfactorily?

- **What connection is there between the decisions that employees are allowed to make and the fundamental objectives?** Do employees make decisions in crucial matters that affect the performance and quality of the work — or are they only allowed to decide on routine chores?

The "We" Feeling

The "we" feeling is the feeling of belonging and identifying with the company, its goals and its "state of health"! It is important in this regard that there is interdependence and respect amongst the people in the organisation, and a sense of shared responsibility with others in the company. The "we" feeling is based on trust and the sense of security in the organisation. How far management encourages the "we" feeling in the workplace can be judged by asking the following questions:

- **What kind of working morale does management promote among employees?** Is there self-discipline and a consensus that "we do what we have agreed on?"

- **Does management encourage employees to help one another — or is the emphasis on competition and egoism, while individual achievements are rewarded?** Are there ground rules for co-operation which have consequences for everyone? Do employees feel that their personal talents and unique contributions are essential to the company — or do they feel that practically anyone can take their place without any great effect on the success of the company?

- **Does management show that co-operation and lower management are developed by "give and take"?** Are employees encouraged through self-discipline to make allowances for one another on the basis of the fundamental principle that "we're in this together" — or does it prefer intrigues, favouritism and allowing a chosen few to advance at the expense of others?

Creativity

Creativity is the last stage of the competence process. The most common definition of creativity is that the person concerned is able to find new solutions on the basis of known factors.

In response to the fact that something has to be done to achieve creative results, many managers continually suggest "new technology" and "higher capital investments" so that this becomes a kind of mantra. Capital investments and technological knowledge are important, but none of them can replace the everyday inventiveness of employees. The fact is that most of the organisation has a greater need for everyday creativity than for the kind that is associated with technological progress and investments.

It might be a matter of suggestions that bring about solutions to irritating everyday problems or spontaneous reflections that provide an impetus for new priorities.

Creativity is a dimension that above all affects the actual work and the way it is done. The factors that support creativity include how the work is controlled and the social environment in the workplace. The methods used to solve problems are important too, i.e.:

- Control of the work

- The social environment

- Problem-solving.

Control of the Work

Managers and employees by and large agree that work needs some kind of structure, that responsibilities and goals must be defined, and that management must assign priorities. There will be differences of opinion on what this means in practice, however — between management and employees and among the employees themselves.

The factors and priorities that employees must take into account are part of the control — for example, matters relating to how the work process is arranged, both physically and psychologically.

The way work is controlled directly affects creativity. Control is the responsibility of management, and can either work as a platform for creativity or make creativity impossible. Information on whether the working environment supports creativity can be obtained by asking the following questions:

- **How is the work distributed?** Is top competence optimally exploited? Is the work delegated through employees choosing for themselves or by co-ordinated group work — or on the basis of personal intuition, or through mechanical choices that locate people without any regard for their personal development?

- **How can the work be described?** Does it have a structure that allows for flexible solutions?

- **How accessible are the resources that employees need to do their work?** Do employees have immediate access to the tools, material and/or capital they need to do their work — or does management constantly decide over their heads what they need for their work?

To control the work satisfactorily, management must be attentive and open to new methods and solutions.

The Social Environment
It is a well known fact that many jobs are done better in the presence of other people. In this way there is an interplay of personalities where new suggestions can be tried out and feedback received, whether positive or negative. This can lead to increased awareness for the employee and a more finely tuned workplace.

The social environment is just as important to creativity as the control of the work. A crucial factor in ensuring a creative environment is that people are frank and speak openly. Good communication is in turn essential to the social environment. When this exists, one feels free to try something new even if one risks failure.

A social environment must start with the personal ability one has to relate to one's fellow human beings. Whether the work is fun and stimulating, whether one looks forward to going to work every day, and whether colleagues are felt to be reliable and supportive, are all factors which affect creativity. The social environment can be investigated by asking the following questions:

- **How does management handle spontaneity and humour at the workplace?** Does management encourage employees to be natural and to feel good together, so that happiness and good humour are typical of the workplace — or does management see this as wasting time?

- **How are feedback and criticism dealt with in relation to work?** Is feedback used as an instrument for the personal development of the employees — or is it simply regarded as management's tool for evaluation and surveillance?

- **How does management handle individuals with originality and an experimental attitude?** Is management happy to see employees making innovations, even if they turn out to be a failure — or do deviations from fixed routines result in displeasure and disciplinary action?

Problem-solving

A central issue in the competence process is how employees get to grips with the challenges that exist. Control of the work may function excellently and the social atmosphere may be stimulating but this is little help if the methods used for problem-solving do not permit creativity. In such cases solutions will tend not to be new and innovative.

Two elements are important in problem-solving. The first concerns the job itself — the information, knowledge and expertise that is important in understanding the problem. This aspect of problem-solving is usually given the most attention.

The second element, which is probably just as important in arriving at creative solutions, is the actual process, that is, the working methods used. For example, it might be a matter of how agreement is to be reached, and which of the employees are to participate. There is much to suggest that the process is of greater value to the creative result than the actual collection of data.

Whether the system is good or not can be judged by answering the following questions:

- **How are shared problems solved?** Does management prefer the people involved to participate — or does it prefer to make unilateral decisions in order to maintain control?

- **What attitudes are stressed when it comes to the ability to solve day-to-day working problems?** Are employees urged to reflect on the way work is organised — or are they expected to tackle the problem in terms of fixed rules?

- **How are conflicts handled when problems are to be solved?** Is disagreement regarded as a sign that not all the facts have been considered, and as an opportunity to look for other, perhaps new perspectives — or is disagreement quite simply "swept under the carpet" to save time and avoid offending anyone?

CONCLUSION

There is nothing new in the ideas and measures described here. Variations on the theme have been typical of behavioural science's treatment of leadership and organisational theory. These are the attitudes and routines which help to create a sound environment for competence development, which in turn encourages achievement and improves productivity. The management of a company will discover that an increased focus on competence requires more of managers than before.

The development of competence will require different kinds of evaluations, routines and skills from those which are usually emphasised. This can mean other priority criteria for the selection and development of management candidates. Competence requires a specialised kind of knowledge. Technical knowledge is no longer sufficient qualification to manage other peoples' collective efforts.

Regardless of the kind of competence that is dominant, a competent manager is someone who masters the social technology of work, i.e. the evaluations, principles and methods that are necessary to create the conditions where people — not machines — cooperate to do what has to be done.

To implement such an effort, one needs managers who are able to handle productively the large amount of human energy — sometimes constructive and sometimes problematical — that is generated in an organisation.

- Management has the main responsibility for developing individuals, divisions and the organisation as a whole.

- Management has the main responsibility for creating an interplay among individual, organisation and society in general.

- Management must be the motive force in developing an organisational training system and in the generation of knowledge.

- Management must ensure that employees are allowed to use their competence.

- Competency development can in many cases be delegated to divisions or working groups.

- Individual employees share in the responsibility for their own competence and career development.

- Individual employees share in the responsibility for the development of other employees in the co-operative relationship.

4

PROCESS CONSULTANCY

INTRODUCTION

Very often, the human element is the determining factor in any consultancy assignment. It would be naive to propose, let alone to try to implement, any recommendations without the involvement of the employees concerned and without taking into account the impact those recommendations are likely to have on people.

Consultants must, therefore, be aware of the human element at all times. *Process consultancy* refers to the role a consultant plays in developing learning processes within companies so that those companies can continue to develop on their own after the consultant has left.

In this chapter process consultancy is looked at under the following headings:

- The Company/Consultant Relationship

- Consultancy Roles

- Communication and Learning

- Communication Techniques

- Some Consultancy Techniques

- Tact and Diplomacy

- Practical Psychology.

THE COMPANY/CONSULTANT RELATIONSHIP

The Importance of Collaboration between Consultant and Client

To achieve success, both consultant and client should be aware of the human and other factors that will affect their relationship, and of the errors to be avoided when working together on an assignment. They must be prepared to make a special effort to build and maintain a relationship that makes the effective intervention of an independent professional possible.

At the outset, the client and the consultant may have different views as to how the assignment should be carried out, as well as having different expectations as to what the final outcome will be. The client may have only a vague idea of how consultants work and may be slightly suspicious — possibly due to having heard about consultants who try to complicate every issue, who require more information than they really need, who ask for more time in order to justify longer assignments and then charge extra fees. Even if there is no suspicion, there is a risk of misunderstanding.

Different situations and client expectations lead to different definitions of the consultant's roles and intervention methods. Nevertheless, whatever choice is made, the overriding objective should always be the creation and maintenance of a true collaborative relationship. This is a golden rule of consulting. The degree and form of client/consultant collaboration will differ from case to case, but there should always be a strong spirit of collaboration, characterised by a shared desire to make the assignment a success, by trust and respect, and by an understanding of the other partner's technical and human roles.

Some clients imagine that by actively collaborating with the consultant they are actually doing the job themselves, and are thus paying the consultant a handsome fee for nothing. Such clients feel that consultants who insist on their clients' collaboration are like "the guy who borrows your watch to tell you the time". The client's commitment to collaboration quickly becomes apparent during the fact-finding stage if the consultant finds that not all data is being made available.

Thus, the need for active collaboration is not automatically perceived by every client and very often various misconceptions will have to be dispelled before an assignment can be successfully undertaken.

The modern concept of consulting methodology assumes strong client collaboration for the following main reasons:

- There are many things that the consultant cannot do at all or cannot do properly if the client is reluctant to collaborate. This happens if the consultant is refused information or cannot exchange ideas with the right people.

- Very often senior management is unaware of all of the competence existing in the organisation, and important strengths may be concealed from it. Through collaboration, consultants help clients to uncover and mobilise their own resources.

- Collaboration is essential so that clients associate themselves fully with the definition of the problem and with the results of the assignment. Consultants emphasise that their client must "own" the problem and its solution. The reason is that human systems often reject changes proposed from the outside. By collaborating on a solution the client is more likely to be committed to it and will not put all the responsibility on the consultant. This commitment will be not only rational, but also emotional. People tend to have different attitudes towards projects into which they have had to put long hours of hard work and a lot of energy, compared to those which they are asked to apply without ever having been consulted on them.

- Most importantly, unless clients collaborate in the assignment, they are unlikely to learn from it. Learning does not occur by defining terms of reference and accepting or rejecting a final report, but by joint work at all stages of the assignment, starting with problem definition and diagnosis, and ending with the implementation and the assessment of the results obtained.

The Client System

With whom, when, and how will the consultant collaborate? The client, in the widest sense of the term, is the organisation which employs the services of a consulting unit. There we have an institutional relationship. But there are also clients in a narrower sense of the term — individuals or groups of persons within the client organisation who initiate the bringing in of the consultant, who discuss the assignment with them, who collaborate during the course of the assignment, who receive reports and make recommendations to higher management whether or not to accept them, and so on. Often a number of managers, supervisors, staff members, workers and liaison officers will be directly involved in the assignment at its various stages, or affected by the conclusions reached. Here the consultant/client relationship is personalised and will be affected by psychological and other factors.

It should be noted that in professional advisory services the consultant/client relationship is always personalised. There may be a formal contract between the consulting firm and the organisation using its services. However, the delivery of that service involves direct contact between persons acting on behalf of the two organisations. This is why the appointment of a new manager, for example, can change the course of an assignment quite dramatically.

The situation is not always clear in that the consultant does not really know who the main client is, and consequently does not know who it is that must be satisfied with the outcome. This can happen when senior management recruit the consultant, but leaves it solely to a functional department to handle the job, or if a consulting assignment is recommended and sponsored by a subsidiary as a pre-condition of assistance from the parent organisation, or if a ministry sends consultants to a public enterprise. In such situations, consultants need to clarify whether they are supposed to act as inspectors, as auditors (financial), as informants or as genuine consultants. A consultant, therefore, should find out at the outset who "owns" the problem that is being addressed and consequently is keen to be helped — this person or organisation will be the consultant's main client.

As can be seen, human relationships are complex and can be fraught with misunderstandings and other difficulties. Sensitivity on the part of the consultant is called for — a consultant must be patient, a good listener, tactful and diplomatic, use non-threatening behaviour, never be sarcastic, and choose words and gestures carefully. There is also a great need to try and understand the client (the other). Trust and openness are cornerstones of a fruitful relationship. A consultant should always try to put clients at ease, to encourage them to give freely of their time and commitment, yet not make excessive demands. The consultant should use the time effectively without being cut and dried, or cold and rigid, in relation to the assignment. It is people who do business together, not robots or organisations. Healthy, sound relationships are generally enjoyable and satisfying, not demanding and non-obligatory. At the end of the assignment the consultant and client should be able to part, each knowing that their needs and aspirations were met in good measure.

This does not mean there are no further problems or work assignments resulting from the initial assignment. There will always be more to do, but in so far as the original brief is concerned the task is completed and client and consultant are satisfied.

Co-created Learning

Co-created learning refers to the process of interaction between the consultant and company employees which results in both parties arriving at a better understanding of the problem under consideration. A model illustrating the co-created learning process is given in Figure 4.1.

The first challenge in the interplay between the consultant and the employees of the company is to put the goal of the consultation process into words. Thus, the first phase in the consultancy process will be to develop an understanding of the issues in cooperation with the management and staff of the company. This can only be brought about through communication between the consultant and the members of the organisation.

At the interface between the company staff's own perception of the issues and challenges, and the consultant's external insight, a *new understanding can be co-created*. The point of reference for the consultant's work is thus formed by the outsider's specialised insight, confronted with the employees' own experience of the issues and options. It should not be the intention that the clarification of the problem will finally match up with the original understanding of one of the parties. A successful process may well result in new understanding for both parties.

Figure 4.1: Co-created Learning in Consultancy Work

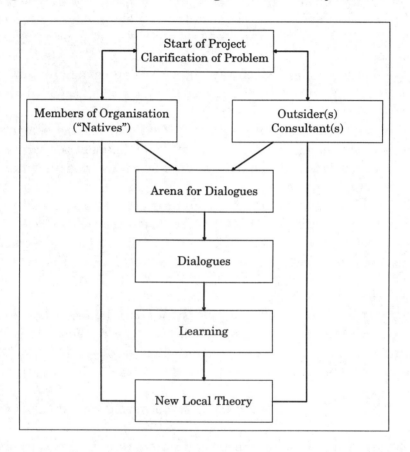

The consultation process contributes to co-created learning. It is important, therefore, to ensure that the consultant's resources and the knowledge and insight of the company combine so that a good, fruitful learning process takes place. This ensures that the result will be a *new local theory* — that is, an understanding of the company's issues and options such that the employees of the company will in future be better able to take their development in their own hands. Every consultation must aim to improve the development environment of a company so that in the long term the company can become ever more self-sufficient.

CONSULTANCY ROLES

Basic Roles: The Expert and the Process Role

The roles of consultants can be characterised in several ways. A common classification is to talk about "expert" and "process" consultants. An expert is expected to have in-depth knowledge of a particular field and gives the company advice, the focus of which is to find solutions based on the consultant's repertoire of knowledge. The dominant perspective in such consultation is the search for the "right" solution. A "process" consultant is often perceived as contributing to learning and development processes which enable the company to solve its own problems.

This twofold distinction is an over-simplification of the situation. An expert's advice is unlikely to have any effect unless the company is capable of turning it into action. So this means that some people in the company must have learnt something by following up on the advice of the consultant. How much has been learnt depends on how the consultant has worked. If the consultant has simply scoured the company for information and then withdrawn to the office to write a report, the consultant's work will have limited potential for learning and development within the company. The learning involved in such a method of working will filter through to the employees only through questions asked during the information-gathering process, or through training in the use of new machinery and equipment if such training forms part of the assignment. In general, an "expert" consultant will be of most use to companies that already have the competence to implement development processes.

A "process" consultant aims to contribute to the solution of problems by arranging things so that the employees of the company can learn something. In the process role, the consultant is the agent of change and attempts to help the organisation to solve its own problems by making it aware of organisational processes, of their likely consequences, and of intervention techniques for stimulating change. Instead of passing on technical knowledge and suggesting solutions, the process consultant is primarily concerned with passing on an approach, methods and values so that the client organisation can diagnose and solve its own problems.

Expressed in simpler terms, while expert consultants suggest to their clients *what* to change, process consultants suggest mainly *how* to change and help the client to go through the change process dealing with human problems as they arise.

Further Refinement of the Role Concept

Reducing the various consulting processes to two basic roles is a simplification that is conceptually useful, but disregards a number of other variables.

For practical purposes it is also instructive to visualise a number of consultative roles along a *directive* and *non-directive* continuum, as shown in Figure 4.2. The term "directive" refers to those behaviours where the consultant assumes a position of leadership or initiates activity. In the "non-directive" role the consultant provides data for the client to use or not to use. Here again, the situational roles are not mutually exclusive and manifest themselves in many ways in different consultant/client relationship. These roles are "spheres of influence" rather than a static continuum of isolated behaviour.

Advocate

In an advocate role, the consultant endeavours to influence the client. There are two quite different types of advocacy:

- Positional or "contact" advocacy tries to influence the client to choose particular alternatives or to accept particular values.

- Methodological advocacy tries to influence the client to become active as a problem-solver, and to use certain methods of problem-solving. The consultant adopting this role is careful not to become an advocate for any particular solution (which would be positional advocacy).

Figure 4.2: Consultative Roles

MULTIPLE ROLES OF THE CONSULTANT

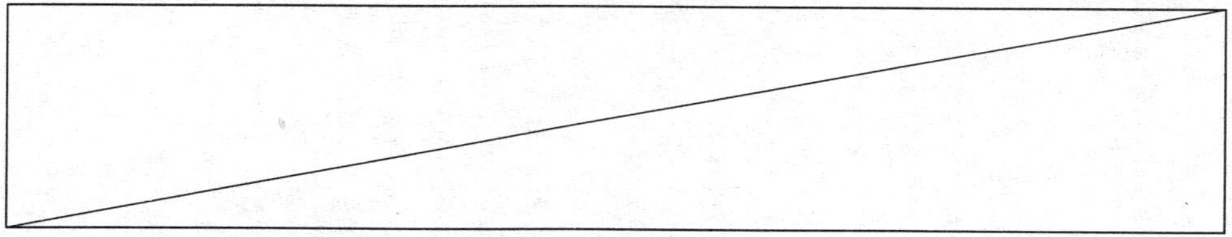

LEVEL OF CONSULTANT ACTIVITY IN PROBLEM-SOLVING

Non-directive							Directive
Reflector	Process Specialist	Fact Finder	Alternative Identifier	Collaborator in Problem-Solving	Trainer/Educator	Technical Expert	Advocate
Raises questions for reflection	Observes problem-solving process and raises issues mirroring feedback	Gathers data and stimulates thinking	Alternatives and resources for client and helps assess consequences	Offers alternatives and participates in decisions	Trains the client and designs learning experiences	Information and suggestions for policy or practice decisions	Proposes guidelines, persuades or directs in the problem-solving process

Technical Expert

One of the roles adopted by any consultant is that of technical specialist or expert. As mentioned above, the more traditional role of a consultant is that of an expert who, through special knowledge, skill and professional experience, is engaged to provide a unique service to the client. The client is mainly responsible for defining the objectives of the consultation.

Thereafter the consultant assumes a directive role until the client is comfortable with the particular approach selected. Later in the relationship the consultant may act as a catalyst in helping to implement the recommendations that have been made. Either the consultant may be a specialist in an area specific to the problem in hand, or a process specialist advising how to cope with a problem and how to implement change. This particular role brings out the consultant's substantive knowledge.

Trainer and Educator

Innovative consultation frequently requires the consultant to initiate training and education within the client system. In this aspect of the helping relationship, the consultant can play a role in bringing to bear the learning process that can best be employed, critically and creatively, depending upon the situation and the need. The consultant may design learning experiences or teach by imparting information directly. This work requires the consultant to be knowledgeable of training methodologies and to know how to develop the potential of those that are being trained.

Collaborator in Problem-solving

The helping role assumed by the consultant uses a synergistic (co-operative) approach to collaborate with the client in the perceptual, cognitive and action-taking processes needed to solve a given problem. The consultant helps to maintain objectivity while stimulating conceptualisation during the formulation of the problem. Additionally, the consultant must help to isolate and define the real dependent and independent variables that caused the problem, and will ultimately influence its solution. The consultant also assists in deciding between alternatives and develops a course of action for an effective resolution. The consultant in this role is involved in decision-making as a peer.

Alternative Identifier

There are direct costs associated with decision-making. While the value of a decision is dependent upon the attainment of a given set of objectives, the consultant can normally propose several identifiable alternatives, along with their attendant risks, when working to find an appropriate solution to a problem. The alternatives, either because of economic or other identifiable implications, should be discovered jointly by the client and the consultant. In this helping relationship, the consultant establishes relevant criteria for assessing alternatives and develops cause/effect relationships for each along with an appropriate set of strategies. In this role, however, the consultant is not a direct participant in decision-making, but a retriever of appropriate alternatives facing the decision-maker.

Fact Finder

Fact finding is an integral part of any consulting assignment, both for developing a database and for resolving intricate client problems. In some cases, the consultant's role can be confined to fact-finding. In such cases the consultant will influence the client system by choosing the sources of data, by using a technique that will get the client more or less involved in gathering and examining data, and by presenting data to the client in a way that will show where and why improvements are needed. In this role the consultant is functioning essentially as a researcher.

Process Specialist

This is the "pure" process role. The consultant focuses chiefly on the interpersonal and intergroup dynamics affecting the process of problem-solving and change. The consultant must bring all their role skills to bear on helping the client. The consultant works on developing joint client/consultant diagnostic skills for addressing specific and relevant problems in order to focus on how things are done rather than on what tasks are performed.

Furthermore, the consultant helps the client to integrate interpersonal and group skills and events with task-oriented activities, and to observe the best match of relationships. In this role, an important function of the consultant is to provide feedback.

Reflector

When operating in the mode of a reflector, the consultant stimulates the client into making decisions by asking reflective questions which help to clarify, modify, or change a given situation. In utilising this attribute, the consultant may be an arbitrator, an integrator or an emphatic respondent who experiences jointly with the client those blocks which provided the structure and provoked the situation initially. In this role the consultant is an "overseer" as well as a philosopher.

COMMUNICATION AND LEARNING

The Ladder of Understanding

The core of a good communication process is that those who talk together understand one another. Different positions and different experience are important factors that influence our perception of reality. In addition, our values and emotions will provide premises for our interaction with other people. An important element in every communication process is to clarify what one is actually talking about. Figure 4.3 shows the "ladder of understanding", which tries to illustrate how communication takes place.

Figure 4.3: The Ladder of Understanding

A's Conclusions		B's Conclusions
Based on A's theories and concepts and the "selected" data		Based on B's theories and concepts and the "selected" data.
A's first reformulated understanding of the situation.		B's first reformulated understanding of the situation.
A's "selected" data — what was said or done		B's "selected" data — what was said or done.
	The Current Situation	

The diagram in Figure 4.3 depicts two people who are communicating. The arguments are presented on the basis of both A and B's conclusions and what they have experienced and understood in relation to the "current situation". These views have been formed through several "rungs" of processing. The first phase of such a process is the choice of data that is relevant. The data which is selected to interpret "the current situation" will in all probability be different for A and B, given that what each sees is dependent on their position in the organisation and on their experience. Thus there is a basis for arriving at different conclusions. On subsequent rungs of the ladder the data is processed so that at the top both A and B have formed conclusions that represent a processed understanding of reality.

The thinking behind this representation suggests that one way of resolving problems of communication is for the participants to move jointly down the ladder of understanding. The closer they come to the core of the "current situation" the greater the possibility that they can understand other people. Processes that can contribute to movement down the ladder will help a consultant to make the consultation better and more in keeping with the expectations and requirements of the company.

The current situation (at the bottom of the ladder) is perceived differently by different people due to differences of experience and position in the organisation. The advantage of the approach illustrated by the ladder of understanding lies in its ability to clarify the core of the different views. In this way, conflicts or misunderstandings can be cleared up quickly. On the other hand, one will also be able to identify real conflicts, understand what they involve and use this as a basis for successful solutions.

The thinking behind the ladder of understanding involves the parties first moving down the ladder. It then becomes important that they can move upwards so that a co-created understanding is achieved. However, if the participants in the dialogue, having "met" each other at the foot of the ladder, move up different ladders of understanding rather than the same one, no progress will have been made.

COMMUNICATION TECHNIQUES

Consultants can increase their effectiveness at human communication through conscious reflection over their own work methods in companies. The communication process is crucial to how one judges one's own success in an assignment, but even more so to the way the client judges it. Three techniques or working methods are presented here. What they have in common is an awareness of one's own role in the communication between the client and oneself. These techniques are meant to contribute to fruitful dialogue and learning for the people involved in the situation under consideration. The techniques are also intended to provide methods of increasing understanding of, and insight into, the way we ourselves and others function and think in a dialogue or interview situation. The three techniques are:

- Active listening

- Model I and Model II behaviour

- Dialogue analysis.

Active Listening

Active listening starts with what the individual can most easily do something about, i.e. how one listens to the people with whom one is talking.

The theme of this discussion is verbal communication between human beings. This does not mean that we are only concerned with what is said out loud. We all know that we tell one another a great deal without using words. The importance of body language is generally acknowledged. Some researchers claim that only 20 per cent of inter-human communication is directly verbal. This is what the technique of active listening tries to do something about. The following rules apply when one practices active listening in a conversation:

- Only you can make the decision to take the responsibility for finding out

    ◊ whether the thoughts and emotions you mean to communicate were received as such

◊ whether the thoughts and emotions you received were the ones the other party meant to send and

◊ whether any misunderstandings not covered by the above are cleared up before the conversation continues.

It does not take much imagination to see that these are rules which can be difficult to follow in practice. The important thing is to be aware that this is in fact a matter of *talking together* or, in other words, it is a *dia*logue, not a monologue or a speech, as "dialogues" often are! A *dia*logue is about the exchange of speech between *two* people, where the point of departure for each should in fact be what the last "speaker" has said. These basic points are of course known to us all. But think about how easy it is to break such a rule. It is easy to see that it is hard to observe the rules of active listening in practice. So it is important that you first and foremost improve your own listening practice in the situations where it is particularly important for you that the dialogue leads to a positive result.

Although active listening is demanding, you can take some comfort in the fact that even small improvements in your own listening practice quickly give results and encouragement to go further. To better understanding what active listening is about, it is useful to divide dialogue into four different phases.

Reformulation of the Message Received (What Did You Say?)
The most common mistake we all make when we hold a conversation (NB: note how language reflects what we in fact often do — we hold a conversation — as if there is a series of defensive positions that different speakers have to hold, which is in fact often the case!) is that we forget to listen to what is in fact being said. Mentally, we are busy preparing our next speech. Instead, we should be busy reformulating what is being said. You can do this simply, for example, by asking questions like:

"Do you mean that . . . ?"

"In other words, you're saying . . . ?"

"So you feel that . . . ?"

The idea of rephrasing what has been said in your own words is to tell the other person how you understand what has been said. Perhaps words and concepts were used where the listener puts a different interpretation on them than the sender of the message. Such situations arise as a rule when people with different specialist backgrounds have to communicate. By rephrasing what has been said in your own words you also give your conversation partner an opening if he or she wants to make corrections.

So far we have been concerned with what is expressed openly and directly — the manifest. We all know that if what is said is sensitive, contentious or emotionally charged, our reaction is crucial to the further course of the conversation. In such a situation, most people will probably try to understand what is actually being said. Then it is very important to reflect the consequences of what is said, and the feelings it creates in you.

Reflecting the Consequences (What Do You Want?)

Often we experience that central parts of what is communicated are not said directly, but conveyed, for example, by body language. In this case active listening means that you try to build up or suggest an implication of the statement which the other party did not fully follow up. This can be done with statements like:

"Does this mean that . . . ?"

"Are you suggesting that perhaps we can . . . ?"

"This would perhaps lead to . . ."

In such a situation it is easy to be misunderstood. When you offer interpretation of what was said by suggesting the results, it is easy for the sender of the message to feel that you are "taking over" the conversation or twisting statements in a direction the other party did not mean. If this happens it will be very difficult for open communication to continue between the two parties. In other words, you must use this technique to show that you have understood, not to "win the debate".

Reflection of Feelings (What Do You Feel?)
If little of a message is communicated directly, and often only hinted at or signalled by body language, this is normally because the message is emotionally charged. In active listening it is important to grasp this aspect also, so that the trust between the conversation partners can be strengthened. This can be done with statements like:

"It must have been a good feeling to . . ."

"I once experienced something similar, I thought . . ."

"It can't have been a very pleasant situation when . . ."

In such a situation we must remember that it is often tone of voice and your own body language that first and foremost communicate, not the words you say! This means, of course, that you must "feel for what you really feel" and then assess what you say. If your feelings are on a collision course with the attitudes that the other party is communicating, it is particularly important that you prevent a breakdown of open communication. Then it is important that you try to find out more about the background of the statement.

Encouraging Clarification (Won't You Tell Me More About . . . ?)
Encouraging further clarification is important in many contexts — for example, as follow-up to an emotionally charged statement. The main rule is that when you think you have not understood enough about a theme to be able to follow up on what was said, you can use statements like:

"Could you explain more about . . .?"

"What happened after . . .?"

"Can you tell me more about . . .?"

With statements like these you indicate both what you have understood from what has been said, and what you want followed up in more detail. This provides an opportunity to correct any misunderstandings, but primarily it signals your interest in what has been said. In a conversation, all parties are responsible for the statements and signals each gives to the other. Deliberate use of active listening skills does not of course exempt you from this shared responsibility.

Active listening is a technique which is meant to improve your communication skills. There are, of course, great variations in the situation in which people meet; some are everyday ones, others are difficult and more critical.

Model I and Model II Behaviour

It is useful to consider two different forms of learning that take place in organisations. The simplest form is called *single-loop learning*. This kind of learning helps the organisation to become better at dealing with the tasks with which it is already working. A classic example of this is the maker of steam locomotives in the USA who through time became world champion at making steam locomotives. The problem arose of course when the market for steam locomotives vanished. *Double-loop learning* is another, more radical type of learning. Central to this learning method is the creation of reflection and learning related to the values and concepts which make up the established goals of the organisation; reflection over the company's business idea and whether it is working on the right markets with the right products is an example of this kind of learning process. Our main point here is that the consultant must help the companies to become capable of acquiring double-loop learning.

The above two forms of learning are associated with two different behavioural patterns. We say that single-loop learning is due to *Model I behaviour* while the behaviour associated with double-loop learning is called *Model II behaviour*. The difference in behaviour patterns in these two models can be described as follows:

- In Model I behaviour there is simple feedback to the person which tells the person where one stands in relation to that person's viewpoint.

- Model II behaviour, on the other hand, will require a change in what people actually do and say on the basis of the feedback the person is given.

Figure 4.4 illustrates the difference between Model I and II throughout a thought process.

Figure 4.4: Model I and Model II Behaviour

In a situation where I think I know what we should do:

Model I	*Model II*
• My task is to get you to see the correctness of my view.	• I will defend my view but create the possibility of revealing weaknesses.
• I will either emphasise my view directly and give convincing arguments,	• I will emphasise my views openly and urge you to reflect on them,
• or I will ask questions formulated so that you will have to come to the same conclusions as I have.	• and I will urge you to present your views, in order to examine your thinking.
• If you still do not see my view is the right one,	• If you do not see that I have anything to offer,
• then I will take this as proof of a lack of intelligence, or of ulterior motives,	• then I will assess the possibility that you see something I do not see.
• and then I will more strongly and more directly, calmly and more shrewdly, or shift from one set of arguments to others.	• If I do not see it, I will not change my mind all at once, but I will encourage you to argue in more detail for your way of thinking which has led to a different conclusion than mine.

Clearly, it is much more demanding to implement Model I behaviour than the logic which Model II represents. So it may be necessary to know when it is appropriate to work to achieve Model I and Model II behaviour respectively. This is illustrated in Figure 4.5. Generally, only Model II behaviour encourages learning in an organisation in difficult situations. It is therefore important to assess the situation before deciding whether a learning process is necessary.

Figure 4.5: Which Model When?

Type of Situation	Routine	Difficult
	• Familiar • Everyday	• Ambiguous • Contentious • Threatening
Model I	Effective	Prevents learning
Model II	Unnecessary	Promotes learning

Dialogue Analysis

Increased consciousness of becoming a better listener and awareness of one's own behaviour in difficult situations is one thing; but
how to actively train to be better listeners and creators of Model
II conditions for learning is another. Figure 4.3 presented the
ladder of understanding as an illustration of how to resolve problems and unclear points in a communication process. In practice
this can be done with the aid of a *dialogue analysis* in which a
third person participates.

Dialogue analysis can be used to improve one's own performance and can also be used as a useful tool in an assignment
situation. Let us first illustrate the procedure to be followed if
dialogue analysis is to be used as a technique for improving one's
own performance.

Choice of Dialogue for Analysis

To learn from a difficult situation, it may be appropriate to recon-
struct the dialogue that took place to analyse what actually happened. It is important to remember the verbal formulation of the
dialogue as accurately as possible. So a normal situation may be
easier to remember well. We can learn just as much from it.

Write the Dialogue Down

Figure 4.6 gives an example of how to write a dialogue down so as
to carry out an analysis. The background for the dialogue is a
consultant's first meeting with the company management after
completing an initial assessment of the company. The question is
whether the management is motivated to carry on with further
consultancy projects.

Figure 4.6: Dialogue Analysis

The Dialogue	Consultant's Interpretation
Consultant: I've had feedback from my colleagues. They are supportive of our work up to now but think we should set clearer goals. Now the project group should meet to start work on the issues already identified. When would it suit you?	My intention was to get further work under way. We were already behind schedule. I knew that the company was in an industry with problems.
Managing Director: We have discussed this internally. We have just had our half-yearly result and it is very weak.	I interpret this as uncertainty about the financial position of the company — not so much the managing director's attitude to my work so far.
Consultant: But the tasks we got together on were chosen to strengthen the company — in the short term too. Surely they can't be less important now?	I would like to get to know more about the resistance to going further.

In the illustration in Figure 4.6, the left-hand side describes the dialogue as the consultant remembers it. The right-hand side shows the consultant's reflections on why certain things were said and how the consultant subsequently interpreted what was being said by the other party.

A Third Party (with Experience) Discusses the Dialogue with You
The point here is that the third party makes you reflect on why you said what you did and whether there are alternative ways of understanding what the second party said. By using the logic of the ladder of understanding we can see that our views build on a set of assumptions that are very often not communicated and thus create obscurities and misunderstandings. This is an illustration of how one can go down the ladder of understanding and up again with new learning.

This technique can also be used actively to resolve poor communication among people in a company. In such situations the consultant will be responsible for implementing the actual dialogue analysis. The main rule is that you cannot carry out a dialogue analysis if you are yourself a party to the dialogue.

SOME CONSULTANCY TECHNIQUES

The consultant has to influence people in order to obtain information, gain confidence and respect, overcome passive resistance, enlist collaboration, and get proposals accepted and implemented. Some general methods of exercising personal influence are reviewed below.

Demonstrating Technical Expertise

Consultants should consider whether they enter the client organisation as a technical expert enjoying prestige, or, on the contrary, as someone totally unknown. Demonstration of theoretical knowledge and practical expertise appeals mainly to technically oriented individuals who are themselves experts in the consultant's field. This can be done in informal discussions, by passing on information on developments in theory, new techniques and equipment, or by referring to successful firms or projects with which the consultant has been involved. Technically superior findings or proposals submitted by the consultant may speak for themselves and influence the client's stance.

Exhibiting Professional Integrity at Work

The consultant's behaviour at work is closely observed by the client, whose attitude can be influenced by the way in which the consultant exhibits commitment, integrity, a methodical approach and efficiency. These are demonstrated at various stages and aspects of the assignment — the way of going about collecting information, self-discipline and perseverance in fact-finding, the ability to discover pitfalls about which the consultant was not informed by the client, persistence in looking for a better technique, rational use of time, tact in handling delicate matters, etc. A powerful effect can be achieved if people see that the consultant is prepared to share knowledge and work methods with them.

Using Assertive Persuasion

This widely applied method uses the force of logical argument to convince the other person that what you want them to do is the right, correct, and effective action to take. As a rule, new ideas or suggestions are put forward followed by reasons for and against, as the consultant presents arguments, facts, and data to support the position adopted. The method is most effective when consultants are perceived to know what they are talking about and are seen to be relatively objective. The consultant should also know enough about the other person's situation to speak in relation to specific needs. Assertive persuasion tends to be overused in the practice of consulting and people often think of it as synonymous with influence.

Developing a Common Vision

A common vision is a shared picture of where you are headed, what you are trying to accomplish, and why it is worthwhile for others to help. Articulating exciting possibilities includes generating images of what the future of the organisation could be like if a specific course of action is followed. In addition, the consultant can influence people by showing enthusiasm for what is to be done and where that action will take the organisation. The method tends to be more effective when the consultant must influence a number of people and generate collective commitment to action. It does not work if it is not clear what the other person can actually do towards achieving a common vision. In contrast to assertive persuasion, common vision tends to be the least utilised method of exerting one's influence.

Using Participation and Trust

This method implies recognising and involving others by asking for their contributions and ideas, by giving them credit for ideas, and building on what others have proposed. This is accompanied by sharing feelings with others and being open about one's own mistakes, shortcomings and lack of knowledge. The purpose is to develop an atmosphere of collaboration and co-responsibility so as to achieve a common goal. The other person involved must believe that your interest in participation and mutual trust is genuine and not just a facade, and that collaborating with you is really the right way to achieve the desired results. Attempts at one-way influence and control should be avoided. Also, participation is hard to achieve when the situation is such that it is not really in the other person's best interest to co-operate. This method is absolutely essential in collaborative consulting styles that emphasise the client's active involvement and their "ownership" of a problem, as well as of the solutions representing the final outcome of the assignment.

Using Rewards and Punishments

Consultants normally do not control the same kinds of rewards and punishments that are available to management in the client organisation. Nevertheless, they can influence people by giving or taking away from them certain things which seem desirable.

It could be a public acknowledgement (e.g. in a meeting) of a person's competence, achievement, or exceptional contribution to the assignment. Enhancing someone's self-esteem is a reward. Omitting to invite someone to a meeting they would probably like to attend, or withholding information from them, could be a punishment. Rewards and punishments which do not motivate people, which are out of proportion to the importance of the issue involved, or which are chosen arbitrarily, produce little effect and should be avoided.

Using Tensions and Anxieties

Although it is not always realised, tensions and anxieties do play some role in consulting. Often, the very presence of the consultant gives rise to tension because people speculate as to what the hidden reasons for the presence of the consultant are and about possible outcomes that could upset the status quo and affect the positions and interests of individuals or whole groups. The tensions that exist in the organisation can be exploited when collecting information so as to obtain a true picture of the situation. Interdepartmental competition can be used when choosing the unit in which to start applying a new method in order to demonstrate its feasibility to other units. In generating and strengthening the desire for change, it may be useful to explain what would happen to the organisation and/or to the individual if the necessary changes are delayed, thus creating a state of anxiety. It may be enough to produce data showing that the organisation already is or is likely to be in difficulties. Here again, a wrongly focused and excessive use of tensions and anxieties will produce negative rather than positive effects. Also, the consultant must be careful not to become involved in internal power struggles within an organisation.

TACT AND DIPLOMACY

It is essential that consultants establish good relations with all of the client's personnel before commencing their studies and investigations.

Any assignment which has such far-reaching effects must obviously be handled with great care and tact. Nobody likes to be made to feel that they have failed, especially in the eyes of their superiors. A feeling of failure leads to a loss of self-confidence and makes people wonder whether or not they may be replaced. Their feeling of security is threatened. At first sight, the result of a consultant's investigations may seem unfair. Managers, foremen and workers, generally speaking, are honest, hard-working people who do their jobs as well as they can. They are certainly not less clever than consultants and specialists. Often they have years of experience and great practical knowledge. If they have failed to obtain the most from the resources at their disposal, it is generally because they have not been trained in, and often do not know the value of, the systematic approach which the consultant brings to bear on the problems of organisation and performance of work.

A consultant will only retain the friendship and respect of the staff if they show from the outset that they are not trying to usurp their place. The following rules should be observed.

1. The consultant should never give a direct order to staff. All instructions should be given through the relevant supervisors. The only exception to this is in matters connected with methods improvements where the worker has been instructed by the supervisor to carry out the instructions of the consultant.

2. Staff asking questions calling for decisions outside the field of the assignment should always be referred to their supervisors.

3. A consultant should never allow themselves to express opinions to staff which may be interpreted as being critical of supervisors.

4. The consultant must not allow the staff to "play them off" against supervisors or to use them to get decisions altered which they consider harsh.

5. The consultant should seek the client's advice in the selection of jobs to be studied and in all technical matters connected with the process (even if they know a great deal about the process). Remember, the staff has to make it work from day to day.

6. At the start of every investigation the consultant should be introduced to the staff concerned by the client. The consultant should never try to start on their own.

The table given in Figure 4.7 lists some of the qualities an effective consultant should possess.

Figure 4.7: Qualities of a Good Consultant

Qualities of a Good Consultant
1. Intellectual ability
• Ability to learn quickly and easily
• Ability to observe, gather, select and evaluate facts
• Good judgement
• Inductive and deductive reasoning
• Ability to synthesise and generalise
• Creative imagination, original thinking.
2. Ability to understand people and work with them
• Respect for other people, tolerance
• Ability to anticipate and evaluate human reactions
• Easy human contacts
• Ability to gain trust and respect
• Courtesy and good manners.

3. Ability to communicate, persuade and motivate
  • Ability to listen
  • Facility in oral and written communication
  • Ability to teach and train people
  • Ability to persuade and motivate.

4. Intellectual and emotional maturity
  • Stability of behaviour and action
  • Independence in drawing unbiased conclusions
  • Ability to withstand pressures and live with frustrations and uncertainties
  • Ability to act with poise and in a calm and objective manner
  • Self-control in all situations
  • Flexibility and adaptability to changed conditions.

4. Personal drive and initiative
  • Right degree of self-confidence
  • Healthy ambition
  • Entrepreneurial spirit
  • Courage, initiative and perseverance in action.

6. Ethics and integrity
  • Genuine desire to help others
  • Extreme honesty
  • Ability to recognise the limitation of one's competence
  • Ability to admit mistakes and learn from failure.

7. Physical and mental health   • Ability to sustain the specific working and living conditions of management consultants.

Dilemma Analysis Ability

Intellectually, the consultant needs the ability to make a "dilemma analysis" because an organisation which uses a consultant is probably faced with a situation that appears insoluble. If the difficulty could easily be solved by the operating manager, a consultant would not be needed. The consultancy must recognise that a dilemma, whether real or not, exists in the minds of those within the organisation. The consultant's role is to discover the nature of the dilemma and to determine the real cause of it, rather than what is thought to be the cause.

In order to make this kind of dilemma analysis, insight or perception and intuition are necessary. Insight or perception is vital because any dilemma requiring outside assistance will be part of a complex situation. The ability to penetrate this complexity and isolate the key situational variables is the toughest task. Unless the important factors can be sifted from the maze of detail, and cause separated from symptoms, accurate diagnosis is impossible.

Sense of Organisational Climate

Intuition or "sensing" must be coupled with perception in order to assess the nature of power and politics in the organisation. Experience with bureaucratic and managerial structures, both public and private, tends to indicate that these are not optimally functional. Underlying and intermingled with the functional operations the organisation performs are the crucial dynamics of internal power and politics. Invariably, people are vying with other people for organisational influence, or for some internal political reason. Very often the consultant has been asked to help, not just to provide needed assistance, but also as an instrument of a strategy designed to secure an objective related to this influence.

Unless the consultant can intuitively sense the organisational climate, they run the risk of being only a pawn in a game of organisational politics. If the consultant has the ability to recognise and understand the dynamics of the internal power and political relationships, the consultant can use these relationships masterfully in pursuit of whatever change objectives the client and consultant conclude are appropriate.

Integrity is Essential

The other important qualities required of a consultant are what we call their personal attributes. Above all, they must be professional in attitude and behaviour. To be successful, they must be as sincerely interested in helping the client organisation as any good doctor is interested in helping a patient.

If the concern of a consultant is primarily to make an impression or build an empire, and only secondarily to help the client organisation, the organisation's leaders will soon recognise that the individual is a phoney and will deal with them accordingly.

People in management generally are astute individuals. They can identify objectivity, honesty, and, above all integrity.

When entering a client system, a strong tolerance for ambiguity is important. The consultant's first acquaintance with an organisational problem tends to be marked by a degree of bewilderment. It takes time to figure out the true situation, and during this period the consultant is going to experience a certain amount of confusion. One must expect this to occur and not be worried by it.

Coupled to this type of tolerance must be the qualities of patience and the ability to sustain a high level of frustration. Curing a client's ills is likely to be a long and trying experience. Substantive changes, full co-operation and complete success are unlikely in the short term. Inevitably, attempts to change people's relationships and behavioural patterns are going to be met with resistance, resentment and obstructionism from those who are, or who think they may be, adversely affected. It is important for the consultant to have that kind of maturity and sense of reality which recognises that many of their actions and hopes for change are going to be frustrated. Such maturity is necessary to avoid experiencing the symptoms of defeat and withdrawal that commonly accompany the frustration of a person's sincere efforts to help others.

Sense of Timing and Interpersonal Skills

Finally, the consulting practitioner should have a good sense of timing, a stable personality and well-developed interpersonal skills. Timing can be crucial. The best conceived and articulated plans for change can be destroyed if introduced at the wrong time. Timing is linked to an understanding of power and of the political realities existing in the change situation, and to the kind of patience that overrides the enthusiasm surrounding a newly conceived idea or training intervention that one is longing to try out immediately. Obviously, consulting involves dealing with people rather than with machines or mathematical solutions. The consultant must have good interpersonal skills, and must be able to communicate and deal with people in an atmosphere of tact, trust, politeness, friendliness, change and stability.

PRACTICAL PSYCHOLOGY

Maslow's Hierarchy of Needs

Managing or carrying out an assignment is a discipline — it is also an undertaking in managing people. Every achievement of management is the achievement of a manager. Every failure is the failure of a manager. People manage, rather than "forces" or "facts". The vision, dedication and integrity of managers determines whether there is management or mismanagement. A consultant therefore achieves their goal by managing personal relationships with client's staff effectively and harmoniously.

Behavioural scientists believe that individuals are motivated to act in a certain way by a desire to satisfy certain needs. One of the most widely accepted notions about needs was developed by Abraham Maslow, who postulated that there are certain essential needs for every individual and that these needs arrange themselves in a hierarchical pattern. Maslow argues that it is only when one need becomes largely satisfied that the next need in the hierarchy will start to exert its motivating influence.

At the bottom of the hierarchy are physiological needs. These are the basic needs that must be met to sustain life itself. Satisfying their physiological needs will be the primary concern of any person, and until they have done so they will not be concerned with any other issues. However, once an individual feels reasonably sure of fulfilling their physiological needs, they will seek to satisfy the next need in the hierarchy, that of security. Security is taken to mean a feeling of protection against physical and psychological harm, as well as security or employment. For an individual who has already satisfied both their physiological and their security needs, the next motivating factor is that of affiliation, that is wanting to belong to a group or an organisation and to associate with others. Next on the hierarchical scale is the need to be recognised, and this is followed by the need for fulfilment (sometimes called "self-actualisation"). This last need expresses the desire of a person to be given an opportunity to use their particular talents.

In practice, most people satisfy some of these needs in part and are left with some that are unsatisfied. In developing countries people are probably preoccupied more with satisfying needs at the lower end of the hierarchy, and their behaviour would appear to reflect this fact. In developed countries, on the other hand, where physiological and security needs are normally largely met, people would seem to be motivated more by needs at the upper end of the hierarchy.

Being Culture-tolerant

Culture is normally defined as a system of collectively shared values, beliefs, traditions and behavioural norms unique to a particular group of people:

> "Culture is the collective programming of the human mind that distinguishes the members of one human group from those of another group."

Culture, in this sense, is a system of collectively held values.

Culture has its roots in basic conditions of human life, including material conditions, the natural environment, climate, and the ways in which people earn their living, and in the historical experience of human communities, which includes interaction with other countries and cultures. People create culture as a mechanism that helps them to cope with their environment and maintain the cohesion and identify of the community in interacting with other communities. In developing countries, in rural areas in particular, traditional cultures reflect the people's poverty and helplessness before the forces of nature. Culture tends to be deeply rooted and therefore cannot be easily changed. Some governments have learned about the power of their own country's culture only after having tried to impose changes that this culture did not tolerate.

Culture is very important to people. Their preference for fundamental cultural values is not rational, but emotional. They may even regard certain social norms and traditions as eternal and sacrosanct. In contrast, a consultant may regard them as anachronistic and irrational. There may be a grain of truth in the consultant's view, since not everything is constructive and progressive in cultures; they often include values that inhibit development and progress. Nevertheless, cultures reflect centuries of society's experience and help people to cope with life. Respect for different cultures and tolerance for values and beliefs alien to one's own culture, but dear to other people, are therefore essential qualities of a good consultant.

In their attitude to other cultures, consultants are strongly influenced by their own. Tolerance towards other cultures is a cultural characteristic too; some cultures are highly tolerant of different cultural values, while others are not. A consultant who has been moulded by a less tolerant cultural environment should be particularly cautious when dealing with delicate organisational and human problems in other cultures.

The spectrum of cultural values and related norms and rituals can be extremely wide and can concern any aspect of human, economic and social life. Of particular importance to consultants are values concerning issues such as:

- The distribution of social roles and the status assigned to them

- The criteria of success and achievement in economic and social life

- Respect for age and seniority

- The role of traditional authorities and community leaders

- Democratic versus autocratic traditions

- Individualism versus collectivism

- Spiritual versus material values

- Responsibility and loyalty to family, community and ethnic group

- Socialisation and communication patterns

- The acceptability and the form of feedback, appraisal and criticism

- Religion, its importance in social life and its impact on economic activity

- Attitudes to other cultures, religions, ethnic groups, minorities

- Attitudes to social, technological and other changes

- The concept of time.

PART II

DIAGNOSTIC PHASE

5

GENERAL STRATEGIC BUSINESS ANALYSIS

INTRODUCTION

This handbook suggests that the diagnosis of a company's problems must first begin with a general strategic analysis. The purpose of this general analysis is to get a broad view of the company so as to identify as quickly and efficiently as possible "where the shoe pinches" before engaging in more detailed survey work. The aim is also to initiate a strategic process in the company and to identify possible areas where competitiveness and profitability can be improved. This brief analysis results in a set of recommendations and guidelines for further work.

It is important to relate company strategy to its business activities. Thus, the consultant must assess the company as a whole, including analysis of its current position and potential so as to decide what strategic direction the company should take. This *business analysis* will clarify what the company's basic business background is — without a clear understanding of the company's business situation, any help a consultant might offer will be severely limited.

The strategic analysis involves three main activities: information gathering, assigning of priorities to issues and options, and finally summarising the company's situation along with recommendations for change.

General strategic analysis is looked at in this chapter under the following headings:

- Business Analysis
- General Strategic Analysis.

BUSINESS ANALYSIS

Structure

A rational working methodology for obtaining the necessary insight into the business situation of a company is to assess the company's:

- Strategic business units

- Business idea(s)

- Strategic position

- Strategic potential

- Strategic direction.

The assessments can be complex, so in the short period available to consultants they will have to rely on being able to draw on sound experience of the industry as well as on the client's own knowledge.

Strategic Business Units

We often find that companies (even small ones) have several separate areas of business without being aware of it. It is always useful to distinguish among the various areas of business because they require different handling and emphases.

As a rule different areas of business meet different market needs. Thus this is often a matter of defining different product/market combinations — often referred to as *strategic business units*. If the strategic business units are not separated within a company, it is often because the company has developed naturally on the basis of its existing business activities.

An example would be an engineering firm that had developed maintenance activities because the company had experts who were in demand in the maintenance market. Engineering series production and maintenance could be handled on a more or less equal footing by company management without realising that they were two different strategic business units.

Another example is a producer of kitchen fittings that over time finds itself in two markets, the construction market and the refurbishment market. These two markets are so different that sooner or later the management of the company will have to decide whether they should be serviced by two different strategic business units.

The Business Idea

The company and/or its management must have a business idea, i.e. a clear specification of the market need the company is to meet.

The consultant should "home in on" this idea rather than create it. It is important that it is clear and precise. An example is the Nobel dynamite company's business idea — not "producing dynamite", but "breaking rocks". This gives a quite different perspective from "producing dynamite". A formulation like this emphasises the needs of the market in a different way, leaving the possibility of alternative products more open, and it is easier to see who the real competitors are. Both the current and future product/market combinations emerge more clearly. This makes it easier to define the company's strategic position.

Strategic Position

Taking the product/market needs as a starting point, we define the company's "who and what" through seeking answers to the following questions:

- What need or group of needs does the company want to meet?
- How should the company meet these needs?
  - ◊ by differentiating its products?
  - ◊ through cost-effectiveness?
  - ◊ in other ways?
- Who are the actors on the market?
- What are the most important competition criteria?
- How are these competition criteria affected?
- Can they be given priorities?
- In terms of which of these criteria has the company an advantage/disadvantage?

The starting point is often a general analysis of the industry, focusing on the basic competitive forces that are crucial to earning potential. These were illustrated previously in Figure 1.3 on page 24.

Strategic Potential

A financial analysis will reveal the commercial situation of the company's products at the present time — but what about the future? How can you arrive at a satisfactory understanding of the future earning potential of the various products? Here it is often useful to use the "product life cycle" (illustrated in Figure 5.1) combined with the "Boston Matrix" (illustrated in Figure 5.2). A modified Boston Matrix is shown in Figure 5.3.

Figure 5.1: Product Life Cycle

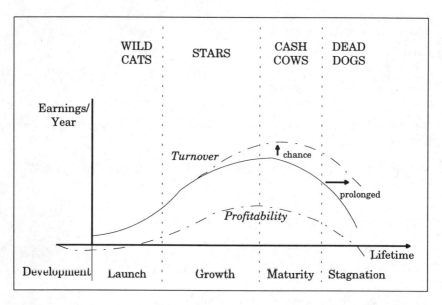

The diagrams of Figures 5.1 and 5.2 are meant to help the consultant find answers to the following questions:

*   Is the product at an early or late stage of the cycle (Figure 5.1)?

*   Can the cycle be influenced?

- What is the "critical success factor" for the product at this stage?

- Is the market attractive?

- How will market needs change?

- What is the relationship between Figure 5.2 and Figure 5.3?

- How can you hasten the progress from "Wild Cats" to "Stars" in Figure 5.2?

- When will the products become "Dead Dogs" on the market, and how can the company delay this process?

The main question in the first instance will be:

- Do you expect future profitability requirements to be fulfilled, and what factors will be critical in achieving this?

Figure 5.2: Boston Matrix

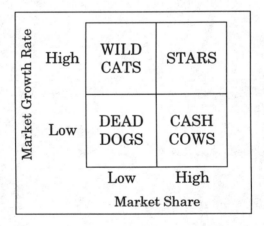

Figure 5.3: Modified Boston Matrix

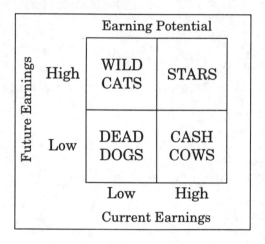

Strategic Direction

If possible, the consultant should be able to indicate the direction in which the company intends to develop within the potential that exists. Appropriate questions in this regard are:

- Should the company grow?
  - ◊ why?
  - ◊ how?
- Which markets should be given high priority?
- Which products should be given high priority?
- Which aspects need further development, and how?
  - ◊ products?
  - ◊ organisational structure?
  - ◊ technology?
- Should the company survive/develop by way of cost leadership and/or differentiation?
- What should not be done?
- What are the critical competition criteria?

Decisions on questions like these in turn raise new questions about consequences and risks. Relevant factors to consider are capital, time, competence and possible sources of error.

Key Questions

A summary of key questions that should be asked during the business analysis is listed below:

1. Does the company have a clear business idea, and what is it?

2. What products does the company "live on" today?

3. What products will the company "live on" in the future?

4. Does the company compete on price or differentiation?

5. What important changes are taking place on the market?

6. What competitors are there, and what are they planning?

7. What are the critical success factors in the industry?

8. What is the situation of the company in terms of these success factors compared with the competition?

9. If the company seems to be at a disadvantage as regards certain critical success factors, can this be remedied by:

   - alliances?

   - technology?

   - fresh capital?

   - building up competence?

10. Is it likely that the company will be able to service its capital this year and three years ahead ?

11. What profitability targets seem natural to aim at, and can these be met?

12. What are the company's most serious problems and how can they be remedied?

GENERAL STRATEGIC ANALYSIS

Goals of the Strategic Analysis
The goals of the strategic analysis are to:

- Identify "where the shoe pinches" — that is, the nature of the main problems being encountered by the company

- Obtain a broad view of the company before carrying out further detailed survey work

- Initiate a strategic process in the company

- Identify possible areas where competitiveness and profitability may be enhanced

- Identify some "quick fixes" — the credibility of the consultant will be greatly enhanced if they correct some minor (or major) problem in the short term

- Prepare a rough outline of how the consultant can continue to assist the company.

Where Does the Shoe Pinch?
The strategic analysis will make great demands on the consultant, because they will have to identify the main problems at short notice and draw clear conclusions based on a limited volume of information.

At the overall level, the analysis normally covers:

- Business idea, goals, business strategies and framework constraints

- The financial situation of the company

- Products and product development

- Markets, customers, suppliers and competitors

- Sales and marketing

- Production and material handling

- Organisational structure, management, staff and competence

- Current technology utilisation in the product, the production process, and management/administration.

Main Components of the Strategic Analysis

The strategic analysis involves three main activities, which are illustrated in Figure 5.4.

Figure 5.4: Phases of Strategic Analysis

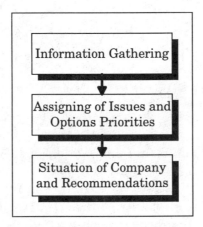

The first activity is a brief information-gathering survey with the emphasis on business evaluation. The aim of the survey is not simply the mechanical collection of information, but the use of the information and views gathered to formulate issues and clear options. This is normally done by interviewing key personnel and reviewing accounting information.

In order to assign priorities to issues and options, the management group in the company takes part in discussions to reach agreement on "where the shoe pinches" and on the options available for addressing the issues. The process creates an awareness of what is important and what is less important to the company. The priorities established form the basis of the conclusions of the strategic analysis.

Finally, the situation of the company and recommendations are summarised in a short report (two or three pages).

The three main components of the strategic analysis are described in greater detail in the following sections.

Information Gathering

During the strategic analysis, information is gathered at a very rough level, using simple tools. An important aim of strategic analysis is to get a "broad view" before any further more detailed survey work is carried out.

During the information-gathering process three key techniques are used. The first two are:

- Structured interviews with key personnel in the company. The interviews are structured in the sense that they follow a definite pattern, during which the interviewees answer a set of key questions before the actual interview.

- Key ratio analysis, during which the consultant seeks to evaluate the financial situation of the company on the basis of accounting data and other information given in the interviews.

The consultant will extract the "essence" of this brief survey by documenting the main points in the form of issues and options. An issue is something the company must decide on, not necessarily because it is a problem at present, but because there is something that remains unclarified. An option is an alternative solution. At this stage of the process we are not yet concerned with the ultimate form of the solution — whether it is a "route" at the overall level or a specific measure.

The issues and options can be correlated in an issues/options list, which is the third key technique in the information-gathering process. At its simplest, such a list takes the form of a two-column sheet with issues on the left and related options on the right.

During the information-gathering process the issues will dominate. Later we will assign priorities to them and focus on finding possible solutions to the issues with the highest priorities.

Figure 5.5 illustrates an example of the way issues can be identified on the basis of the interviewee's answers to two key questions. In this case two clear options were also pointed out during the interview. These solutions have been assigned the status "possible" — which means that their practical feasibility has not been discussed. In the subsequent process of assigning priorities some options are recommended, others are rejected, while others again will need further examination.

Figure 5.5: Identification of Issues and Options

Standard Questionnaires	Answers
How often is key financial data reported to management?	Quarterly for all information. Some figures every month
Is profitability measured by division, by product/product group or only as a whole for the company?	As a whole for the company.

Issues	Options/Strategies/Measures
• The current financial control system is inadequate. • Profitability is only measured at company level, and reporting frequency is too low to allow efficient control. • Divisional managers and those responsible for sales lack the information necessary for on-going follow-up on earnings and costs.	• Introduction of new financial management system at all levels of the organisation [*possible*] • Quick training of all sales staff in simple follow-up principles for their own areas. Model development with spreadsheet. [*possible*]

Assigning Priorities to Issues and Options

The process of assigning priorities during the strategic analysis is a short one, involving an interplay between systematic evaluations and the generation of creative ideas. The point of departure is the interviewee's and consultant's assessments of the situation of the company, as documented in an issues/options list (without priorities).

The process is important for winning acceptance for the conclusions of the strategic analysis. The priorities are assigned in group discussions with company management, supplemented if necessary by other key staff members. In the discussions, agreement is reached on:

- The factors that are to determine the priorities given to issues and options — that is, the relevant priority criteria, and the internal weighting given to them. For example, "increased short-term profitability" may be a high-priority criterion, while "improved working environment" may perhaps (but not necessarily) be given lower priority.

- The most critical issues in terms of the criteria agreed on. Looking at Figure 5.5, for instance, solving the current problem of inadequate financial control might be given very high priority if it represents a direct threat to the survival of the company in the shorter term.

- The most relevant options for addressing the issues with the highest priority. Although some options will already have been identified during the information-gathering process, creative generation of ideas with the management group will generally be the best approach.

During the process, it is important that the consultant notes arguments and assumptions for evaluations made by the group and the priorities assigned.

The prioritising process is a kind of initial screening of issues and options. During the strategic analysis the number of issues and options specified will never be exhaustive — nor is this intended. Remember that the idea is to find out "where the shoe pinches" at the overall level, and to direct the focus of the subsequent planning process towards these areas.

Company Situation and Recommendations

The last activity in the process is the summarising of the situation of the company and recommendations in a brief report. The intention is not to produce a comprehensive document based on the strategic analysis. Nevertheless, the summary is very important, because it forms the starting point for further work. If the consultant fails at this early stage to direct the focus to the correct areas, it is highly likely that subsequent work will at best involve unnecessary survey work and will achieve poor results.

The summary report should document:

- The main problems of the company

- The most relevant solutions to these problems

- How any subsequent work should be implemented, including a rough schedule, statement of focus areas and a specification of the resources, participation and administration necessary

- Any "quick fixes" the company can implement in the short term

- The arguments and assumption on which conclusions are based.

6

INFORMATION GATHERING

INTRODUCTION

Strategic analysis, as previously mentioned, can be broken down into three main activities: information gathering, assigning priorities to issues and options and recommendations. In this section, the first of these activities, *information gathering*, is considered.

Given that consultants are generally working under pressure of time, it is important that relevant information be extracted as quickly as possible from key personnel in the company. Information is acquired during the consultant's visit through talking to company employees at all levels and through observations made during time spent in the production facility. Communication with company employees takes place during both formal and informal interviews. In this chapter, we concentrate on how interviews can be structured so as to enable the consultant to gather information as efficiently as possible.

Structured interviews employ the use of standard questionnaires which can be tailored to each situation by the consultant. The questionnaires deal with most of the company's activities and its relationships with its environment. Answered questionnaires give consultants an important basis for identifying the critical issues so that they can offer the right recommendations at the end of the strategic analysis. In this way, structured interviews can be a very effective analytical technique — provided one asks the right people the right questions.

It is proposed here that structured interviews should follow a set pattern where the interviewees answer a set of key questions before the actual interview. In this way, key personnel in the company do much of the "spadework" so that the interviews can be kept brief and can concentrate on critical areas, without any loss of essential items of information.

Structured interviews can also be used during the actual strategy and planning process. In this part of the process, though, the consultants must themselves define the key questions on the basis of the issues and options given priorities in the strategic analysis.

In this chapter, information gathering is looked at under the following headings:

- The Interview Process

- Selection of Interviewees

- Questionnaires

- Conducting the Interviews

- Processing after the Interviews.

THE INTERVIEW PROCESS

The interview process is shown diagrammatically in Figure 6.1.

Figure 6.1: The Interview Process

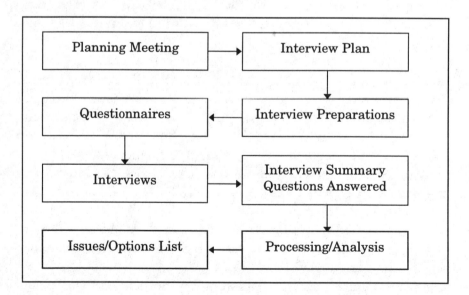

The process consists of the following typical stages:

- A short planning meeting with the chief executive, to decide who is to be interviewed and what kind of key questions are to be asked. If important issues are already pointed out during this meeting, the consultant must ensure that the necessary questions are asked later to address these issues.

- A period of preparation for the interviews, during which the consultant selects appropriate key questions from the standard lists. The questions are distributed to the relevant people, who answer them in advance.

- The interview itself, which is kept short and concentrates on critical areas.

- A processing period, during which the consultant formulates the issues on the basis of the answers given by the interviewees.

SELECTION OF INTERVIEWEES

The mix of people to be interviewed is judged on a company-to-company basis, both because of the importance of the areas to be clarified and because of the differences between companies.

It may often be expedient to interview people across line function (divisional) boundaries, even when specialised topics have to be discussed. For example, the Financial Manager may have much to say about the marketing function which will not emerge from the interview with the Marketing Manager, and vice versa.

Representatives of employee organisations can also be included among interviewees if this is relevant for "political" reasons or helps to answer questions.

In general, consultants should allow between a half-day and a day per interview, including preparation and processing.

If conducted properly, structured interviews can reveal 80 per cent of the most important issues in the course of the first four to six interviews. This is important. With the "right" questionnaires and the right choice of key interviewees, a large increase in the number of people would not have a significant effect on an understanding of the high-priority issues.

It is important to have a balanced selection of interviewees, where management and any other strong opinion-formers in the company are represented. If the selection of interviewees is too one-sided, the consultant will not get an accurate picture of the situation in the company with consequent limited acceptance of any conclusions that are formulated.

QUESTIONNAIRES

The content and formulation of the questions are critical to the success of the interviews. As an aid in interviewing, we have therefore drawn up a "standard" questionnaire which can be adapted to each organisation. A copy of the questionnaire is given at the end of this chapter. How the standard questionnaire will be adapted will depend on:

- The issues and options that emerged during the introductory planning meeting.

- Key questions given in many sections within this manual. Many sections include a list of key questions associated with the area discussed. These are often more specific and detailed than those in the standard questionnaire.

- Which financial key ratios have to be collected. Chapter 9 on Financial Key Ratio Analysis gives an account of relevant key ratios.

The standard questionnaire covers the following main areas:

- Overall goals, strategies and constraints

- Existing products

- Current use of technology in general

- Organisation and management

- Product development

- Purchasing and general relations with suppliers

- Sales, marketing and general relations with customers

- Production and material handling

- Finance

- Quality

- Environmental conditions.

The questions cover a broad spectrum of business-oriented activities. Normally different questionnaires are used for different categories of key personnel. However, it is important that interviewees not only assess issues and options in their own areas, but also try to look beyond them.

The list includes questions that will enable the consultant to:

- Discover strengths and weaknesses in the current situation, in order to identify potential problem areas

- Bring out the interviewees' individual ideas and views on future goals, strategies and measures. The questioning here should, among other things, build on "typical" option areas that have been exploited by other companies.

CONDUCTING THE INTERVIEWS

Ideally, all interviewees should answer the questions in writing in advance. In some cases the questionnaires are returned before the interview, while in others they are not. This depends in particular on how well the key personnel know the aims and implementation principles of the analysis in advance. The consultant must decide whether the questionnaires should be returned in advance on the basis of his knowledge of the company and the dissemination of information that has taken place.

If the questions are sent out and answered in advance, this means that:

- The interviews can be kept brief and can concentrate on the most important points. "Trivial points" will already be documented in writing.

- The interviewee will be very well prepared. The focus can very quickly be directed to the important points and towards creative thinking.

The interviews should be conducted informally, so one gets the most frank and "honest" picture possible of the interviewee's view of the company and its situation.

It is important that the interviewees are guaranteed anonymity as far as possible, given the limited number of people involved. The subsequent prioritisation of issues should concentrate on objective matters, not on a search for scapegoats or arguments about who said what.

PROCESSING AFTER THE INTERVIEWS

After the interviews the consultant will formulate issues and options, based on answered questionnaires and on interview notes. For this, an issues/options list is used, as described in Chapter 8 on Prioritisation of Goals, Issues and Options. Processing will often be done as a whole, not after each interview.

Issues can typically be identified by:

- The pointing-out of an issue by the interviewee, directly or indirectly

- No answer or an inadequate answer may indicate an issue

- Very different answers from two interviewees (to the same question) may indicate an issue

- The consultant may deduce the issues by analysing the basic information given in the interview. For example, the interview will provide the necessary information for the financial key ratio analysis, which in itself may raise important issues.

To avoid a long and unmanageable list of related issues, the consultant should do some combining of issues during processing.

Figure 5.5 in the previous chapter (see page 149) illustrates an example of how the transition from answered questionnaires to an issues/options list is brought about. In this example, the lack of financial management was taken up as a main issue during the discussion with the interviewee. This resulted in several obvious options, as shown in the illustration.

In general, the options pointed out by the interviewee are documented automatically on the right-hand side of the issues/options list, without significant processing. At this stage the options will not necessarily be "linked" with the issues, although this was the case in Figure 5.5.

STANDARD QUESTIONNAIRE

Overall Goals, Strategies and Constraints

A company must set its sights on certain goals. The goals of the company determine the overall choice of routes which are to lead to the goals. One of the assumptions for the formation of the correct strategies is knowledge of the general constraints under which the company works.

1. Does the company have a clear business idea, and what is it?

2. How do you think the present business idea contributes to the development of the company?

3. Has the company specified its overall goals (e.g. requirements with regard to return on investment) and what are these goals?

4. What market trends do you think represent threats or opportunities for the company? What has the company done to meet these developments?

5. How do developments look with regard to the availability of raw materials and work in progress? What about price development?

6. What major changes are taking place in the industry with regard to product technology, process technology and information technology? What has the company done to meet these developments?

7. Are any new laws or regulations being prepared which are likely to affect the company's goals, strategy or tactics?

8. What is the attitude of the market to the company and the products it makes?

9. Do you see any changes that are likely to affect the company in lifestyle patterns and values in the industry and among the consumers?

10. What do you think are the critical success factors (conditions that *must* be fulfilled) for your company?

11. Does the company have a monitoring system which provides the management with relevant information on a regular basis? What kind of information do you think is lacking, if any?

12. How often is financial key data reported to management?

13. Is profitability measured by division, by product/product group, by customer/customer group, by distribution channel or only for the company as a whole?

Existing Products

Products are goods or services which can be offered to a market for its attention or for sale, use, or consumption, and which satisfy desires and needs. Products are created, developed and die. It is of paramount importance that the company has a range of products or services which "match" the requirements of the market.

14. How have turnover and profits been distributed over individual products (or product groups) over the last three years?

15. How many sales orders has the company had in each of the last three years?

16. How big do you think the total market for your company's products is in the geographical areas where the company is represented?

17. How do you think this market will develop in the next few years (indicate yearly change as a percentage)?

18. What is the budget/forecast for the products/product groups in the next two years?

19. How is the range of products distributed over growth markets, stagnating and/or declining markets?

20. Which are the most important geographical markets today and in the future?

21. What alternative products/services can be substituted for the company's products?

22. Which products do you think should be phased out? What kind of products should be added?

23. How much do customers know about, and what is their attitude to, the company's and competitors' product quality, product features, design, name etc.? Which product strategies do you think should be improved?

24. What factors do you think the customers attach most importance to when buying your or your competitor's products?

25. As far as these factors/buying criteria are concerned, what do you think are your strengths and weaknesses in relation to your competitors?

26. What are the advantages of your company's products in relation to those of the competitors?

27. How many complaints/claims has the company had in each of the last three years?

Current Use of Technology in General

The technical soundness of system solutions is no guarantee that they can be successfully introduced and used in the company. Implementation and use of new technology may also require an increase in competence and organisational changes. This is why investment in the organisation and user environment is at least as important as investment in machinery and software.

28. How is technology used in the company today for:

- production

- production documentation

- product development

- financial monitoring systems

- stock control systems

- ordering/invoicing systems

- sales and customer follow-up

- etc.

29. Would you say that your company is very sophisticated or far behind in its use of technology in relation to the competition?

30. In what areas do you think the use of new technology will give your company competitive advantage?

31. Does the company have any technology which is not being used at present?

32. Has the existing use of technology resulted in any competitive advantages? Can you give any examples of this?

33. Do you know of any contracts which have been lost as a result of insufficient use of technology?

34. What technology-oriented projects have been implemented over the last three years? How have these worked out in terms of

- investment costs

- implementation time

- benefit

- competitive advantage

- competence requirements in the organisation

- etc.

35. What factors do you think should determine where new technology is to be implemented?

36. Do you feel that key personnel in the company have sufficient knowledge of technological trends and options to take the initiative with regard to strategically important system solutions? If you think there is a lack of information, how can this problem best be solved?

Organisation and Management

Organisational structure is determined by the people available and the tasks that need to be performed.

37. What does the organisational structure of the company (organisational chart) look like?

38. How many people have been employed (man-years) by the company (in each of the last three years), and how are these employees distributed over the various functions?

39. How many people have left the company on average over the last three years?

40. Does the company have a system for establishing personnel goals?

41. What kind of management goals has the company had, and what results have been achieved? If the results have been negative, what do you think is missing?

42. Can you imagine any organisational changes that would have a positive effect on the company's profitability? What would these changes be?

43. What is done to make the company's employees (management in particular) identify with company goals?

44. Have job descriptions been drawn up with clear definitions of responsibility for critical jobs?

45. Do you have regular talks with staff? How often?

46. How would you assess the level of competence in the company? Are management and staff sufficiently qualified to do their jobs satisfactorily? If not, what do you think could be done about it?

47. Who normally takes part in the strategy work?

48. Are there any key staff members who are "irreplaceable"?

49. Do you see any possibilities for using new technology in organisational development to:

    • create better links between different units in the organisation?

    • support decentralisation?

    • create more meaningful job content for individual members of staff?

    • automate dangerous jobs?

    • reduce administrative work?

Product Development

Successful product development requires that the company has a clearly formulated strategy for the development of new products. This strategy must specify the general guidelines for product development and form the framework for detailed decision-making.

50. Is company organisation such that it can easily pick up, generate and screen new product ideas?

51. How is product development organised? Who participates?

52. Does the company carry out concept studies and business analyses before investing in new ideas?

53. Does the company carry out adequate product and market testing before launching new products?

54. Do you feel that sufficient attention is paid to "production-friendliness" when new products are developed? What, if anything, do you feel should have been done differently?

55. How great a proportion of turnover in each of the last three years can be ascribed to products developed by your own company?

56. Do you see any potential for new or significantly-changed products in the use of new technology?

57. How much time normally passes from idea to finished product? What kind of time-scale is required if the product is to be competitive?

58. What do you consider to be the most important limitation on product development as it functions at present?

59. Do you see any possibility of making product development more efficient by using new technology?

Purchasing and General Relations with Suppliers

Purchasing raw materials, parts and equipment for production is a significant source of costs. One way of ensuring rational purchasing is to exploit the competition between suppliers. Stating and meeting specifications which are adequate but not too stringent or comprehensive is another aspect of good purchasing.

60. Has the company formulated any kind of purchasing strategy? If so, what is this strategy?

61. Has the company developed any kind of purchasing routines? If so, what are these routines?

62. How would you describe your company's purchasing function: as passive acquisition of goods, or as active and professional?

63. Is the responsibility for the quality of goods delivered clearly defined? If not, what measures do you feel should be taken to monitor quality from suppliers?

64. How much is your current stock worth in money terms? What is the situation in terms of marketability and real value?

65. Is it your impression that your company gets favourable prices from its suppliers? If not, what do you think could be done to change this?

66. Do you see co-operation with the suppliers as working smoothly, or are there aspects which you think should be changed? If so, what aspects?

67. What is the delivery time (average and maximum) for critical components?

68. How often does production run out of purchased goods (once a day, once a week, several times a week)?

69. How many times a year does the company have to complain about purchased goods (estimate)?

70. How many suppliers does the company have for critical components?

71. Do you see any potential in using new technology in relation to suppliers, in terms of

   - obtaining better information about alternative suppliers?

   - making the company less dependent on specific suppliers?

   - reducing raw material costs?

   - increasing raw material quality?

   - reducing delivery times from suppliers?

Sales, Marketing and General Relations with Customers
"In future, countries will become industrialised not by building factories, but by building up markets." In order to be successful with its marketing, the company must have clear goals and strategies based on analyses and plans, as well as an efficient monitoring system.

72. Is the business idea clearly formulated in market-oriented terms? Is it feasible?

73. Are the company's goals defined so that they can be converted into activities and milestones in market plans that can be followed up?

74. Are the market goals realistic, given the competitiveness, resources and options of the company?

75. Does the company have a clear strategy for reaching its market goals?

76. Is the strategy convincing? Is the strategy related to the life cycle of the product, the strategy of the competitors and the financial situation of the company?

77. Are the company's market activities optimally structured with regard to functions, products, end-users, distribution channels and sales districts?

78. Are there any problems between sales/marketing and production, R&D, purchasing, finance etc., and/or external suppliers of services which should be rectified?

79. Does the company have a market information system that provides accurate, adequate and timely information on market developments as regards customers, projects, distributors, dealers, competitors, suppliers and different customer groups?

80. Are monitoring procedures such that they can ensure the realisation of the budget goals?

81. Does management analyse the profitability of products, markets, districts, sales and distribution channels on a regular basis?

82. Should the company enter or withdraw from any business areas, or expand or reduce activities in some of its business areas, and what would the short and long-term consequences of this be in terms of profitability?

83. Does the company have quantified goals for the sales organisation? What are these goals?

84. Is the sales force big enough to fulfil the company's goals?

85. Is the sales force organised according to the "right" criteria (district, market, product)?

86. What has the average turnover per customer been in each of the last three years?

87. Is any single customer so important for the company that the loss of this customer would cause problems for the company?

88. Do you see any possibility of making use of IT vis-à-vis the customers by:

    - identifying potential customers and projects?

    - obtaining earlier, better information about the customers the company is making a profit or a loss on?

    - reducing internal costs in order to increase the contribution margin?

    - reducing internal costs in order to make the products more price-competitive?

    - making it easier for the customer to order goods and services?

    - increasing product quality?

    - developing products which are more in keeping with the customer's needs?

    - increasing flexibility with a view to quicker adaptation to changes in buying patterns?

    - creating more long-term customer relations?

Production and Material Handling

Having an efficient production layout and material-handling system reduces the time and costs involved in moving goods in production within the production system. Costs are related to the way divisions and operational units are organised as well as the way materials are actually handled.

89. By what key indicators is production measured?

90. What measuring criteria do you think are the most important for assessing the efficiency of production?

91. Has a general plan been drawn up for transporting raw materials to the machines, work in progress to the next stage in the production line, and finished goods to stock?

92. Does the company have production and storage in several places? If so, does this create bottleneck problems?

93. Do you feel that the quality specifications for the products are detailed enough and fulfil the expectations of the customers?

94. What main routines are used for quality control?

95. Does the company have a documented process layout for production?

96. What is the stock turnover for raw materials?

97. What is the scrapping percentage in production?

98. How often are there production stoppages as a result of machine failure or other circumstances relating to production?

99. What analytical tools or system support are at present available for production planning in your company?

100. What routines or system support are at present available for quality assurance in your company?

101. Does co-operation between the production department and other departments function satisfactorily, or can you point to specific problems you consider to be of importance for productivity?

102. Do you think the quality of the data used as a basis for production planning and control is adequate?

103. How long is the change-over time from production of one se-ries of products to another? Do you think that this can be improved? If so, how?

104. How long is the throughput time for goods in production?

105. Do you think that the company is ahead of / on a par with / behind the competition in terms of professional competence in production?

106. What do you consider really important in the organisation of the company's production plant (give examples)?

107. Are enough allowances made for all the important consid-erations, or do you think anything is missing (give exam-ples)?

108. How great a proportion of production costs is made up of wages and salaries?

109. Has an overview of the potential rationalisation benefits of new technology been drawn up?

110. To what extent do you think the implementation of new technology will increase your company's competitiveness (a lot / somewhat / insignificantly)? What type of technology, if any, do you think will have the greatest impact?

Finance

Finance includes earnings, costs and assets. Good financial man-agement means continuously ensuring that there is a balanced re-lationship between resource production and resource consumption. Another aspect of financial management is ensuring that there is a balance among cost, quality and the time factor. Good financial management and monitoring require the right choice of measur-able control criteria.

111. What financial measuring criteria and indicators does the company use as monitoring parameters?

112. Are the financial measuring criteria related to the overall goals of the company?

113. What is the general financial situation of the company with regard to:

    • equity ratio

    • debt ratio

    • operating margin

    • rate of return on total capital

    • rate of return on equity

    • profit as percentage of turnover

    • cash flow

    • quick ratio.

114. How do the key indicator values compare with those for the industry in general?

115. What investment ceilings is the company operating with this year? What will these ceilings be next year? Are they realistic?

116. Has the company laid down routines for the budgeting process?

117. Who takes part (at what organisational levels) in the budgeting process? What is the cut-off date for the budget?

118. Does the company prepare revised budgets? When are these available?

119. How often are turnover, margins and operating profit or loss reported?

120. Is the present accounting system geared to providing the current information the management needs to make the right decisions?

121. How are costs distributed (absorption/full costing method vs. the contribution margin method)? Can costs be directly traced to their sources? if not, are the distribution keys used realistic?

122. What is the company's turnover per employee?

123. What is the usual turnover per employee in the industry?

124. What are the company's guidelines for the use of various types of capital and financing sources?

125. To what extent do long-term investments form an obstacle to new investments in, for example, high-profitability plant and machinery?

126. Does the company use computer-based aids in its financial management at present? Does this function satisfactorily?

127. What methods (e.g. cost-benefit analysis) are used at present to evaluate new projects, and what is your experience of these methods?

Quality

Quality has become a more important competitive factor than it was ten or fifteen years ago, and this tendency will continue. Work on improving quality requires a determined effort over an extended period. Nevertheless, those who have made the effort have found that the rewards are great compared with the work involved.

128. The attitude of management:

- Does the company have a written quality policy?

- Does the company have prioritised buying criteria in the quality area?

- Are there quantified goals for quality?

- Is development towards these goals registered and reported?

- How does the quality of the product rate compared with leading competitors?

- Do the authorities, customers or others demand formalised quality assurance systems?

129. Quality control:

- Is the distribution of responsibilities in the company documented?

- Are company activities organised so that planned quality can be achieved?

130. Are market conditions used as a basis for developing new products?

131. What measures are used to verify new products?

- Design reviews?

- Reliability analysis?

- Testing?

132. Purchasing:

- What does the purchasing policy have to say about quality?

- Are quality assessments of suppliers used?

- How is goods reception control organised?

133. Are the capabilities and limitations of the production process known?

134. What are the routines for:

- Process control?

- Quality control?

- Treatment of faults/discrepancies?

135. How are the following reported:

- Quality costs?

- Complaints/claims?

- Internal faults/errors?

- Control results?

136. Quality development:

- Has the company introduced a formal quality assurance system?

- Are quality reviews used?

- Is there training in quality?

- Is systematic quality improvement done?

- Specify any other development measures in the quality area.

Environmental Conditions

The importance of environmental factors as general constraints and competitive factors in industrial business activities is increasing. The background for this is the development of greater environmental consciousness throughout society, nationally and internationally, inasmuch as:

- *the consumers are reacting to environmental selling points in marketing — consumer patterns are changing*

- *the authorities are tightening their requirements — with public opinion behind them*

- *environmental activists have become "acceptable" — they get media coverage and sympathy for their actions.*

137. Is the company in any way environmentally exposed — in a positive or negative sense?

138. Does the company have a permit to emit discharges from the relevant authorities?

139. Has the company had any orders/mention from the environmental authorities, been reported to the police for causing emissions, had complaints from neighbours, or has it been subject to action by environmental activists because of environmental factors?

140. Has the company done any material flow analysis for minimisation of waste/effluents?

141. Does the company use materials in any products, packaging or work in progress that would give rise to negative environmental associations on the market?

142. Does the company have products that can use the "Green Swan" or similar national environmental approval symbol for sales-promoting?

143. What would it mean for production costs or the profitability of products if there was a substantial rise in energy taxes, stricter requirements/higher duties on discharges of gas into the air, or increased and differentiated sewage and dumping charges/taxes?

PRIORITISATION OF GOALS, ISSUES AND OPTIONS

INTRODUCTION

"I often say that when you can measure what you are speaking about, and express it in numbers, you know something about it; but when you cannot measure it, when you cannot express it in numbers, your knowledge is of a meagre and unsatisfactory kind." — Lord Kelvin, 1883

Inherent in the need to establish goals is the wish for qualitative knowledge for which Lord Kelvin had such a high regard. This chapter aims to show the relationship between strategy and goals, and how the establishment of goals can be used to find out "where the shoe pinches".

The *issues/options list* is probably the simplest and the single most useful tool available to assist with the planning process. The technique of using issues/options lists can be applied at all levels of the strategy process, from the initial general business analysis all the way down to the identification of measures and the drawing-up of action plans.

The work on strategic analysis (business idea, goals, strategies etc.) and action plans is rarely a straightforward process which simply begins with the formulation of the business idea and overall goals and ends with plans for the implementation of specific measures. On the contrary, the typical process involves a considerable amount of iteration and a constant need for reformulation and reassessment of assumptions and consequences. The issues/options list is a tool which allows a method of working, so it is a very important aid to the practical implementation of the analytical work.

The aim of the prioritising process is to identify which problems are most critical for the company, and which solutions are best suited to solving them.

The starting point for this prioritising process can vary. During the initial overview of the company, issues are generated from interviews, key ratio analysis, product/market analysis with buying criteria, and business analysis. During the course of the consultancy assignment issues are generated from a more detailed analysis of the same areas, plus more in-depth internal and external analyses.

Whatever the stage in the process, it is important to employ a *prioritising methodology* so as to ensure the best possible result. In this section we focus on the practical groupings and prioritising of issues and options that come up in the preliminary phases of the consultant's work.

The prioritisation of goals and of issues and options is looked at in this chapter under the following headings:

- Establishment of Goals

- Issues/Options Lists

- Prioritisation of Issues/Options

- Prioritisation, a Numerical Method.

ESTABLISHMENT OF GOALS

Goals Defined
The concept of a goal can be defined as follows:

> "A goal is a mental image that provides a focus of attention. It should specify a direction and a result".

Well-formulated goals should also be:

- Ambitious (but not impossible)

- Specific

- Achievable (not just "fancy words")

- Relevant (company management and staff must feel that the goal is "their concern")

- Accepted

- Measurable/verifiable.

Company goals are laid down at the same time as company strategy — and may well be at several levels. The more progress the company has made in formulating and trying to achieve goals, the simpler it should be to define what is wrong or what is particularly encouraging about the company.

The Goal Hierarchy
A simple goal hierarchy is illustrated in Figure 7.1. The "how" questions (means) are answered on the way down in the hierarchy, and the "why" questions as one moves upwards.

Figure 7.1: Simple Goal Hierarchy

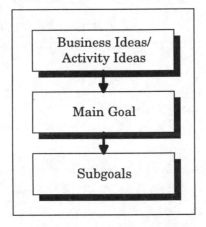

The main goal of business activities is to increase the value of the company to the owners in the longer term. We can rarely see more than three years ahead. The main goals are as a rule means of realising the business idea. In most cases it is natural to use "return on capital" as the overall goal, in which case the priorities of main goals are as follows:

- Return on capital

- Earnings

- Capital utilisation.

In financial circles, "earnings per share" — i.e. return on equity — is often used as the ultimate overall goal.

If one begins with return on capital, all the other subgoals take their natural place as means of achieving the main goal. A reasonably coherent goal hierarchy is very important.

Use of Goal Hierarchies

Within this manual goal hierarchies are used at several stages during the consultancy process:

- The assessment of the business during the strategic analysis uses goal hierarchies to identify areas where the company lacks goals, where the goals are inadequate, where goal achievement is poor, or where goals are obviously contradictory. This helps us to find out "where the shoe pinches".

- During the identification of options, the goal hierarchy is used to identify potential solutions which will give strong support to the company's goals.

- During the prioritisation of issues and options, the goals are potential prioritising criteria.

Establishment of Goals

In order to see the interrelationships between goals and means of achieving them, it is useful to refer to the *value chain* as illustrated in Figure 7.2.

A value chain shows the company's primary activities and support activities as a linked "chain" from supplier to customer. Figure 7.2 only shows the main activities of a *general* industrial company. The SWOT Analysis in Chapter 9 on Product/Market Priorities gives a more detailed account of value chains.

All quantification of productivity and competitive position can be used directly in the value chain and can provide useful subgoals for the company. Normative figures for the industry in general or for individual competitors (assuming such data is available) can be compared to figures for the company under scrutiny, so as to provide a good point of departure for quantifying the situation of the company in specific areas.

Figure 7.2: The Generic Value Chain

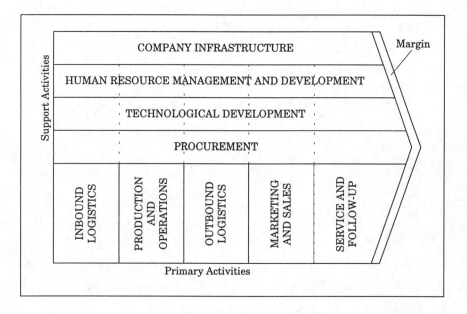

For example, consider a company which deals in marine electronics. The company's primary option for success on the market is to differentiate its products and ensure high quality and the right delivery times. Each of the areas in the value chain sets up its own subgoals. In differentiation strategies, the subgoals will often be a result of the company's perception of the customers' buying criteria. "High quality" and "right delivery times" are examples of such criteria.

Figure 7.3 shows how goals for each activity depicted in the value chain can be established. On the basis of a table like this, it is easier to co-ordinate subsequent subgoal priorities.

Figure 7.3: Subgoals for Various Activities

AREA	MAIN GOAL	SUBGOAL 1	SUBGOAL 2	SUBGOAL 3	SUBGOAL 4
Primary Activities					
SALES AND MARKETING	Contribution Margin	Market Share	Marketing Activities	Quotes and Follow-up	Customer Visits
PRODUCTION AND OPERAT.	Capacity Utilisation	Delivery Capability	Number of Complaints	Units per Day	Unit Costs
INBOUND LOGISTICS	Product Quality	Punctuality	Price	Stock Turnover	
OUTBOUND LOGISTICS	Delivery Times	Product Quality	Transport Quality	Stock Turnover	
Support Functions					
HUMAN RESOURCE DEVELOPMENT	Productivity	Competence	Precision	Efficiency	
TECHNOLOGY DEVELOPMENT	Competitive Advantage	New Product	Improved Production Method		

Key Questions

- What sort of return on capital must the company have in the short term to survive?

- What return on capital should the company aim for in order to develop further — and what about the industry as a whole?

- What is the company's equity ratio and what should it be?

- What operational parameters/subgoals would be most effective and most realistic to work on to achieve goals as regards return on capital and equity ratio?

- Can the company's capital structure be improved?

- Can its capital turnover be increased?

- What is the company's relationship with its customers compared to its competitors?

- Is the company on the right markets?

- What is needed to increase:

◊ sales volumes?

◊ sales prices?

- How can the products be improved?

- What sort of cost structure does the company have in relation to its competitors?

- What are the strengths and weaknesses of the company?

- Which subgoals are most technology-intensive, and what priorities do these have?

- Are there clear conflicts between some of the company's subgoals, or between subgoals and the main goal?

- Are there important areas where there are no goals at all?

- Do the subgoals tie in with critical success factors in the industry and the competitive profile of the company?

ISSUES/OPTIONS LISTS

Overview
Figure 7.4 shows a typical sequence during the analytical process. First we work with the issues, then gradually shift the focus to the assessment of the options, so as to finally end up with a coherent hierarchy of goals, strategies and measures. In its simplest form, the issues/options list consists of two parts:

- An **issue**, i.e. something on which a decision has to be made

- A **possible solution** (option), which may be at the goal, strategy or measure level.

For any issue there may be many alternative (wholly or partially overlapping) options. In the same way, one option can address several different issues.

Figure 7.4: From Issues to Goals and Strategies

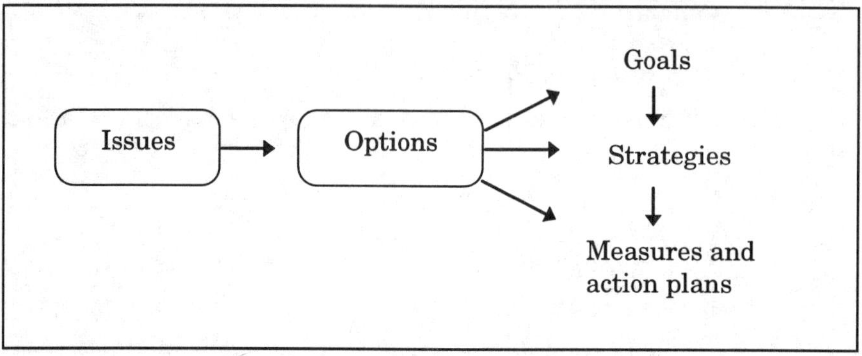

Figure 7.5 shows a typical extract from an issues/options list.

Figure 7.5: Extract from Issues/Options List

Subject: Ordering/Stocks/Invoicing/Buying

Issues	Options/Strategies/Measures	
How can we exploit computerisation better to achieve lower prices, better service and more favourable delivery terms from our suppliers?	• Expand the current purchasing system to give us an overview of supplier contracts	Possible
	• Link up with three-part supplier and goods database.	Possible
	• Co-ordinate purchases of equipment for better exploitation of volume discounts	Adopted

The Issues/Options List as a Management Tool

The issues/options list is a very effective management tool that can be used during the planning process. In the context of this manual, it will constitute a guiding principle which will be used to identify issues during the general business analysis, which will then be expanded with priorities and details as the various other techniques are phased into the process. Thus, at any given time there will be a prioritised set of issues which defines what lies within and outside the scope of the project.

It is important to note that issues are not the same as problems. Issues define something on which you have to make a decision — not necessarily because it is a problem at present, but because something is unresolved.

The formulation of the "right" issues is one of the most important factors for success in the planning process. Early identification of critical issues directs the analysis towards the right areas. Detailed survey work without a focus on issues and options results as a rule in "surveying for its own sake", with results that cannot be applied to practical planned measures.

Establishment of Issues and Options

This manual presents a number of techniques that can be used in connection with the general strategic analysis and the establishment of strategies and action plans. In addition to these techniques, consultants are expected to have their own range of techniques and experience to draw on. So it is important to have a mechanism that can combine and systematise the results of the work with the various techniques. The issues/options lists are very well-suited to this work.

Note that an experienced consultant will often identify the issues and options directly, without using additional techniques.

The different techniques interact with the issues/options list as shown in Figure 7.6. The techniques used generally fall into one of four categories:

- Category 1: Techniques which help to identify issues. Structured interviews and financial key ratio analysis are typical examples of these.

- Category 2: Techniques which help to identify options. Analysis of buying criteria, scenario techniques and value chain analysis are examples.

- Category 3: Prioritising techniques which can be applied to issues, options or specific measures. Cost-benefit analysis and risk analysis are examples.

- Category 4: Techniques which help to get from rough option analysis to clear specifications of goals, strategies and measures. The goal hierarchy technique is a relevant example.

Figure 7.6: Issues/Options List and Other Techniques

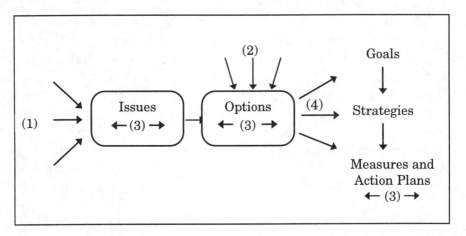

Some techniques fall into more than one category. Goal hierarchies, for example, will help to find areas where the company's goals are inadequately fulfilled or where they conflict with one another (Category 1). During the assessment of options, the same technique is used to identify potential uses of technology for better fulfilment of the company's targets, and as support for decisions on better goal-orientation (Category 2). As part of the prioritisation process we will look for applications which will give as much support as possible to the company's goals (Category 3). Finally, the goal hierarchy technique forms a basis for establishing goals and strategies for the company's exploitation of technology, and linking these with business goals and strategies (Category 4).

Examples of Issues
Issues can often be formulated by combining statements (about the current situation, trends and/or goals) and questions about how one should approach these. Nevertheless, the most important thing is that the issues are at the *right level*, are precise, and that they are formulated to allow for coherent relationships between goals, strategies and measures.

Some typical examples are listed below.

From the Identification of the Business Idea and Goal Hierarchies:

"Our business idea is very product-oriented, in a situation where the market is changing and is making new demands on our business activities. How can the use of new technology make us better at facing change?"

"Our targets are relatively clear, but many of them are very difficult to quantify. How can we deal with follow-up and documentation so it can show us how to achieve our goals?"

From the Analysis of the Industry Structure and Competitors

"The present structure of the industry, with many small competitors of similar size to ourselves, is threatened by two or three large groups which are assessing our market niche as a possible new area of business. What are our options for taking up a good position in relation to this threat?"

"Our worst competitor has production costs that are 20 per cent to 40 per cent lower than our own as a result of investments in technology. But these investments have put a lot of pressure on their equity ratio. How can we avoid a similar situation if we invest in new technology?"

From the Analysis of Financial Key Ratios

"The key ratio analysis indicates that our return on capital is sufficient in the short term — but with ever-greater pressure on margins and stiffer price competition, the long-term perspectives for return on capital are rather doubtful. What are our options for improving this situation?"

Grouping Issues

As the issues are identified, it becomes natural to group them to systematise the content of the documentation. This grouping should be adapted to the individual case, and there is no standard model for classification. Some examples of group topics are:

- Product/market combinations (e.g. "construction market", "kitchen fittings")

- Technology areas (e.g. communications systems, robotics, control automation)

- Functional areas or groups of activities (e.g. material control, production control, logistics, financial management.)

It is not necessary to stick rigidly to one particular type of classification. Grouping should be done in terms of topics that the consultant and working group consider natural. After all, the most important thing is to identify the crucial issues quickly, so one can focus on future work that will have the best impact on the company.

Establishment and Assessment of Options

The use of an issues/options list has much potential at all levels, from strategy and policy-making, down to setting goals and establishing specific measures. Options in principle have the status "possible" — that is, they are ideas that have been thrown up but usually have not been discussed as real measures. Eventually, one reaches a point where the options change status from "possible" to "recommended", and then a selection of the recommended options achieve "adopted" status.

This makes the issues/options list a *living document*. The number of new issues decreases gradually throughout the process, and the number of possible strategies grows, while the existing options change status.

Discussion and brainstorming meetings are useful tools for identifying options. The participants are normally the same key personnel who were interviewed. This is a great aid to creating acceptance of the conclusions. The conclusions become not only the consultant's advice, but recommendations that have been identified, discussed and assigned priorities by selected personnel in the firm.

This process is alternately *systematic* and *creative*. A typical course of events is:

- Systematic assessment of whether the issues are "right" in the opinion of the group. A number of issues are removed or combined as a result of this.

- Creative identification of alternative prioritisation criteria for assessing the issues, with internal emphases and arrangement.

- Systematic prioritisation of options on the basis of agreed prioritisation criteria and value scales.

- Creative identification and definition of possible solutions (strategies and possible measures) for addressing the issues. This is normally done on a priority-to-priority basis.

- Creative identification of alternative prioritisation criteria for assessing options.

- Systematic prioritisation of identified options on the basis of agreed prioritisation criteria and value scales.

PRIORITISATION OF ISSUES/OPTIONS

Issues and Options during the Strategic Analysis

The aim of the strategic analysis is to find out "where the shoe pinches", and to define the framework and limits of future analytical work. To facilitate this work we carry out the following analyses:

- Business analysis
- Key ratio analysis
- Product/market analysis
- Structured interviews.

This line of approach ensures that the business issues are brought into focus. The relevant opportunities and threats, along with the company's strategic position, will therefore play a decisive role in the initial prioritising of the issues.

So the question that has to be asked is "What is most important for the company?"

In some cases the answer may be obvious through analysis of
key financial ratios. In other situations it may be much more difficult to carry out correct prioritising immediately. This is especially so for companies where the situation is a complex one, and
where it is difficult to find a sure frame of reference for the company's position and situation. Often, issues and possible solutions
are at different levels as far as detail and specifications are concerned. It is therefore important to bear in mind that the initial
prioritising must be based upon overall business criteria.

Examples of relevant overall business criteria include:

- Cost reduction

- Reorganisation

- Product restructuring

- Value chain considerations/strategic alliances

- Increased production capacity

- Increased value to customers by better satisfaction of buying
  criteria.

Identifying and Evaluating Criteria for Prioritising Issues
In a strategic analysis this is a critical point, in that the criteria
are an expression of how both consultant and company view the
company's position and the direction it is necessary to take in order to improve it. In this phase then, the prioritising criteria can
be said to represent the overall critical success factors.

It is important that their number is not exaggerated; between
three and five is appropriate.

Determining the prioritising criteria is a job that must be done
together with the company's management. The consultant's task
is to initiate the process so that both the management and others
engaged in the strategy process come to have the same understanding of the company's situation, and agree on what is most
important on this basis. It is important to bear in mind that this
is a process, and that different points of departure and information create different understandings of the situation. The consult-

ant should therefore make sure that all those participating in the process have the same basic information.

The final decisions on what constitutes these criteria should be taken at a meeting with the company's executive management. The consultant should lead this meeting. A brainstorming process should be used with the consultant acting as a catalyst.

It is worth remembering that the issues brought up during the analysis will have different values depending on how they are generated. Key ratio analysis will typically focus on the company's financial situation; product/market combinations will focus on buying criteria; business analysis on the strategic position; and interviews will typically concentrate on issues related to daily operations. Assigning priorities without first carrying out these analyses will at best lead to sub-optimal results, at worst to incorrect prioritising.

It is natural to select prioritising criteria from all of these areas, and the following questions may be helpful in reaching sensible criteria:

- What are the critical factors for improving the company's competitive position in the most important product/market combinations? Examples include higher entry barriers in the market, increased customer loyalty, etc.

- What are the critical success factors for satisfying customers' buying criteria? Examples of criteria are those that improve customer service, improve quality, etc.

- What are the critical success factors for improving the company's financial position? Examples of these are less tying-up of capital, improved liquidity, increased turnover, etc.

- What are the critical success factors for improving product development and restructuring? Examples of this include more stringent control of development projects, more production-friendly design, integration of market and purchase analyses into product development, etc.

- What are the critical parameters for meeting other company goals? These goals might include an improved working environment, improved communications, slower staff turnover in key positions, etc.

Grouping Issues and Options in the Analysis Phase

During the strategic analysis, prioritising is done at an overall level. It is therefore not usual to sub-prioritise into special areas at this stage. Later on this might be necessary in connection with detailed proposals for special functions or areas.

Usually during the analysis phase, issues and options are grouped according to how much they satisfy the main criteria. Priority criteria themselves, therefore, provide a good grouping system at this stage.

Different products/market combinations, however, can produce different priority criteria. Buying criteria can vary, and if priority criteria basically mirror these differences, it may be a good idea to group issues and options accordingly.

The consultant must be able to evaluate how the criteria ought to be used in the ensuing work of identifying the most important issues. A normal methodology is to write the priority criteria on a flip-over or white board that can be seen by all those participating in the prioritising meeting. Meeting participants can then glance at these criteria while evaluating the issues, and go on to assign priorities accordingly. In other cases it may be necessary to take a more methodological approach (see below).

As the work of the consultant progresses, many issues and options will be generated in different areas. The initial analysis will have ensured that the focus is on problem areas.

If the conclusion from the initial analysis is that one should concentrate on cost reduction for product/market combination A, and improving service for product/market combination B, then it may be difficult to compare the importance of the various options available for both areas. In such a case it would be natural to group options before the prioritising takes place.

Questions during the interview phase are grouped according to topic, and this may form a natural starting point for grouping options too. The company's organisational structure is another starting point.

Some common ways of grouping are:

- **Product/market combinations with the same buying criteria** can be grouped together, and issues/options within these areas can be given priorities according to the same priority criteria.

- **Functional grouping**. For example, issues and options within product planning and monitoring, finance/accounts, material administration, etc.

- **Technological basis**. This involves grouping within the various technological areas such as communications, office automation, production automation, etc.

In organisations that focus heavily on the use of information technology, the following points can serve as a starting point for grouping:

- Strategy and management (decision support systems)

- Administration (basic/transaction systems)

- Marketing/sales (forecasting/strategic systems)

- Product development/engineering (control systems/CAD, etc.)

- Production (CIM, planning, MPS, etc.)

- Purchasing (value chain, strategic systems)

- Organisation

- Training.

The most important aspect of this division of the issues/options is that the groupings simplify the priority process by allowing you to use the same criteria within each group.

In most cases, the same criteria can be used in several groups (consultants must use their judgement to decide whether this is so). It is also necessary to combine options that address one or more issues, either because they are covered by the same technological solution, or because they are dependent upon each other in achieving a total solution.

Criteria for the Choice of Possible Solutions

In addition to the criteria for identifying the most important issues, the consultant must also identify the criteria for deciding how realistic it would be to implement any proposed solutions. The following factors should be taken into account in this regard:

- **Apparently simple realisation**. In many cases the options can appear simple to realise — "It's just a matter of doing it." This applies to typical (straightforward) changes in company procedure.

- **Rough cost-benefit evaluation** that indicates whether an investment appears to be profitable or unprofitable.

- **Rapid realisation**. This is especially true for issues that receive a high priority in order to produce immediate results. This may be because something is a "burning issue" or because further progress on development of strategy may be dependant on its solution.

- **Dependency**. The option must be implemented because other high-priority solutions are dependent on it. The option itself may not be a decidedly profitable one.

- **Implementability**. This is a matter of the evaluation of accessible technology, company competence, company maturity, accessible external competence, the risk of failure, probable cost compared with financial constraints, implementation schedule, etc.

With reference to the last point, some practical consideration could be:

- What type of organisational changes will have to take place as a consequence?

- How large and complex is this project going to be, and is company competence good enough to control such a project?

Implementing the Prioritising Process

The implementation of an effective prioritising process demands correct organisation, a good mix of participants and competence, and a great deal of work from the person who is to lead the process. It is important not to search for scapegoats, but rather to focus on how one can best deal with the present situation.

The guidelines outlined in this section are precisely that — guidelines. Consultants must use their own experience, both to control the process and to discover what are the most important issues and options. This section, together with the following one which describes a numerical method of implementing a prioritising process, can therefore only help to clarify the assumptions behind the priorities and prioritising criteria so the company will have a clear focus on these.

This is a good starting point for meaningful prioritisation of issues.

PRIORITISATION, A NUMERICAL METHOD

The prioritising methodology described here may appear complicated at first glance, but is quickly learnt through use on specific cases. However, this numerical method is clearly aimed at the consultant, and is not suited for general distribution to managers or participants in work groups in the company.

The methodology should be seen as a tool for facilitating the process, not as a straitjacket. The process (i.e. the structured discussion) the methodology brings out into the open is just as important as the numerical results. It is likewise important that the method's numerical values do not become a substitute for common sense.

Steps in the Prioritising Process

The process for assigning priorities to issues and options is comprised of the following steps:

- Identifying and evaluating the criteria for prioritising issues

- Assigning priorities to issues on the basis of the selected prioritising criteria

- Identifying and evaluating the criteria for prioritising options

- Selection of the most relevant options for each issue

- Prioritising among the selected options.

These steps are described in further detail below.

Identifying and Evaluating the Criteria for Prioritising Issues
The aim here is to decide which criteria to apply when prioritising the issues and their relative importance. The selected criteria should reflect what is important for the company, so that the most important issues can be selected at a later stage. Deciding on the criteria to use is of critical importance for the final result, and must therefore be taken seriously. It is also very much a process of "consciousness-raising" with value in its own right.

Before this process starts, the issues should already be grouped by relevant topic, and it follows that prioritising criteria should be decided upon within each topic accordingly. If an appropriate topic grouping has not already taken place, then such groupings should be formed before prioritising criteria are selected.

Brainstorming is a good technique for generating ideas for assigning priority criteria. Examples of the types of questions that can bring these criteria out in discussion are given in Chapter 11 on Problem-solving.

After the criteria have been selected (the ideal number being between four and eight), they need to be listed in order of importance. Figure 7.7 shows a value table that can be used for this purpose — each criteria is assigned a number from 1 – 5 with 5 being the most important.

Figure 7.7: Values for Use in Assigning Priority

Category	Importance
Critical	5
Very important	4
Important	3
Less important	2
Unimportant	1

The criteria selected are placed in a matrix (illustrated in Figure 7.8), to be used later to assist with assigning of priorities. A similar matrix can be used for assigning values to the criteria as (illustrated in Figure 7.9).

Figure 7.8: Matrix for Prioritising Issues

Company: Topic:										Date: Page:		
Importance (1–5)												
Prioritising Criteria ⟍ Issue	Reduces Bottlenecks	Increases Turnover	Reduces Costs							Numerical Result	Intuitively Correct	Result

Figure 7.9: Matrix for Assessing Criteria

Company: Topic:									Date: Page:		
Importance (5–1)							⑤ ◀ - - - - - -				
Prioritising Criteria ⟍ Participants	Increases Revenue	Reduces Costs	Removes Bottlenecks	Means Comp. Advantage	Profiles the Company	Better Work Environment	Increases Competence	Simple/ Quick Implement.	Numerical Result	Intuitively Correct	Result
Participant 1	5	4	5	4	4	4	3	5			
Participant 2	4	3	3	5	3	2	4	5			
Participant 3	5	5	4	5	2	2	4	4			
Participant 4	5	2	1	3	5	1	2	4			
Result	5	4	③ ↑ After Discussing	5	4	2	4	⑤ - - - - - -			

There should also be an evaluation based on what seems intuitively correct ("gut feeling") in addition to these more specific criteria. The result of this step is a set of general prioritising criteria that can then be used to prioritise issues in a specific prioritising process.

Assigning Priorities to Issues on the Basis of the Selected Prioritising Criteria

The object of the exercise is to select the issues that are most important for the company. Each issue is given an importance value in accordance with the previously-defined prioritising criteria. The value should be an expression of a combination of the issue's importance and how far it satisfies the criteria in question.

When issues are being prioritised each participant gives each issue a value, and the average determines the final order of importance. In practice, much discussion takes place during this "voting" process. If there is much difference of opinion the voters must attempt to explain their point of view and try to reach agreement. The matrix contains the selected criteria with their relative importance (weighting). The weighting can be used to give a numerical basis for final prioritising. There is also a column for intuitive evaluation, i.e. evaluation based on common sense. The final or total result should therefore be the result of an evaluation of both of these factors.

It is important that attention is concentrated on the issues and their importance. It is especially important to differentiate between symptoms and actual issues. A discussion of possible solutions should be avoided at this stage. This way one separates the "whats" from the "hows". But this in turn makes demands on the person leading the process. A time schedule for implementing the priorities must be agreed at the start so that everyone is aware of how much time has been set aside for each issue. Between two and four minutes per issue is sufficient if the group already knows the methodology.

Material handed out to participants at this stage should only contain a description of the issues.

An example of the matrix being used to prioritise issues is illustrated in Figure 7.10.

Figure 7.10: Use of Prioritising Matrix

Company: BUNT VVS & Contractor   Date:
Topic: Operating Systems   Page:

Prioritising Criteria / Participants	Increases Revenue	Reduces Costs	Removes Bottlenecks	Means Comp. Advantage	Profiles the Company	Better Work Environment	Increases Competence	Simple/ Quick Implement.	Numerical Result	Intuitively Correct	Result
Importance (5–1)	5	4	3	5	4	2	4	5			
1. Can a reorganising of jobs lead to saving in production, and between administration?	—	3	—	2	2	4	3	5	3.1	5	5
2. An "experience database" containing technical information on earlier projects would contribute to increased quality. How should such a "database" be implemented?	—	5	5	5	4	2	4	3	4.1	5	5
3. An "experience database" with financial key ratios from earlier projects would contribute to better calculations when drawing up tenders. How should this be implemented?	—	5	5	5	4	2	4	3	4.1	5	5
4. A cost database containing information on subcontractors would contribute to a quicker tendering process. Is this an important strategic tool, and if so, what resources would be necessary to establish such a database?	—	3	3	3	4	4	3	3	3.2	3	3
5. In the past, various methods have been used for charting computerisation costs to customers. Which guidelines are to be followed from now on?	4	—	—	—	—	—	—	4	4.0	4	4
6. The company wishes to maintain its image of a company working in a technically sophisticated environment and with high-quality products. How can the use of technical calculation programmers contribute to this? How should the company evaluate tenders in the market?	—	4	4	5	5	5	3	3	(3.9)	5	5

Result = Sum[value * importance]/Sum[crit. importance]

Participant 1	4
Participant 2	3
Participant 3	5
Participant 4	3

Category	
Critical	5
Very Important	4
Important	3
Less Important	2
Unimportant	1

Identifying and Evaluating the Criteria for Prioritising Options
Prioritising options also requires guidelines or criteria. This process must determine how well-suited or realistic an option actually is when faced with solving the issue in question. Here a matrix similar to the one used for prioritising issues also forms the starting point for assigning priorities to options.

In other words, the starting point is the same criteria as those used for prioritising issues. These can, if required, be summarised in a single column entitled "Address issue?" in a prioritising matrix.

In addition to these criteria, a matrix may also be supplemented with criteria for how realistic implementation of the given options would be. Factors to be considered should include:

- Ease of implementation

- A rough cost-benefit evaluation

- Speed of implementation

- How other options depend on a given option.

Thus the overall *implementability* of the different options is assessed by evaluating accessible technology, company competence, company maturity, accessible external competence, risk of failure, probable cost against financial constraints, implementation schedule, etc.

Criteria should be selected by starting with this approach. After selection, they are placed in a prioritising matrix and evaluated for importance. Even if the importance of the criteria is not given a numerical value, the form can still be used as a checklist. The actual process of deciding what the criteria are to be is in itself important, as it creates a common understanding of the prioritising criteria.

Figure 7.11 shows an example of a matrix being used to prioritise options. The columns for status and cost-benefit evaluation are explained in the next two sections.

Figure 7.11: Matrix for Prioritising Options

Company:
Topic:

Date:
Page:

Importance (5–1) / Prioritising Criteria / Participants	Increases Revenue	Reduces Costs	Profiles Company	Improves Work Envir.	—	Low Complexity	Simple/ Quick Implement.	Establish Technology	Numerical Result	Intuitively Correct	Result	Status before Cost-Benefit	Total Cost	Total Benefit	Cost-Benefit	Status after Cost-Benefit

Selection of the Most Relevant Options for Each Issue

Initially, all options are given the same status: "possible". For each issue we need to classify the related options in one of the following categories:

- **"Adopted"**. The option can be adopted immediately without any further evaluation. This typically applies to solutions that can be applied straight away, without any significant implementation problems.

- **"Recommended"**. The priority assignment group recommends that this option should be followed up.

- **"Interesting"**. The option appears to be an interesting one, but closer evaluation (e.g. cost-benefit) is necessary before it can be designated "recommended" or "rejected".

- **"Rejected"**. The option can be rejected straight away. This typically applies to options that are "politically unimplementable" in the organisation.

During this prioritising phase, the issues are gone through one by one in order of importance, using the prioritising matrix as a checklist. As there are a limited number of options per issue, a "numbering drill" is often unnecessary. Usually a "limit" is set to the number of issues that can be dealt with, so that only those issues above a certain priority are included in the process.

After the assigning of priorities has been completed, all the "rejected" options are removed. The same goes for the "adopted" options, which can immediately be "changed" to recommended measures without further prioritising.

Prioritising among the Selected Options

Now priorities have to be assigned to all the "recommended" and "interesting" options in relation to each other and independently of the issues they "belong to". The result of this final round of assigning priorities should form the basis for specific plans. This final prioritising is done in two steps:

- An evaluation of each option in relation to the actual prioritising criteria. This provides both a qualitative and very rough quantitative evaluation.

- A rough cost-benefit analysis for those options that have survived Step 1. This provides a purely quantitative evaluation in real money terms.

Step 1 of the implementation takes the same course as with the prioritisation of issues. Options are proposed by project participants, and the average functions as the numerical expression of priority. Here too it is important that sufficient notice is taken of quantifiable criteria and common sense.

Sufficient time must be allocated for a certain amount of reformulation or regeneration of options. Actual prioritisation will be a repetitive process given that options will most probably be interdependent or will affect one other. Several rounds are often necessary before the prioritisation is completed.

After Step 1, many of the "interesting" options will have altered status to either "recommended" or "rejected", while a number will of course continue to be "interesting". It may also happen that a "recommended" option is given a new status.

And then it is time for Step 2. In Step 1, statements have been of the type "we believe this option will mean a strong/slight increase in turnover", or "we believe this option involves low/medium/high costs". Step 2 should include rough estimates of cost-benefit effects for the "recommended" and "interesting" options. The cost-benefit column in Figure 7.11 summarises the result, and this in turn can lead to a change in status for some of the remaining options.

The final result of this last prioritisation of options should be a list of options that have to be acted upon. In practice, this means that measures and action plans for implementing these options have to be decided on later.

Note that the whole prioritising drill has involved a gradual narrowing of the focus area for the project. Effective handling of prioritising is therefore critical if manageable, realistic plans are to be obtained from it.

We began with a set of unprioritised issues. Gradually, the less important issues were given lower priorities or removed altogether. For the issues that remained, the number of options was drastically reduced, first issue by issue, then in an overall evaluation in terms of qualitative and quantitative criteria, and finally in a quantitative cost-benefit evaluation of the remaining options, if only at a very rough level. In our experience, after such an exercise high priority issues are down to 20 to 40 per cent of the original volume, and high priority options are cut down to 5 to 10 per cent.

The result is a manageable number of issues and options that can form a basis for realistic goals, strategies, and measures to bring about improvements within the company.

Implementing the Prioritising Process

The implementation of an effective prioritising process makes great demands as regards good organisation, the right mix of participants and competence, and requires a great deal from the person who is to lead the process.

It is important not to search for scapegoats — one should focus instead on the best way of dealing with the present situation.

And finally, a word of warning. It is often more difficult to calculate accurate cost-benefit figures for issues and options that deal with strategic issues than it is with rationalisation measures. Make sure that this does not become a pretext for doing nothing. It is only by addressing the strategic issues that the company can ensure its long-term future. This is also why a purely quantitative evaluation is carried out after one has finished an overall prioritising process that takes the "strategic bonuses" into account.

8

FINANCIAL KEY RATIO ANALYSIS

INTRODUCTION

In this section *financial key ratios* are discussed. A company's financial key ratios are linked with the financial goals of the company. The company will also have a number of goals with related non-financial key ratios. Typically these goals will be linked loosely with company finances in the short term. This applies in particular to long-term goals meant to improve the competitiveness of the company by improving its ability to meet customer or market needs. The following section relates to financial key ratios only.

Financial key ratios can be used to:

- Illustrate whether company finances are developing positively or negatively

- Give early warnings of potential problems (i.e. "switch on red lights")

- Lead to the implementation of necessary corrective measures.

Financial key ratio analysis plays an important part during the consultant's initial assessment of a company, since it can be used to identify "where the shoe pinches". The choice of key questions during the information-gathering process is influenced by the key ratios about which the consultant wants information.

In this chapter, a number of the most commonly used financial ratios are defined. The application of some of these ratios is explained through the use of two forms:

- The (modified) DuPont model, and

- A (modified) Boston matrix which gives insight into the strategic direction.

Both forms are filled in using financial key ratios which the consultant will have worked out during the initial general strategic analysis. In this way the work of the consultant can be related back to the commercial situation of the company. Special emphasis is given to information on products and markets, so that strategies and measures both start with and focus on the combinations that are most attractive to the company in terms of competitive advantage and profitability.

In this chapter, financial key ratios are looked at under the following headings:

- Financial Key Ratios

- The DuPont Model (a financial model used to compare the company's financial key ratios).

- Use of the DuPont Model for Ratio Analysis

- Use of the Modified Boston Matrix.

FINANCIAL KEY RATIOS

The following questions are answered through assessment of the financial key ratios:

- Whether *liquidity* is sufficient to meet the company's current commitments

- How the company's assets are *financed*

- Whether the *equity ratio* is satisfactory

- Whether *profitability* is satisfactory

- Whether *return on investment* is good enough to provide adequate returns on invested capital.

Liquidity/Working Capital

"Liquidity" refers to current assets that can be turned into liquid assets so that current liabilities can be paid. The two ratios normally used are:

$$\text{Current ratio} = \frac{\text{Current assets}}{\text{Current liabilities}}$$

$$\text{Acid test ratio} = \frac{\text{Current assets - stock}}{\text{Current liabilities}}$$

Traditionally, the requirement has been that the first ratio — the current ratio — should have a value of 2 or greater than 2, and the second ratio — the acid test ratio (or quick ratio) — should have a value of 1 or greater than 1. These requirements, however, should be seen in relation to prevailing level of turnover and credit terms available.

The working capital of a company is defined as current assets less current liabilities. Working capital requirements can therefore be reduced by a reduction in effective credit terms to customers, a reduction in the time goods are tied in stocks, or an improvement in the agreed credit terms from suppliers. These factors can be expressed in the five ratios listed below:

$$\text{Credit turnover for creditors} = \frac{\text{Average supplier debt x 365}}{\text{Goods purchased incl. VAT}}$$

$$\text{Credit turnover to customers} = \frac{\text{Average accts receivable x 365}}{\text{Operating turnover incl. VAT}}$$

$$\text{Stock turnover} = \frac{\text{Average stocks x 365}}{\text{Raw materials used}}$$

$$\text{Work-in-progress (WIP) turnover} = \frac{\text{Average WIP x 365}}{\text{Prod. cost of annual sales}}$$

$$\text{Finished goods (FG) turnover} = \frac{\text{Avg. FG stocks at prod. cost x 365}}{\text{Prod. cost of annual sales}}$$

Financing

A minimum requirement for financing is that fixed assets should be financed by long-term capital. The ratio below relates long term capital to total fixed assets:

$$\text{Long-term capital as\% of fixed assets} = \frac{(\text{Long-term debt} + \text{equity}) \times 100}{\text{Fixed assets}}$$

Equity Ratio

The equity ratio expresses the company's ability to withstand strains or to absorb losses. It indicates how much of the assets are financed with the company's own capital. It also shows how much of the assets could be lost before the creditors' receivables are threatened.

$$\text{Equity ratio} = \frac{\text{Equity} \times 100}{\text{Total capital}}$$

Profitability

Analysis of a company's costs and earnings will give a measure of the profitability of the company's products and services.

The *contribution method* of costing is relevant to most companies. With this method, costs are classified as being either *variable* or *fixed*. Variable costs are those that are directly attributable to a given product or service, and which vary in proportion with the level of turnover and activity (the cost of raw materials, for example). Fixed costs are those costs which do not directly change with the level of turnover/activity (rent and administration costs, for example).

Use of the contribution method ensures that, products, markets or divisions are assessed on the basis of their contribution margin:

$$\text{Sales price per unit - variable unit costs} = \text{Contribution marg. per unit}$$

> Total contribution margin - fixed costs = Earnings

The contribution method enables the consultant to extract the following key ratios from company records:

- The *contribution margin* (per product, per division and for the whole company)

- The *contribution ratio* (the contribution margin as a percentage of turnover)

- The *break-even point*, i.e. a turnover that exactly balances costs

- A *safety margin* (the percentage that turnover can drop before the company runs at a loss).

The relationship between the above ratios are illustrated in the example given in Figure 8.1.

Figure 8.1: Relationship between Key Indicators

Turnover   ECU 150,-
-Variable units costs   ECU 105,-

Contribution   ECU 45,-

Turnover: ECU 10.0 million per year
Fixed costs: ECU 2.4 million per year

$$\text{Contribution ratio} = \frac{\text{Contribution margin (45,-) x 100\%}}{\text{Turnover (150,-)}} = 30\%$$

$$\text{Break-even point} = \frac{\text{Fixed costs (2.4 m) x 100\%}}{\text{Contribution ratio (30\%)}} = \text{ECU 8m}$$

$$\text{Safety margin} = \frac{\text{Turnover (10m) - break-even (8m) x 100\%}}{\text{Turnover (10m)}} = 20\%$$

The example in Figure 8.2 illustrates how the contribution method can be applied to a company manufacturing a range of products (A to E) in two separate departments (1 and 2).

Figure 8.2: Contribution Method Illustrated

Department	Department 1				Department 2			Sum
Product	A	B	C	Sum (A-C)	D	E	Sum (D-E)	Total (A-E)
Turnover	50	80	70	200	100	200	300	500
– Direct material costs	25	40	15	80	20	80	100	180
– Direct payroll costs	10	20	40	70	25	50	75	145
= Product contribution	15	20	15	50	55	70	125	175
Contribution ratio	30%	25%	22%	25%	55%	35%	42%	35%
– Fixed department costs				25			100	125
= Department contribution				25			25	50
Contribution ratio				12.5%			8.3%	
– Fixed company costs								20
= Profits								30
Profit ratio								6%

Return on Capital

Return on capital or profitability can of course be judged by looking at profit or loss in simple money terms. However, a better insight into a company's situation is gained if profitability is seen in relation to turnover and capital employed. The ratio, *return on total capital*, illustrates this relationship. It gives a measure of the *profitability of ordinary operations*, and is normally defined as follows:

$$\text{Return on capital} \ = \ \frac{\text{(Earnings before extraordinary items + financial costs) x 100}}{\text{Average total capital}}$$

The owners of a company will frequently be interested in what yield is being attained from equity capital — that is *return on equity*. This ratio is defined as:

$$\text{Return on equity} \ = \ \frac{\text{Earnings before extraordinary items x 100}}{\text{Equity capital}}$$

Another key ratio of interest is the *rate of capital turnover* — that is, how many times a year the capital at our disposal will be used. This ratio is calculated by dividing annual turnover by total capital:

$$\text{Rate of capital turnover} \ = \ \frac{\text{Total operating turnover}}{\text{Total capital}}$$

We may also want to look at net earnings in relation to operating turnover. This is referred to the *rate of return on net sales*. Here we are not concerned with how much of the capital is borrowed. The net earnings in normal accounting contexts are earnings before financial items and extraordinary items.

$$\text{Return on net sales} \ = \ \frac{\text{Net earnings before interest x 100}}{\text{Operating turnover}}$$

Interest cover gives an indication of the extent to which the company is able to meet its interest commitments. If the result of the formula is 100, this means that the surplus before financial costs is just enough to cover financial costs. If the result is less than

100, this indicates that the company cannot meet its interest commitments.

$$\text{Interest cover} = \frac{(\text{Interest costs} + \text{earnings before extraordinary items}) \times 100}{\text{Interest costs}}$$

Finally, a word of caution. Management will be able to extract a whole range of ratios from the published accounts as well as having access to unpublished information which may be even more useful. Over-emphasis on a single ratio should be avoided. Instead, when ratios are being evaluated the following points should be considered:

- How does the particular ratio fit in with the trend over the past few years?

- How does the ratio compare with other ratios obtained form the same set of data?

- What influence does the type of business activity have on the ratio?

THE DUPONT MODEL

The factors that influence the finances of a company can be tabulated to illustrate simple relationships between the various factors and the final financial outcome. Figure 8.3 shows how the return on total capital (surplus/total capital) is affected by various factors. The model, referred to as the *DuPont model*, compares the financial data of a company in terms of a capital side and an operations side. The financial model can be used as a general tool for overall analytical purposes. In its capacity as a ready-made model it can be an effective aid to monitoring the critical factors and financial key ratios, and can be tailored to the individual company's products/markets and divisions.

Figure 8.3 The DuPont Model

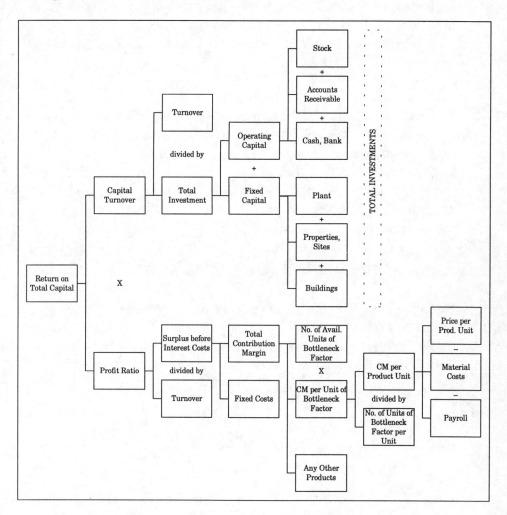

The Capital Side of the Model

Total capital is analysed in terms of how the capital is used — not how it has been procured. In the DuPont model, total capital is divided into:

- Operating capital
- Fixed capital.

Operating capital is further subdivided into stocks, accounts receivable and cash/bank deposits whereas fixed capital is further subdivided into plant, land and buildings. Return on capital can thus be influenced through influencing how that capital has been employed.

The Operations Side of the Model

The operations side of the model reflects the contributions method of costing, in that costs are classified as being either fixed or variable. If the model is to be used as an internal management tool, it is important that it is tailored to mirror the internal divisions within the company, so that the various financial key ratios that are extracted from the model will reflect the different areas of responsibility within the company.

USE OF THE DUPONT MODEL FOR RATIO ANALYSIS

Need for and Principles of Reporting on Projects Using Ratio Analysis

The consultant must assist the company in gaining a realistic understanding of:

- The situation it is in (strengths and weaknesses)

- Why the company has got to where it is (issues)

- And what it can do in the future (opportunities and threats, options).

It is thus necessary to find simple forms of reporting based on known data from the company, which make it easier to keep the overall perspective. This handbook emphasises the use of just a few concepts, and has kept them at such a general level of detail that most people should be able to see the benefit of using the forms.

In many cases, both the company and the consultant may experience problems with finding facts for the following reasons:

- The accounts may not include the cost breakdowns necessary to calculate the contribution margin.

- There may have been major changes in operations that make historical data useless.

- The evaluation of raw materials stocks will invariably require attention in more detail.

In such situations it will be necessary to provide assistance with practical solutions which ensure that the real aim is achieved:

- To arrive at a specific, simple description that gives an integrated picture of the company's business activities.

In drawing up the forms used in this section, emphasis has been given to the use of normative figures (industry "norms") and to the company's own estimates. Again, the importance of information on product/market combinations is stressed, in order to ensure that the company makes the right strategic choices.

The forms are designed to be used for both analysis of the current situation and as tools for prioritising and following up on measures in the time ahead.

Time Perspectives

For the purposes of project reporting, three time perspectives are relevant:

- The past (the last 1-3 years)

- The present (this year)

- The future (in 1-3 years times, i.e. in terms of budgets/strategy).

A consultant should be interested in the past because when analysing the current situation it is useful to bring out the strengths and weaknesses that have placed the company where it is today. One does not go further back than to the point where the factors that led to the present situation first arose (normally 1-3 years).

In all cases, the most practical approach is to stick to figures for the whole accounting year. There must be adjustments for seasonal fluctuations and extraordinary events, so that the figures will represent a "normal" operating situation.

This means that figures for the current year must be constructed. Normally one would build on the figures "so far this year" and add figures for probable developments in the remaining part of the year. Alternative methods are to:

- Add budgets for the rest of the year

- Find a multiplication factor based on the remaining part of the year (e.g. half-year accounts × 2)

- Make a forecast based on the present situation.

Data Collection

One cannot always find exact figures in the financial statements for use in the forms. In such cases some creativity and the ability to adopt estimates are necessary. The following guidelines will assist the consultant in this regard:

- Problems of estimating "cost of goods sold" can be solved by obtaining statistics from supplier current accounts, comparing cost estimates for some typical products or looking at withdrawals from stocks over a given period.

- Estimates of variable payroll costs can be done by distributing man-years according to production statistics, or by using a few samples of time consumption.

- The difference between variable and fixed costs can be used as a rough Contribution Margin, where only those costs that are substantial and vary with product and volume are distributed — that is payroll costs (direct payroll costs) and material costs (direct material costs).

- The breakdown of other costs combined in the financial statement can either be done by sampling the vouchers or finding some logical distribution basis (e.g. kw/hr per machine, weight or volume of goods produced in kilos /metres etc., hours or days from start to finish, etc.).

Use of the DuPont Model

The DuPont Model is used as a basis for key ratio analysis. The advantage of this is that the diagram can show at a glance the relationships among the various factors, and one avoids discussions of factors of lesser importance.

We have chosen to use fewer elements in the figure than in the theoretical model shown Figure 8.3. This is done for the sake of achieving a focus on, and assigning priorities to, the things that will normally be considered to have important consequences.

The diagram allows for the use of directional arrows instead of exact specifications of changes in key ratios. The advantage of this is that the conclusions can be seen at a glance. It does require, however, that the person filling in the form be able to distinguish between what is perceived as being positive or negative.

Carrying Out the Key Ratio Analysis

Two forms are presented:

- The first form is used to document financial data and to calculate a number of key ratios (10 different ratios will be of interest), which is presented in Figure 8.4.

- The figures from this form are then transferred to the modified DuPont model, which is presented in Figure 8.5.

The following notes/guidelines apply to the use of these forms:

- The forms can either be used for historical data up to "now" or for plans up to "one to three years ahead" (budgets/strategy).

- The development of each figure/key ratio must be drawn in as an arrow from left to right as shown in Figure 8.6, from the start to the end of the period.

Figure 8.4: Accounting Information and Financial Key Ratio Analysis

	#	ACCOUNT GROUP	CALCULATION	– 2 Yrs	– 1 Yr	Curr. Yr	
OPERATING ACCOUNTS	A	Number of Employees	Man-Years (or Persons)				
	B	Turnover					
	C	Payroll	Dir. Payroll Costs in Pr.				
	D	Materials	Dir. Mat. Costs in Prod.				
	E	Contribution Margin	B–(C+D)				
	F	Fixed Costs	Operating and Admin.				
	G	Depreciation					
	H	Net Oper. Income	E–(F+G)				
	I	Interest	Net Interest				
	J	Profit	H–I				
BALANCE SHEET	K	Cash, Bank, etc.					
	L	Acc. Receivable					
	M	Stocks	Raw m/semim/fin goods				
	N	Current Assets	K+L+M				
	O	Fixed Assets					
	P	Current Liabilities					
	Q	Long-Term Liabilities					
	R	Cont. Tax-Free Prov.					
	S	Equity					
	T	Total Capital	N+O				
KEY RATIOS		Contribution Ratio	E:Bx100%				
		CM per Payroll Unit	E:C				
		Acc. Rec. Turnover	L:(B+20%)x360 days				
		Stock Turnover	M:Dx360 days				
		Quick Ratio	(K+L):P				
		Financing	(Q+R+S):O				
		Equity Ratio	(Rx50%+S):Tx100%				
	U	Profit Ratio	H:Bx100%				
	V	Capital Turnover	B:T				
		RO Total Capital	UxV				

Figure 8.5: Modified DuPont Model

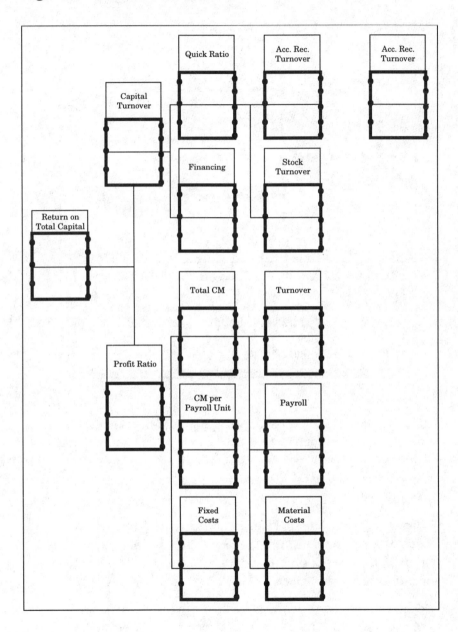

Figure 8.6: Illustration of Current Situation and Trends

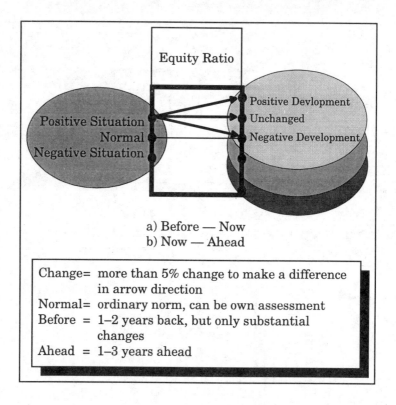

Equity Ratio

Positive Devlopment

Unchanged

Negative Development

Positive Situation

Normal

Negative Situation

a) Before — Now
b) Now — Ahead

Change= more than 5% change to make a difference
in arrow direction
Normal= ordinary norm, can be own assessment
Before = 1–2 years back, but only substantial
changes
Ahead = 1–3 years ahead

- The key ratio is assessed on the basis of how favourable it is for the company, such that low costs are considered positive, and thus start above the line, while an increase in costs is considered negative and means that the arrow must move downwards.

- It can be seen that there are more points at the end of the period than at the beginning. This enables the arrow to show that if the starting point was good, further development can be/has been even better.

- It is not necessary to have the arrow pointing up or down if the relative change in the ratio has been/will be less than 5 per cent of its value. We call a contribution margin of 40 per cent "unchanged" even if it has changed from 38 per cent or 42 per cent.

- It is conceivable that there are other factors in the company's business activities that need special attention (for example, the development of finished goods stocks). In this case there is space to include one's own figures in addition to these (NB: this should be used to bring out the factors most relevant to the company!)

Use of the Key Ratio Analysis

Once the modified DuPont model has been filled in, reasons for a rise or drop in profitability can be traced back to "previous" points in the structure. This will provide a basis for knowing where to intervene to improve the situation. So it will also be useful to use the sheet for future developments.

For example, supposing it is evident from the model that the company does not have the capital base necessary for growth, one can quickly see that a focus on growth will not lead to satisfactory profitability. In such a case, it would be important to give a high priority to releasing capital (for example, by reducing stocks or rationalising the collection of accounts receivable).

USE OF THE MODIFIED BOSTON MATRIX

Strategic Development

A strategy describes the measures a company will take to achieve its overall goals. When analysing the company and assigning priorities to new measures, it will therefore be crucial to show how the development of:

- Products and technology

- Prices and volume

- Production, administration and financing costs

can collectively contribute in to the planned development of the business.

Companies live on their products, and the products often have a limited lifetime. So an analysis of the profitability potential of the products is an important basis for drawing up the company's action plans.

Each of the stages in the lifetime of the product requires its own kind of focus and resource deployment from the company. Rather too often, one sees that investments and managers' "priority time" are spent on marginal areas where it is either too late to affect developments or where the effects that can be obtained are too insignificant.

Thus, a new diagram is required that will show how the profitability development of the products will contribute to the overall result. Using this diagram and the DuPont model together we can see whether resources are being deployed by the company in areas in which they are most important (i.e. most profitable).

The diagram in Figure 8.7 can be used to illustrate a company's strategic direction. The diagram builds on the Boston matrix, but there is a difference: no use of external market information is required. The reason for this is the practical problems one often has with defining markets and obtaining relevant statistics.

By placing the products in a matrix where the axes are contribution margin and turnover development, one can still use the perspectives given by the Boston matrix for each of the stages of the lifetime of the product.

The company/consultant can select for themselves the products to be included in the diagram. They must consider which grouping provides most information. They may:

- Only show the company as a whole because the products are uniform

- Classify the products in main groups

- Show a major product separately and the rest in groups

- Distribute turnover and contribution margin over market groups, segments (product /market combinations).

The point of grouping is to show the effect of strategic measures on market development and profitability.

Figure 8.7: Modified Boston Matrix for Illustrating Strategic Direction

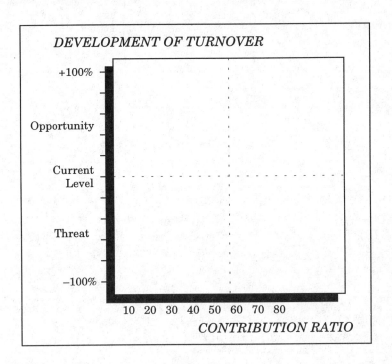

Filling in the Modified Boston Matrix

The diagram consists of two axes — contribution margin and turnover development.

The axes are placed so that the middle of the lines represents the normative figures for manufacturing companies (trading companies usually have contribution margins around 30-40 per cent and distributors/wholesalers around 10-20 per cent). If the company has unique features, one should choose other, suitable dimensions for the axes to reflect the norm.

Information on the development of turnover per product group/market segment can be recorded on the form given in Figure 8.8. The diagram can be used both for development up to the current year or for the plan period ("in three years").

Figure 8.8: Development of Turnover and Profitability

#	Product Group/ Market/Segment	Current Year		In 3 Years	
		Turnover	Contrib.	Turnover	Contrib.
1					
2					
3					
4					
5					
6					
7					

Turnover development for future years will have to be estimated. Here a prudent assessment is best. Estimates should assume that "the world will stay the way it is" and the overall market will develop more or less as in the current year. There should be good arguments for any other basis.

1. Draw a thick arrow from the intersection point for current turnover/contribution margin to the intersection point for turnover/contribution margin in three years.

2. Draw in each product group as a circle in the diagram, where the size of the circle shows the importance of the product group as a percentage of current turnover. Place the circles with their centre at "in three years".

Interpretation of the Modified Boston Matrix

When the diagram is finished, there are several features one should pay attention to:

• Have investments to date contributed to an increase in turnover or profitability?

• Have investments supported high-growth or stagnating products?

• If any products change their turnover without any change in the contribution margin, there may be reasons to look more closely at pricing policy or the effect of technological measures.

Finally, use of the modified DuPont model and the matrix for strategic analysis/direction should give the project manager essential indications as to whether:

- Measures are being given the right priorities

- Investments are leading to sufficient benefit

- The measures are helping to strengthen the company's position in the market.

9

PRODUCT/MARKET PRIORITIES

INTRODUCTION

A preliminary, general prioritisation of the different product/market combinations that a company is engaged in is important for the consultant to achieve good goal-orientation of planning and analysis. One only does in-depth work in areas with a potentially high impact.

This chapter describes how such a preliminary prioritisation can be carried out. The following is most relevant in situations where the company in question has a differentiated range of products.

The material presented complements other aspects of the consultant's work including:

- Business evaluations in the strategic analysis.

- Prioritisation of issues and options. Support for strategically important product/market combinations naturally receives a high priority.

- Determination of the extent and focus of a full strategy and planning process — that is, to ensure good goal-orientation during planning work.

When trying to arrive at product/market priorities, it is important to take *buying criteria* into consideration.

The term "buying criteria" refers to the primary factors that a customer takes into consideration when buying goods or services. Examples of buying criteria include price, "quality" (which can mean many different things), delivery times, proximity to the supplier, the supplier's reputation, etc. Some typical buying criteria are listed in Figure 9.1 — not necessarily in order of priority.

Figure 9.1: Typical Buying Criteria

- Purchase Price
- Other Initial Costs
- Supplier's Reputation
- Customisation
- Delivery Times
- Delivery Reliability and Punctuality
- Closeness to Supplier
- Product Quality
- Supplier's Financial Situation
- Ease of Installation
- Training Requirements/Use Friendliness
- Capacity for Upgrading
- Standardisation/Compatibility
- Technological Sophistication
- Level of After-Sales Service
- Personal Customer Service
- Low Operation/Maintenance Costs
- Supplier Competence
- Rate of Innovation/Renewal
- Wide Range of Products
- Status Value
- Design/Appearance
- Product Lifetime
- Operational Reliability
- Impulse

The material in this chapter is discussed under the following headings:

- Product/Market Priorities: An Example
- Identifying Product/Market Combinations
- Assigning Priorities to Product/Market Combinations — Business Considerations
- Competitive Strategies
- Buying Criteria
- Key Buying Criteria and Fundamental Buying Criteria
- Buying Criteria: Main Principles.

PRODUCT/MARKET PRIORITIES: AN EXAMPLE

The initial assigning of priorities to product/market combinations can be carried out using the following procedure:

- Identify the company's product/market combinations
- Assign priorities to each product/market combination on the basis of business considerations
- Evaluate the company's competitive strategy for the prioritised product/market combinations and identify the issues that arise as a result.

After an introductory example, each of the above points will be explained in more depth.

Introductory Example

A medium-sized company sells kitchen units. Traditionally, it has supplied standard units to the construction industry with large contractors as its main customers. In the past, the company has benefited from a "building boom" that allowed it to produce large series of kitchens at competitive prices.

In recent years, the market for new housing dropped dramatically. To survive, the company felt that it must make greater efforts in selling to the restoration market, which is less sensitive to market trends. However, both customers and distribution networks are radically different from those in the building sector proper. The potential customer base is large and often consists of proper. The potential customer base is large and often consists of individuals who do their own restoration work. Even though each kitchen unit is part of a standard module, the end product will in general be unique. In addition, fewer goods are delivered directly from the factory. So the company will become more dependent on indirect distribution outlets (dealers), and must now "nurture" this business relationship more than previously.

The company described above should be divided into two primary product/market combinations:

- Kitchen units/new homes, and

- Kitchen units/restoration.

The different areas have different commercial levels of importance. Assuming that the new homes market will continue to shrink in the next few years, while restoration will continue to be relatively stable, then in the short term, the company should probably view restoration as its top priority, and this will in turn affect its competitive profile, the company's competence, and company resources.

The manufacturing requirements for both product/market combinations are different. This is demonstrated by some key points listed below.

Market for New Homes:

- Requires the company to concentrate on cost-effective production (because of price competition).

- Requires simple systems to handle customer base (few customers).

- Requires simple distribution network, with the exception of stock control and pure transport.

- Requires the production strategy and control to be adapted to mass production with limited requirements for rapid readjustment of production.

Restoration Market:

- Requires the company to focus on product differentiation, with individual customer specifications being an important element.

- Requires advanced systems, both for dealing directly with customers (large customer base) and for market surveying, market planning, and marketing.

- Requires advanced systems for dealing with stocks and transport, and for follow-up on dealers.

- Requires the production strategy and control to be adapted to "customer-driven" production, with production lot sizes of down to one per order. Great need for rapid readjustment of production units.

IDENTIFYING PRODUCT/MARKET COMBINATIONS

Figure 9.2 shows an example of a company's products and markets laid out in a matrix. A product/market combination, often equated with a strategic business unit in the company, is an intersection point in the matrix.

The matrix can be made to work at different levels of detail. We are interested in a level where products, market, market forces, customers, suppliers, and competitors are different enough to constitute a meaningful basis for different strategies for each product group. In the introductory example, kitchen units were seen as constituting a suitable product level; we did not separate large cupboards from small, or drawers from shelves, etc.

Some guidelines for the identification of product/market combinations at a "suitable level" are:

- If the company is already organised in terms of products or markets, this can be used as a starting point.

- Combinations of approximately the same competitive forces can be grouped together. The five forces of competition are described in more detail in Chapter 5 on General Strategic Business Analysis and in Chapter 22 on Marketing.

- Single products are, as a rule, at too detailed a level.

Figure 9.2: Product/Market Combinations

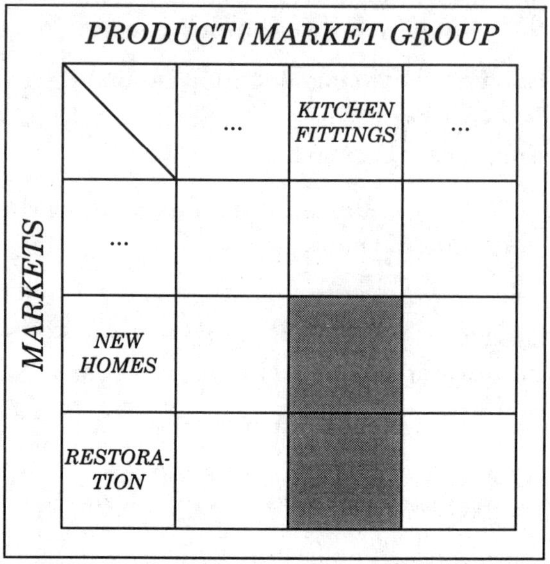

ASSIGNING PRIORITIES TO PRODUCT/MARKET COMBINATIONS — BUSINESS CONSIDERATIONS

A company that understands its strategic position as well as its potential for development has the basis for determining its business strategy in terms of which product/markets should the company concentrate on in the future, how should it do so, and how much should it invest?

Assigning priorities to product/markets is ultimately a question of:

1. In which areas does the company earn money today, and

2. Where is it going to earn money in the future?

The first question can usually be answered with the help of financial key ratio analysis, as described in Chapter 8. The second question requires consideration of the following factors:

- Demand development in the product/market combinations in which the company operates.

- The product's position in its life cycle.

- The company's market share, and the market size in comparison to the company's own capacity.

- The company's competitive strength, i.e. how competitive is the company in each of the product/markets in question?

The future income potential for each product/market combination needs to be evaluated with reference to a general evaluation of the above factors.

A company often places its product/market combinations in a matrix similar to the one shown earlier in Figure 5.3 (see page 144) — the so-called "modified Boston matrix". The company used as an example earlier would expect that developments in kitchen units/new homes and kitchen units/restoration are likely to be as shown in the figure. The importance of the new homes market is diminishing with the product/market combination heading for a period of modest profits, while the opposite will hopefully be the case for the kitchen unit/restoration combination.

If one pays sufficient attention to demand development and competitive strength, the concepts in the Boston matrix begin to resemble the phases "introduction", "growth", "maturity", and "stagnation" in a product life cycle as shown earlier in Figure 5.1 (see page 142).

Goal-oriented utilisation of resources typically results in:

- Long-term, intensive efforts in growth product/market combinations ("stars"). Special attention is paid to ways of prolonging a product's lifetime.

- Short-term efforts in development of product/market combinations in the mature phase ("cash cows"), primarily aimed at milking as much as possible out of the situation before it stagnates. Typically, efforts concentrate on how to achieve the most rational and cost-effective system of production possible, but with a limited amount of investment. If the product has a long maturity period with a "flat" curve, then prolonging product lifetime may also become a possibility worthy of attention (assuming that demand development has not stagnated).

- Long-term investment in products in the development and introduction phases ("wild cats"), assuming that they have "the right to live".

- Little or no investment in product/market combinations that are stagnant ("dead dogs").

When comparing product life cycles it is important to bear the time scale in mind. The maturation phase for some products is a matter of years; for others, all phases of the life cycle occur within months. New generations of computers offer a good example of products with short life cycles — the period is now down to one year from introduction to stagnation.

COMPETITIVE STRATEGIES

The last step in the prioritising process is to identify issues after an evaluation of the competitive strategies for the prioritised product/market combinations.

A company can generally compete in one of four ways, as shown in the matrix model in Figure 9.3. It can compete primarily on price or by differentiating its products, and in a broad market or in a niche. Many companies have difficulty in becoming fully conscious of their competitive strategies.

It is important to note that different product/market combinations may require different competitive strategies. Thus, a company must identify its competitive strategies, and produce issues and options in the light of these findings.

A cost/price leadership strategy will focus on how to make in-house production processes more efficient, whereas a differentiation strategy will focus on how to provide the customer with a product that is significantly different from the competitors' products. The introductory example of the kitchen unit manufacturer clearly shows this.

Differentiation is expensive, and it is not a good idea to focus on costs and differentiation at the same time.

On the other hand, different competitive strategies can be used with different customers/markets within the same product area. This is, for example, typical of electronics manufacturers who make off-the-shelf products for a wide market and at the same time offer customised products to large, important customers e.g. offshore companies. In the latter case, the customer's buying criteria will include factors other than price, and the strategy should be to differentiate.

Figure 9.3: Competitive Strategies

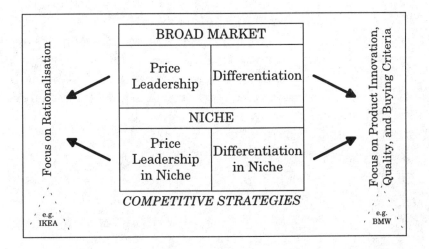

Once we have classified and prioritised product/market combinations and identified what competitive strategies are appropriate, we will have succeeded in reducing the focus of further analysis. We have already found the areas we should concentrate on. Analysis of organisational units and activities that are not part of these areas should therefore be put aside or given a lower priority.

We now know which product/market combinations are important for the company in the light of a business evaluation. We know, too, that the types of solutions we are primarily looking for are cost-saving solutions or solutions that increases the value of certain products to the customers. On the basis of this evaluation we can identify the issues that will be central to the analytical and planning work that will follow. An issue in the kitchen supplier example might be:

In the course of the next two years we must adapt our production facilities from mass production to customer-initiated orders of the "unique" type. How can we improve our systems for processing orders, product development, production, and production control in order to be able to provide "tailor-made" kitchen units?

BUYING CRITERIA

Buying criteria, and especially their relative importance, vary considerably within industry, product area, product, market, and buyer group. Understanding buying criteria is critical for business and market strategies. The consultant can uses the analysis of buying criteria as a key technique in identifying ways of improving a company's competitiveness.

Competitiveness is determined by two key factors:

- The company's ability to satisfy the customer's needs better than its competitors

- The company's ability to satisfy the customer's needs just as well as its competitors but more efficiently.

Buying criteria analysis focuses on the first factor: *the ability of the company to satisfy the customer's needs better than its competitors*. An analysis of buying criteria will also help the consultant to assign priorities to the options identified

The initial identification of buying criteria for each product/market combination is an important aspect of the business evaluation carried out during the strategic analysis. The linkage of buying criteria with the company's activities is continued during the formulation of the strategy and action plans. When the company has identified the crucial criteria and its position in relation to these, they are linked even more closely with activities in the company's value chain.

KEY BUYING CRITERIA AND FUNDAMENTAL BUYING CRITERIA

Not all buying criteria are of equal importance. After an initial screening, a number of possible buying criteria will be found to be less important and can be discarded. Those remaining can be classified in two main groups:

- Key criteria which are vital for the company's actual competitiveness, because they determine the customer's final choice

- Fundamental buying criteria, which determine a product's "general standard", market segment/customer group, and which ensure that the company will be considered as a possible supplier.

Reputation and image in the market, a supplier's financial situation, closeness to the supplier, the general level of quality and price class are in many situations examples of fundamental criteria. These are necessary if the company is to be considered, but not sufficient for it to be selected.

To improve competitiveness, however, it is necessary to identify the key criteria and then meet these needs better than the competition. This is what increases the customer's perception of value.

Figure 9.4 illustrates the relationships between the competitive situation and the fundamental/key criteria. First and foremost it is necessary to concentrate on areas in the company where investment will help to satisfy customers' *key criteria* better than competitors do.

Typically between four and eight key criteria should be identifiable. What determines customer choice differs widely from one product/market combination to another, so generalised examples of key criteria cannot be given, as with fundamental criteria.

Figure 9.4: Relationship between Concepts

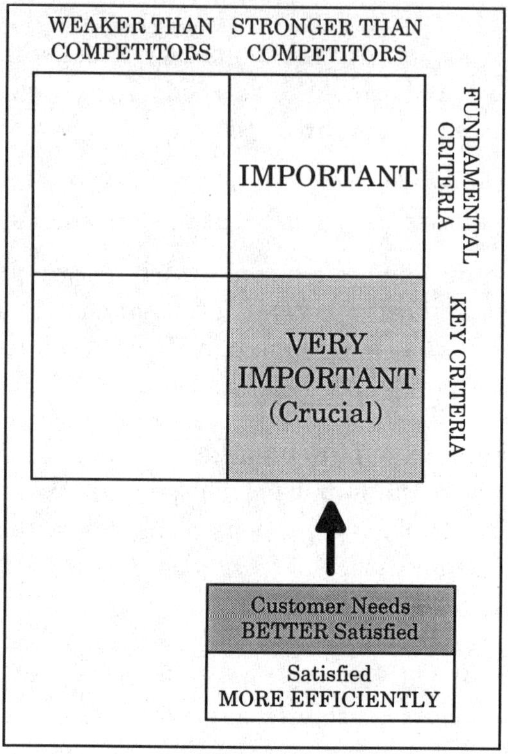

BUYING CRITERIA: MAIN PRINCIPLES

The principles for analysing buying criteria are relatively straightforward:

- Start with the prioritised list product/market combinations.

- For each product/market combination, evaluate what the customer considers to be important, i.e. the customer's buying criteria. Try to work out which of these are key criteria and then rank these in order of importance. There may be a significant difference between what the customer sees as being important and what the company thinks is important.

- For each criterion (in order of priority), critically consider which of the company's activities contribute or could contribute significantly to meeting the criterion.

- For each activity identified, evaluate what measures are required so as to increase the customer's perception of value.

In other words, try to follow the chain from buying criteria through to activities within the company. Figure 9.5 shows a matrix which relates buying criteria to company activities.

Figure 9.5: Buying Criteria/Activity Matrix

BUYING CRITERIA	ACTIVITIES		
	...	Production	Order Processing
...	...	...	...
Wide Product Range	...	Order-Driven Production Short Changeover Time Integration of Design and Production Control	System Support for Customer-Specified Orders
Closeness to Supplier	...	...	Use of Communications Network for Direct Order Registration by Customer

A buying criteria analysis will typically entail:

- Assigning high priority to measures that support "value creation" activities.

- Assigning lower priorities to measures that do not significantly contribute to "value creation".

An analysis of buying criteria can be used to identify issues and to evaluate and prioritise issues that have already been identified. Where buying criteria are used in connection with option evaluation they will help to give a "true" prioritisation on the basis of business needs.

Different Buying Criteria Lead to Different Priorities
Different buying criteria lead to different priorities being assigned. Buying criteria will vary with product area and market segment, even in the same company. Some examples would include:

- A company competing on price will look initially at ways of rationalising its production methods. In the area of information technology this typically leads to efficient transaction systems for supporting high-cost activities, plus decision-making support for tight financial management.

- A company competing on product customisation, will look at ways to integrate order processing and design/product development activities, and order-driven production will be given high priority.

- A company competing on the basis of product quality will focus on methods for following up quality assurance plans, spot testing and similar activities, the introduction of more high-precision production plant, or the reduction of fault sources by integrating stand-alone machinery units.

10

TOOLS FOR OPERATIONAL ANALYSIS

INTRODUCTION

In this chapter some tools that can be used during a consultant's analysis of a company's operations are described. More specifically, the tools presented cover activity analysis, information analysis and material flow analysis. A description of how to carry out a SWOT (strengths, weaknesses, opportunities and threats) analysis is also described.

Activity analysis aims to show what the company *actually does*, irrespective of its organisational structure and its present way of doing things. By activities we mean a group of logically related decisions made and actions carried out to manage products, services or resources. Traditionally, activities are thought of in terms of the "divisions" or "functions" that already exist in a company. These concepts, however, are often tied up with a particular organisational pattern. In this section, the aim is to look at the company without reference to the existing organisational structure. Thus the term "activity" will be used to refer to the work the company *actually* does.

The aim of the information analysis is to describe the information requirements of individual activities and the flow of information among the activities that have been identified.

Material flow analysis is carried out with a view to identifying how to bring about (a) more efficient use of capital, (b) better exploitation of resources and (c) better delivery service.

The subject material in this chapter is presented under the following headings:

- Activity Analysis

- Information Analysis

- Implementation of Activity and Information Analysis in Practice

- Material Flow Analysis

- SWOT Analysis.

ACTIVITY ANALYSIS

Introduction

During the general strategic business evaluation, we analyse the company in an overall perspective at a high level, i.e. we do not go down to the level of the individual operations that constitute a single task in the company. We delve deeper by carrying out an activity analysis in the areas we believe will have the greatest impact by virtue of their:

- High relative importance for the company's cost position

- Potential importance for realising the company's goals

- Potential importance for increasing satisfaction of the customer's buying criteria.

If, for example, the company's production activity accounts for 55 per cent of its operating and investment costs, and one of the most important buying criteria is the ability to gear production quickly to respond to the signals and needs of the market, this is obviously an activity that should be given a high priority in the analytical work.

Value Chains

There are many relevant techniques that can be used in activity analysis. Here we will concentrate on a combination of the "value chain". The actual analytical work is normally done by the company itself, whilst the consultant acts as the driving force and adviser during the process.

A value chain illustrates the company's overall, customer-perceived value creation, with emphasis on the work that has to be done to produce, market and deliver/support the products and services offered. These activities are grouped in a "chain" from the supplier to the customer side, and this gives a picture of the total work done to satisfy the customers' buying criteria. An example of a value chain is illustrated in Figure 10.1.

One of the most important points about the value chain as a descriptive and analytical tool is that the representation is independent of the formal organisational structure of the company. This means one avoids traditional "pigeonholing" by focusing on value creation as a unified process.

Figure 10.1: Example of Value Chain

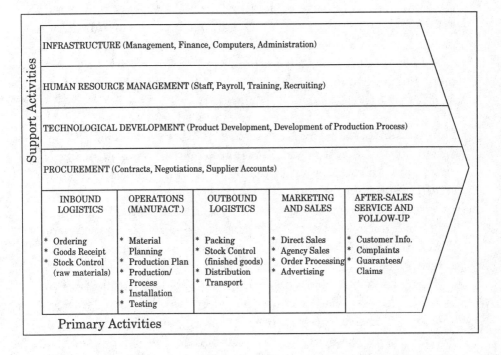

The value chain is divided into activities which are part of the direct product manufacturing process (primary activities) and activities which provide support for the primary activities (support activities). To illustrate this, the support activities are drawn horizontally in relation to the primary activities — that is, each primary activity to a greater or lesser degree "draws on" the support activities in its work.

The primary and the support activities can both be further subdivided into sub-activities (as shown by the points below/beside the name of the activity in the figure). This way one obtains a hierarchical breakdown of the activities in the company's value chain. However, one must be careful not to go too far with this breakdown, as the degree of detail can quickly become unsuitable for the further analytical work. During a typical strategy and planning process it will be sufficient to describe features one level below the actual primary or support activity.

In a "standardised" value chain the terms as shown in Figure 10.1 are often used (inbound logistics, operations (manufacture), outbound logistics etc.). However, it is important to establish terms which match the company's own terminology and reality before getting down to the analysis in earnest. This will make it easier for the individual participants to relate the value chain to everyday reality, and they will quickly see it as a useful instrument for describing their work — both how it is done today and how it perhaps could/should be done.

Relationship with the Rest of the Strategy Process

Arising out of the analysis of the forces of competition in the industry and the strategy selected by the company (cost leadership or differentiation oriented towards a broad market or a niche) a clear need emerges to analyse the company's individual components to identify where there is most to be gained from increasing the customer's perception of the value of the company's products and services.

Using the value chain one can assess the activities one by one in the light of overall competitive and strategic considerations, and identify areas for high-priority effort and/or investment. By comparing the company's value chain with the established goal hierarchies and buying criteria one can set up a matrix as in Figure 10.2. (The matrix given in Figure 9.5 of Chapter 9 on "Product/Market Priorities" is a simplified version of this matrix.)

The most important function of activity analysis is not to break down or describe the company's activities as such, but to allow you to *use* the description to discover issues and options, which can then form the basis for the establishment of goals, strategies and action plans. The issues/options lists is therefore a key technique for "extracting the essence" of the activity analysis.

Figure 10.2: Linking Goal Hierarchy, Buying Criteria and Activities

GOAL HIERARCHY

1.
2.
3.

BUYING CRITERIA

* Price
* Delivery Times
* Customisation
* _____
* _____
* _____

INFRASTRUCTURE

HUMAN RESOURCE MANAGEMENT

TECHNOLOGICAL DEVELOPMENT

PURCHASING

| INBOUND LOGISTICS | OPERATIONS (MANUFACT.) | OUTBOUND LOGISTICS | MARKETING AND SALES | AFTER-SALES SERVICE AND FOLLOW-UP |

Primary Activities

Support Activities

ACTIVITY / BUYING CRITERIA	Inbound Logistics	Operations (manufact.)	Outbound Logistics	Sales/ Marketing	After-Sales Service/ Follow-up	Infra-structure	Human Resource Administr.	Technology Development	Purchasing
• Price	X	X X X	X X X						X X
• Delivery Times		X X X	X X X	X	X X				X X
• Customisation		X X		X				X X	
• _____									
GOAL									
1. _____	X	X X X	X X	X	X				X
2. _____		X X X	X X	X X	X X				
3. _____	X	X		X	X				X

PRIMARY ACTIVITIES

SUPPORT ACTIVITIES

INFORMATION ANALYSIS

The most useful tool for this task is an information flow diagram. These diagrams are meant to show how the activities in the value chain are linked (that is, what information they exchange) and how the information is used within each activity.

It is important to restrict the work of information analysis to a general level — that is, to the flow of information among the activities in the identified value chain and at most one level below this (the "sub-activity level"). In addition, using the matrix set-up in Figure 10.2, we can prioritise the activities that should be described in detail, and those that should be described in more general terms. Figure 10.3 illustrates this point: in the example in Figure 10.2 it is first and foremost the activities "operations (manufacturing)" and "outbound logistics" that have the highest density of crosses, and which are thus most important for the realisation of goals and satisfaction of buying criteria.

When the flow of information has been described down to the relevant level, one should stop to think about the following questions (and possibly formulate relevant issues and options):

- Which single activities stand out as being clearly information-intensive (i.e. receive, use and send out a lot of critical information)?

- Which interfaces among activities are particularly information-intensive (i.e. are used to receive/send out particularly high volumes of information among the activities defined in the information analysis)? The options for introducing modern methods to establish closer and more efficient linkages among such activities are often clear sources of competitive advantage.

- If you compare the company-specific value chain with the existing organisational structure, do you see obvious "barriers" to efficient exploitation of the flow of information? Can you find appropriate ways of reorganising the company's business to take advantage of the lessons learned from this?

Figure 10.3: Flow of Information among Important Activities

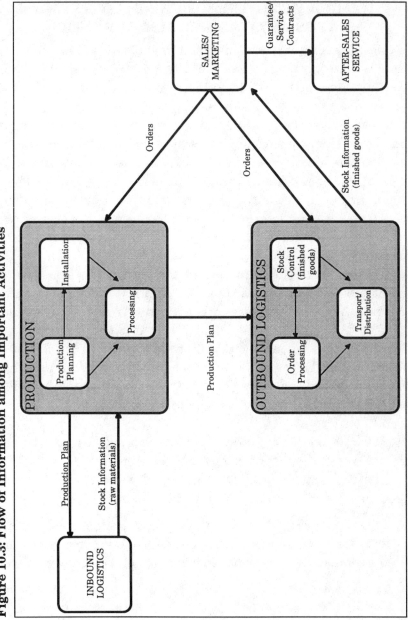

IMPLEMENTATION OF THE ACTIVITY AND INFORMATION ANALYSIS IN PRACTICE

Typically, an activity and information analysis will reveal quite a few "sacred cows" and traditionally or historically determined routines and methods of working and organisation. The most critical success factor in this respect is that the company employees themselves help to identify these disparities and suggest changes. Often one encounters "aha! experiences" of the type "I've thought about this many times, but was never able to put it into words". It is important to watch out for these — and to develop them further into constructive formulations of issues and options!

An activity and information analysis (even at the overall level) makes great demands on knowledge of "how things work" in the company.

Those who are to take part in the work must also have the ability to "look at things in a new light" without being bogged down in historically determined patterns ("We've always done it that way, and it's the only right way"). In small companies it is likely that top management will be well aware of the flow of information in the company. In larger companies it will usually be necessary to involve more employees who are thoroughly familiar with individual activities and the corresponding flow of information.

The role of the consultant will be to guide the process and provide input in the form of methods and experience.

The following "checklist" sums up the procedure for implementing an activity and information analysis:

- Identify the main activities in the value chain — both primary activities and support activities. (NB: Make sure you reflect the company's own terminology and reality as far as possible!)

- Break down the main activities into sub-activities. Between two and five sub-activities per main activity is a reasonable level of detail.

- Assess the importance of the company's goals for each main activity. Try to identify any conflicting goals, or activities for which no clear goals exist. Reformulate the goals if necessary.

- Set up a matrix (see Figure 10.2) which links the activities of the value chain with buying criteria, any other competitive factors and company goals.

- Identify the linkages among the activities and buying criteria/competitive factors/goals that are most critical. Cross these off in the matrix. Use the key questions at the end of this section to reformulate the crosses as issues.

- For each issue (each cross in the matrix), critically assess how changes could be implemented that will affect the buying criteria, other competitive factors and goals. Formulate these ideas as options.

- Establish an information flow diagram where each of the most important main activities and/or sub-activities in the value chain is represented in a box. Be critical about the number of boxes: there should be no more than a total of twenty in the diagram.

- Draw in and name the most important flows of information among the activities in the diagram.

- Identify information flow options on the basis of the key questions and a systematic review of the buying criteria, other competitive factors and goals. For example, "We cannot manage to keep delivery times down to an acceptable level because information transfer between order processing and production control is done manually with a delay of x days".

- Identify options by "applying" the buying criteria, competitive factors and goals to each of the arrows in the figure. For example, "How can we improve the transfer of information between order processing and production control so we can reduce delivery times?"

Key Questions

Issues and options can be "extracted" from the activity and information analysis — among other ways by asking the following key questions (as well as the three mentioned in the section on information analysis):

- Which activities in the value chain are, relatively speaking, most closely associated with the realisation of the business goals set out for the company?

- Which activities are, relatively speaking, particularly cost-intensive, and thus offer great potential for rationalisation benefits through investment. For example, we are not primarily interested in activities that account for 1 per cent of costs if others account for 40 per cent.

- Which activities create what our customers perceive as "value" in relation to their buying criteria? With investments in specific areas, can we increase this customer-perceived value — for example, by clearer differentiation of our products and services than our competitors?

- What sort of system coverage is there for the most crucial activities? Are there important functions that are particularly poorly covered?

- How can the present organisational structure and division of work among the company's activities be changed?

- Do strategic decisions in the business area suggest that some of the current activities will be dropped, or perhaps redefined, and will new ones take their place?

MATERIAL FLOW ANALYSIS

Introduction

Following on from the activity and information analysis described earlier, it is necessary to analyse the critical issues associated with the flow of materials in the company.

The value chain approach provides an integrated focus for material flow. In Figure 10.4 we have supplemented the value chain with boxes representing: Suppliers, Purchasing, Raw materials stocks, Production, Distribution, Customer. These primary activities must be dealt with in the analysis.

Figure 10.4: Material Flow Value Chain Analysis

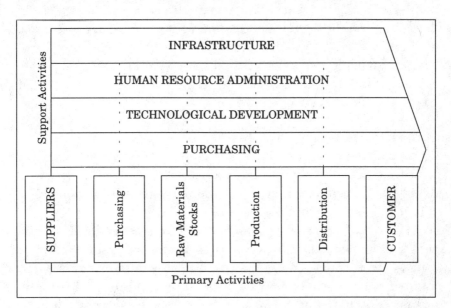

In this context we have chosen to call purchasing a primary activity. This only means that we stress the importance of focusing on the purchasing function as an element in material flow. In the general value chain — such as that given in Figure 10.1 — purchasing is often regarded as a support activity. This means that we have seen purchasing as rather more than just purchasing for production. This approach is particularly relevant for large corporate groups with a centralised purchasing division which also deals with the inflow of knowledge, technology, quality control etc., while in SMEs the purchasing function can usually be directly related to production.

One definition of the specialised field of Material Administration is:

> "The planning, development, co-ordination, organisation, control and monitoring of the flow of materials from the raw materials supplier to the final end-user."

This definition confirms and underscores the need for co-ordination across the traditional functional boundaries and activities in the value chain.

More efficient use of capital, increased exploitation of resources and *better delivery service* are the main areas we want to tackle by using material flow analysis. Dealing with all three of these areas of focus will lead to better profitability for the company. Given that achieving improvements in all three together can give rise to conflict, it is essential to have a strategy that tells us what should be given highest priority and when.

Differentiated Material Control

An important precondition of achieving capital rationalisation, improved delivery service and increased resource utilisation is deliberate prioritisation of areas where work is to be done. Not everything is important all the time!

The "20/80" rule turns out to be "true" in most cases. This rule says that 80 per cent of the company's products account for 20 per cent of its turnover. More cautiously, we can say that a large number of products account for a small part of the turnover. The technique is based on a classification of the company's products into classes — A, B and C.

The "20/80" rule can also be used with customers and suppliers. The rule is often used in association with a so-called ABC distribution.

Figure 10.5 shows a situation in which "A" articles account for 20 per cent of the product range and 80 per cent of turnover. The "B" articles make up 50 per cent of the range and are responsible for about 15 per cent of turnover. Finally, the "C" articles account for 30 per cent of the range and less than 5 per cent of the turnover.

Given that the company has a product/turnover distribution like this, is it wise to treat an "A" article in the same way as a "C" article in terms of planning, follow-up, service etc.? The answer to this question should be no, one should prioritise — in other words introduce deliberate, *differentiated* control mechanisms to optimise the flow of materials.

An example of a way of defining the ground rules on the basis of the ABC analysis would be *delivery service*. The "A" articles should be stocked in all district stores. The "B" articles should only be stocked at central stores. The "C" articles should be transferred to the supplier and withdrawn as required from the supplier's stocks. The "A" articles should be counted twice a month to reduce back-up stocks. The "B" articles should be counted twice a year — here we can accept higher levels of back-up stocks.

Figure 10.5: ABC Analysis According to 20/80 Rule

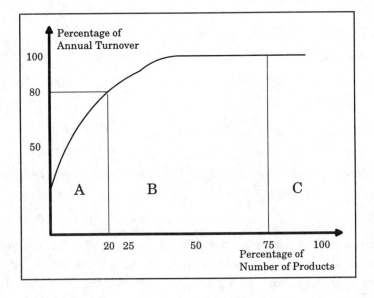

This kind of differentiated stock control allows for lower costs/better resource exploitation, less tying-up of capital and, not least, better delivery service for products with the highest percentage of turnover. The ABC principle as we have presented it takes volume value as its point of departure:

> Volume value = Number of units of a product sold × unit price

From the delivery service point of view, the "A" products are particularly important. For example, they should be able to bear the cost of both high stock availability and short delivery times. The "C" products, on the other hand, we can store in one place and thus also have longer delivery times than for the "A" products. The "B" products should be somewhere between the "A" and "C" products in terms of delivery times.

For most companies, differentiated material control will be more than a matter of volume value and ABC analyses. In many cases it will be just as important to focus on:

- Frequency of withdrawals

- High-value articles

- The contribution margins of the different products

- The life cycle curve — new products need special control

- Critical products — for example, some products may be critical for production.

The point of differentiated material control is to concentrate on a *few* articles that make a *large* contribution. These variants must be given high priority in terms of the level of service and must therefore be strictly controlled.

Capital Rationalisation

The demand for higher profitability in the company can be met by various means. Often companies resort to increasing prices and volumes (through an intensified sales effort) to achieve the established goals. But in the short term there is also potential to increase profits through monitoring of cost and through releasing "dead capital" — capital rationalisation. Figure 10.6 illustrates the relationship between options for increasing company profits.

Capital can be divided into two categories:

- *Physical* capital — which includes buildings, machinery and stock (raw materials, work-in-progress and finished goods), and

- *Financial* capital — which includes cash, bank deposits, customer receivables and unpaid advances.

In this section we will concentrate on physical capital and in particular capital tied up in all kinds of stocks.

The cost of stocking goods will vary from industry to industry and from company to company, but something between 30 per cent and 40 per cent of the annual cost price of stocks is typical of most companies today. These costs are referred to as "storage costs", and they consist of the following elements:

- Capital costs (overdraft)

- Insurance

- Risk of obsolescence

- Power and heating

- Various warehousing costs

- Wastage

- Administration and control costs.

Figure 10.6: How to Increase Profit?

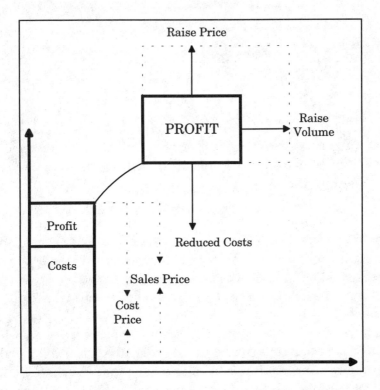

Storage costs should be used as a measure of what it actually costs to store goods. A company with goods in stock worth ECU 20

million could have current storage costs of ECU 6-8 million (i.e. 30 per cent to 40 per cent of cost of stock).

It is very important for the company to obtain a picture of how capital is utilised. A simple way of tabulating how capital is distributed is given in Figure 10.7.

Figure 10.7: How Capital is Utilised

Analysis of Tied Capital					
Type of Tied Capital	Figures from	Tied Capital in Money Terms	Value of 10% Improvement	Potential in % or Money	Priority
Machinery	Buildings				
Buildings	Balance sheet				
Stocks: Raw materials Work in Progress Finished Goods	Balance sheet/ stocktak. Balance/ sheet/stocktak. Balance sheet/ Stocktak.				
Customer Receivables	Balance sheet/ Accounts-current				

The release of capital obtained by increasing stock turnover will be a critical factor for many companies in the time to come. In fact, for many firms the only real goal in the short term will be to increase stock turnover.

By definition, stock turnover means "input cost of goods sold divided by average stock volume". Many companies battle with stock turnovers of 1-3 times a year whilst the better companies often achieve stock turnover of in excess of ten times a year. These examples focus on the total turnover of stock — it is impor tant to note, however, that it is always more "expensive" to stock finished goods than raw materials. This is because the wage component is high, and high costs accrue during processing, which means that the relative price of the finished goods are far higher than the raw material price. It also means that the chance of the product becoming unsaleable increases with the processing of the product. Raw materials are usually more flexible than finished goods, as raw materials can often be used in several different processes.

It follows that storage costs for raw materials should be treated differently from storage costs for finished goods stocks. The stock turnover requirements should also be differentiated. The turnover requirement for raw material stocks could, for example, be three times a year, while the requirement for finished goods stocks could be ten times a year. The level of stocks must be based on a balance between capital rationalisation and short delivery times.

Resource Utilisation

Traditionally, increased capacity utilisation has been a major production goal. Capacity utilisation is often defined as production divided by resources used. This tells us nothing, however, about delivery times and the meeting of deadlines, or about throughput times and capital rationalisation. Strictly speaking, one does not need to produce saleable goods to achieve "good" productivity figures.

Thus, instead of only using capacity utilisation as a measure of production one should consider the following as more appropriate measures:

- Delivery service

- Quality

- Reliable delivery times

- Level of intermediate stocks and work in progress

- Quantities delivered compared with plan.

Delivery Service

Delivery service is defined as:

> "the company's ability to deliver products and services that match the customer's expectations as regards delivery times, delivery reliability, volume, quality (in relation to the price the customer is willing to pay), information on the progress of the order and flexibility."

Good delivery service is one of the most important competitive parameters companies must work on in the time to come. Studies have show that meeting delivery schedules is one of the most important buying criteria the customer has. This will of course vary from industry to industry, but meeting delivery schedules is always important.

Delivery service is not just something to work on in relation to an external customer. Service elements are something one already has internally in all the links of the value chain. A consultant should ask the following key questions in this regard:

- What demands do raw materials and component stocks make on the suppliers?

- What demands does production make on raw materials and component stocks?

- What demands do finished goods stocks make on production?

- What are the customer's demands on the company as regards delivery service?

Conflicting Goals?

The three objectives of (a) *more efficient use of capital,* (b) *increased exploitation of resources* and (c) *better delivery service* are often in conflict with one another. Typical issues that arise when trying to satisfy all three are illustrated in the table in Figure 10.8.

Procedure and Key Questions

For practical analysis of material flow the following procedure and key questions can be used:

- Find out where the company stands today in terms of material flow — use the value chain approach. Here we have selected some general key questions that may be relevant:

  ◊ What is important to the customer (the customer's buying criteria)?

  ◊ Delivery capability to customers (real deliveries as opposed to planned ones)?

  ◊ Delivery capability from production?

Figure 10.8: Conflicting Goals?

Delivery Service versus Capital Rationalisation	Capital Rationalisation versus Resource Utilisation	Delivery Service versus Resource Utilisation
A company will often want to offer a high level of delivery service whilst keeping the level of capital tied up to a minimum. High delivery capability can be achieved by having large finished goods stocks or stores at the intermediate level. High storage levels means that a high level of capital is tied up and the risk of obsolescence is increased. Important focuses/possible solutions: • Low throughput times • Storage points/processing value • Small stocks/small series • Good forecasting • Increased capacity through more flexibility • Differentiated material control through ABC analysis	If the company wants high capacity utilisation, this will often involve producing in long series with few/no changeovers. In some cases this can be dealt with by having "buffer stocks" ahead of machines so that they always have something to work on. But this means that machines produce for stock rather than standing idle. Important focuses/possible solutions: • Short changeover times, more flexible production plant • Differentiated control of materials at the raw materials, intermediate and finished goods levels	High capacity utilisation will mean large buffer stocks. This means that the goods often have to wait their turn in queues before the production process. The queuing time will often be long, and this leads to long throughput times — and very probably to poor delivery capability. Important focuses/possible solutions: • Analysis of throughput time — why is throughput time as long as it is at present? • Small series • Observance of plans, combination of centralised/decentralised planning • Choice of intermediate storage points • Standardisation in areas which do not affect the customer.

◊ Suppliers' delivery service — how often do the suppliers deliver on time and in the right quantities?

◊ How does one differentiate in terms of products, customers and any suppliers?

◊ Stock turnover rate (input cost of goods sold divided by average stock holdings). It is useful to divide stocks up into raw materials, semi-manufactured goods, work in progress and finished goods.

◊ What governs production today? Capacity utilisation? Capital rationalisation? Delivery service? Does it vary from time to time? Are you not quite sure?

◊ Capacity utilisation. How much, for example, are the company's machine groups "booked up" over a given period of time?

This description of the present situation is important for understanding why and how one should prioritise further analytical work. The present situation should always be related back to the analysis of buying criteria. If the buying criteria analysis, for example, concludes that delivery times and delivery capability are clear key criteria for the company's customers then this means that one should measure production on this basis. A "traditionally important" factor like capacity utilisation (which has nothing whatsoever to do with the customer's buying criteria) is not an area to focus on in further work!

Once the most important problem areas have been pinpointed (use the "20/80 rule" here too) these can be linked with possible solutions and given a status. In order to view this in the profitability perspective, one should link the information to the DuPont model (see Chapter 8 on "Financial Key Ratio Analysis"). The model can be used to establish figures for stock levels (raw materials, work in progress and finished goods), turnover of both total capital and stocks, the effect of costs on overall profitability etc.

Routines for reporting and follow-up on the prioritised areas should be established.

The value chain and the DuPont model are two specific techniques that will ensure that you have the integrated perspective you should be aiming for.

SWOT ANALYSIS

This section describes the operation of a workshop to identify the Strengths, Weaknesses, Opportunities and Threats (SWOT) in SMEs and the subsequent analysis. The object of the exercise is to produce a report with recommendations that will enable the client company to develop their business in future years.

The factors that make up the SWOT analysis are illustrated in Figure 10.9.

Figure 10.9: "SWOT" Analysis

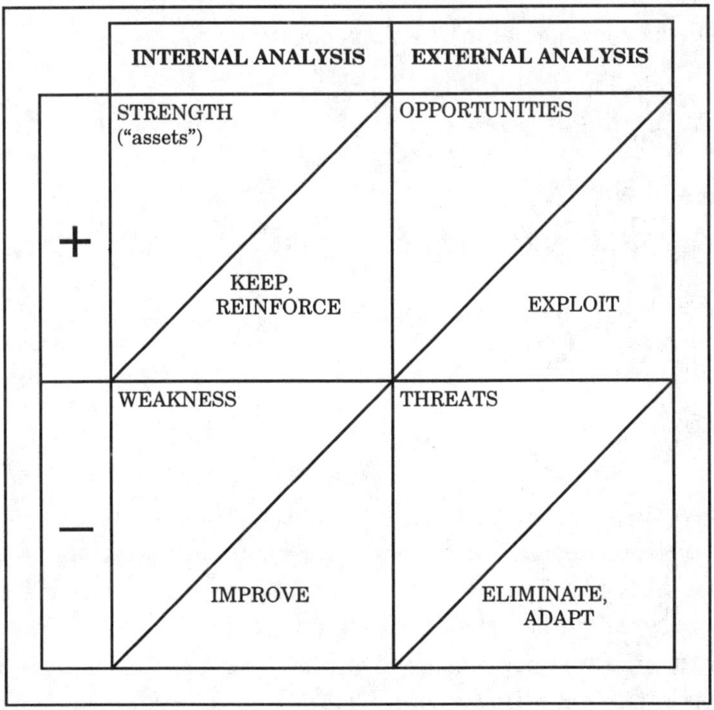

	INTERNAL ANALYSIS	EXTERNAL ANALYSIS
+	STRENGTH ("assets") KEEP, REINFORCE	OPPORTUNITIES EXPLOIT
—	WEAKNESS IMPROVE	THREATS ELIMINATE, ADAPT

Set-Up

It is suggested that a two-member consultancy team will do the work. Prior to the workshop the consultants should seek a meeting with company management to outline the procedures to be followed, and to obtain documentary information to familiarise themselves with the company, this will consist of:

- Accounts for two years

- Organisation chart

- Business plans

- Marketing plans

- Operational plans

- Factory layout.

It would also be important to have a factory tour and an introduction to management participants at the workshops, normally this would be the function head or senior nominee, such as:

- General management/Chief Executive

- Finance/Administration

- Sales/Marketing

- Personnel

- Production

- Distribution

- Product development

- Engineering.

Prior to the workshop, the consultants should divide the functions between them and carry out a relatively informal discussion with each function head. The methods, programme intentions and objectives should be explained. Using knowledge gained from a technology audit or other prior knowledge of the firm, the consultants should encourage each head of function to express their opinion of the road the company is taking, its needs etc. It is quite interesting to hear the sometimes conflicting views expressed, and the information and views gained can help the consultants in the conduct of the workshop.

If all views follow a pattern this can be taken as an indication of "priming" by the Chief Executive. This may also assist the consultants in determining how to conduct the workshop.

It would also be useful to identify a suitable room or premises for the workshop and state the "rules of play" by which the workshop will be conducted, the most important being:

- The consultants chair the workshop.

- There will be no interruptions by staff, telephone calls or paging etc. The consultants may facilitate the company by agreeing to have breaks for coffee at regular intervals so that messages can be received.

- Hierarchy will be irrelevant during the workshop sessions.

- All ideas will be welcome and of equal importance until scoring or weighting. Use "brainstorming" techniques.

- The workshop will take two days and management must agree to devote the time.

The consultants will send the agenda for the workshop in advance.

Preparation Work for Participants

Each participant should prepare a short page of their perception of the company from the functional point of view, i.e. how their function is affected by other functions within the company, by the outside environment and how they perceive their function affects other functional areas. Each participant should consider their function under the following headings:

S	Strengths	
		Internal environment
W	Weaknesses	
O	Opportunities	
		External environment
T	Threats	

During the morning session of Day 1 each participant will be asked to provide their analysis of the SWOT. This should typically take 10-15 minutes. The balance of the time allocated to that function will be used by the other participants to debate the analysis to criticise, to support, to discuss, etc. The facilitators will prompt the discussion and record the results.

Workshop

The two consultants will take the roles of facilitator/catalyst and recorder. These roles will frequently rotate. The recorder will use a flip-chart and pen.

Day 1 — Diagnosis

The facilitator will tackle each company function in turn and a single flip page will be used to list each function parameter, e.g. Production Strengths, Production Opportunities, Finance Threats etc.

The facilitator should foster a climate of debate, isolate disagreements, look for agreement. The catalytic role can be fulfilled by the odd interjection or shrewd question. Where opportunities and threats are concerned, the consultants prior to the workshop should have given some thought as to how, for example, external economic circumstances may affect the particular business being analysed. It is surprising how an independent input can bring up factors to which the company has given little thought.

As each flip page is completed it should be taped around the walls of the room with a full space between each page. This is to allow second pages to be fixed alongside during the next stage of the workshop.

As with any well run brainstorming session there should be no questioning or analysis at this stage unless it has relevance to a new or innovative idea.

Day 2 — Solutions

Again using the facilitator/catalyst and recorder roles (frequently interchanged) the consultants should bring the participants through each item of each function highlighted at the diagnostic stage to attain a practical solution or exploitation ploy. Recording is again carried out on a flip chart and the page when completed should be attached opposite the page put up earlier.

Consultants should endeavour to reduce the solution/exploitation options to one agreed ploy if possible as this will save work later. A watch should be kept for inter-relationships of ploys and practicality should be questioned where, for example, a particular solution to one problem would have a major effect elsewhere.

This process should not take all day as time will be needed at the end of the session to prioritise the solutions and suggest an implementation plan.

Day 2 (continued) — Prioritising Solutions

The analysis of the SWOT will have identified possible methods of maximising the strengths and opportunities and providing solutions to the weaknesses and threats. These must be placed in order of importance so that a plan for implementation can be made.

The most simple method of identifying priorities is to weigh or score the ideas. The company management will form a weighting committee, it may or may not comprise all those who took part in the workshop. The consultants will not vote but will direct the exercise and record the results.

It will be important for those who are doing the scoring not to be influenced by more senior management or more experienced personnel. Each member will have score cards, say $1 - 5$, which they will hold up at the direction of the consultant on each subject raised while the other records the total score. The result of this exercise will be a list of suggestions, each with a numerical score.

It is now necessary to compare this list against a set of important criteria which the company chooses, such as the following:

- Cost
- Time to implement
- Technical ability
- Availability of personnel
- Competition
- Policy
- "Gut feeling".

One useful method is to compare all other suggestions against the best scoring suggestions using the criteria specified to see if it is indeed the best. The scoring here is:

- Better than

- Worse than

- Same.

The top suggestion will have all others with a higher percentage "worse than" or the "same".

At the close of the workshop consultants should leave the flip pages with the company, having of course recorded their contents (perhaps by camera).

Report

The consultants will meet back at their base to prepare their report. This will consist of the following deliverables:

- A summary of the discoveries made. The strengths and weaknesses of the company and the opportunities and threats of the outside environment, as perceived by the management.

- An analysis of the SWOT into a coherent document which condenses the large quantity of detail down to several ideas and solutions.

- A list of priorities for the company.

- A recommended implementation plan taking into account the financial and technical ability of the company to achieve success. A suggested timescale with realistic targets.

- A copy for each member of management who took part in the workshop.

It is recommended that the report be personally delivered by the consultants and discussed in detail with the participants to ensure that it is fully understood and acceptable.

11

PROBLEM-SOLVING

INTRODUCTION

This chapter gives a description of the principles of creative problem-solving. Emphasis is placed on those aspects that lead to a creative process in the company, and especially on how one can get participants to work optimally together in group discussions and "brainstorming" sessions. During a consultancy assignment creative problem-solving is used in almost all situations where it is important to make a group of people as goal-oriented and effective as possible. The techniques described below can be used in a number of different situations.

In this chapter, problem-solving is dealt with under the following headings:

- Different Phases of Problem-solving

- Creative Problem-solving

- Formulation of Issues

- Analysis of Causes

- Generating Ideas and Possibilities

- Brainstorming

- "Wallcharting" as a Key Technique

- Selecting Participants.

DIFFERENT PHASES OF PROBLEM-SOLVING

When a problem becomes so complex that a solution is not immediately evident, it is necessary to concentrate on its causes. It is not enough to attack the symptoms of the problem. There are two aspects, therefore, to the process of solving the problem, as illustrated in Figure 11.1:

- From symptom to cause, and

- From cause to solution.

Figure 11.1: Phases of Problem-solving

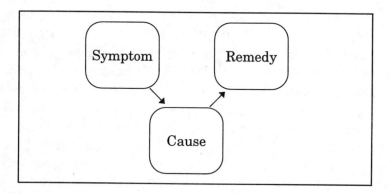

The first requirement, however, is to clarify what the problem is that has to be solved. Also, when the solution has been chosen, it has to be implemented in practice. So the process can be broken into four phases overall:

- Formulation of the issue

- Finding the cause or causes of the problem

- Choosing a solution

- Implementation of a permanent solution.

The implementation in turn involves (a) planning, (b) implementation and (c) setting up a monitoring system to make sure the solution remains permanently in place.

This chapter concentrates on the use of creative problem-solving in the first three phases. Implementation is dealt with in greater detail in Chapter 16.

CREATIVE PROBLEM-SOLVING

The creative phases in the problem-solving process fall into two parts:

- A "divergent" part

- A "convergent" part.

Figure 11.2 shows how this is repeated throughout the process. In the divergent part we attempt to produce as many ideas as possible, while in the convergent part we try to assign priorities to those ideas so we can move on in the process.

Figure 11.2: Creative Problem-solving

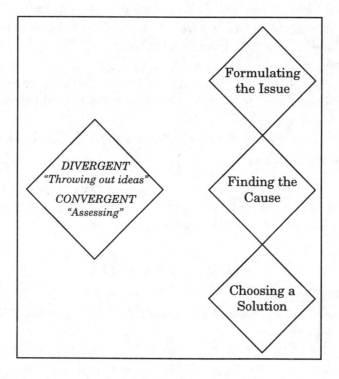

In this way the entire analysis can be seen as a creative process that leads to specific action plans.

FORMULATION OF ISSUES

The way an issue is formulated affects the solutions which will be found. An issue formulated as "the Stores Manager is always complaining that he can't find things he wants" is not likely to generate a lot of ideas. A better formulation would be:

> "How can we organise and structure our stocks better and what systems can we put in place to bring this about ?"

The object of correct issue formulation is twofold:

- It describes the actual issue

- It leads to creativity.

Problems that are revealed during interviews and conversations are often superficial symptoms. Thus the emphasis should be on stating the issue as precisely as possible.

In this regard it is important to collect factual information about the problem. Try breaking down the problem into several sub-problems, and concentrate on the most important aspects. Solve one problem at a time.

Thus, the above problem could end up end up being more precisely formulated as:

> The way in which the stores for semi-manufactured goods is organised does not facilitate the finding and withdrawal of goods, and it takes too long to find individual parts.

ANALYSIS OF CAUSES

The next step in the problem-solving process is analysing the causes. This is perhaps the most important part of the problem-solving process.

A good aid in analysing causes is the so-called "fishbone diagram" developed by Professor Ishikawa in Japan (see Figure 11.3). Using the fishbone diagram, the problem is described in terms of key words at the right in the diagram. Usually the most important causes are among the "four Ms":

- Materials
- Machinery
- Manning
- Methods.

Figure 11.3: Analysis of Causes

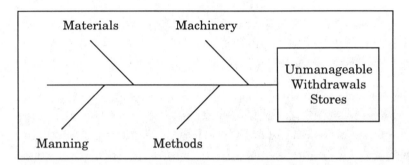

Draw the diagram on the board and get the members of the group to contribute specific suggestions for possible solutions. Group the proposals along the main branches and make smaller branches and twigs as you go along. Follow the ground rules for creative idea generation (see below) during this phase.

When you feel that a sufficient number of ideas have emerged review the proposals critically, group those together that belong together and use group discussions to bring out the most likely causes (i.e. the convergent part of the process).

In this phase, there may also be a need to gather factual information so as to check whether the group's understanding of the causes is accurate.

GENERATING IDEAS AND POSSIBILITIES

In all three creative phases we need to generate as many ideas as possible. Solutions and options are best generated in groups in which everyone is given the opportunity to present their own ideas for discussion by the group It is important that the meeting takes place in a pleasant atmosphere, and that participants are positive about the process.

If the process grinds to a halt, the process leader must try to inspire the participants. Some techniques that can be used in this regard are:

- Reformulating of the issue

- Generating ideas from a picture

- Producing similar issues from other areas and finding approaches to these.

It often helps to reformulate an issue. This can widen the perspective so that the participants see issues from different points of view. It often produces sub-issues that can contribute to a total solution.

Picture association is a good technique that often produces totally different solutions to those already "brought to light". The technique involves giving each participant a picture and asking them to formulate one or more issues/solutions based on associations the participant gets from looking at the picture. The best results are obtained if participants are supplied with pictures that differ widely from each other.

Pictures can also be used to formulate similar issues from other areas and afterwards find approaches to these. When solutions are found, try to re-apply them to the actual issue that is being dealt with. This technique is time-consuming, but at the same time especially well-suited to finding new solutions to technological problems.

BRAINSTORMING

Brainstorming is a creative technique for generating a large number of ideas. During the process, no demands are made on the ideas, but the point of departure is an objective that must be reasonably precisely formulated.

The actual brainstorming is followed by a critical assessment, but it is important to make sure that the critical comments are not made during the actual brainstorming process. We must create an atmosphere of creativity as described in more detail below.

The procedure for brainstorming is outlined below:

1. Establish the objective.

2. Appoint a process leader who will be responsible for writing down all ideas, making sure that the members of the group are active, and ensuring that all the rules are observed.

3. State the method to be used — structured or free (in a structured brainstorming session everyone contributes in turn in a predetermined order, in a free brainstorming session everyone is free to make comments at any stage).

4. Allow time for reflection and idea creation before starting (a few minutes).

5. Register all ideas on a wallboard — without changes, editing or questions.

6. Build on one another's ideas.

7. Do not discuss, ask questions or criticise during the process. Avoid destructive remarks (see below).

8. Keep going until there are no longer any new ideas. Normally one gets 50-100 suggestions, and it takes between half an hour and an hour.

9. Destructive remarks can ruin a brainstorming session so they must be avoided. Examples of destructive remarks are:

"It won't work (won't do)."

"You must be joking/You can't be serious."

"That's stupid."

"You're talking nonsense."

"It won't work in practice."

"We don't have time for that."

After a brainstorming session all of the ideas that participants have come up with have to be put into some sort of order. This involves the following stages:

- **Sorting**. "Duplicate" ideas are eliminated. Similar ideas are gathered together.

- **Discussion**. Clarify what is meant. Find ways of improving suggestions.

- **Editing**. Gather the ideas in groups.

- **Prioritising**. Select the suggested solutions that have the greatest potential. Make a list — in order of priority if possible.

The techniques described for creative problem-solving are simple. Simple techniques are often best in cases where you have to focus on creativity and problem-solving.

The process leader's job is to guide the group through the process, maintain a neutral position with respect to the case in hand, and exercise authority only with respect to the process itself. The leader should accept all proposals without evaluating them, and write them down just as they have been proposed. The leader should contribute to creating a pleasant, positive atmosphere in the group through maintaining an amenable, inspiring manner at all times. Everyone should be encouraged to contribute. Make sure there is a relaxed atmosphere — smiles and laughter are fine. In many situations the consultant will act as process leader, especially if the company has little experience of creative problem-solving themselves.

"WALLCHARTING" AS A KEY TECHNIQUE

"Wallcharting" is a simple technique that requires nothing more than a board and the so-called "Post-It" self-adhesive and detachable labels that we all know from our everyday work. The technique makes it easier to order ideas in an analysis of causes or in a brainstorming session.

The group should use the wallchart as a shared communication medium. The notes are stuck on the board, and can later be manipulated and moved around. If there are not too many participants, they should stand during the process, actively taking part in the "moving".

When working with issues and options this technique can be used to classify and group them into activity areas or other topics.

Issues can be subordinated to each other and then prioritised. The notes are easy to move, and if colour coding is used, another manipulative dimension is added to the process.

Generating options from buying criteria, and then tying these into the company's activities, is another area where the technique can be very beneficial. Here, the chart functions as a matrix, and the notes describe options. Colour codes can designate option status. A Polaroid camera can be another useful aid in documenting things written on a wallchart.

SELECTING PARTICIPANTS

Creative problem-solving techniques can be successfully used when working with a project group on the strategy and planning processes. The strategy and planning process can also benefit from a periodic meeting of the reference personnel in an idea-generating session.

Participants in a group should be selected on the plurality principle. It is important that different competences are present in the group. Good specialised skills are important, but it is also important to include creative people with different backgrounds and different areas of expertise. The number should not be too high — a maximum of six participants plus the process leader.

It is important that the process can take place without being interrupted by daily routines, the telephone, etc. So find comfortable rooms where participants can relax and be free from interruption. Refreshments and a relaxed atmosphere are important ingredients if a brainstorming session is to function successfully.

Controlling a process in which many inventive people are taking part is often easier than controlling one where the ideas have to be "dragged out" into the open. The problem with a very creative group, however, is to prioritise the ideas during the convergent phase. This work can be helped by using simple techniques like "wallcharting".

PART III

STRATEGIES AND ACTION PLANS

12

ESTABLISHING STRATEGIES AND ACTION PLANS

INTRODUCTION

This chapter aims to give companies and consultants an idea of what a strategy and planning process (the process of establishing a strategy and action plan) involves. It also presents an outline of a methodology that can be used for this purpose.

The general strategic analysis carried out during the initial diagnostic phase of an assignment is meant to quickly reveal "where the shoe pinches". It should result in a set of recommendations and guidelines for further work.

During the general analysis, a financial key ratio analysis will have been carried out which gives the consultant a picture of the current competitive situation of the company and its products. Consultants will have further identified the business areas and products/services that they want to evaluate in more detail in terms of potential for the introduction of change. They will also have identified the two or three most important issues and some possible solutions (options).

Before proceeding with a description of the planning process, it is appropriate to recall some definitions:

- Company *goals* are the results the company wishes to achieve after implementation of its strategies and plans.

- The *strategy* is a general plan for the way it is intended to achieve the goals. The strategy describes general "routes". A related action plan describes the specific measures that must be implemented.

- *Strategic planning* (or the strategy and planning process) is a *process* of determining goals, choosing strategy and creating an action plan for the introduction and use of measures which directly support the company's business goals and strategies.

In this chapter, the establishment of strategies and action plans is considered under the following headings:

- The Strategy and Planning Process
- Drawing Up an Action Plan
- Project Implementation
- Critical Success Factors for Project Implementation
- Suggested Structure for a Strategic Plan
- Concluding Remarks.

THE STRATEGY AND PLANNING PROCESS

What is the Result of the Strategy and Planning Process?

The strategy and planning process is about determining goals, selecting strategies and drawing up action plans for the introduction of measures in the areas that have been highlighted by the strategic analysis.

The primary result is a plan with specific measures in accordance with the selected strategies. Apart from the written report presented by the consultant which gives a description of the selected goals and strategies, the process itself will often be of great value to the company.

What is a Strategy and Planning Process All About?

As with other planning processes, there are three questions (illustrated in Figure 12.1) that must be answered:

- Where do we stand today, and why?
- Where do we want to be?
- How do we get there?

This handbook proposes to split the work of finding answers to these questions up into a four-stage process. Each stage forms a milestone and involves a number of activities. Each stage must lead to interim results and genuine points to be decided which will affect further work. The four stages are:

- A business analysis, where the work of the preceding strategic analysis is continued with more detailed evaluation and quantification of goals, success factors and scenarios for the future.

- An evaluation of options, supported by analysis of the competitive situation in the industry and of the company's internal situation and background.

- Establishment of goals and strategies to support the results of the business analysis.

- Establishment of an action plan for the practical implementation of strategies, and thus of goals.

Figure 12.1: Key Questions

The four stages are illustrated in Figure 12.2. The external and internal analyses shown in the figure are "support activities" for collecting information (and issues) relevant to various external and internal factors. Such analyses may be necessary during the business analysis and are a precondition of the evaluation of any options that are identified.

Figure 12.2: Stages of Establishing Strategies and Actions Plans

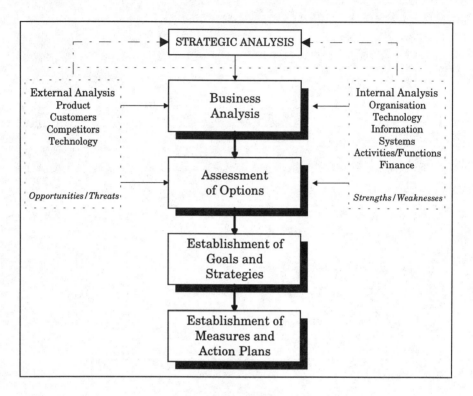

By analysing the company from several different angles we will discover the issues that it are most important for the company to deal with. Then we will look for, and select, the options that are most appropriate to those issues. This is an iterative process which requires a mix of analysis/survey, creativity (generation of ideas) and prioritising work. Finally we will end up with a specific plan for implementing the options that have been considered "best".

The first three stages illustrated in Figure 12.2 — "business analysis", "assessment of options" and "establishing goals and strategies" — have been covered in detail in previous sections. The fourth stage — "establishing measures and action plans" — is described in more detail below.

DRAWING UP AN ACTION PLAN

The planning process often stops when general strategies have been established. Yet strategies are of little value unless they are put into practice and thus the establishment of an action plan with specific measures is essential. An action plan shows the measures and projects adopted, scheduled in time, with responsibilities allocated, and with a statement of resource requirements.

The drawing up of the action plans must be done with due regard for an assessment of benefits based on time and cost estimates. All these analyses are specifications of strategies and general goals. Specifying these at an adequate level of detail helps to ensure that realistic decisions are made.

Action plans should have sensible milestones. A proposal for more specialised and financial follow-up must be established and the necessary quality assurance criteria must be stated.

The plan should have a two or three-year perspective and should be updated before budgeting is done. The work should be done in connection with a review (confirmation/update) of the overall goals and strategies.

Emphasis should be given to achieving a balance between short-term and long-term measures. Important problems cannot wait for an ideal solution to turn up some time in the future. Short-term problem-solving also increases acceptance of the plan, because results are available sooner. Clear goals and strategies make it easier to select those short-term solutions which best fit in with the long-term goals.

What Should an Action Plan Show?

An action plan should be worked out for each project or measure. The plan should be drawn up so that it at least includes the following information:

- The activities the measure consists of at a general level

- The dates for starting and finishing an activity

- Estimated resource requirement (based on time estimates) for the duration of the time required to implement the measure, itemised per activity per week/month or some other appropriate unit of time

- How the available time resources have been allocated to cover the estimated requirements

- Total cost consequences (based on time and cost estimates)

- Expected result on completion of the activity — results can be referred to as milestones.

Measures, Activities, Projects and Implementation Phases
Specific action plans can vary greatly in accordance with the complexity of the job to be done. Above (and in the examples given below) we talk, for example, about a measure consisting of activities — in other words, we are using a grouping at two levels: measures subdivided into activities.

It is important to keep the number of measures and activities down to a controllable level. If the number becomes too large, the result is often that little or nothing is accomplished. Thus strict prioritisation and grouping of measures is necessary. There is no "easy answer" as to how such a grouping should be done, but we can give some guidelines:

- The number of "units" in an action plan should never be more than twenty. Ten is considered "suitable". The "units" may be projects, measures or activities.

- Consider whether related and/or interdependent measures and activities can be grouped together in projects.

- In general, avoid subdividing the measures into detailed activities if this will lead to an unmanageable number of units.

- If detailing down to the level of individual activities is necessary, and this means that the number of units becomes difficult to handle, establish separate versions of the action plans with different levels of detail. At the highest level, for example, the plan could only show projects, while the description of each project would include a plan for the individual activities in the project.

- Consider whether measures/projects should be grouped together if their phases of implementation coincide in time.

Figure 12.3 shows a form for activity specification. This form can be used in two ways:

- As an aid while drawing up the action plans

- When filled in, as documentation of the assumptions on which the plan is based.

Figure 12.3: Form for Activity Specification

Activity Specification
Name of Activity
Evaluation of quotes for CAD workstations
Brief Description
The evaluation is based on quotes received from a total of five suppliers. *The activity involves a review and comparison of the quotes with a view to a systematic comparison of prices and technical parameters.*
Participants
Chief executive to attend at meeting with each of the suppliers. *Evaluation to be done by group consisting of: The Design Manager, Engineer X from the Design Division, Consultant Y from CAD Consult. Ltd.*
Results
Recommendation giving the pros and cons of various alternatives. Criteria to be agreed in advance. The final outcome will be a proposal for a purchasing alternative.
Duration (Start/Finish)
1½ months
Resource Requirements
Chief executive   5 man-days *Design Manager   12 man-days* *Engineer X   20 man-days* *Consultant Y   10 man-days*

Similar forms can be used at the project and measure level. Again, it is the consultant who should recommend the level of detail in each situation, on the basis of, among other things, the number of measures the company has decided to implement.

Figure 12.3 shows the sample form already filled in giving an activity specification. It concerns the introduction of a CAD/CAM system in the company. The form describes one of the activities — i.e. the one that consists of evaluating relevant quotes.

Resource Time and Calendar Time

A major problem in action planning is illustrated in Figure 12.4. The horizontal axis represents calendar time. The vertical axis represents resource time, i.e. the time resources required to carry out the activities. Available resources are also indicated on the vertical axis — five man-weeks per calendar week in the example.

Figure 12.4: Resource Time and Calendar Time

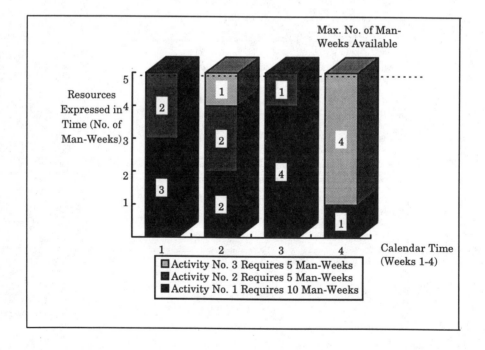

It is estimated that the three activities together will require twenty man-weeks, that is, ten man-weeks for Activity 1, and five for each of the others.

With the capacity to use five man-weeks per calendar week — in Week 1 distributed over three man-weeks for Activity 1 and two man-weeks for Activity 2 — it will thus take four calendar weeks to carry out the three activities.

We can see that in carrying out the measure or project, delays in the use and distribution of time can be due to two factors:

- More time used per activity than estimated — i.e. an increase along the vertical axis in Figure 12.4. If the project is not given more resources in such a situation, the total time consumption must be distributed over more calendar time.

- The resources planned for the project may not in practice be allocated to the project — i.e. the broken line in Figure 12.4, which marks a capacity of five man-weeks per calendar week, will be moved down to a lower level. If this happens without any corresponding reduction in estimated time required to carry out the various activities, completion inevitably will be delayed.

Activity Plan in the Form of a Gantt Diagram

To illustrate how an action plan looks in terms of calendar time — in other words to indicate specifically when we plan that an activity will start and finish — we can use a Gantt diagram.

Figure 12.5 shows such a diagram for the same example as given in Figure 12.4.

In the diagram in Figure 12.5 we have included a column to show who is responsible for carrying out the activity. We have also included a column for total costs estimated for the various activities. This may be useful for checking that we have not forgotten important costs.

If the company plans to implement many measures, it may be useful to group these on a separate Gantt diagram which gives an overview for each group of measures (i.e. projects).

Figure 12.5: Example of a Gantt Diagram

Activity Plan									
Activity	Respon-sible	Cost (ECU)	Week No.						
			1	2	3	4	5	6	7
Activity No. 1	NN	55000							
Activity No. 2	NN	30000							
Activity No. 3	NN	23000							

Interdependence of Activities

In a measure with many activities, various relationships will often exist between the different activities so that they become interdependent on one another. A typical example of interdependence would be the case in which one activity cannot start before another has been concluded.

To resolve such problems, one can supplement the techniques described above with special network diagrams. In practice, though, it often emerges that where measures are not too complex, it is possible to allow intuitively or less formally for interdependencies while drawing up — for example — a Gantt diagram.

Key Questions for Action Planning

In drawing up action plans, it may be useful to ask the following key questions, among others:

- How many simultaneous measures and projects can the company handle in practice? One is often the limit for smallish companies, because the same key personnel will have to be involved.

- Which measures should be carried out through line management, and for which should special project groups be set up?

- Where projects are established, who should manage them? The number of potential project managers often imposes a practical limit on the number of projects. This can in turn mean a stronger concentration of measures within projects than would otherwise have been natural, and can mean shifts in the time perspective.

- Can mutually independent measures be grouped naturally in the same project?

- Which measures must be implemented before others? Interdependencies can cause radical shifts in the timescale.

- Can one find a natural classification into implementation phases?

- What kind of personnel and competence are required to implement which measures? Often, periodised capacity for a given personnel group will impose limits on the speed at which measures can be implemented. If, for example, company management can only set aside a maximum of five man-days a month for the implementation of the plans, and these require a total of fifty man-days from this group, the measures cannot be implemented in less than ten months. It helps very little in this case if, for example, the total resource requirement is for a hundred man-days and the other personnel can put in a hundred man-days a month.

- What periodised capital requirement can the company bear in connection with implementation? It may be necessary, for example, to phase two measures after each other in time, because they both need outside consultancy assistance and the company cannot pay too much in monthly fees. In addition, it may be necessary to extend the calendar schedule for each of the measures.

PROJECT IMPLEMENTATION

Organisation

The work on the strategy and planning process is organised as a project. The best way of organising the project will depend on the size of the company, the availability of internal competence, and the consultant's own experience and preferences. A typical organisational structure for a project is shown in Figure 12.6.

Figure 12.6: Typical Organisational Structure for a Project

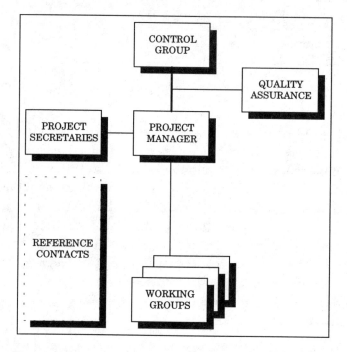

The Role of the Consultant

A consultant will have a dual role:

- As a *process* consultant — a "backup player" for the project manager

- As an active *resource* (or *expert*) consultant in the work of drawing up and assessing options

The work involves the roles of creative generator of ideas, "Devil's advocate", co-ordinator and mediator.

Implementation Phases

The grouping of measures and projects into implementation phases can help to create acceptance and motivation in the organisation, while at the same time making the plans at the general level easier to understand and communicate to others.

Often the division into phases is based on the length of time required for implementation. This leads to natural grouping of measures as follows:

- Measures to be implemented in the course of the first six months

- Measures to be implemented in the course of the first year

- Measures to be implemented during the remainder of the timespan of the plan.

This provides a clear focus on "quick fixes" (in the first six months) — often simple measures which solve the everyday problems. Quick results (no matter how banal the solutions are) create acceptance of the overall plan in the organisation, because they show that "planning pays". This often helps to create better motivation for the more extensive and difficult measures in later phases.

CRITICAL SUCCESS FACTORS FOR PROJECT IMPLEMENTATION

The effect of planned changes or innovations can be seen in broad terms as a product of several factors: the quality of the plan, the acceptance of the plan in the organisation, and the resources available for its implementation. Some of the factors that are critical for ensuring satisfactory quality, acceptance and resources are listed below:

- **Motivation and commitment of management.** Motivation and commitment from top management is necessary for ongoing decision-making, for ensuring acceptance by the organisation and for allocation of the resources necessary for implementation.

- **Proper organisation and participation.** We recommend that the work on the strategy and planning process should be done in project form. The work makes great demands on the project manager, on the composition of the project group and management committee, and on the use of reference contacts.

- **Well-defined, flexible methodology.** A methodology is important in ensuring a structured approach. The methodological material presented in this manual includes a comprehensive toolkit of techniques. This gives the consultant a range of choices on the basis of the specific assignment.

- **Understanding general constraints** is important in making realistic plans. The company must have the financial, organisation and competence-related preconditions for implementing the plans.

- **Balance between short-term and long-term measures.** Proposals must be realistic. It is also important that results are not too long in materialising. Similarly, it is important to choose the right level for strategies and measures.

- **Efficient communication of results.** A strategic plan has to be communicated to others to gain the necessary acceptance. Make allowances for the fact that some "active marketing" will be necessary internally in the organisation.

- **A strategic plan requires regular updating.** The strategy and action plan must be updated at least once a year. A consultant should always try to help to create a "climate" for long-term planning in the company. This means that key personnel in the company must be trained in the methodology used.

SUGGESTED STRUCTURE FOR A STRATEGIC PLAN

A possible structure for a strategic plan is presented in Figure 12.7. A list of key concepts/questions is also given below which the consultant can use to assist with the preparation of a report. The list includes many more questions than will be necessary to use in writing a report. This is deliberate so as to force the consultant to tailor the content to the company concerned — it is important to spend time reading through the list and critically selecting/adapting the questions raised to suit a given assignment.

Figure 12.7: Suggested Report Structure

List of Contents
1. Introduction and résumé
2. Company goals
3. Issues
4. Options
5. General strategy
6. General implementation plan
7. Investment requirements/financial consequences
Appendices

List of Contents and Key Questions

I. Introduction and Résumé

(a) Background of the planning project

- Why was the work on a strategic plan initiated?
- What are the goals of the planning process?
- What issues and options formed the point of departure?

(b) Scope

- What is the timescale of the plan?
- Which of the company's activities and/or product/market combinations have been in focus?

- Does the plan cover all areas (business activities, organisation, technology, information systems) or only some of these? What priorities have been given to each of these?

(c) Résumé of goals, strategies and recommended measures

- What are the most important goals, strategies and measures?

- What are the most important issues and weaknesses, and how can these be dealt with?

- What quantifiable and non-quantifiable bonuses can be seen in realising the goals in the short and long term?

- What are the risk factors, and what are the critical success factors for successful implementation of the plans?

(d) Basic assumptions and constraints

- What assumptions is the plan based on with regard to developments in, business activities, markets, social, political and economic trends and technology?

- What possible changes in the surrounding constraints could invalidate the plan?

II. Company Goals

(a) Strategic goals

- In what activities and/or product/market combinations should changes be implemented to establish competitive advantage through:

  ◊ cost reductions?

  ◊ differentiation (better satisfaction of the customer's buying criteria)?

(b) Financial goals

- What goals have been set for return on investments?

- How does the company want to be positioned in relation to its competitors in the industry with regard to return on investment?

(c) Organisational goals

- How should the company's activities be controlled?
- What goals exist for competence, recruitment, personnel development and training?
- What goals exist for the development of the organisational structure? How much influence should individuals have on the shaping of their own work situations?

(d) Technological goals

- What goals have been set for the spread of technology throughout the organisation?
- Does the company want to be at the leading edge in technology use in the industry, or does it want to concentrate on well-tried technology?
- What goals exist for standardisation of technology and linkages between different technologies?

(e) Information goals

- What information should be available to whom in order to make what decisions, and when?
- What goals exist for the spread of access to information throughout the organisation?

III. Issues

Issues related to company goals, with the focus on areas where there are substantial discrepancies between goals and the present situation, and on areas with clear potential for improvement.

(a) Assessment of business and competitive aspects

- What primary customers, suppliers and competitors exist in the company's areas of business?

- What is the situation of the company in relation to these competitors with regard to:

  ◊ investments in technology?

  ◊ economic stability?

  ◊ human resources/competence?

  ◊ use of technology to gain competitive advantage?

  ◊ general strengths and weaknesses?

- What primary and support activities are involved in the production of goods and/or services? Which of these activities:

  ◊ have a particularly high customer-perceived value (great importance in the satisfaction of buying criteria)?

  ◊ are particularly costly?

  ◊ are particularly information-intensive?

(b) Organisation and staff

- Are company activities well-organised? Are all the necessary tasks covered, and are redundant functions avoided?

- How is competence ensured by recruitment and training and how are key personnel kept in the company?

- How are development projects organised? Is there a good balance between internal and external resources? Is the work organised in projects with clear goals and satisfactory control?

(c) Technology

- Is technology use standardised, or are many incompatible technologies used?

- Are communication systems used appropriately to increase the accessibility of information in the organisation?

- Is a technology used that generates high operating and maintenance costs?

- How does current technology use fit with general trends in development? Is technology being used that will not survive the next 3-5 years?

- How operationally stable are the company's technical installations?

- Does the current use of technology match adopted technology strategies?

(d) Information and information systems

- What information systems exist, and what systems are planned or being developed?

- What system software and hardware is used in the systems? How old is it, and what is its technical quality?

- What do the systems cost, distributed over development, operation and maintenance?

- Are the users satisfied with the various systems? Are there many unfulfilled system needs/wishes in the organisation?

- Are the systems satisfactorily integrated? Is there inconsistency or redundancy between information used in different systems?

- Is there existing basic information which cannot be put to use because it is not available at the right time and place?

- Is there information and/or information systems that could be used to gain competitive advantage?

- Does the company avoid expensive in-house system development where application packages could do the job just as well or better?

IV. Options

(a) Options to gain competitive advantage

- What changes will strengthen the company's position vis-à-vis its customers, so there will be a higher demand for its products/services?

- How can the company "lock" on to customers, so that the threshold for them changing suppliers is raised?

- Could the company raise entry barriers to the market for potential new entrants?

- Could technology change or remove potential substitute products/services or make it generally more difficult for the company's competitors to survive?

- How can the company reduce its dependence on specific suppliers?

- Could the company achieve synergy effects by directly linking its information systems with the systems of its customers and/or suppliers?

(b) Options for differentiation

- What can the company do so that it will be in a better position to supply products/services that satisfy the customer's buying criteria better than those of the competitors?

(c) Options for rationalisation

- How can the company reduce costs and/or provide better support for higher volumes and market shares?

- Can the company reduce the price of products through internal rationalisation?

- Could more efficient linkages between existing technologies reduce costs?

- Are there already areas where the company's expectations for savings have not been realised because of poor integration/co-ordination of changes to date?

(d) Technological options

- What technological trends are most important in general and in the industry? Is there new technology that could be used cost-effectively in the company?

- Are there any trends that pave the way for standardisation of technology in ways that will have consequences for the company's future use of technology?

(e) Alternative strategies

- What are the most important alternatives for areas of focus (product/market combinations) during the plan period?

- What are the advantages and disadvantages of each alternative?

V. General Strategy

The company's (and each product/market combination's) goals, and related issues and options, form the key components in a strategic plan. The work of establishing, documenting and prioritising these components will have created a basis for the company's strategy for the next 3-5 years.

(a) Principles, measures and action plans. The strategy will be a summing-up of the conclusions from the previous sections, and will have a threefold structure:

- Basic strategic principles in areas such as:

  ◊ organisation and control of the company's (and each product/market combination's) use of technology

  ◊ prioritisation criteria for technology investments

  ◊ technological standards for communications, systems/solutions, interfaces to users/the environment, upgradability, flexibility etc.

- Measures and plans that will have effects in the medium or long term (3-5 years)

- "Quick fixes" (current year).

(b) Consequences of the strategy

- What will be the financial consequences of the general strategy?

- What kinds of organisational development will be necessary to achieve full realisation of the bonus potential?

- How will the strategy affect the company's customer relations and relationships with suppliers and competitors?

- How will the strategy affect the company's range of products and services?

(c) Assumptions and general constraints

- On what assumptions about developments on the business and market front is the strategy based?

- On what assumptions about technological development is the strategy based?

- What changes in general constraints and assumptions would make a rethinking of plans and strategies necessary?

VI. General Implementation Plan

This section covers the co-ordination of measures and plans in the short, medium and long terms. Measures and projects defined by them are prioritised on the basis of:

- General strategies and principles

- Relationships with other measures and systems

- A phased plan for the implementation of measures/projects.

VII. Investment Requirements and Financial Consequences

- Summary of the cost-benefit analysis for prioritised measures and projects in the plan period

- Investment analysis

- Summary of investment requirements for:

    ◊ systems

    ◊ personnel

    ◊ technology

- Basic estimation parameters for financial analysis, including an assessment of the reliability of the parameters

- Estimate of decrease in returns in the event of changes in basic parameters.

Appendices

A. Organisation and scheduling of the work

- Project organisation and participants

- Composition of control group

- Mandate of the project (directive)

- Brief description of tasks

B. Detailed financial analysis

C. Detailed risk and benefit assessment

D. Detailed project description for the highest-priority (and most pressing) measures.

CONCLUDING REMARKS

The strategy and planning process is difficult — for both the company and the consultant. Every company is different and needs individual treatment. What works for one company may not necessarily be suitable for another.

The work involved in implementation of action plans should not be underestimated. The very principle of working with consultants is that the company is to undergo a process of change, and for a period it may be necessary to support the company with knowledge and experience in the area of change management.

But the first and biggest obstacle has been overcome. Once a company has decided to approach a consultant for assistance, it will have seen the need to assess its present method and systems and will have initiated a strategy and planning process.

13

THE PLANNING PROCESS, IDENTIFICATION OF MEASURES, SUCCESS FACTORS

INTRODUCTION

This chapter deals with the process a company must go through after having completed the initial general strategic analysis and before starting on further strategy and planning work. The aim of this planning process is:

- To set realistic goals for the introduction of changes

- To devise a strategy and to evaluate its consequences

- To devise plans for carrying out any projects that are identified, including project description (goals, tasks), cost-benefit analysis, schedules, and project organisation for the impending investments in technology.

Thus, the company must devise a plan of action at the same time as a strategic, action-oriented process is being initiated in the company. In doing so, the consultant must assist the company at devising specific measures out of the prioritised list of options that have been generated. The consultant should understand how such a process is planned, organised, managed and carried out, and what the critical factors for successful implementation are. A detailed discussion on success factors is presented in this section.

The material in this chapter is under the following headings:

- Organisation/Control of the Planning Process

- Identification of Specific Measures

- Success Factors.

ORGANISATION/CONTROL OF THE PLANNING PROCESS

Activities/Phases of the Planning Process

The strategy and planning process can be carried out in four phases as illustrated in Figure 12.2 in the previous chapter (see page 282). Each phase represents a milestone in the process. The four phases are:

1. **Business analysis**, during which the company continues the work from the initial strategic analysis towards a more detailed evaluation and quantification (via key ratios) of the goals, success factors, and future scenarios.

2. **Evaluation of options**, supported by analysis of the competitive situation in the industry, and of the extent to which the company is able to establish and prioritise relevant issues and options.

3. **Defining goals and strategies** in support of the business analysis.

4. **Devising measures and action plans** for the practical implementation of the strategies and thus the achievement of the goals set for the project.

The above activities are backed up by a series of techniques for analysing the company and the market in question, as well as the systematisation of any data that is collected. The work can be carried out in various ways, using everything from structured interviews to creative "brainstorming" sessions.

Participants in the Strategy and Planning Process

One of the greatest challenges with the implementation of strategy and planning processes is ensuring that company management is actively engaged in it. The work should be regarded as a natural part of normal managerial responsibilities. Apart from this, it is difficult to define in advance who the participants in a typical strategy and planning process should be. The most important factor should be arriving at a good balance between product/market competence, technological competence and experience of the actual production process.

The consultant must also be aware of the legal and statutory consequences of introducing changes in the company. Employee representatives generally have strong views and have a right to say what they think about the strategy process. Accordingly, they should be kept up-to-date, and even involved, in the actual project work.

The Consultant's Role in the Strategy and Planning Process

The most important aspects of the consultant's job in the process are to provide professional know-how and to function as a driving force and source of inspiration.

In general, the consultant should not be the project manager. The company itself must take the responsibility for work on the project. Should a consultant take over too much control and initiative in the main project, it could result in a weakening of the company's "ownership" of the problems, options, and the results of the project. The company would then experience major problems in implementing the planned measures and action plans after the consultant has left.

The consultant must also have the ability to analyse the company and its environment, in order to be able to place it in a strategic perspective. Accordingly, the consultant should be in possession of a set of tools that will facilitate quick and effective implementation of the project.

The consultant's role as inspirer and advisor on the project can be summarised by the following qualities:

- **A generator of ideas** who, through using various techniques and methods, is capable of getting the company's project team to "think out loud", "think new", and "think different".

- **The devil's advocate** who, on the basis of their own experience and general competence, is able to create discussion sessions, try out the general issues and options, and bring out into the open the various points of view and consequences.

- **A co-ordinator** who is able to gather together the more or less "loose" ideas and disconnected arguments into an integrated explanation of the company's issues and options.

- **A mediator** who, as a neutral party, has the ability to solve any conflicts of interest that may arise.

- **A network-builder** who, through their own competence and knowledge is able to establish the necessary contacts between these and the company.

- **A catalyst** who ensures that there is continuity in the process, and who keeps those involved aware of the main threads in the project.

Organisation and Delegation of Work

The optimum way of organising a project and the allocation of associated jobs will very much depend on the following parameters:

- The size of the company

- Availability of in-house competence

- The consultant's own preferences and experience.

A typical project organisation will, however, resemble that shown in Figure 12.6 in the previous chapter (see page 290). Each component of this organisation model is briefly described below:

- **The control group** has the overall, controlling responsibility for the project, and will generally include the company's chief executive, as well as key personnel who are central to company operations. The project manager and consultant will also be in the control group. It may be relevant to have one or two employee representatives in the control group. The control group must not be too large: a maximum of six people, but preferably no more than four (*including* the project manager and consultant).

In most cases, the company's chief executive will be the chairman of the control group. The control group will usually hold meetings once every two or three weeks, depending on the size and duration of the project.

- **The project manager** is responsible for keeping the project going, and for costs and results. It is a prerequisite that the project manager is a central figure in the company in order to ensure that the necessary changes can be carried out in the organisation.

- **The consultant**, because of their more process-related role, will function as "project secretary", with responsibility for summarising, systematising, and documenting work in the project.

- **Quality assurance** will be necessary to monitor the progress of the project.

- **Project/Work groups** are put together in accordance with the planned project activities.

Planning and Controlling the Project

Projects in general should be planned and followed up in as simple a form as possible. At the same time as the obvious need for satisfactory control of the project is taken care of, it is also necessary to keep methodology and reporting at a level suited to the limitations of the project.

An activity plan is illustrated in Figure 13.1. The plan is drawn up for each of the four milestones shown in Figure 12.2 (see page 282), and provides an overview of:

- Which activities have to be carried out in order to reach the milestone in question.

- Who is responsible for each activity, including a categorisation of each area of responsibility.

- Expected calendar time for each activity.

- Resources (man-hours, days or weeks) necessary for implementing each of the activities.

Figure 13.1 is an example of a completed activity plan for a milestone after the evaluation of options has been done.

Figure 13.1: Example of a Completed Activity Plan

Time Schedule　　　　**Responsibility Chart**　　　　**Persons/Bodies**

Responsibility Chart legend:

- D Does Work
- M Main Decision
- I Interim Decision
- O Ordinary Work Supervision
- W Work Supervision with Assistance
- i Must be Consulted
- m Must be Informed
- d May be Called for Discussions

Dates on Time-Scale (MAY/JUNE) H/D/W: D								Estimate	No.	Activities/Factors	Project Manager	Consultant	Control Group	Work Group 1	Work Group 2	Quality Assurance	NTNF	Technolog. Environm
2	8	16	22	29	5	12	19											
	▮	▮						8	1	Activity and Information Analysis	A	R		U		I		
			▮	▮				2	2	Analysis of Organisation/Competence	U	R			U			
				▮	▮			3	3	Quantification of Benefits	A	R			U	I		
				▮	▮			2	4	Risk Factor Analysis	A	R			U	I		

Approval Date

Reporting dates should be set for each project — it is often practical to use the control group meetings as fixed reporting dates. A report should include the following considerations as regards the activities planned for the reporting period in question:

- Has the activity been implemented?

- How much work is remaining?

- Will the implementation schedule for this activity be met?

- Is the quality of the work acceptable (to the project manager)?

- Was the responsibility chart for this activity adhered to?

- Are there changes/additions to the activity?

- Are there other special problems in implementing the activity?

These key questions should, where necessary, be supplemented with further problem descriptions, reasons, consequences and any relevant proposals for measures to get "back on the right track".

IDENTIFICATION OF SPECIFIC MEASURES

Introduction

Before identifying specific measures, we will have been through a process of prioritising issues and options. We are thus left with a number of options which have been prioritised on the basis of their commercial importance. What we now have to do is to identify a number of specific measures to do further work on.

So far we have not done much to distinguish between whether the options actually represented goals, strategies or measures, or whether they were at different levels. Everything has been treated as "options", regardless of level. On closer inspection, the options described may turn out to be:

- Directly or indirectly formulated goals

- Strategies or parts of strategies

- Indirect proposals for measures

- Specific proposals for measures.

The theoretically "correct" sequence of work should be as follows:

- Establish what business goals are to be affected positively by the introduction of changes.

- Establish goals for the introduction of the proposed changes, and link these with business goals and strategies. In practice, this means ensuring that the proposed changes are compatible with the company's other goals and choice of routes.

- Establish overall strategies, i.e. the primary routes to the desired goals.

- Work out the detail of the overall strategies to make them into specific, scheduled measures (actions) which can and must be realised during the plan period.

- Group measures into projects, and link these together into action plans and phases of implementation.

- Incorporate the action plans into company budgets.

During the initial strategic analysis the consultant will skim over the overall goals and strategies and identify "quick fixes" directly from the options list. During the strategy and planning process itself the consultant will work in a sequence closer to the above "ideal", but here again goals, strategies and measures will often be found in a "less ideal" order than described above. In particular, there will be an interaction between establishing goals and establishing strategies and between identifying measures and linking them to actions plans and budgeting.

Specific measures will often emerge directly from the overview of options, so one can work on these specific actions while establishing goals and strategies. This can have clear benefits, because it will result in greater awareness of costs and other consequences prior to and parallel with documentation of the strategies.

In this chapter the focus is on how to identify measures on the basis of an issues/options list. Assessment of cost, benefit, risk, time consumption, priority etc. are not dealt with in depth here.

Descriptive Techniques

Two main techniques are normally used to describe the specific actions that the planning work should lead to:

- Descriptions of measures and projects which, in addition to a textual description, also include cost and time estimates, risk assessment, assessment of quantifiable and non-quantifiable profits, assessment of rate of return together with assumption and consequences.

- Action plans (phase plans) showing recommended measures and projects on a time-scale (see example in Figure 13.2) with scheduled resource consumption (especially capital and staff). The action plans are often divided into three or four implementation phases, the first of which usually includes measures which must be implemented within six months ("quick fixes").

Figure 13.2: Example of an Implementation Plan

Project	1992	1993	1994	1995
Introduction of develop. method	▬			
Establishment of career plans	▬			
Stock control requirements	▬			
Establ. standard architecture req.	▬▬			
Stock control installation		▬▬		
Customer system installation			▬▬	
Ordering system conversion			▬▬	

The consultant can use both these techniques during the strategy and planning process. The general strategic analysis will only uncover very simple action plans including:

- "Quick fixes" with or without the use of technology

- Actions/activities for implementation of a full strategy and planning process.

It is important to keep the number of specific measures low by means of strict prioritisation and grouping. It is not the intention to document all minor tasks as measures in an action plan. If the number becomes too large, the result will often be that nothing or very little is actually implemented. In the strategy and planning process, twenty measures is a practical maximum — ten is considered "suitable". In a strategic analysis the number should be even lower.

Use of the Issues/Options List

Figure 13.3 shows an extract of a typical issues/options list. When consultants are engaged in the planning of measures they should concentrate on the right-hand side of the list, i.e. the *options*.

Figure 13.3: Use of Issues/Options List

Issues	Options/Strategies/Measures	
How can we exploit computerisation better to achieve lower prices, better service and more favourable delivery terms from our suppliers?	Expand the current purchasing system to give us an overview of supplier contracts.	*Possible*
	Link up with three-part supplier and goods database.	*Possible*
	Co-ordinate purchase of equipment for better exploitation of volume discounts.	*Adopted*

At this stage the project group will have examined and prioritised the options (using some of the techniques discussed in Chapter 8 on "Prioritisation of Goals, Issues and Options"), and these will also to some extent have been dealt with by the management group. Efforts will have been concentrated on options with the status of "recommended" and "adopted", since the prioritisation of issues and options in the strategic analysis will have removed those ideas which were not good enough or not realistic.

The formulation of options will depend on who writes them — the formulations in Figure 13.3 are "typical examples". Generally, options will fall into one of the following categories:

- Simple measures or decisions which do not involve a significant amount of work (for example, better follow-up on existing routines, purchasing of special equipment etc.)

- Changes in work, methods, manual routines which involve personnel development requirements

- Organisational changes

- Changes in management or control principles

- New or changed system solutions and ways of using information

- Changes in technology (software, system software, communication solutions, automation equipment, robots etc.).

The two latter categories appear directly in Figure 13.3. Categorisation of options is not always "cut and dried", however. "Co-ordination of purchasing" implies both organisational changes, changes in work tasks and new system solutions (for "collection" of orders). The purpose of identifying measures is to find out what the recommended solutions actually mean in the form of specific actions.

Formulation of Measures
Most measures can be seen in terms of a simplified "life cycle" with phases for:

- Planning

- Specification of requirements

- Evaluation of alternatives

- Acquisition/adaptation/development

- Implementation in (new parts of) the organisation

- Evaluation of effects

- Phasing out.

This division into phases can be used to describe all types of measures, including the purchase of industry-specific technology, in-house development of computer systems, purchasing of package solutions, use of tools and methods (e.g. development methods and project management methods), training, information distribution, organisational development etc.

An example will make the principles clearer. Suppose that the following option has been formulated:

> Use a robot to place a silver spoon blank in the mould in which the spoons are made.

If this option is adopted and implemented, this will involve a number of activities as follows:

- Preparation of a specification of requirements for the robot's range of movement, accuracy, programming, peripheral equipment etc.

- Evaluation of alternative robots on the market

- Visits to selected suppliers of robots plus some relevant robot installations

- Selection and possible borrowing/hiring/purchasing of a robot for test installation

- Installation of robot for testing in the co-operating partner's laboratory

- Development/adaptation of grippers, magazines for blanks etc.

- Demonstration of finished test installation in the laboratory — this is done by realistic simulation of production

- Installation at the company's own premises

- Adaptation/adjustment in the operating environment

- Formal acceptance test in real large-scale trial run.

In an action plan a number of these measures can be grouped together in projects. The above measures could, for example, be the main activities in the project description for the project "implementation of robot for spoon blank feeding", whereas the overall project definition is the only thing that appears in the action plans from the strategy work.

SUCCESS FACTORS

The Effect of the Strategy Work

The effect of any plan can be said to be a product of several factors — the quality of the plan, its acceptance in the organisation and the resources available for its implementation. Mediocre plans, limited acceptance and limited resources are unfortunately more the rule than the exception, and mostly result in poor returns. On the other hand, an excellent plan is useless if its implementation is not accepted by the organisation or if the necessary resources are not available.

The factors listed below are critical for the achievement of satisfactory quality, acceptance and use of resources — so they in turn will determine whether the planning work will be successful.

Motivation and Involvement of Management

"Management involvement" is a cliché to some extent, but is still relevant and critical. Motivation and involvement on the part of senior management is necessary for making ongoing decisions during the strategy work, gaining acceptance throughout the rest of the organisation and getting resources allocated for implementation.

The consultant must watch out for flagging motivation and involvement in the strategic analysis. If management is not "100 per cent behind the idea", the process should be stopped after the initial strategic analysis.

Good Organisation and Participation

Participation in the planning process is important for subsequent acceptance in the organisation. Gradual maturing through active participation is necessary. Successful planning processes do not happen in closed rooms.

In the strategic analysis, little importance has been attached to the process. The participants have generally been limited to a small number of people interviewed, and there have been brief discussions in the company's management group, but this has not been part of any formal project organisation. In addition, the strategic analysis is too short to promote any maturation in the organisation.

Even though acceptance through participation should be the goal in all consultancy assignments, there is still a clear limit to how many people can participate. This applies both to the direct, goal-oriented work and to the process as a whole. Having too many participants will often have a negative effect on goal-orientation and progress.

As described earlier, it is useful to divide the tasks between a control group (decision-making group) and a working group (executive group). This limits the number of people in each group and at the same time makes reasonable allowances for the need for participation. The use of reference contacts in specialist areas may also increase participation and result in better treatment of prioritised subjects.

Good organisation is critical for success. Classic errors are:

- Control groups that think their role is to receive information, not to make decisions. Sometimes this will be because the members of the control group are not at the appropriate decision-making level in the organisation. A control group for consultancy projects in SMEs should generally be run by the chief executive of the firm.

- Working groups with too many people and without proper management. Five or six people is a practical limit.

- Reference contacts are appointed on the basis of age and seniority, not on the basis of a critical assessment of their expected contribution. The working group's time is spent on "courtesy interviews".

Clear demands must be made on the participants in each group, both with regard to their effort (in terms of man-days), specific work distribution and responsibility for results. It is common for companies to promise too much participation by key personnel. The consultant must:

- Obtain binding promises of participation in the main project as part of the completion of the strategic analysis. It is necessary that this participation requirement is understood and accepted both by the chief executive and the persons committing themselves before the assignment is started.

- Follow up on significant deviations from the planned efforts which are threatening the success of the project.

The Right Competence Mix

The competence of the working group is also important for a successful result. Ideally, a combination of participants with professional competence in management, industry, important areas of activity and technology is needed, and the type of person with a strategic bent and the ability to "see the woods as well as the trees". In practice, this need must be met by including several people with different backgrounds.

The consultant's competence, experience and ability to act as a catalyst during the process is also decisive. All experience tells us that a company needs competent, external assistance to carry out a strategy process even though the issues and to a certain extent the options are generated by the company itself.

In addition to functioning as a process consultant, the consultant must master the techniques that are going to be used, and must have the ability to instruct others in their use. There are limits to the amount of effort the consultant can put into the strategy and planning process. The process will fail if they keep knowledge of the techniques to themselves.

Efficient Control of the Work

Strategic planning is difficult because it is about selecting routes on the basis of assumptions about a future, uncertain situation. At first, goals and scope are loosely defined, the options are many and there is a large, disorganised body of data. Even though the initial strategic analysis will have defined the scope and areas of focus, strict control of the scope is required because there is an obvious risk of the work "expanding".

Project managers in the planning process must above all have a professional approach to project management. This is considerably more important than whether the person is from a data processing environment, line management or has been brought in from the outside. Project management must not be awarded as a prize for long and faithful service!

In practice, the consultant will not have time to function as project manager. Often this is not desirable anyway, since in certain situations it may make the company distance itself from the project. However, the consultant must function as a "background figure" for the project manager and help them actively with the management and control of the work.

In comparison with many other projects, planning processes often require less initial planning effort and more effort in connection with ongoing adjustment of scope and focus, re-planning and strict prioritisation. This is because the scope is at first rather loosely defined, regardless of the quality of the conclusions after the strategic analysis.

So one of the control group's most important tasks is ongoing prioritisation of issues. This also includes the necessary downward prioritisation. One-sided prioritisation of new issues (continuous increase of scope) is a classic managerial error, both in planning work and in other types of project.

The scope and focus will change during the process. It is just as well to realise this at the beginning and establish mechanisms for handling changes in scope.

Well-defined, Flexible Methodology

The fact that the scope and focus are initially loosely defined means that a structuring procedure or method will be necessary if the planning process is to succeed. The material presented in this manual, along with the consultant's own techniques, should constitute the necessary basis. However, there are two important premises:

- Consultants must master the method. Especially before the first assignment, it is important that consultants familiarise themselves with the material on their own and in their own time, and decide what material they will want to use in the job.

- Consultants must "control themselves" and beware of trying to use all of the methodological material. It is not the intention that all the techniques presented in this handbook should be used in every assignment.

Efficient Use of Reference Contacts

The strategic analysis will have exposed important issue areas and quite a few central options. When these areas are to be examined further, additional information gathering will be necessary, even from people outside the working group. These people will have an advisory role in relation to the project. They will have no responsibility for results, but will have both a duty to give some of their time and a right to be asked.

So we must expect the strategy and planning process to include several interviews, discussion meetings and some collective work on ideas.

The reference contacts selected must be key personnel for bringing out issues and options. It is quite possible to hold dozens of interviews without getting any closer to focus areas or strategies. Generally, the maximum effect will be achieved as follows:

- Limit the number of reference contacts to those really in a position to add something substantial. (If you end up with more than ten people, start again!)

- Use structured interviews during the survey work, like the ones held during the initial general strategic analysis. Formulate the key questions on the basis of issues and options that have already been identified. Avoid situations where interviewees are direct "opponents" as regards the issues. Guarantee full anonymity to the sources of the individual points of view. Controversial issues come up in private, not in plenary sessions!

- Work on ideas collectively in working groups when you want to find solutions to problems. Avoid large groups and give the groups clear mandates. Emphasise that it is not the group's job to find scapegoats.

- Prepare the meetings thoroughly by laying down the agenda in advance and defining what is to be achieved during the meeting.

Be particularly aware of the transition from individual work to group work when going from the problem to the solution.

The above procedure will reveal critical issues very quickly. A brief, goal-oriented survey is achieved and the work then moves on to the creative generation of solutions.

Understanding Constraints

Important constraints are finances, existing technology, organisation and competence. These are factors which must be assessed and understood in the planning work in order to create realistic plans, i.e. "you must learn to crawl before you can walk". It is particularly important not to recommend advanced technology for which the company is not ready!

The key questions used in the strategic analysis address all the most important aspects of constraints. So both the consultant and the company should have a clear opinion about the level of ambition even before the assignment starts.

The relationship between financial constraints and project costs, and risk and benefit assessments, are dealt with in Chapter 15 on "Risk Factors and Risk Assessment".

Balance between a Systematic Approach and Creativity

Planning processes require a balance between systematic surveying and creative idea generation. A lack of balance usually results in a disproportionate amount of survey work. Surveying only serves its purpose if it directly reveals issues and options for bringing about improvements in the company. This requires clear targeting of the surveying work.

Disproportionate surveying is usually the result of inadequate project management and/or inadequate methodology. As a rule of thumb, survey work as such should not take more than one-third of the total process.

Balance between Short-term and Long-term Measures

It is easy to build "castles in Spain". The castles in Spain syndrome is in many ways the exact opposite of the "survey syndrome": a result is obtained which is full of creative ideas but has no roots in reality.

The castles-in-Spain syndrome is usually caused by:

- Inadequate analysis of issues, constraints and realistic possibilities on the basis of the present situation. This can take the form of inadequate survey work or too much survey work, in which the original purpose of the survey has been forgotten.

- Inadequate level of detail during the planning of measures. Measures must be specified, backed up with estimates and scheduled in order to form a basis for realistic plans.

- Inadequate screening of existing tasks. If resources are to be available for the implementation of new measures, and no new resources are added, other tasks must necessarily have a lower priority.

The time scale for strategic plans is usually five years, and two to three years for detailed measures. As a rule it is impossible to create motivation for something which will only happen in three-to-five years' time, unless it is directly linked with measures with a time scale of a few months. The balance between short-term and long-term measures is therefore critical. A goal-oriented analysis of the current situation results in quick prioritisation of issues. Make sure that the most important of these will be resolved within six months. This will show that the plan is being implemented and will also create long-term motivation.

Right Level of Detail for Strategies and Measures

Planning is only part of a cycle aimed at efficient goal-orientation. The completion of planning work is an important milestone which marks the beginning of the actual job. Strategies, project and measures must be implemented and followed up. Deadlines, use of resources and results achieved must be followed up and assessed against the plan. The cycle is completed when this comparison results in corrective measures and the plan is updated.

At best, plans which are not realised represent wasted work. The actual implementation of the plan requires a level of detail that can be used in making decisions and controlling implementation. This in turn requires specific, scheduled, prioritised measures with clear allocations of responsibility based on the estimated use of resources and cost-benefit assessment.

It is too easy to agree on vague "principles and goals". The actual decisions are made when specific actions are to be undertaken and others are consequently assigned a lower priority. A strategy without an action plan has a minimal effect, because resources will not be made available for implementation of the strategies.

Efficient Communication of Results

Strategies and plans must be read, understood, remembered and implemented at all levels of the organisation. Voluminous, densely written, detailed reports are devastating obstacles to efficient communication.

Final documentation must be concise, brief and conclusion-oriented. A strategy process results in a great deal of information. Keep the detailed information outside the final report. Only information which is crucial for the understanding of the conclusions — and even then only in easily grasped form, preferably using graphs/illustrations — should be included. Suggested contents and structure of a report are presented in Chapter 12 on "Establishing Strategies and Action Plans".

The plan will need to be "marketed" within the organisation. Active "promotion" is important for acceptance. Start from the top and work your way down, and let line managers keep a large proportion of the responsibility for the "marketing" work within their own organisational units.

It is difficult to create motivation afterwards, regardless of the quality of the plan, unless the people affected have had a reason to participate along the way. So activities connected with the promotion of the plan should be an integrated part of the progress plan for the process.

Strategic Plans Require Regular Updating

It is utopian to believe that the plan will remain unchanged throughout the entire planning period. It is therefore absolutely essential that the strategy and implementation are adjusted at regular intervals. This adjustment is in itself a "miniature" strategy process and must be part of company management's natural area of responsibility.

The consultant should help to create a long-term planning "ambience" in the company. This is impossible unless the consultant actively trains key personnel in the company in the methodology used.

In addition to this, the action plans themselves should always include updating of the technology plan. Annual revisions prior to budgeting are sensible.

Conclusion

The strategy and planning process is difficult, both for the company and the consultant. Understanding of the critical success factors will help the consultant to avoid the pitfalls described above.

If the strategic plan is to be implemented, the company must understand and accept the process of change that is about to take place. However, there are examples of unsuccessful implementation even though management has been involved in the process and results have been communicated to others involved. So it may be necessary to assist the company with knowledge and experience of change management for a while in order to ensure that the necessary "non-technical" development takes place.

14

ASSESSMENT OF OPTIONS USING COST/BENEFIT ANALYSIS

INTRODUCTION

Cost/benefit analyses play an important role in a company's general planning process. The work on the strategic analysis and the strategy and planning process itself will identify various measures which will have to be implemented in order to realise the company's general goals and strategies. The cost/benefit analyses are used at three levels in the process (as illustrated in Figure 14.1):

- **In prioritising options**, before the options with the highest priorities are assigned the status of strategies and measures. The cost-benefit analysis here helps to screen the options, so that the least profitable alternatives are "filtered out". The prioritisation of options is part of both the general strategic analysis and the later, more detailed strategy and planning process. During the general strategic analysis the focus will be on the most obvious options, and from then on future work will be structured on the basis of these options. During the strategy and planning process, a number of new options will appear in the course of further analysis of various business requirements, assessment of alternative technologies and analysis of internal and external factors and constraints.

- **In the prioritisation of alternative measures and projects.** The cost/benefit analysis fits in here after identification of possible specific measures. Generally, this will take place after goals and strategies have been established at the top level.

- **In the prioritisation of implementation alternatives** for specific measures or projects. Typically a project can be implemented in several ways, and a number of different proposals for performing the tasks will normally be made. So for each of the projects it is necessary to carry out cost/benefit analyses for each alternative solution before giving the final go-ahead for implementation or, if relevant, stopping the investment. Thus, this type of cost/benefit analysis forms part of the implementation of measures.

Figure 14.1: Levels of Cost/Benefit Assessment

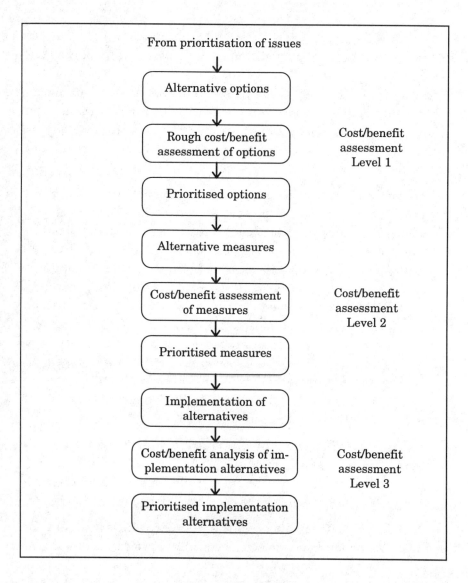

The material in this chapter is presented under the following headings:

- Rough Cost/Benefit Analysis

- Quantification of Benefits

- Detailed Time and Cost Estimates

- Investment and Liquidity Analysis.

ROUGH COST/BENEFIT ANALYSIS

Rough Cost/Benefit Assessment in the Prioritisation of Options

Criteria for prioritisation of options can be both *qualitative* and *quantitative*. A rough cost/benefit assessment can thus be described as a *quantitative* assessment of the most promising options after an overall assessment has been made.

We should first recall the prioritisation process as described in Chapter 7 on "Prioritisation of Goals, Issues and Options":

- Identification and evaluation of criteria for prioritisation of *issues*

- Prioritisation of *issues* on the basis of the selected prioritisation criteria

- Identification and evaluation of criteria for prioritisation of *options*

- Prioritisation of all selected/interesting *options*.

Rough cost/benefit analysis is carried out to assist with the last step above. At this point the remaining options will have the status of "recommended" or "interesting". "Rejected" options will have been removed, and "adopted" options are normally used without further prioritisation.

In the overall assessment of options, priorities will have been allocated on the basis of statements like "we believe this option will contribute significantly/minimally to an increase in earnings", or "we believe this option involves low/medium/high costs".

The prioritisation and status given to the options reflect this assessment.

As for options with the status "recommended" or "interesting", we will verify these claims on the basis of a rough quantitative assessment with benefits and costs calculated in monetary terms.

Remember that at this stage we are not at the level where measures are implemented — we are only looking at options, so we do not have sufficient information to calculate these values precisely.

We are interested in rough estimates, so we can further reduce the number of options. Options that are obviously among the least profitable need to be "screened out", and we must ensure that what we proceed with stands a good chance of being profitable.

Procedure

The procedure is best illustrated by way of an example. The prioritising matrix shown in Figure 14.2 illustrates a suitable example accordingly.

The company BUNT VVS and Contractor has established that, among other things, increased earnings, a better company profile, an improved working environment and simple/quick implementation are important prioritisation criteria. "Reduced costs" have been given medium priority, probably because the company believes it is already reasonably efficient such that this is not where the primary profits are to come from. "Low complexity" and "established technology" have been given low priorities. This could mean that the company believes its competence is high in both technology and project implementation, and that these factors will not have much significance in prioritisation.

The figure shows a single option, namely potential integration of CAD systems for product design with a goods/product registration structure and production control. This option has been given medium priority in terms of the criteria "reduced costs" and "established technology" and the lowest value for two others.

The figure does not show the numerical result, but compared to other alternatives this result is obviously so good that the option has been given the provisional status of "interesting". Options with the status of "interesting" or "recommended" are candidates for rough cost/benefit assessment.

Figure 14.2: Prioritising Matrix for Options

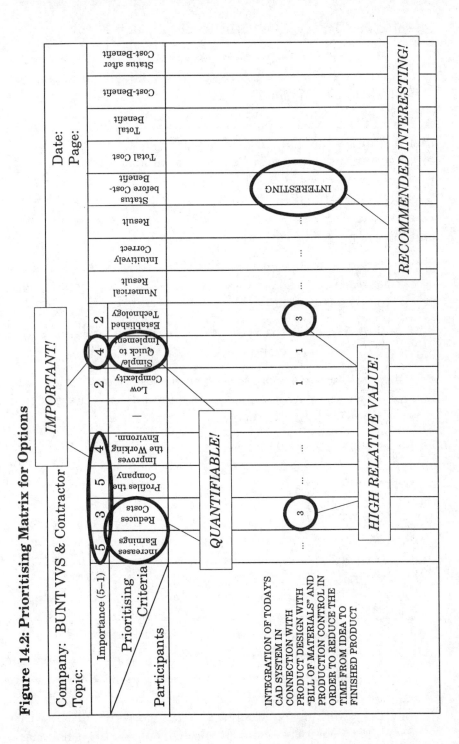

The procedure for rough cost/benefit assessment is as follows:

> **Step 1:** For each subject in the options list, select the prioritisation criteria which are important and quantifiable in terms of financial profit or loss.

"Important" should mean a priority of at least 3. It can be seen from the figure that "profiles the company" and "improves working environment" are not considered quantifiable. Instead we will use the criteria "increases earnings", "reduces costs", and "simple/quick to implement" as the basis for rough cost/benefit assessment. The first two criteria are related to the benefit side and the last one to the cost side.

> **Step 2:** For each subject in the options list, select only the options that have the status of "interesting" or "recommended".

This is simple to do in the present case, since the potential CAD system is the only option and has the status of "interesting".

> **Step 3:** For each option selected, choose the criteria that have a high relative value (in relation to the value assignment for this option in general).

As far as the CAD system is concerned, it can be seen that this option gets a "medium score" for "reduced costs" and "established technology". However, "established technology" is not included in the list from Step 1, so is ignored. Against this background, it is evident that the potential CAD system should be quantitatively assessed for its benefit on the basis of reduced costs alone, and that the benefit must be considered in relation to the implementation costs.

Step 3 may mean that no criteria are fulfilled. If this is so, then the process is stopped on the basis that it is not possible to make a sensible cost/benefit assessment. This means that either:

- The option is "interesting", but only from a qualitative point of view. This would be the case if, for example, the CAD system had not been given points for "reduces costs" but only for "improves working environment". This does not necessarily mean that the option should be rejected, only that it is not easy to assess the cost/benefit aspect. "Improves working environment" is, of course, important in its own right. Or,

* The option should have been "rejected" in the first part of the overall assessment, but was (erroneously) given the status "interesting". This is the case if the option cannot be defended, either on a cost/benefit basis or by means of purely qualitative assessments. If, for example, the CAD system had not been given points for "reduces costs", and a value of 2 or lower for "improves working environment", it is likely that the option should have been rejected. Generally speaking, one must always be wary of options which pass Step 2 but not Step 3.

Steps 1 to 3 can be performed fairly automatically. Steps 4 and 5 are more difficult:

> **Step 4:** For each of the remaining benefit criteria from Step 3, we should assess how the fulfilment of these criteria would affect the company's accounting figures and financial key ratios.

The comparison with the company's accounts and key ratios is important because it facilitates simple quantification of benefit. We therefore want to know what the general description "reduced costs" means in reality as far as the CAD system is concerned. This requires experience. We must understand which cost elements are affected by integration of CAD with the other systems.

In this example, let us assume that the consultant has experience of previous CAD investments and a matter-of-fact attitude to cost reduction. The consultant estimates that the five staff of the product development department spend ten man-days a month on manual handling of data to and from the goods register and production system. The consultant believes there could be savings of 10 per cent here because one of the staff works at hourly rates. The saving is therefore considered realistic. Ten per cent is estimated to amount to about ECU 250,000 a year. As far as the consultant can see, no other cost-reducing factors would be affected significantly.

Step 5: Calculate the company's "net profit period" (the company's usual payback period minus the estimated time before the option becomes profitable). This is multiplied by the estimated annual benefit and results in the *aggregate benefit of the investment*. (For the time being, internal interest requirements, inflation and other complicated aspects are to be disregarded).

Insert *aggregate benefit* (in money terms) into the table in Figure 14.2 (in the "Total benefit" column).

In this example, let us assume that the company BUNT VVS and Contractor operates with a standard payback period of five years. The consultant believes it will take at least one year before the change becomes effective in terms of reduced staff costs. Being careful, the consultant therefore estimates the "total benefit" to be ECU 750,000 over the five-year period, on the assumption that the effect will not appear until the beginning of the third year.

Step 6: Calculate the aggregate cost of the investment in the same period as in Step 5. You must also make the necessary allowance for other prioritisation criteria involving costs in the options matrix, regardless of priority/weight. Insert aggregate costs (in money terms) in the table in Figure 14.2 ("Total cost" column).

The consultant sees that the CAD investment gets a "low score" on "easy/fast implementation" and takes this into consideration by estimating the implementation time at more than one year. At this stage the cost estimate must be based on experience. The consultant had a similar problem in a previous job, and on that basis estimates the investment costs at ECU 200,000. In the absence of more exact calculations, the annual operating costs are estimated to be 10 per cent of the initial investment cost. Total investment over five years will therefore amount to ECU 300,000.

Step 7: Calculate the cost/benefit ratio in the prioritisation matrix, and assess the consequences for the status given to the option.

In the above example the cost/benefit ratio is 2.5 to 1, and the investment therefore appears to be profitable.

Companies will often find that the process of assessing the benefit (especially Steps 4 and 5) will in itself raise awareness of the costs involved in a given option. Prioritisation criteria may be affected as a result and may have to be re-assessed during the process accordingly.

QUANTIFICATION OF BENEFITS

The above procedure describes a very simple method for rough cost/benefit assessments. However, this procedure does not provide a sure estimate and should only lead to confident conclusions when the investments concerned are either clearly unprofitable or very profitable. If the result is "borderline", a more detailed cost/benefit assessment will be required as described below.

In order to carry out a profitability analysis of an investment, we must have some idea of the yield/cash inflow of an investment and its costs/cash outflow. This is not a matter of calculations based on sophisticated methods, but of making estimates — expressed in money terms — in which one can have confidence, given the available data.

In the previous section we made some very simple, rough estimates for both the cost and benefit aspect, primarily in order to exclude options that are obviously among the least profitable.

Here benefit appraisal is taken a step further. This level of detail is primarily used midway through a prioritisation process where we successively consider alternative options, alternative measures and alternative methods of implementation.

The procedure is to first estimate what the total benefit of a project or investment must be to make it profitable. On the basis of this estimate we must systematically assess whether and to what extent possible benefit factors are relevant to the investment. This involves an initial verbal description as the basis for a quantitative analysis.

It is also recommended that the quantification should be done with the aid of the financial key ratio calculations in the strategic analysis. This means that benefit analysis will be done at an overall level, and we can assess how the investment or measure will contribute to the general financial development of the company.

What are Benefits?

"Benefits" are what we call the potential contribution of investments to the improvement of the company's financial position. When the benefits are quantified they will constitute the earnings side of the profitability analysis.

As illustrated in Figure 14.3, the sum of benefits must exceed the sum of costs if the investment is to be profitable. If an existing solution is replaced by a new one, it may be more appropriate to measure the new solution's added cost against the benefits of the investment — for example, in the form of new earning potential and direct cost savings.

Figure 14.3: Benefits Must Exceed Costs

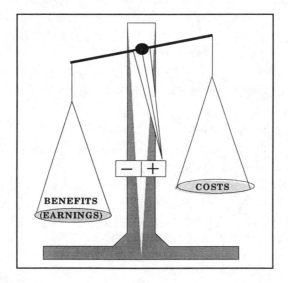

Procedure for Quantifying Benefit

The following procedure is suggested for quantifying the benefit of a project or investment (NB: a project is also an investment):

1. First estimate the total benefit that must be generated annually if the investment is to be financially profitable. This estimate is done on the basis of requirements as regards either the internal rate of return or the payback period of the investment.

2. Then go through the list of potential benefits and assess which will be relevant to this investment. You can supplement the list with your own ideas.

3. Then systematically go through the benefit factors you have thus singled out for quantification. Each of the benefits must be quantified. This can done on the basis of key ratio analysis so as to make the assessments more realistic. In addition, such a procedure may make it easier to focus on the overall goals of investment — for instance, winning a market advantage. For example:

   Supposing a company invests in a CAD/CAM system to adapt part of its production capacity (let us say one-third) to production of customised solutions. The price of customisation is assumed to be substantially above that of the standard products — of the order of 8 per cent. Current turnover is ECU 15 million (key figure). The benefit in the form of "market impact" is therefore set at ECU 0.4 million a year (15 x .33 x 0.08), assuming that material consumption, changeover costs etc. remain constant.

4. Calculate the sum of the benefit factors which have now been quantified. If the investment is to be profitable, this sum must be at least as much as the total benefit requirement calculated to begin with.

Calculating Annual Benefit

By "annual benefit" we mean the annual value the benefit must have to satisfy the company's requirements as regards the profitability of new investments.

Several methods are used to calculate annual benefit. We will look at two alternatives here:

- **The payback method**. Profitability requirements are formulated as a requirement for the number of years it will take for the investment to "pay for itself" (payback period). The formula is shown in Figure 14.4.

Figure 14.4: The Payback Method

Calculation of Annual Benefit
Payback Method

$$B \quad = \quad C \quad + \quad \frac{U}{N}$$

Where:
B = Annual benefit required for the investment
C = Annual operating costs
U = Amount invested (one-off cost)
N = Payback period required (no. of years)

- **The internal rate of return method.** The profitability re-quirement is formulated in terms of the investment's internal rate of return. The formula is shown in Figure 14.5.

Figure 14.5: Internal Rate of Return Method

Calculation of Annual Benefit
Internal Rate of Return

$$B \quad = \quad C \quad + \quad \frac{U}{Y} + (U \times r) \times \tfrac{1}{2}$$

Where:
B = Annual benefit required for the investment
C = Annual operating costs
U = Amount invested (one-off cost)
Y = Financial lifetime of investment (years)
r = Internal rate of return required

As the formulae show, we need the following data in addition to the profitability requirements:

- The initial amount invested

- Financial lifetime of the investment

- Operating costs arising out of the investment.

These methods of calculation are based on a number of simplifi-cations, including the following:

- Earnings and costs are equated with cash inflow and outflow

- With the payback method (Figure 14.4) we disregard interest costs

- Profit inflow is assumed to remain constant over the lifetime of the investment

- Inflation and price rises have been disregarded.

Types of Benefits

An investment made by a company should not be regarded as an end in itself, but as a means of achieving other ends. The goals to be achieved through investment can be many: cost reductions, new products and services, better control, new organisational structures, quicker caseworking, better working environment, better customer service, etc. These factors can in turn be elements in a general strategy for improving the financial situation of the company. In reality we are dealing with a hierarchy of goals.

Benefits can be of different types as listed below:

Strategic/Market Benefits

By strategic and market benefits we mean benefits in the form of increased earnings due to investment in market-oriented activities. Examples of such investments and related benefits are:

- Investments made such that the company gains a new image

- Investments made so as to distinguish the company from its competitors

- Investments in new products

- Investment in customer service systems to achieve a competitive advantage

- Investment in information systems to give improved information on competitors, markets and products

- Investments in communications with the customer to influence the customer's attitude to the company.

Control Benefits

By control benefits we mean benefits in the form of better deci-sion-making. Control benefits are quite crucial if it is a matter of starting to use computerisation. Examples of such investments and related benefits are:

- Better future capacity utilisation through investment in plan-ning and forecasting systems

- Higher capital turnover and less tied capital through invest-ments in stock control systems

- Shorter lead times and more reliable observance of delivery schedules through investment in systems for processing cus-tomer orders and production orders

Rationalisation Benefits

The benefits will mainly be a matter of getting jobs done with less personnel input. Other arguments we can cite are that jobs can be done quicker and with fewer errors. The typical example is the automation of manual routines. Examples of such investments and related benefits are:

- Reduced personnel costs due to automation of routines for-merly performed manually

- Increased production with continuous "staffing" due to auto-mation

- Less rejects and complaints due to the transition to mecha-nised tools and robots

- Better working environment due to the transition to the use of robots and automation in environmentally hazardous and health-hazardous areas of production.

Example — Calculation of Benefit

Here is an example of how to calculate the benefit associated with investing in a computer software for order processing, stock con-trol and invoicing.

Some key figures and ratios for the company in question are given in the table in Figure 14.6. The company carries out both serial and unit production.

The total investment is estimated to be ECU 490,000. This includes a user licence fee of ECU 180,000 and costs of ECU 310,000 incurred for modifications to the standard software package.

Figure 14.6: Key Financial Data and Ratios

Key Figures (Extract) (amounts in ECU '000)	
Operating Earnings	
1. Sales	60,000
2. Direct Costs (payroll + material.)	35,000
3. Contribution margin	25,000
4. Fixed manuf. costs payable	5,000
5. Fixed sales costs	5,000
6. Earn. before depr. and fin. costs	15,000
7. Ordinary depreciation	5,000
8. Earnings before fin. costs	10,000
9. Net financial costs	6,000
10. Earnings after fin. costs	4,000
Balance sheet / Capital fig.	
11. Accounts receivable	10,000
12. Raw material stocks	5,000
13. Work in progress	5,000
14. Finish goods stock	5,000
Tied Capital Periods	
15. Accounts receivable	60 days
16. Raw materials storage time	90 days
17. Production time	45 days
18. Finish. goods storage period	45 days
Other Key Issues	
19. Average order size	100
20. Number of customers	600

Operating Costs

Operating costs are assumed to amount to 10 per cent of the once-off investment — i.e. ECU 490,000 × 10 per cent = ECU 49,000. The make-up of operating costs is described in detail later on.

Profitability Requirements

For illustrative purposes, profitability is assessed here on the basis of both the internal rate of return requirement and payback period assuming a payback requirement of three years and an internal rate of return requirement of 10 per cent (low, because inflation is disregard). The financial lifetime of the investment is assumed to be five years.

Value of Total Annual Benefit

Using the formulae given in Figures 14.4 and 14.5, the total annual benefit required works out to be as follows:

Payback Method:

$$B = 49,000 + \frac{490,000}{3} = 212,000$$

Internal Rate of Return Method:

$$B = 49,000 + \frac{490,000}{5} + (490,000 \times 0.10) \times \frac{1}{2} = 171,500$$

The annual benefit value requirement will be about ECU 171,000 on the basis of the internal rate of return criterion, and about ECU 212,000 according to the payback method. If the payback period requirement was four years, the two methods would give the same result — ECU 171,000 — given that all other assumptions remained constant.

Quantification of Different Types of Benefit

The problem with the following is the systematic identification of relevant factors that will result in benefits and therefore should be quantified. As mentioned above, key ratio analysis is a good aid to quantification.

The sum of the quantified benefit must be at least as much as the benefit requirement. In this example we have calculated that the annual benefit requirement will be of the order of ECU 171,000 – 212,000.

Quantification of Strategic / Market Benefits

The order processing and invoicing components of the system will be active in the interface between the company and the customer. We have a strong conviction that the system will improve the level of service and the customer's confidence in the company. Among other things, the company receives a number of complaints over incorrect invoices, late deliveries, incorrect labelling of consignments and unnecessary out-of-stock notes. The last problem is due to inadequate updating of information on stock levels, so the company is sending out-of-stock notes when the goods are in fact in stock!

It is difficult to quantify the effect of better service and more customer confidence, but to exemplify the issue we can cite two factors in benefit quantification, i.e.:

- Increased sales due to better information given to customers at the actual time of the sale

- Increased sales due to less customer "turnover".

The staff who process the orders and who are in direct contact with the customer say that they are losing a number of orders because they are unable to give fast, reliable enough information on whether the goods are in stock — and if they are not, when delivery can be effected. The customer then contacts other suppliers to place their order.

After a discussion with the sales staff, we estimate that the company is losing an average of ten orders a year because of this. If we assume that the lost contribution margin can be regained by investing in the new system, we can quantify the benefit as follows:

Quantification of Benefit No. 1 — Increased contribution margin: 42 per cent (contribution ratio) of ten orders @ ECU 50,000: ECU 210,000.

From the key figures we can see that the company has 600 customers. Calculations show that the company loses an average of 60 customers a year, and gains the same number. Once more we discuss this with the sales and marketing staff, and arrive at the conclusion that one-tenth — six customers — of those they lose every year go over to the competition because of direct dissatisfaction with the firm's invoicing and stock control routines etc. If we assume that their ability to win new customers remains constant, the above-mentioned improvement will make an average contribution as follows:

Quantification of Benefit No. 2 — Increased contribution margin: 42 per cent (contribution ratio) of average turnover (ECU 100,000) for six customers: ECU 252,000.

Quantification of Rationalisation and Control Benefits
An investment in a new system for order processing, stock control and invoicing has clear control and rationalisation benefits. We will attach most importance to these benefits in the case of this investment.

The control benefits in particular are interesting. Quantification is related to the savings on interest costs due to less tying-up of capital.

Figure 14.7 shows the general development of accrued tied capital throughout the lifetime of the products. As is evident from the figure, the potential for improvement is considered to lie in finished goods stocks and accounts receivable.

Because of better stock control we think it is realistic to reduce finished goods stocks substantially. At present the average stocking period is 45 days. After reviewing the factors that cause this we think that it is possible to reduce this period by ten days by means of better control. This gives us ECU 1.1 million less in tied capital. So we note:

Figure 14.7: Tied Capital

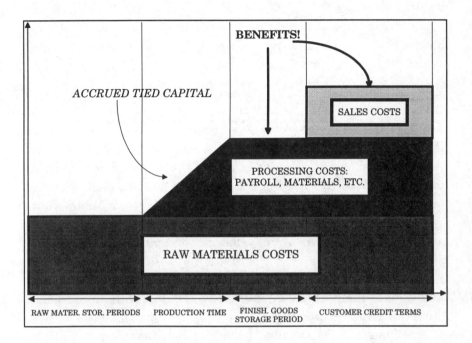

Quantification of Benefit No. 3 — Savings on interest costs (15 per cent p.a.) because less capital is tied up in stocks: ECU 1.1 mill × 0.15 = ECU 165,000.

The new invoicing system means quicker invoicing and better follow-up on uninvoiced amounts. We estimate the improvement in invoicing time as one week. We also think that the period when capital is tied up can be reduced by a further week because of better administration of accounts receivable (using reminder routines, for example). At present customer receivables amount to ECU 10 million. A reduction of two weeks in the period when capital is tied up here releases ECU 2.4 million.

Quantification of Benefit No. 4 — Savings on interest costs (15 per cent p.a.) because less capital is tied up in customer receivables: ECU 2.4 million × 0.15 = ECU 360,000.

Summary of the Example

The sum of the values of Benefits 3 and 4 — perhaps the most reliable ones — is ECU 525,000. For purposes of comparison, we calculated an initial benefit value of ECU 171,000 – ECU 212,000 on the basis of profitability requirements. In other words, the investment is clearly profitable. If we also include Benefit 1 and 2 the total value of benefits will be ECU 987,000.

DETAILED TIME AND COST ESTIMATES

In the previous section we did rough cost estimates for both investment and operating costs as part of the calculation exercise in connection with the quantifications. So when we deal with detailed cost estimation in the following, we are in other words talking about drawing up cost estimates for projects and investment ideas that have already passed several preliminary tests along the way.

In general, it is only relevant to draw up detailed cost estimates for options which we are very likely to decide to realise in the form of specific measures.

The result of the detailed time and cost estimates should be used in the investment analysis.

General Points about Costs

In business economics costs are usually defined as resource consumption (goods and services) expressed in monetary terms. Defined this way, costs are different from expenditure, which is the same as payment obligations; and costs should also properly be distinguished from payments, which make up the specific outflow from the company cash holdings or bank accounts.

In this section we will not operate explicitly with the above definitions. Given the uncertainties inherent in analyses like these, costs, expenditure and payments will stand for the same thing. As will be evident from the discussion on "Investment and Liquidity Analysis" later in this chapter, the calculations in the investment analysis will be based on cash inflow and outflow.

How to Group Costs

Costs can be classified according to where in the "life cycle" of an investment they are incurred. This is illustrated in Figure 14.8, which shows accrued costs in two different periods:

- The investment period

- The operating period.

During the investment period, there will normally be no generation of income, only costs.

The operating period follows immediately after the investment period. The operating period is characterised by the fact that income must be created which will cover both the operating costs which now accrue, and the capital costs which are calculated on the basis of the accrued costs from the investment period.

Figure 14.8: Investment and Operating Costs

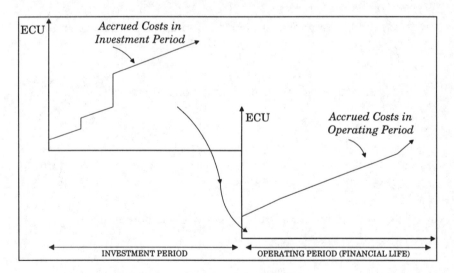

Costs can also be grouped another way:

- One-off costs

- Running costs.

In cost estimates for many investments it will be appropriate to work with a group of costs that are a combination of one-off costs and running costs:

- Periodical maintenance and modernisation costs.

These types of costs are easy to overlook in the original profitability estimates. But, almost without exception, there will be upgrading and ongoing development costs before the financial life of the investment is over.

We should base cost estimates on the following:

- During the investment period, both one-off costs and running costs will accrue. This is illustrated in Figure 14.8 by the fact that the curve for accrued costs takes a number of "upward leaps" when one-off costs fall due. Otherwise the curve rises evenly as the running costs accrue. When the investment and project period is over, the total accrued costs will be treated as "one-off costs" which will form the basis for capital costs throughout the operating period (indicated by an arrow in Figure 14.8).

- During the operating period, we will assume that running costs, and upgrading and ongoing development costs, will accrue.

Figure 14.9 shows the relationship between the cost concepts introduced above. The shaded areas in Figure 14.9 show the main areas covered by cost estimates.

Figure 14.9: Relationship between Cost Concepts

	One-Off Costs	Running Costs	Upgrading Costs
Investment Period	▓	▓	
Operating Period		▓	▓

One-off Costs

The distinction between one-off costs and running costs must not be taken too literally — it is first and foremost an aid in the estimation work. After the project or investment period is over, all costs which have accrued in the meantime will normally be regarded as one-off costs. This is logical, inasmuch as a project as such is defined as a one-off operation meant to deal with a task.

Typical one-off costs for investment projects are costs related to:

- Plant/buildings

- Machinery/equipment

- Control systems/software

- Adaptation/modification

- Development work in general

- Initial training.

Running Costs

Running costs can be related to the use or consumption of particular resources (such as electricity and consumables, for example), or they can be purely time-dependent (for example, rental costs depending on the rental period). Payroll costs are also normally time-dependent. The characteristic feature of running costs is that they can be estimated by the year, the month or whatever time unit one wishes. In most analyses it is appropriate to operate with years as the time interval.

When an investment requires a development period before it can be exploited commercially, current costs can make up a substantial proportion of the investment costs. This is a factor that is often underestimated, and can make the basis of the investment analysis and profitability estimates unrealistic.

Typical running costs for investment projects are costs related to:

- Technical maintenance

- All operating costs

- All consumption of materials, accessories etc.

- Ongoing training.

Upgrading and Ongoing Development Costs

The costs of upgrading and ongoing development will normally accrue at regular intervals — every 2-4 years — in the course of the financial lifetime of the investment. Upgrading and ongoing development can also prolong the financial lifetime of the investment.

To decide what kind of ongoing development costs should be included in the cost estimate, one must use one's judgement. If ongoing development costs are very extensive, it may in reality be a matter of a new investment, and should in that case be treated as such.

The costs that should be included in the estimate must in other words be foreseeable. This means that when we make the estimate we have an idea of the total development of costs as in the graph in Figure 14.10. Unlike the total cost curve in Figure 14.8, this curve takes a leap to a new level every time upgrading and ongoing development costs accrue.

Figure 14.10: Cost Development during the Operating Period

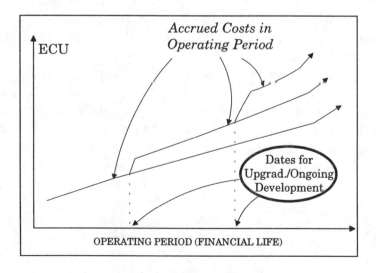

OPERATING PERIOD (FINANCIAL LIFE)

Typical upgrading and ongoing development costs are costs related to:

- Various kinds of capacity expansion

- Establishment of new capacity

- Replacement with more modern technology

- New versions of software.

Tips for Working with Cost Estimates

The work involved in estimating costs should begin with a review of the company's financial or costing situation to see whether key ratios or "rules of thumb" can be worked out that will be useful as estimates are being prepared. The following questions can be asked so as to establish "rules of thumb":

- Can current accounting figures for the relationship between operating costs and fixed/current assets be used in the estimate? For example, if the company traditionally has operating costs of 7 per cent of its investment in fixed assets, can this percentage be applied to new investments?

- How long has the time between initial investment in technical equipment, etc. and the start of operations been in the past? During this time, one knows that costs in the form of payroll costs etc. will accrue — it is a matter of expressing these costs as figures.

- Presumably the company has previously drawn up cost estimates for investments. If there has been no formal pre- and post-costing, there should at least be some figures based on experience to build on. Has the company previously been too optimistic or pessimistic? Lessons can be drawn from this and certain safety margins can be included.

- If it is a matter of purchasing new equipment that has to be installed, it will be useful to get the supplier's views of costs — also of those for which he is not responsible.

- Very often there are other companies that have been through the same process. They may be prepared to share their positive and negative experiences.

Time Estimates

Time estimates refers to the appraisal of what resources various activities will require expressed in time, i.e. the number of man-days, man-weeks, man-years etc.

These time estimates form the basis for cost estimates as given by the formula in Figure 14.11, being the number of man-weeks multiplied by the price per man-week. Resource requirements expressed in time must not be confused with implementation time — that is, the calendar time over which the project or investment will last. Implementation time depends on the number of people assigned to the job. If the number of people is doubled, the implementation time is halved.

Figure 14.11: Estimates of the Cost of Time

$$\text{Cost Estimate} = T \times P$$

Where:
T = estimated time (man-weeks, man-years, etc.)
P = price of T

Many cost elements are largely dependent on time consumption, such as the cost of a company's own employees, the cost of consultants and training costs. Thus, a significant part of the work of preparing cost estimates can be done by estimating the number of days and months an activity is likely to take. In general, estimates should be based on average figures:

- Time estimates should be done in terms of the number of man-days or man-weeks per job or per phase. The sum of the amounts that such sub-tasks cost should be subjected to a reasonability assessment. For example, after totalling the time estimates for several sub-activities one should ask "Does this seem intuitively reasonable, given the size of the company, the benefit of the measure, etc.?"

- In establishing prices of time units one should avoid too much differentiation among staff groups. In most cases one price (an average) is enough for one's own staff. This means, for example, that a man-week is costed at the same rate irrespective of the type of personnel involved in the job.

- One should "round up or down" appropriately in the estimation work. For example, if a smallish job requires non-continuous effort over several weeks, it will be reasonable to round the figure up to include a margin for "start-up time".

Finally, an important consideration is that the longer the time span in an analysis, the greater is the uncertainty/risk. It is reasonable, therefore, that high uncertainty/risk levels be taken into consideration in the cost estimates in the form of a specified margin of risk.

Example of a Detailed Cost Estimate

An engineering company markets and sells agricultural machinery which it designs and sells itself. The company has 80 employees, 3 of whom work with design, 7 with administration and 70 in production.

The company has two digitally-controlled machine tools. Administrative routines, including material control routines, are "run" on an IBM System 36. The company has decided to purchase a CAD system and it is this investment that is the subject of the following cost estimate

Pilot Project

The basis for the decision to buy a CAD system was a completed pilot project. In the pilot project the company's own designers had worked with an outside consultant to assess the benefits a CAD system would bring, the main requirements the system would have to fulfil, and the profitability of the investment. These were rough estimates and calculations — but accurate enough for management to feel that the investment would be a wise one.

In the context of this manual, we would say that the idea of investing in the CAD system is in the process of being detailed into measures to be implemented. Some of the requirements specified for the system are listed below:

- A drawing tool allowing three-dimensional visualising with additional modules

- An open interface to the digitally-controlled machine tools and to the IBM system

- Document handling facilities (desktop publishing)

- Two workstations, one for the regular use of the system manager (engineer) and one to be shared by a draughtsman and the design manager

- A communications link between the two CAD terminals.

On the basis of the above requirements, quotes were invited from relevant suppliers. The average prices quoted are listed in Figure 14.12.

Figure 14.12: Summary of Quotes Received

Quote for Hardware and Software	
	ECU
Workstation #1:	
Hardware	230,000
Software	150,000
Workstation #2:	
Hardware	160,000
Software	50,000
Cables for Network, etc.	10,000
Pen Plotter, A1	50,000
Matrix Printer	5,000
Total	655,000

Assumptions Used for Preparation of Estimate

A small working group had the job of drawing up proposed estimates for the other costs. This group used reference installations in other companies as well as advice from a consultant to help with the work. A summary of the cost estimates thus arrived at is given in Figure 14.13. These estimates are used to fill out a standard cost estimating form as illustrated in Figure 14.14.

The following assumptions have been used:

- Cost of the company's own staff: ECU 3,840 a day (ECU 400 an hour, eight-hour day, 20 per cent national insurance costs etc.)

- Cost of consultancy assistance: ECU 4,400 a day (ECU 550 an hour, eight-hour day).

Figure 14.13: Working Group Estimates

Summary of Time and Cost Estimates (in ECU)	
Training and Start-Up:	
3 basic courses, 5 days on the CAD system	92,500
2 basic courses, 3 days on the operating system	42,000
10 days consultancy at 4,400 per day	44,000
System mgt.: 22 days at 3,480 per day	76,560
New Inventory Services:	
Ergonomic desk	5,000
New partitioning	5,000
Indirect lighting	2,000
New power points	3,000
Fireproof safe	10,000
Annual Running Costs:	
Service contract on hardware & software	45,000
Materials: paper, pens, etc.	10,000
Insurance	4,000
System mgt.: 1½ days/week	
Upgrading Costs:	
Courses/seminars: to be attended every 2 yrs	

We choose to distribute the first section of Figure 14.13, Training and Start-up, over Lines 4, 5 and 6 of the cost estimate form (Figure 14.14) on the basis of the following calculations:

- The basic courses in the CAD system and the operating system cost ECU 1,000 per participant per day. The basic course in the CAD system is to be taken by three of the company staff, the operating system course by two. This gives us total course costs of ECU 51,000 (three persons for 15 days plus two persons for

3 days). In addition the estimate must include the cost of the employees' lost normal working time, ECU 195,840 (51 man-days @ ECU 3,840). Alternatively, we could include this cost in Line 4 of the estimate form, but we choose to regard it as part of the training costs. So we itemise a total of ECU 246,840 as "initial training" (Line 6 of the estimate form).

- The consultancy assistance, estimated at ten days, involves the use of a consultant with special CAD competence. This is a one-off cost of ECU 44,000 (ten days @ ECU 4,400) — and is itemised in Line 5 of the estimate form.

- System management in the start-up period, estimated at one man-month, will be done by the company's own staff. The cost, ECU 76,560, is itemised in Line 4 of the estimate form.

Figure 14.14: Cost Estimate Form Filled in for the Example

Project: CAD System   Estimate date: 1/5   Drawn up by: NN

	Cost Element	Cost

Costs in Investment Period	Investment period:
	Start: 1/7 Finish: 1/11
	1. Purchase value
	   Price
	   Investment tax
	   Customs/carriage and other purchasing costs
	2. Additional equipment
	3. Installation costs
	4. Const. own employees
	5. Consultancy assistance
	6. Initial training
	7. Other costs in investment period
		
		655,000
		65,500
		0
		27,500
		0
		76,560
		44,000
		246,840
		0

	Total Costs, Investment Period	*1,115,400*
Costs in Operating Period (Cost per Year)	8. Personnel costs 9. Technical service/maintenance 10. Operating materials, lighting, heating 11. Premises 12. Ongoing training 13. Other costs in operating period	288,000 45,000 10,000 0 0 2,000
	Total Cost per Year (Operations)	*345,000*
Upgrading and Ongoing Development Costs	Frequency: Every 2nd year 14. Ongoing specialised development (courses, etc.) 15. Technical equipment/installations 16. Other ongoing develop. costs	 190,200 0 0
		190,200

The next section in Figure 14.13, New Inventory/Services, includes both equipment and services, but these are purchased as "package deals". We itemise the costs, estimated at a total of ECU 27,500 in Line 2 of the estimate form. Some of these costs could have been itemised separately as installation costs in Line 3 of the estimate form.

This means that the costs for the investment or start-up period have been estimated, and amount to a total of ECU 1,115,400.

The next section in Figure 14.13 — Running costs per year — is based on the following calculations:

- The service contract price — ECU 45,000 — is an average figure from the suppliers' quotes. The cost is set at 8 per cent of the hardware and software costs, and covers annual maintenance of the actual workstations and the software. The cost is itemised in Line 9, Technical service/maintenance, of the cost estimate form.

- Material costs, including power, are estimated at ECU 10,000 a year. The estimate is very rough, and is based on figures experienced by other companies. The cost is itemised in Line 10 of the costing form.

- The insurance premium is assumed to be 0.3 per cent of the insured value. The company has chosen to insure most of the equipment components, so the annual premium will be ECU 2,000. The cost is itemised in Line 13 of the form.

- Personnel costs means the cost of the system manager's time. The requirement is estimated at 1.5 man-days a week, i.e. about 75 man-days a year. This gives us a cost in Line 8 of the form of ECU 288,000 (75 man-days at ECU 3,840).

The last section in Figure 14.13 — Upgrading/ongoing Development Costs — is meant to cover courses and specialist seminars. The working group assumes that these are costs which will be necessary every two years. Assumption:

- It is assumed that three staff members will attend for an average of ten days each, which means 30 man-days.

The cost of the actual course is assumed to be ECU 2,500 a day, including accommodation and other costs. This gives us course costs of ECU 75,000 (30 course days @ ECU 2,500). Then comes the estimated cost of the employees' lost working time, ECU 115,200 (30 man-days @ ECU 3,840).

This amounts to a total of ECU 190,200, which is itemised in Line 14 of the cost estimate form.

INVESTMENT AND LIQUIDITY ANALYSIS

Investment and liquidity analysis involves two areas of analysis:

- Calculating the profitability of the company taking the aspect of time into consideration. The term *capital budgeting* is used for this kind of analysis. In an investment situation there is a time interval between the purchase/use of resources and revenues earned by those resources. Thus an investment can be defined as a financial disposition which leads to future cash inflows and outflows.

- Calculating liquidity-related consequences in the form of capital requirements which must be met in a financial plan. This is called *cash budgeting*.

The treatment of risk and uncertainty is critical in capital budgeting. This is dealt with in more detail in Chapter 15 on "Risk Factors and Risk Assessment".

Overview of Investment and Liquidity Analysis

An overview of investment and liquidity analysis is presented in Figure 14.15.

Cash budgets are drawn up on the basis of time and cost estimates, revenues, quantified benefits, action plans and figures based on experience that the company has gained in the past.

The cash budgets at the level of measures are the basis for calculating the net cash flow for the measure. The net cash flow is the basis of the actual capital budgeting, which can be based on several methods: present value, internal rate of return and payback. We will concentrate on the present value method.

The appraisal of financing will not normally be done at the level of individual measures. This is indicated in Figure 14.15 by the fact that the cash budgets for the individual measures are combined in an overall cash budget. This budget, which shows the capital requirement for all the measures, forms the basis for assessments related to financing.

Figure 14.15: Overview of Investment and Liquidity Analysis

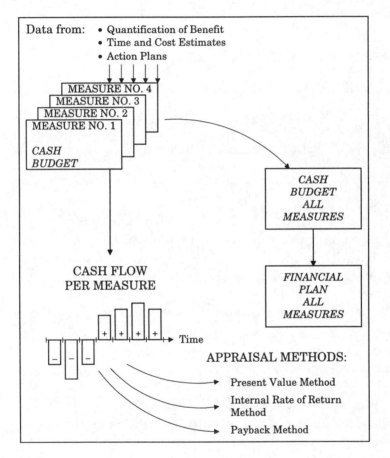

Cash Budget
The cash budget should be drawn up at two levels:

- The "measures" level

- The "overall" level.

The company's cash budget should show the expected developments in cash inflow and outflow incurred by the company.

Figure 14.16 shows an outline that can be used as a template for cash budgeting. The profitability estimates are related back to this budget (capital budgeting).

Figure 14.16: Template for Drawing Up a Cash Budget

	Period				
Cash inflow: Revenues/quantified benefit Sales value of inv. obj. on repl.					
Total Cash Inflow					
Cash outflow: One-off cost (investment sum) Operating capital (increase) Running costs payable					
Total Cash Outflow (2)					
Net Cash Flow (1-2)					

In the cash budget for individual measures one rarely sees great fluctuations from year to year in terms of the cash inflow and outflow for the operating period. By contrast, the costs in the investment period (the company's one-off costs) will normally vary a lot.

Similarly, one will see great fluctuations in the net cash flow when all the measures are taken together. So it is important to draw up a cash budget at the overall level too. The main aim of this is to obtain a basis for assessing financing requirements.

Example of a Cash Budget for a Measure

As mentioned above, it is useful to base the calculation of the cash value of a measure on the results of:

- Time and cost estimates

- Quantification of benefit

- The action plans.

This is illustrated in Figure 14.17, which includes some of the main items from these analyses. These items form the assumptions for the cash budget drawn up in Figure 14.18, in which the template given in Figure 14.16 has been used.

Figure 14.17: Assumptions for Cash Budget

Assumptions - cash budget

<u>Data from time and cost estimates</u>
Costs in the investment period:

— Equipment/installation	ECU 500,000
— Annual running costs in inv. period	ECU 60,000
Upgrading cost in Year 3	ECU 100,000

<u>Data from quantification of benefit</u>

Benefit Factor No. 1 per year	ECU 300,000
Benefit Factor No. 2 per year	ECU 200,000

<u>Data from action plan</u>
The investment period extends over two years.
The running investment costs will begin with the commencement of the project/measure. The equipment is acquired the year after the initiation of the measure, i.e. in Year One of the cost budget.
The financial lifetime of the investment is set at four years. So we must reckon with a total of six years — the commencement year, which we call Year 0, and a further five years.

<u>Additional considerations</u>
At the end of the fourth year of operation, it is expected that the equipment can be sold for 15% of the historic cost price.

To ensure that the plans are realistic, the liquidity consequences of each measure must be calculated as part of the company's regular liquidity planning. This is illustrated in Figure 14.19, where we see that the budgets for the individual measures have been added together. In this case we have periodised in units of years. In practice one should use the periodisation and timescale that the company uses in its ordinary cash flow monitoring routines.

Figure 14.18: Example of Cash Budget

	Year					
	0	1	2	3	4	5
Cash inflow:						
Revenues/quantified benefit			500	500	500	500
Sales value of inv. obj. on repl.						75
Total cash inflow (1)			500	500	500	575
Cash outflow:						
One-off cost (init. invest. sum)	60	560		100		
Operating capital (increase)						
Running costs payable			200	200	200	200
Total cash outflow (2)	60	560	200	300	200	200
Net cash flow (1-2)	-60	-560	300	200	300	375

The overall cash budget is not used for profitability estimates. So there is no reason why the cash flows calculated at the "measures" level should not continue beyond the timescale that applies to the overall cash budget.

Figure 14.19: Overall Cash Budget

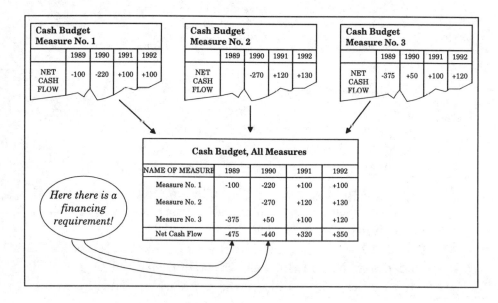

Financing

Even if profitability is satisfactory, we do not have the go-ahead for starting the project. The capital requirement shown by the cash budget must be financed.

In the example in Figure 14.19 we see that the three measures mean a financing requirement in 1989 of ECU 475,000 and a new requirement in 1990 of ECU 440,000. As of 1991 we anticipate a positive cash flow. Although this is a hypothetical situation it is still realistic. When a company enters a period of intensive development and investment, it will accumulate a negative net cash flow at first. This must be financed on the basis of anticipated revenues and profits.

In practice, it only becomes necessary in very few cases to finance measures and the project separately. Financing is normally done as a whole for the company. So it is best to tie the assessment of financing requirements to the overall cash budget for all measures.

Besides assessing the financing requirement, it is important to carry out a key ratio analysis at the overall level to ensure that the company's debt situation is not such a burden that key ratios like financial strength, equity ratio and interest cover are unacceptable. This is dealt with in more detail in Chapter 15 on "Risk Factors and Risk Assessment".

Profitability Appraisal Methods

By profitability appraisal methods we mean ways of estimating the profitability of the measure or project. Figure 14.15 shows that on the basis of the net cash flow of the measure we can do calculations based on:

- The present value method

- The internal rate of return method

- The payback method.

The Present Value Method

In the present value method — also called the "discounted cash flow" (DCF) method — the cash flows are carried back (discounted) to the investment date. This is done by using a discounting rate of interest.

The sum of the discounted cash flows and the initial investment is called the *net present value* of the measure.

The interest rate one uses should be realistic, in the sense that it should be representative of the company's capital costs. The discounting rate in this context can also be interpreted as an interest requirement.

The criterion for profitability in the present value method is whether the calculated net present value is positive or negative. If it is positive, this means that the company will get wealthier. If it is negative, this means that there will be a reduction in the company's capital.

Figure 14.20 shows an example of the use of the present value method. On the basis of the given cash flow, we have calculated that the net present value is +ECU 169,000 at a 15 per cent discounting rate. By raising the discounting rate to 20 per cent we reduce the net present value to ECU 93,000 — which is natural enough, as the higher the interest requirement, the poorer the profitability.

The net present value can easily be worked out with a spreadsheet or one of the more sophisticated calculators. If you do not have tools like these, you can use the manual procedure described in Figure 14.20.

We have made certain simplifications and assumptions in the treatment of the present value method:

- Cash inflow and outflow are calculated for the end of the year

- Inflow is equated with revenues and outflow with costs/expenditure

- We disregard financial issues like the debt-equity ratio — in other words, we only concern ourselves with total capital

- We disregard price rises and taxes. Tax issues are discussed in more detail later on.

Figure 14.20: Example of Present Value Calculation

Calculating Net Present Value
(all amounts in ECU 1000s)

Basis of estimates:
Net cash flow from cash budget:
-60, -560, 300, 200, 300, 375

Net present value at 15% discount rate: ECU 169
Net present value at 20% discount rate: ECU 93

Manual calculation of net present value (15% interest):
We begin with the last year (Year 5) and find out what the
net cash surplus is worth a year before this (Year 4) by
dividing by 1.15 (15% interest). The figure we arrive
at is added to the cash surplus for Year 4. Then we find
out what this is worth a year earlier (Year 3). We continue
this way until Year 0, thus arriving at the net present value.

The calculations are as follows:

Year 5: 375 : 1,15   = 326
Year 4: (326 + 300) : 1,15   = 544
Year 3: (544 + 200) : 1,15   = 647
Year 2: (647 + 300) : 1,15   = 823
Year 1: (823 - 560) : 1,15   = 229
Year 0: (229-60)   = 169

The Internal Rate of Return Method and the Payback Method
The formulae for both these appraisal methods have already been
presented in Figures 14.4 and 14.5 earlier in this chapter.

The internal rate of return method focuses on finding critical
values for return requirements. The internal rate of return for a
measure is the discounting rate that gives a net present value of
zero. If the measure is to be profitable, the calculated internal
rate of return must lie above the company's interest requirement.

In looking at the formula for the internal rate of return in Figure 14.5, it is important to note that it is not exact — it represents
an approximation. If fluctuations can be anticipated in the cash
inflows and outflows, this kind of simple formula should not be
used.

The payback method is not a method of finding profitability,
but it may be useful in doing an initial screening of projects. By

the payback period for a measure we mean the number of years that will pass before the investment has been earned back (has "paid for itself"). If, for instance, a measure has a net cash flow of -100, +10, +90, +70, the payback period is two years.

The Time Aspect

All the factors in an investment analysis have related risks. An analysis of uncertainty is very much a matter of studying how the profitability of the measure or project would be affected by changes in one or more of the assumptions on which the investment analysis is based.

Another important issue is the timescale of the analysis. This is especially true of development projects.

As the examples above show, first there is an investment period with pure cash outflow. Only in the operating period will the project generate cash inflow — hopefully, an inflow that is greater than the outflow, so that the net cash flow will be positive.

If, for instance, the investment or development extends over time so that the flow of revenues is delayed while the other assumptions remain unchanged, this will mean poorer profitability.

Tax Factors

It is not within the scope of this manual to cover all aspects of taxation in detail. However, it is important to be aware that tax can be an important factor which in certain circumstances can be crucial for whether an investment will be profitable or not.

Tax factors enter the picture in two ways:

- Tax on profits reduces the annual cash inflow surplus by the tax amount. In other words, the present value is reduced if the discounting rate remains constant. Or, as a corollary, the discounting rate must be reduced if the present value is to be maintained.

- The authorities in many countries use tax regulations as a tool to encourage certain types of investment. Examples are investments in regional development, in marketing work abroad, etc.

When estimating the annual net cash flow after taxes it is important to remember that tax is assessed on profits after depreciation. So compared with the calculations we presented above, we can set up a formula as shown in Figure 14.21.

Figure 14.21: Adjustment of Net Cash Flow for Taxes

> **Net cash flow adjusted for taxes**
>
> Simplifications:
> Cash inflow = Revenues (1)
> Cash outflow = Costs payable (CP)
>
> Formulae:
> Net cash flow after tax =
> Net cash flow before tax – tax
>
> Tax = (1 – CP – depreciat.) x tax rate

Summary of Procedures
Finally, here is a brief summary of the procedures to be used in investment and liquidity analysis:

- Draw up a cash budget for each measure to find the measure's net cash flow.

- On the basis of the net cash flow, estimate the profitability of the measure. You can use the present value method.

- Compare the net cash flows of the individual measures in an overall cash budget.

- On the basis of the overall cash budget, assess the financing requirement.

- Make the necessary adjustments in the action plans (commencement dates, priorities etc.) on the basis of the results of the analyses.

15

RISK FACTORS AND RISK ASSESSMENT

INTRODUCTION

Risk can be defined as a deviation from expected values. Deviations can be both positive and negative. However, this handbook will only deal with those deviations that create problems: the negative ones.

The purpose of risk analysis is twofold:

- First, to identify and evaluate possible risk factors. The purpose of this exercise is to screen out measures with a risk profile the company is unable to cope with, and to increase awareness of and take risk-reducing action against the risk factors that the company accepts.

- The results of this analysis and the assumptions on which it is based form a very important foundation for the way management follows up on the plans. Management's main task in this regard is therefore to make sure that plans are altered if and when there are changes in the factors that affect them.

So changes in risk factors and the current status of risk factors must be detailed in the progress report when measures are being carried out.

It often appears that to evaluate the uncertainty factor in plans extending over several years is an insurmountable task, and consequently many people choose to act in accordance with a quote from Keynes:

"In the long run we are all dead."

The result of this is that many people limit themselves to calculating whether there is sufficient liquidity to see the company through the development stage and then the first few years of normal production. The consequences of this can be disastrous. Many product development projects have come to a sticky end, for example, because when the product was ready there was no money left for marketing.

It is not always necessary to carry out a large, sophisticated risk analysis in order to avoid such a fate. But it is necessary to look systematically at the risk issues.

Risk factors are discussed in this chapter under the following headings:

- What is Risk?

- How to Carry Out a Risk Analysis and Establish Risk Management

- Implementation Risk

- Financial Risk

- Risk Related to Cost/Benefit Estimates — Sensitivity Analysis

- Key Issues in Risk Identification.

WHAT IS RISK?

We have just defined risk as a deviation from expected values. Such deviation is created by two elements:

- Probability

- Consequence.

Figure 15.1 shows a simple formula for measuring risk. If, for example, a company invests ECU 0.5 million in an area where the chance of success is one in ten, then the loss risk is ECU 450,000 (ECU 500,000 x 0.9).

Figure 15.1: A Formula for Measuring Risk

$$\text{Risk} = \text{Consequence} \times \text{Probability}$$

This chapter will not deal with the mathematical calculation of risk as such, but will rather use the definition to help identify and analyse which risk elements ought to be considered.

HOW TO CARRY OUT A RISK ANALYSIS AND ESTABLISH RISK MANAGEMENT

Figure 15.2 shows a general model for planning and analysing risk. In principle, this form can be used for all the three areas of analysis mentioned in the introduction, but is probably most useful for dealing with implementation risk.

Figure 15.2: Model for Risk Analysis

Model for Surveying and Analysing Risk				
Measure:_____				
Risk Factor	Probability	Consequences	Possible cause	Action

The risk issues can be dealt with in the following steps:

- Identify the risk factors

- Consider the probability and consequence at a general level

- Carry out a sensitivity analysis of the main elements in the cost/benefit analysis, and consider the financial risk, using ratio analysis

- Consider the possible causes of identified, unacceptable risks, and propose actions to reduce risk by dealing with the causes

- Drop measures with risk factors that the company would be unable to deal with through action

- Adjust the priorities of measures in accordance with the risk assessments

- Set up an apparatus for regular monitoring and reporting of risk factors.

IMPLEMENTATION RISK

By implementation risk we mean the risk associated with the implementability of the measure on the basis, for example, of:

- Project size

- Technical complexity

- Organisational and personnel-related factors.

In practice, one will find that many apparently good measures and projects cannot be implemented because of the reasons outlined above.

The purpose of this section of the risk analysis is to ensure that unimplementability is noticed early enough to stop the company wasting its money. The model in Figure 15.2, the diagram in Figure 15.3, and the key questions at the end of the section can help in this process.

Figure 15.3: Diagram for Classifying Risk Factors

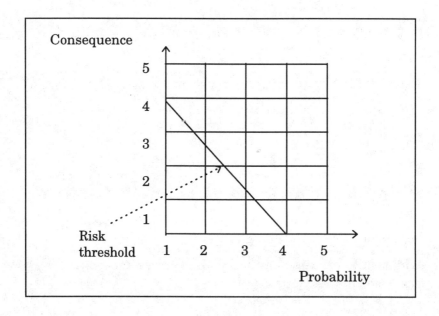

The key questions should be answered for each of the measures. Where there is a risk factor associated with a measure, the next step is to evaluate the risk factor's probability and consequence.

The probability and consequence assessment should be done at a general level — for example, by classifying on the basis of a rough scale. Figure 15.4 shows a scale with values in the interval 1 to 5 grouping first probabilities, and then consequences.

Figure 15.4: Probability and Consequence Evaluation Scale

Scale for Grading Probability	Scale for Grading Consequences
1. Not expected to occur 2. May occur, but very rarely 3. Fifty – fifty chance 4. Expected because it is a common phenomenon 5. Will most probably happen	1. Of little (negligible) consequence 2. Minor damage 3. More damage — aggravated financial position 4. Major damage — serious financial problems 5. Disaster — threatens the company's survival

The identified risk factors together with their respective probabilities and consequences can then be plotted on the diagram of Figure 15.3. The axes of the diagram are the two elements that go into the make up of risk — probability and consequences.

The diagram also includes a straight line between the two axes. This line represents the level of risk the company is prepared to accept. Risk-reducing action should only be defined for risks with a risk factor above this threshold. Along the actual risk threshold, the risk is constant, i.e. the sum of assessed probability and assessed consequences is constant.

Once we have plotted the risk factors in on the diagram, the problem is to find out which of the risks (i.e. probability and consequence taken as a whole) are unacceptable.

The unacceptable elements of risk appear where they exceed the level of risk the company is prepared to accept. It is these risk factors that the company first has to take a closer look at, and then define, risk-reducing actions for (see the right-hand column in Figure 15.2).

Should it prove impossible to define actions that would bring the unacceptable risks under the company's risk threshold, then the company must drop the measure that involves the risk factor in question.

Figure 15.5 provides an example of the result of such an analysis.

Figure 15.5: An Example of Risk Evaluation

Measure: Develop an Electric Door-locking System				
Risk Factor	*Prob.*	*Conseq*	*Possible cause*	*Action*
1. Dependent upon a few key people	3	4	Intensive "head-hunting activity by competitors	Spread competition via training/ education
2. Technological obsolescence	2	5	New competing technologies	Work together with companies
3. Price reduction due to tough competition	1	2		

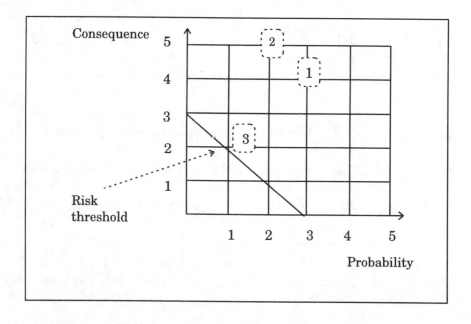

The three risk factors identified are plotted on the diagram with their respective probability and consequence values. The risk threshold has been set at 3 (i.e. low) — note the straight line that starts at the value 3 on both axes. We can see that Risk Factors 1 and 2 exceed the limit, so the company needs to be able to devise risk-reducing actions for these risk factors. The other alternatives are to either drop the measures in question or raise the risk threshold.

FINANCIAL RISK

Financial risk should be understood as meaning risk related to the company's financial structure, primarily debt/equity capital. Simply put, the larger the company debt, the more it will be at risk from fluctuating net earnings.

The purpose of this section is therefore to ensure that the company does not put itself in a financially unacceptable position because of the implementation of a measure.

We can shed light on this with the help of the following key figures:

- Equity ratio

- Working capital

- Interest cover.

The formulae for the key figures are given in Figure 15.6.

The equity ratio is often seen as a measurement of the company's financial strength. And financial strength can be seen as something to "lean on" should losses occur at any stage. If many measures are implemented and these are basically financed by borrowed capital, then a company's financial strength may be affected detrimentally.

Many people claim that an industrial company's equity ratio should be between 35 per cent and 40 per cent.

Working capital is that part of current assets (operating capital) financed by long-term loans. If the company finances expansion with its own funds (which are part of the long-term capital), the working capital will be reduced. For the sake of liquidity it is therefore important that management has figures for both working capital and liquidity reserves.

Figure 15.6: Example of Some Key Ratios

$$\text{Equity ratio} = \frac{\text{Equity x } 100}{\text{Total capital}}$$

$$\text{Working capital} = \text{Current assets - current liabilities}$$

$$\text{Interest cover} = \frac{\text{Profit before interest and tax x } 100}{\text{Interest costs}}$$

Interest cover tells us how many times earnings before the deduction of financial costs will cover financial costs. This is an especially important key ratio. It is quite easy to show that the total return on investment is satisfactory, but things are still bad if all earnings (and perhaps more) are used to cover interest costs. A rule of thumb often used by banks is that a satisfactory interest cover value should be at least 3.

Where the total number of measures involves significant expenditure for the company, a full key ratio analysis should be carried out as described in Chapter 8 on "Financial Key Ratio Analysis".

RISK RELATED TO COST/BENEFIT ESTIMATES — SENSITIVITY ANALYSIS

Risk related to cost/benefit evaluations can be divided into two sub-groups:

- The risk that costs exceed original estimates
- The risk that the benefits are lower than estimated.

Risk evaluation for cost/benefit estimates is often called sensitivity analysis. What is analysed here is how sensitive a measure's profitability is to changes in one or more of the assumptions on which the profitability estimates are based.

The cost/benefit estimates in turn form the basis for the investment estimates, where the estimates make up the cost and benefit sides respectively. In the investment analysis we operate with the cash inflow and cash outflow of payments which together comprise the net cash flow.

In many consultancy assignments, the consultant will not always carry out an investment and liquidity analysis of individual measures that can be implemented in a relatively short period of time. We will therefore illustrate two kinds of sensitivity analysis. The first is relatively simple and can be used no matter how "advanced" the earlier cost/benefit analysis has been. The other is based upon possible changes in the measure's present value, and requires that an investment analysis has been done.

The simple sensitivity analysis disregards the time factor. This means, for example, that it will not register changes in the measure's profitability due to fact that the project runs over the planned time and the beneficial effects thus come later than expected. Though this is a serious limitation, it plays only a minor role for the measures where we have decided to use only simple estimates. Remember that investment analysis ought to be carried out for those measures that extend over a long period of time, or where there is a long delay between investment and the realisation of benefits.

The procedure for a simple sensitivity analysis is:

- List all factors relating to costs/benefits in a table as shown in Figure 15.7, together with the estimated values.

- Make both a pessimistic and optimistic estimate for each factor relating to costs and benefits.

- Calculate the cost/benefit ratio of pessimistic to optimistic estimates.

- Adjust the estimated (e.g. most probable) cost/benefit values so that this column reflects an average of the pessimistic and optimistic estimates.

- Identify risk-reducing actions for those cost/benefit elements that represent the greatest deviation from the estimated values. Assess both absolute (money) and percentage deviations

Figure 15.7: Form for Simple Sensitivity Analysis

Sensitivity Analysis for Cost Benefit			
Measure: _____			
Factor	Estimate	Pessimistic	Optimistic
Cost Factors: ------------------- ------------------- -------------------			
Benefit Factors: ------------------- ------------------- -------------------			
Cost/benefit			

Sensitivity Analysis by Cash Flow Appraisal

In order to deal with risk and uncertainty in cost/benefit estimates it may be a good idea to start with the net cash flow and
then do an analysis where we deal with the two main factors (on
the cost/benefit side) that affect cash flows — and thereby profitability. An investment's present value is an expression of its
profitability; investments with positive present values are profitable. The calculation of present value is explained in Chapter 14
on "Assessment of Options using Cost/Benefit Analysis".

For a present value analysis to have any merit, the implementation of the measure and the realisation of the beneficial effects
have to extend over a period of time. If, for example, both costs
and gains are basically of the "one-off type" and occur in the current year, then a present value evaluation would be like "using a
sledge hammer to crack a nut".

The method is easy to understand and use. However, it may
lead to a great deal of calculation work if special tools are not
available. We strongly recommend the use of a spreadsheet when
working with sensitivity evaluations. And we should also mention
a weakness in the method: its starting point is partial, inasmuch
as we alter one factor and expect all the other factors to remain

constant. Using a spreadsheet certainly improves the chances of being able to "play" with several factors at the same time.

The result of the method can be displayed in the form of a "star diagram" like the one in Figure 15.8. The centre of the "star" is the starting point for the calculations. The measure's present value is shown along the vertical axis and changes (expressed in percentages) in the factors we wish to see the results of are shown on the horizontal axis. In this example we change the factors by plus/minus thirty per cent.

Figure 15.8: Star Diagram

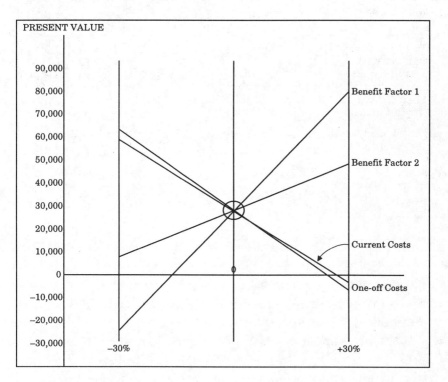

Our starting point for Figure 15.8 can be seen in the investment analysis in Figure 15.9. The net cash flow has a present value of ECU 29,550, which we have plotted in over zero on the horizontal axis. The investment is thus in principle profitable.

We have changed the main factors (Benefit Factors 1, 2 and one-off and current costs) as shown in Figure 15.9 by plus/minus

30 per cent. The corresponding changed present values are plotted in the diagram. We can see that if the value of the measure's once-off costs or current costs rises by thirty per cent, the present value (e.g. profitability) is negative. Similarly, the present value is negative if the value of Benefit Factor 1 is reduced by 30 per cent.

Figure 15.9: Key Figures from Investment Analysis

Year	0	1	2	3
Cash inflow				
Benefit Factor 1		80,000	80,000	80,000
Benefit Factor 2		40,000	40,000	40,000
Residual value on replacement				30,000
Cash outflow		120,000	120,000	150,000
One-off costs				
Present costs	-150,000			
Net cash flow		50,000	50,000	50,000
Net cash flow	-150,000	70,000	70,000	100,000

Interest rate: 15%
Present value: ECU 29,550

Setting up a sensitivity analysis in a star diagram focuses attention on those factors that have the potentially greatest effect on the investment's profitability. These factors will have steep curves in Figure 15.8, and will therefore intersect the zero level (profitability limit) quickest.

If the investment estimates in Figure 15.9 are entered onto a spreadsheet, changes can also be made in the time factor. As a supplement to a percentage change in cost and benefit factors, we can then also evaluate the consequences of the factors occurring at another time than planned. For example, in Figure 15.9, there is a risk that Benefit Factor 1 will not realise ECU 80,000 a year in the first two years. This will in turn have a negative effect on the investment's profitability.

KEY ISSUES IN RISK IDENTIFICATION

Implementation Risk

- What is the extent of the measure (in man-days) in comparison to other tasks the company has dealt with in the past? Has the company potential project managers who can cope with a task of this magnitude?

- What is the extent of the measure (in man-days) in relation to the available work input? Is there a chance that key personnel will not be able to spend the necessary time working on the project?

- Which key personnel is the measure dependent on? How has the company ensured the project will not be endangered if any of these key personnel leave the company?

- Is the implementation of the measure dependent on resources over which the company itself has no control? If, for example, the measure is implemented in co-operation with several other companies, what will happen if one of these companies quits the project?

- How will the measure's costs come to affect the company financially? Is the measure significantly more costly than tasks undertaken by the company in the past?

- How do the owners/management assess the investment? How has it been ensured that the necessary decisions will be taken at the right time? Will a project control group be set up in accordance with the requirements for ongoing control?

- Is the measure dependent on other measures, e.g. the development of better production planning, delivery routines, material administration, financial management, etc.? To what extent will the delay or failure of other measures affect the success of this one?

- Is the measure dependent on radical replacements of production equipment or a new company infrastructure?

- How does the measure's technical complexity compare with tasks the company has previously dealt with?

- What is the opinion of the implementation of this measure in the ordinary organisational apparatus of the company? Is it possible for particular groups of employees to "sabotage" it?

- Has sufficient consideration been given to competence-building, changes in manual routines, and any necessary organisational changes that are to take place concurrently with or before the proposed changes?

- How have the measure(s) been dealt with internally in the company in order to ensure that in-house conflicts do not hinder implementation?

- Is the measure dependent on the recruitment of new personnel, and if so, what are the chances of employing people with the necessary qualifications?

- Is the success of the measure dependent on official regulations and laws governing the environment, tax, customs, imports/exports, etc.?

Financial Risk

- How is the implementation of the measure to be financed? Is, for example, the company dependent on public grants and subsidies? What would happen if it was necessary to finance the project in another way?

- How much more expensive (expressed as a percentage) could the measure be before being halted by lack of funds?

- Are there elements on the measure's benefit side that would lead to a serious detrimental effect on company finances if they were not realised? If, for example, start-up problems with a new invoicing system actually increased effective credit terms for customers for a time, how would that affect liquidity/working capital?

- Is there a risk that the measure will reduce the company's equity ratio for a while? What would be the general effect of the measure being stopped after the introductory phase, so that all costs continued to accrue, but there was no profit?

- How will the financing of the measure affect the company's ability to meet its interest obligations?

- Are the financial risks involved closely related to other measures that are being implemented parallel with or after this measure? What happens if these other measures cannot be implemented (e.g., product development projects where insufficient funds are available for final implementation)?

Risk Related to Cost/Benefit Evaluation

- Generally speaking, are cost estimates judged as being reliable or unreliable?

- How much of the costs are related to time spent working on the project? How has this been estimated? Have the estimates been reached on the basis of experience from earlier measures implemented in the company?

- Which events in and outside the company could affect cost estimates? What, for example, would be the financial consequences of a prolonged training programme, a need for more input from external consultants, price rises on important components, and so on?

- What percentage of possible beneficial elements have been included in the benefit evaluation? Generally speaking, have estimates been very optimistic regarding full utilisation of all beneficial elements? What would happen if the most important benefit factors were removed?

- Is there doubt as to when the beneficial effects will be realised? What would happen if all the benefits were delayed by a year?

- Is income dependent on other, parallel measures? Is the measure dependent, for example, on increased sales and marketing because the company's production capacity increases? What happens if these measures fail?

- In cases where the income aspect of the measure is dependent on external customers, what is the composition of the customer base: only a few customers, many small, etc.? What if part of the customer base did not yield an increased profit? Risk is generally greatest with a few, large customers and/or a few, large single orders.

- Will the measure alter the working situation of either customers or suppliers? Can the company be reasonably sure that they will accept this? If, for example, the benefit estimates are based on reducing credit terms from thirty to ten days, what if customers do not accept this?

- What is the competitive situation and who are the competitors? Does the company operate in a broad market or in a niche? Is price an important buying criterion? Is there a chance that competitors might squeeze prices so that the income estimated for the investment is not realised?

PART IV

IMPLEMENTATION

16

PROJECT IMPLEMENTATION

INTRODUCTION

This handbook has recommended that consultancy assignments relating to strategic planning be carried out in three phases.

- The first phase is a *general strategic analysis* and is meant to establish quickly "where the shoe pinches" and should result in a set of recommendations and guidelines for further work.

- The second phase involves more comprehensive survey and analysis work aimed at identifying the "right action" for the company to take. The result of this phase will be the establishment of *strategies and action plans* for the implementation of innovation and change.

- The third and final phase covers the *implementation* of the various measures that have been identified during the strategy and planning process.

The implementation process is defined as those activities necessary from the time when an action plan is ready until the measures have been implemented and responsibility for them has been transferred back to the ordinary organisational apparatus of the company.

This chapter deals with the implementation of projects under the following headings:

- Consequences of Strategic Innovations

- What does the Implementation Process Involve?

- Funding

- Planning and Organisation

- Company-internal Organisational Activities

- Supplier-oriented Technical Activities

- Company-internal Technical Activities

- Follow-up

- Evaluation.

CONSEQUENCES OF STRATEGIC INNOVATIONS

The introduction of strategic innovations in a company always means changes. The company (or parts of it) must be adapted to "work in a different way". It is important to realise that such a transformation affects more than just the technical manufacturing process. The people in the organisation, and the organisational structure itself, must undergo an adaptation process.

It is a precondition for the successful introduction of change that these aspects too are addressed. New ways of working may require new kinds of co-operation, changes in the distribution of responsibility or other organisational changes. So one is likely to encounter resistance in unexpected areas. "Rocking the boat" can lead to insecurity and/or changes in the power balance in the company. There may be established "territorial rights" or "king of the castle" situations that will result in resistance based on quite different criteria from those that motivated the establishment of the action plan for implementing the measures.

One of the keys to success here lies in building up the individual's understanding of the company's success factors. It must be understood that changes are necessary and that they help to increase security more than they spread insecurity. If the company is able to adapt to market conditions on an ongoing basis its competitive potential improves, and this in turn increases job security for the individual. "Security through change" can be the motto for the message that has to be conveyed.

WHAT DOES THE IMPLEMENTATION PROCESS INVOLVE?

Innovation and the implementation of changes in a company involves work at different levels within the company organisation. Figure 16.1 gives an overview of the activities that must take place during the implementation process.

Figure 16.1: Overview of Implementation Activities

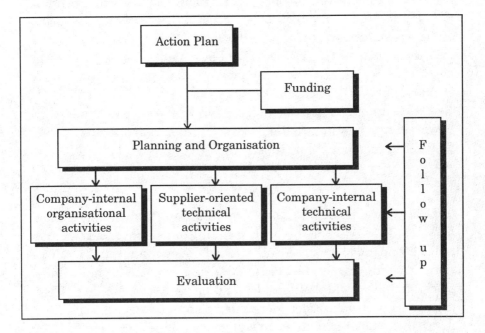

The activities in the figure which must be planned and followed up are divided into three groups.

Company-internal Organisational Activities

This group of activities includes informative, motivational and general competence-raising work. The aim of the activities is to prepare the organisation for change, to remove uncertainty and antagonism, and to get the whole organisation "hooked" on the idea that "we can manage this together".

Supplier-oriented Technical Activities

This group of activities includes the evaluation of alternative solutions, formulation of requirement specifications, asking for quotes and selecting suppliers.

Company-internal Technical Activities

In this group we find the company's own specialised work. This may mean changes in the physical environment for the reception of new equipment (for example, constructional changes, cabling). Other purchases may also be necessary. The activities also include specialised training of directly-involved personnel (users and those responsible for running equipment). Finally, there is the actual delivery of the equipment from suppliers, and its installation and initialisation.

This kind of activity concludes when the responsibility for the new equipment/system is taken over by the organisational apparatus of the company (line functions).

FUNDING

Typically the implementation of projects to introduce innovation and change will involve costs. Funding must be ensured, and must be included as a central element in planning and evaluation. It is important that the capital requirement is accurately calculated to avoid both underfunding and overfunding. This applies to both investment and operational aspects. A cash flow forecast can be drawn up as an effective aid in this context.

Projects can be funded in many different ways. They may be based on external and/or internal funding. External funding includes a number of public and semi-public sector funding institutions which can help with subsidies and/or loans.

Chapter 21 on "Project Financing" gives an overview of ways of estimating funding requirements and of sources of funding.

PLANNING AND ORGANISATION

Planning

The aim of planning is to ensure that activities and resources are co-ordinated over time so that goals can be achieved with as little resource consumption as possible. Planning must be done so that the progress of the plan can be monitored at regular intervals.

The Planning Process
Planning takes place in several stages and at several levels. Figure 16.2 is a flowchart for the planning process.

Figure 16.2: The Planning Process

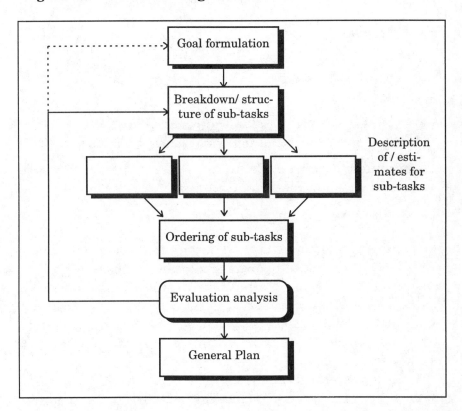

Planning is an iterative process, so it is shown here as a "loop" where there are several "rounds" on the way towards the final plan.

The point of departure for the plan is the formulation of the goal. Both an overall goal and subgoals must be defined.

Who Should Do the Planning?

Planning should be the responsibility of the project manager, who should prepare a plan at an overall level. The breakdown work will result in the identification of sub-tasks (activities or sub-projects). Responsibility for the individual subgoals will be defined by the project participants. One gets the best result in implementation if the person responsible for the goal (sub-goal) plans the activity or activities necessary to achieve it.

Extent of Planning

Planning at all levels includes the following elements:

- **Scheduling**, i.e. specifying the start, duration and end of the various activities

- **Personnel resource planning**, i.e. allocation of staff /distribution of responsibilities and resources/man-hours

- **Equipment resource planning**, i.e. identification of types and need for equipment resources

- **Cost planning**, i.e. which and when.

The process of combining all these factors into one whole is important. It is not difficult to make "impossible" plans. The project manager must make sure the plan is consistent. This means that the activities must come in a logical order. No resources (equipment or staff) should be "double-booked". Time and cost plans for the sub-projects should be fitted in so that the overall time and cost ceilings are observed.

There are several methods and tools for planning. The best known are (a) milestone planning, (b) Gantt techniques and (c) network techniques. In small projects the work can easily be done with pencil and paper. In larger projects the planning process can be rationalised with computer support (there are several products available in this area).

The final plan will include activities, responsibilities, a progress schedule and a budget.

Organisation

The implementation process requires an effort to which the normal organisational apparatus of the company is not geared. So it is natural to establish a special organisational structure in the project for handling the implementation process. There are several ways of doing this. The traditional organisational structure for a project was shown earlier in Figure 13.6 (see page 294).

The project is manned by people from the base organisation, and it is important that they are given sufficient freedom from their usual tasks during the project period.

Who should lead the project? The project manager is the central figure in all projects. When choosing a project manager, it is the person's leadership qualities that are most important; detailed specialist knowledge is also an advantage, but is less important.

There are also "reference contacts" in the figure. This is a group of "support" figures outside the actual project. It may consist of people with special competence, or groups representing the employees who need to be informed or consulted along the way.

An important job for the project manager is ensuring that the project organisation is always properly staffed in terms of both competence and capacity.

Use of Consultants

The need for outside help in the implementation process will vary from company to company. Consultancy services which may be relevant can be divided into three groups:

- **Help with implementation**, i.e. a catalyst and "right-hand man" for the project manager

- **Special competence**, e.g. for product evaluation

- **General resources**, i.e. competence which the company has, but cannot release enough of for the project.

Of these, general resources can perhaps be bought from suppliers along with the equipment, while the first two categories should be hired from independent consultancy firms.

COMPANY-INTERNAL ORGANISATIONAL ACTIVITIES

Activities oriented towards the internal organisational structure of the company are important for several reasons. The introduction of new methods of working can mean changes and a need for new competencies. Attitudes in the company may make special informative and motivational work necessary.

To avoid resistance and uncertainty it is important to get information out quickly. Employee representatives and other people directly affected must be won over. Training needs must be mapped out and planned. There may be a need for both specialist training of users and maintenance personnel, and everyone may need a general introduction to what the proposed change involves. This kind of general introduction can help to "demystify" the proposed innovations and create positive expectations about new and more efficient tools.

Figure 16.3 is a model of factors that should be taken into account in the planning of training.

Figure 16.3: Model for Planning Training Requirements

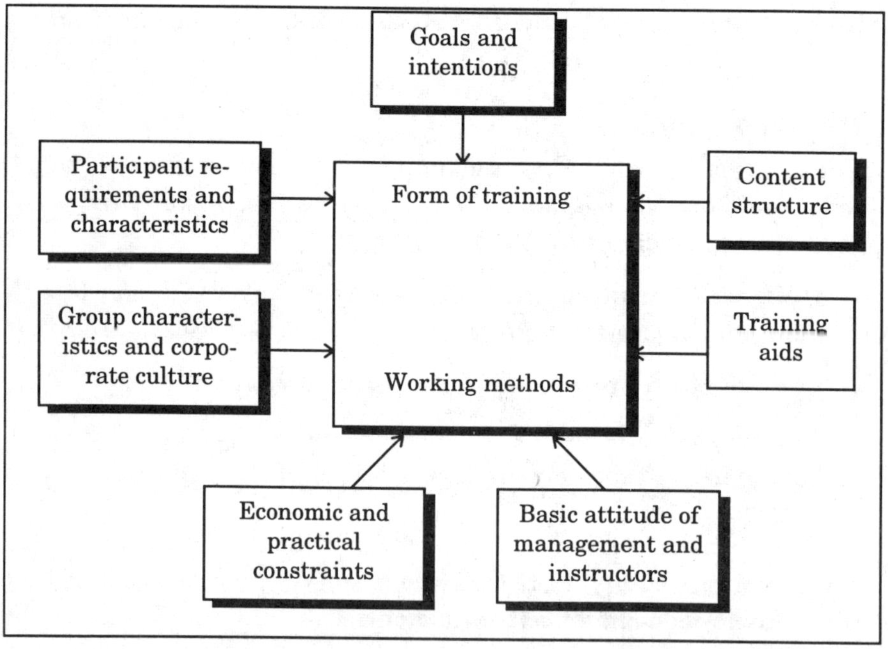

SUPPLIER-ORIENTED TECHNICAL ACTIVITIES

Specification of Requirements

The specification of requirements is often the nucleus of a good system. However, there are innumerable examples of bad specifications of requirements. There are many reasons for poor quality in this area, but the most important ones are:

- Failure to understand the importance of spending a significant amount of time on the formulation of the specification of requirements

- Failure to understand what a specification of requirements should contain.

The most important function of the specification of requirements is to convey *what* the equipment/system is to do. It is primarily the functional requirements for the equipment that must be described. Thus the main message to be conveyed by a specification of requirements is which needs the equipment is to meet. Strictly speaking, one can say that if the specification of requirements tells suppliers *what* the system has to do, it is the responsibility of the suppliers to find out *how* their equipment will solve the problem. The main error made in drawing up requirement specifications is that people begin describing solutions in addition to stating functional requirements.

The situation is often such that the equipment/system has to interact with existing equipment in the company. In addition, the company may already have defined a number of standards for "the way they want things done". The specification of requirements must also get this across.

Content of the Specification of Requirements

The specification of requirements must state:

- The context in which the system/equipment is to function

- Constraints of the surroundings (co-ordination, environment etc.)

- What the equipment has to do (functional features)

- How well the functions have to be performed (quality and performance requirements).

Drawing up the Specification — An Ongoing Process
The drawing-up of the specification of requirements is an ongoing process. While it is being drawn up it may emerge that other requirements can also be met.

The drawing-up of the specification of requirements is an area where assistance from experienced outside consultants can be useful.

Choice of Equipment/Supplier
In many cases, consultancy assignments will identify new technology or services that the company should purchase in order to implement proposed innovations. Most companies believe that if they can get a firm quotation, they can feel secure that the cost ceiling will be observed. This is only true to a certain extent!

Success in this respect depends on the quality of the specification of requirements and how one handles quotes and suppliers.

The experience of many companies can be summed up in the following statements:

- Inaccurate specifications lead to expensive modifications

- The cheapest offers are based on "minimum solutions" which only partly meet needs

- The combination of vague specifications and a minimum solution is a dangerous one for both company and supplier.

When making enquiries to suppliers, the consultant should be aware of how complete a delivery they want. What can be achieved is directly related to the level of the specification of requirements. Be aware that partial solutions can lead to very expensive modifications later.

How to evaluate offers should be thought through in advance in order to ask for information that can form a basis for comparison. In the event of deviations from specifications and from the quote, one should have a conceptual framework for evaluating them so that a final comparison and selection can be done as far as possible on an identical basis.

In addition to the actual solution offered, the supplier's delivery capacity, service apparatus and the overall impression should be evaluated in comparing suppliers.

Of course, it is also possible not to make general enquiries. If the company knows suppliers it has confidence in, a co-operative project may be a sensible alternative. In this type of co-operation the supplier comes in as a consultant at an early stage and helps to ensure that their solution will be the optimum one for the company.

Contracting

Contracting in this context means entering into contracts with suppliers for the delivery of equipment, systems or services. The aim of the contract is to ensure that the right product is delivered at the right time and at the right price.

The formulation and signing of the contract require co-operation among several groups in the company, and with the supplier. Put rather simply, one can say that the contract must deal with three topics:

- **Legal aspects**, i.e. the formulation of the contract

- **Specifications**, i.e. the definition of *what* is to be supplied and *when* (the obligations of the supplier)

- **Financial aspects**, i.e. the price (the obligations of the company).

There are strong links between the work of formulating the specification of requirements, asking for quotes, the choice of supplier and the contract work. If the foundation given by the specification of requirements is weak, what is actually being ordered may not be clear.

COMPANY-INTERNAL TECHNICAL ACTIVITIES

The Company's Own Preparations

When innovations/changes are being introduced, whether they consist of information systems or other equipment/systems, good interrelations among company, supplier and possibly a consultant will be necessary.

Many companies have experienced surprising delays, even though deliveries from the supplier have been punctual. This is very often due to the low priority given to the company's own work. So it cannot be emphasised enough that co-operation between the supplier and the company is important.

Two areas in particular should be emphasised:

- Is the company ready to receive the equipment when it is delivered?

- Has the company used training to build up the competence necessary to operate the equipment?

Preparations to receive equipment have a tendency to foul up because of apparent trifles:

- Are the physical conditions for receiving, installing and starting to use the system ready?

- Has the responsibility for the reception and checking of the equipment been given to a specified person?

The most common source of failure is that the planning work has not been focused on the *overall* project.

Specialised Training

Specialised training must be planned so that the company is ready to start using any new equipment or systems that it has ordered. One must evaluate whether training should be completed before starting to use the equipment, or whether training can be done on an ongoing basis. To motivate the new users, it may be relevant to try out similar equipment (for example, by visiting the supplier) so that the users can gain experience for themselves by looking, by trial and error, and by talking to the experts.

Installation and Start-up

The installation and starting up of new equipment or systems is always exciting. It involves interaction among the supplier, the project participants and the organisational apparatus of the company. This phase must be planned to create minimum disturbance of the ordinary operations of the company. In some cases it is possible to phase in the use of the new equipment/system gradually. This can be useful for ensuring a "softer" transition. In other cases installation constitutes a "point of no return".

In this phase it is still the project organisation that is responsible, but it is important that the normal organisational apparatus of the company is involved, because they will soon have to take over the formal responsibility.

The participation of the normal organisational apparatus of the company is particularly important at this stage, but it is also important throughout the implementation phase. Many apparently successful projects have lost some of their impact when the project apparatus is dissolved. If the normal company apparatus does not perceive the project as "its own", there may be a "vacuum" when the momentum given by the project itself is gone.

FOLLOW-UP

Project Management, Reporting and Follow-up
Good project management in the company is by far one of the most important preconditions of successful implementation. Project management is a specialised subject in its own right, and here we will only emphasise a few individual elements that are significant.

While the work is in progress, how is the project manager to ensure that the schedule and resource consumption are observed as planned?

The essential requirement for following up on the situation and initiating any necessary corrective measures is good reporting. The reports should focus on any deviations from the plan. We have previously mentioned that the plans include starting and finishing dates, resource requirements and the distribution of responsibilities. It is any deviations in these respects that must be pointed out. So follow-up should concentrate on:

- **Activity**. It is too late to follow up on an activity once the date when it should be finished has arrived. Deviations from the planned work should be reported from the starting date.

- **Resource consumption and completion estimates**. Reports on time and resource consumption must include current consumption and what will be necessary for completion of the work. NB: The budget ceiling minus current consumption is *not* necessarily the same as the remaining resources necessary for completion!

- **Staffing**. Are the right people doing the work? Is the work being done by competent people? Have resources been "stolen" from other areas, and can problems therefore be expected in those areas?

Quality Assurance, Dealing with Ongoing Modifications

What is quality? Ask different people about this and you will get different answers. In a project context it is better to ask the question "What is real quality?"

Real quality is when the product is delivered at the agreed time, at the agreed price and with the agreed specifications.

Quality assurance has gradually grown into a whole specialised field. The need certainly exists. However, we have seen many examples of the way a strong wish to introduce quality assurance routines has led to "massive bureaucracy" and a quality that only exists "on paper". Having the paperwork in order has become more important than the state of the product itself. Of course, this is not a general situation — but it is a possible pitfall.

Companies about to embark on the implementation of new and innovative change have a need for quality assurance. If the company already has an existing scheme, this should be used. If there is no quality assurance scheme, one should be introduced — *but do not introduce unnecessary bureaucracy*. The most important thing is to identify the routines and tasks that are most critical, and to establish a *simple* system for ensuring that the routines are properly observed.

How does one deal with ongoing modifications? All projects experience changes. In the first place, we must distinguish between wishes for change and changes that have actually been adopted and must be implemented. There will always be a number of wishes for changes. As people in the organisational apparatus become involved, they will want some things done differently. One should be aware of this in advance, so that one has a strategy for dealing with proposed changes. The most important thing is that one should not allow people a free hand to make changes. The rule must be that modifications have to be approved. Before approving a change, one must analyse its consequences and any alternatives. If the change is accepted, information to that effect must be distributed in an pre-arranged way. The point is to ensure that there is never any doubt as to what the current specification of requirements is.

EVALUATION

The last task is the final evaluation of the project. Unfortunately this is a phase that is often "forgotten". At the start of the project everyone is agreed that a final evaluation has to be done, but when the project is over the people are involved in other tasks and "don't have the time".

Why is it so important to evaluate? The whole implementation has been focused on the definition of goals, and planning to achieve the goals. So it is now quite logical and necessary to ask "Did we achieve these goals?"

The evaluation must show whether the goals were achieved, and if necessary analyse why we did not achieve them. On the basis of this analysis and the lessons learned along the way one should be able to document:

- To what extent were the goals reached?

- What lessons did we learn?

- What did we do well?

- What did we do badly?

It will be very useful to have this experience for the next project related to new technology.

17

CRITICAL SUCCESS FACTORS FOR THE IMPLEMENTATION OF MEASURES

INTRODUCTION

The introduction of innovation and new methods of working in the form of equipment and systems can be crucial to a company's development and future survival. New solutions and systems can have an influence on the jobs and working conditions of employees. When this is the case, it is important that any proposed changes are assessed not only in technical and financial terms, but also in organisational and personnel-related terms.

This kind of overall view must be used as a basis for the implementation of new measures in a company. The period of transition from an action plan to the implementation of measures is often the time when opposition and conflicts arise, and this must be regarded as a critical period in the project. Several of the factors that emerge here have their background in earlier phases of the project, while others are directly related to the actual way the implementation work is done.

This chapter focuses on important factors that will lead to more successful implementation. The critical success factors for implementation are discussed under the following headings:

- Critical Success Factors in the Preparatory Phases.

- Critical Success Factors in the Implementation Phase.

CRITICAL SUCCESS FACTORS IN THE PREPARATORY PHASES

Management Commitment

It is important that management supports the project work and makes its support known throughout the organisation. In practice this is best demonstrated by allocating the necessary resources to the preparatory work. Here it is not enough to pick out key personnel; management must also consider the consequences this work will have for everyday operations, and must then make resources available so that both the project and normal operations can function properly.

Providing the Staff with Information

Transformation work of this kind can easily create uncertainty and resistance among the staff. Most of this resistance has its background in uncertainty about what the project will mean for individuals and the environment they work in. Information about the importance of the project and the way the company will tackle the personnel-related consequences (for example, will there be redundancies or not?) should be made available as quickly as possible. The employee representatives must also be involved in this informative work — this is often a matter that is regulated by law — and they will also make a great contribution to creating a more secure mood about the project.

Employee Representatives Should Quickly Be Involved in the Project

Employee organisations and employee representatives are important elements in the balance of "power" within a company, so they must be involved, to avoid conflicts, in both the planning and implementation phases. Many of these factors are also regulated by law or collective bargaining/employee contract agreements, so this aspect must be carefully assessed right at the beginning of the project. As an example, we can take Norwegian legislation:

> Working Environment Act, Section 12: "Employees and their elected representatives shall be kept informed of systems used in the planning and implementation of work, including

planned changes in such systems. They shall be provided with the training necessary to familiarise themselves with the systems, and shall be involved in the design of the systems."

In most countries the various parties that make up the labour market, the Trade Unions Council and the Employers' Association or national equivalents have realised how necessary it is to have a good relationship of trust between companies and their employees.

Consensus

Major or minor disagreements will very probably arise during the project work. Most of these are solved along the way without leading to major conflicts. Many sections of this manual describe ways of working that may be appropriate in this regard. All the same, it is important to stress that a critical success factor for the implementation of a project is that company management, elected employee representatives and users reach some sort of consensus about the project goals and implementation methods.

By consensus here we do not necessarily mean that everyone should agree 100 per cent, but that they must respect the decisions that are worked out. In practice this will mean that objections to parts of the project will emerge on an ongoing basis, and the parties will have a chance to influence the course of further work. So important conflicts in the area to be analysed must not be swept under the carpet or covered up.

Understanding General Constraints

Even before the strategy and planning process begins, the company should have an idea of the general constraints to which the project will be subjected. By "general constraints" we mean, for example, financial ceilings, the limitation to the scope of the project, etc. The information provided throughout the company should be adapted accordingly so as not to create unrealistic expectations amongst company staff.

The Right Level of Detail for the Action Plans

When action plans have been drawn up, they must be specific, scheduled and must contain prioritised measures with a clear distribution of responsibilities.

Effective Dissemination of the Results of the Strategy Work

Once the action plans have been drawn up, they should be easy to read and should contain clear conclusions. The conclusions and goals will then have to be "marketed" within the company.

CRITICAL SUCCESS FACTORS IN THE IMPLEMENTATION PHASE

Reserve Enough Time for the Planning of Project Implementation

Once the action plans are available, it is tempting to start work right away. To ensure good results for the company, though, time must be set aside for planning the actual implementation.

Experience of many projects has shown that too little thought has been given to planning — resulting in stress and a hectic implementation phase. In such a situation it goes without saying that the potential for finding the best solutions often simply does not exist. If the implementation phase is typified by stress and hurry, the more human aspects are often forgotten in the rush, and this results in a backlash from the affected parties.

Training and Competence-building

The issue of training is very often overlooked and is thus not addressed until too late a stage in the process of introducing new methods of working. When the changes are minor this is usually not a problem, but if the new system makes great demands on new thinking from the people who are to use the new systems or equipment, it is important to have training in mind at an early stage of planning.

A good deal of the user training will be purely practical — i.e. letting the user see the equipment, try it out and talk to experienced people. Planning must also allow time for the necessary study of the level of competence and competence requirements. Resources and time must be allocated to training.

Surveying the Organisational and Personnel-related Consequences

In general, the amount of opposition and scepticism in a company increases with the scope of changes. This applies to both management and other employees. The cause is often fear of the new and unknown and/or of losing the benefits one already has.

It is natural that no one wants to be "changed", whereas most people will go along with changes they can influence themselves. During the survey work one should also assess the work-related opportunities and challenges created by the new equipment or systems that are being proposed.

The consultant should start surveying and working on the organisational and personnel-related consequences as soon as they have specific enough information from the analytical work.

Organisation of the Project

The consultant must ensure that key personnel have time to take part in the project work. The Project Manager should be a person who can direct this work, and should not be chosen just because of their specialised skills. The Project Manager must be given the necessary authority and must have a mandate to act.

Clear agreements must be reached about reporting and follow-up, and the differences between these two parts of the project work must be made clear.

Reported Results Must Be Measurable

An implementation plan must be established where measurable progress can be reported — not just finishing dates for parts of the project, but also for example the level of activity and the estimated amount of work remaining. Control in terms of dates alone can lead to unpleasant surprises.

Close Follow-up on Measures

The best way of ensuring good progress in the project is regular reporting by the project group. A sense of responsibility for time and budget ceilings is best ensured by having the project participants themselves help to create the framework that concerns them.

The control group for the project must be active, and management must participate.

Motivation of Personnel in the Implementation Phase

Users and line management must be involved in the implementation phase. A project will always involve extra burdens on the company. This will mean that individuals will at some point raise doubts about the justification of the project.

In many cases, people are against the project because they are in doubt about whether they can master the new working environment or the new technology that is being introduced. The company's training plans and personnel policies will be important factors to be taken into consideration when dealing with this kind of resistance.

18

SPECIFICATION OF REQUIREMENTS

INTRODUCTION

The purpose of this chapter is to provide an overview of requirement specifications and show how the company can produce such a document. The qualities that characterise a good specification of requirements are emphasised, and typical pitfalls to be avoided are listed.

This section deals with the drawing up of a specification of requirements under the following headings:

- Why Compile a Specification of Requirements?

- Evaluation of Alternative Requirements

- Contents of a Specification of Requirements

- Characteristics of a Good Specification of Requirements

- Pitfalls to be Avoided when Drawing Up Requirements

- Who Should Work on Drawing Up the Specification?

- Pitfalls to be Avoided when Drawing Up the Specification

- Quality Assurance.

WHY COMPILE A SPECIFICATION OF REQUIREMENTS?

Many consultancy assignments will seek to identify ways in which a company can improve through acquiring new technology in one form or another. A specification of requirements is one of the most important documents in projects that involve the acquisition of new equipment, services or systems or the introduction of new technology of any kind, and thus it is important for the consultant to ensure that comprehensive specifications are prepared by companies accordingly. The purpose of such a specification is to:

- Define what the system/equipment is to do
- Enable the company to obtain fixed-price tenders
- Provide necessary information on planned purchases
- Minimise expensive alterations at a later stage.

The target groups for the specification of requirements are:

- Potential suppliers
- Users
- Decision-makers in the company.

EVALUATION OF ALTERNATIVE REQUIREMENTS

During the work of drawing up the specification of requirements a number of alternative wishes and options will arise. The various proposals will have different financial effects, so it will be necessary to carry out a cost/benefit analysis before selecting the requirements that will form part of the specification.

Figure 18.1 shows an ideal procedure, in which the process of drawing up a specification is split up into stages. At the same time, it is important to be aware that writing specifications is an ongoing process, and it is often difficult to see all the possibilities at the beginning. In practice it is often necessary to do a new round of cost/benefit evaluation as work on the issues generates new wishes and possible solutions.

CONTENTS OF A SPECIFICATION OF REQUIREMENTS

The specification should not describe the design of the system in question. The messages to be communicated are the functional requirements for *what* the equipment should be able to do, the quantitative requirements for *how well* the functions should be carried out (performance), and further requirements describing what *environment* the system/equipment is to operate in.

Figure 18.1: Stages in the Drawing Up of Specifications

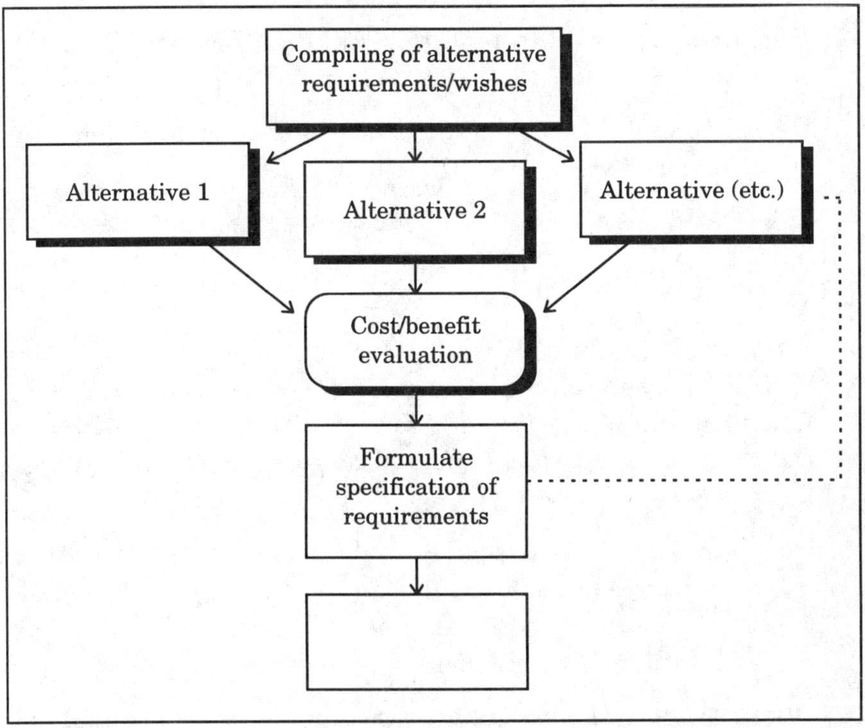

A simple but illustrative example of what is meant by functional requirements is the specifications for a chair. A typical mistake would be to make the following requirements:

- Has legs

- Has a seat

- Has a back.

This would impose restrictions on the design of the chair. Functional requirements on the other hand would be:

- Can bear weight

- Has the correct sitting height

- Supports the back.

The following is an example of how to organise a specification of requirements:

1. **Purpose**. A general introduction outlining the main goals for the system.

2. **Definition of concepts**. A list of words to explain how the words and expressions used should be understood.

3. **Integration**. A description of what the system is to become a part of. It may, for example, constitute one part of a production line.

4. **Functional capabilities**. This is the main section in the specification, and describes *what* the system is to do. Direct functional requirements are detailed here, along with requirements for operating the equipment /system (user interface).

5. **Performance**. Details the requirements as to how functions are to be carried out. Typical requirements deal with speed, capacity, precision, and so on. Such requirements can be formulated with minimum and maximum values.

6. **Operating environment**. This section is used if a special operating environment is required for the equipment (e.g. temperature, humidity, electrical interference etc.).

7. **Other properties**. Here it is possible to specify any other requirements that are not directly related to function. These might include maintenance, service, modularity, expansion potential and security.

CHARACTERISTICS OF A GOOD SPECIFICATION OF REQUIREMENTS

It is not enough merely to include certain points in the specification — it is also necessary to formulate them in a certain way. A good specification is characterised by being:

- **Unambiguous**. All requirements must be formulated in a way that allows for only one meaning. Words or expressions that might be interpreted in several ways should be defined so as to avoid ambiguity.

- **Complete**. All functions, limitations, capacity specifications and integration requirements are detailed. Phrases such as "no decision taken at this stage" must not appear in the specification.

- **Verifiable**. It must be possible to measure the requirements. In other words, it must be not only a qualitative, but also a quantitative formulation.

- **Consistent**. Requirements should not contradict one another. A function must be described with the same word/name throughout the document.

- **Modifiable**. The specification must be structured in a way that allows a requirement to be altered without having to restructure the whole document.

PITFALLS TO BE AVOIDED WHEN DRAWING UP REQUIREMENTS

The following examples are, unfortunately, typical of many specifications of requirements, and do not live up to the characteristics outlined above:

- "When the customer information menu is called, it should automatically show information on the last customer." This sentence is *ambiguous*. Is the "last customer" (a) the customer whose data was last viewed by the user or (b) the customer who has been most recently registered in the system, or (c) a reference to the most recent incoming order?

- Phrases such as "not decided", "decision to be reached later", and "will probably be" are inconsistent with a *complete* specification.

- Phrases such as "the system should have a short response time", "screen update should be fast", and "the buffer memory must be big enough for incoming goods" are not *verifiable* requirements. Such phrases must either be rewritten or followed by explanations that make them measurable.

- One often sees requirements for the system's memory capacity formulated as, for example, "the database should have a capacity of 100 mb." But this is a matter of design (how). Requirements for memory capacity should be formulated as the necessary number of transactions of each type, with a description of the amount of information in each transaction (what). The supplier can then decide how many megabytes are necessary to fulfil the requirement.

WHO SHOULD WORK ON DRAWING UP THE SPECIFICATION?

Users
The biggest mistake is to "forget" the people who will have to use the system. The old saying that "everyone knows best where their shoe pinches" is appropriate here. Not consulting the users can easily lead to alienation and scepticism when it comes to changing to the new system. Involving users also provides a means of motivating this group.

Technicians
It is very important that technical staff with a knowledge of the possibilities and limitations are involved in the process.

Project Manager
The person responsible for compiling the specification of requirements should also have a good overview of the financial implications of the proposed requirements. Without this, "active technicians" might easily specify a "Mercedes" when a "Volkswagen" would have done nicely.

Operation/Maintenance
Those responsible for operations and maintenance must be involved to ensure that no requirements are stated that are incompatible with the company's philosophy and guidelines.

External Consultant
The stage during which specifications are being drawn up is a time when help from outside the company can produce good results. Such a consultant can act as an inspiration and catalyst in the process.

The efficiency of the work can be influenced by the number of people involved. So it may be a good idea to split the work up into smaller areas. The most important thing is that all the groups involved are given the opportunity to comment on their particular area.

PITFALLS TO BE AVOIDED WHEN DRAWING UP THE SPECIFICATION

- Users of the system not involved

- Failure to understand the purpose and importance of the specification of requirements

- Not enough time assigned to the work. This results in "shoddy" work concluded before the specification is complete

- Technocrats are "given a free hand" and specify "their dream system"

- No competence involved that can see the financial consequences of the requirements.

QUALITY ASSURANCE

Two areas must be kept in focus when compiling a specification of requirements:

1. **The Quality of the Contents**. The document needs to be critically reviewed for the qualities mentioned earlier for a good specification. Check, too, that the stated requirements are not inconsistent with other strategies in the company (for example environmental, maintenance, data processing, and security strategies).

2. **Document administration**. The process of compiling a specification is iterative, and several versions of the document are produced. Before starting it is a good idea to define a system for keeping control of the various different versions. There should be no doubt as to which is the current version. Rules should also be defined for dealing with proposed alterations.

19

PROJECT PLANNING

INTRODUCTION

The aim of this chapter is to provide an overview of what project planning involves, to indicate some techniques that can be used and to offer advice, tips and checklists that can be used in the planning and organisational work.

This section also discusses techniques used for scheduling during the implementation of and follow-up on relatively simple projects assumed to be most relevant in the context of consultancy assignments in SMEs. The scheduling of large and complex projects where many parties must co-operate over an extended period may require more comprehensive competence and tools.

The subject material in this chapter is looked at under the following headings:

- The planning process
- Project organisation
- Reporting and follow-up
- Project scheduling
- Organisation of the schedule
- Establishing the schedule
- Follow-up and monitoring against the schedule
- Checklist for individual schedules.

THE PLANNING PROCESS

The planning process is an iterative process made up of many different phases. Figure 16.2 on page 389 shows the process as a "loop".

The result of the planning process is a general plan covering activities, responsibilities, scheduling and budgets. Organisation, reporting and follow-up are closely linked with the planning process

Goal Formulation

The planning of a project starts with the definition of overall goals. Since goal formulation is the point of departure, it must meet certain requirements. Goal formulation must:

- Determine the results to be achieved by the project

- Define and delimit the tasks in the project

- Form the starting point for planning at various levels

- Provide a basis for follow-up on results

- Create general understanding and acceptance.

The goal formulation can (and should) include goals for several different areas (for example technical, organisational and competence-related goals). Goals are defined at several levels (hierarchically). The goal formulation can also be used for informative purposes.

Breakdown and Structuring of Sub-tasks

On the basis of the goal formulation, the project is broken down into sub-tasks and these are structured. Depending on their size, these may be sub-projects (which should again be broken down) or direct activities.

Breakdown Tips:

- Do the breakdown in several steps (hierarchically)

- Group logically-related activities together

- The breakdown should be "balanced" — i.e. final activities should be about the same size

- Identify the person responsible for each sub-task (activity or sub-project).

The breakdown/structuring should be carried out by the Project Manager, since they will have to follow up at this level.

When the breakdown/structuring has been done, each sub-task has to be described and estimates have to be done for it. If the sub-task is a sub-project (consisting of several activities), these must be broken down first. Description and estimates must be done by the person responsible for the sub-task.

Extent of Planning (What Should Be Planned?)
At each level the following should be included in the plan:

- **Scheduling.** The start and finish dates for the sub-task and the estimated time consumption.

- **Personnel resource planning.** Person responsible, participants, co-ordination and information requirements.

- **Equipment resource planning.** The equipment that must be available.

- **Cost planning.** Purchases, travel, courses etc.

There are strong links between the above four planning areas.

Ordering of Sub-tasks
Ordering the sub-tasks is essential before one can do evaluation/analysis work. It involves establishing:

- **A schedule.** The sub-plans ordered along a time axis.

- **A resource plan.** Calculated burden on staff and equipment.

Evaluation/Analysis
The combined schedule and resource plan must be evaluated in terms of practical feasibility, whether it is financially acceptable, and whether it is suitable for follow-up.

The analysis of practical feasibility includes asking the following questions:

- Are there interdependencies among the sub-tasks?

- Is the timing of the sub-tasks logical?

- Are resources available at the times when they are to be used according to the plan?

- Is the overall time perspective acceptable?

There are several techniques that can be used to analyse the plan.

Gantt Diagrams

A Gantt diagram shows all the activities drawn as lines along a time axis. This gives an overview of how the work is distributed over time. An example is shown in Figure 19.1.

Milestone Planning

The aim of a milestone plan is to identify "control stages" for progress. Milestones are stages the project must pass on the way to the goal. Milestones can be related to precise events or situations that are easy to verify. The plan defines the date by which each milestone must be reached. The milestones must be selected to meet the following requirements:

- Important decisions/control points must be milestones

- They must be "natural"

- They must be verifiable

- There should not be too many milestones

- There should not be too many different activities between milestones.

A milestone plan can be drawn up separately, but the commonest approach is to combine a milestone plan with a Gantt diagram. The milestones are drawn in with special symbols in the diagram. An example is also shown in Figure 19.1.

Figure 19.1: Example of a Gantt Diagram with Milestones Shown

Activities	Week 10	Week 11	Week 12	Week 13	Week 14	Week 15
Activity 1						
Activity 2						
Activity 3			∇	2		
Activity 4			∇	1		
Activity 5					∇	3

∇ = Milestone

Network Planning

Network planning focuses on the interdependencies between activities. The diagrams used show the preconditions for starting an activity (for example, the conclusion of another activity). This reveals whether interdependencies make planned starting and finishing dates impossible. Network plans may be event-based or activity-based.

From the network diagram one can derive the so-called "critical path" of the project. This consists of the activities that must come in a certain order, and which as a whole take the longest time. Activities on the critical path should be given special attention in follow-up. Delays in activities on the critical path lead to corresponding delays in the project as a whole.

Network planning is described in more detail in the discussion on Scheduling below.

Responsibility Chart

The analysis of resource consumption and distribution of responsibilities can be made easier by setting up a responsibility chart. An example of such a chart is given in Figure 19.2. If the plan does not "fit" the financial framework established, one must go back to the breakdown and description of the sub-tasks and consider alternatives.

Figure 19.2: Responsibility Chart

Activities	Clark	Davis	Baker	Kelly
Activity 1	D	I	C	R
Activity 2	R			
Activity 3			RD	
Activity 4	I			RD
Activity 5	RD			

R = responsible   I = must be informed
D = doer   C = must be consulted

PROJECT ORGANISATION

A project has the following characteristics:

- It has to deal with a one-off task

- Work is done towards a defined goal

- The work is done in a defined time/cost framework

- It often needs a co-ordinated interdisciplinary effort

- It involves some degree of uncertainty

- The project is run independently of the company.

An organisational structure for the project is established in addition to the base organisation for the duration of the project. Linkages between the base organisation and the project organisation can be made in several ways:

1. Separate, independent project organisation

   - Staffed by people without other tasks

   - The project has full responsibility

   - The base organisation only has an advisory function

   - Best for major projects (e.g. offshore).

2. Matrix organisation

- Staffed by people from the base organisation

- The staff are released from other duties for sufficient periods

- Project participants report to both line management and project management

- The project organisation is responsible for both the goals and results of the project

- The base organisation has the specialised responsibility.

3. Individual organisation

- Only a Project Manager is appointed

- The Project Manager "buys" services as required from the base organisation

- The base organisation is responsible for the results

- The Project Manager is responsible for co-ordination.

Whatever the linkage with the base organisation, Figure 12.6 on page 290 shows the traditional organisational structure of a project.

Responsibilities of the Control Group

- Setting a goal for the project, and making sure it is made clear and understood

- Appointing a Project Manager

- Providing guidelines for project organisation

- Approving the project schedule (time, staff, costs)

- Allocating resources from base organisation as per approved plan

- Making sure the project is run according to the plan

- Supporting the Project Manager in relations with the base organisation.

Responsibilities of the Project Manager

- Planning the project

- Making sure the project achieves the goals within the established plans and framework

- Creating understanding and acceptance of project goals and plans among project staff

- Creating good working relationships internally in the project and with surroundings

- Reporting to the control group

- Following up on the project and taking corrective action as required.

Possible Pitfalls in Organisation

- Project Manager given no formal authority

- Alternative organisational structures not considered

- Unclear delegation of responsibilities

- Unclear principles of co-operation

- Key personnel not available when required

- Project participants not released sufficiently from other duties

- Line management and key personnel not motivated

- Wrong person as Project Manager (may be good at their specialisation but has no management talent)

- Total competence of participants does not cover the field

REPORTING AND FOLLOW-UP

If the plan is to be implementable, it is essential that it allows for follow-up. Analysis in this area consists of a critical review of the following factors:

- Has the reporting procedure been defined?

- Are the milestones suitable as checkpoints?

- Is it easy to report on progress as planned?

- Are the individual activities balanced?

- Are responsibilities clearly defined?

- Are co-operation principles clearly defined?

Reporting and follow-up must not be confused. Reporting is describing progress in terms of the plan. Follow-up is action — that is, analysing information and initiating corrective measures.

Many people see reporting as a burden. At the same time, good reporting is the main precondition for effective follow-up. The following tips may help to make reporting simpler and follow-up more effective:

- Leave space for reporting in the plan — i.e. make the report a copy of the plan with information filled in for the relevant period.

- Report on deviations from the plan — i.e. dates, time consumption and resource consumption.

- Report on both "time consumed" and "time necessary for completion", since "budgeted time" minus "time consumed" may of course be different from "time necessary for completion".

- Base follow-up on activities — i.e. activities which do not consume the resources allocated to them at the right times will probably be delayed.

- Focus in particular on activities on the "critical path". Be aware that the critical path may change during implementation.

PROJECT SCHEDULING

Main Principles of Scheduling
To establish a good schedule for a project, it is necessary to understand:

- The intention of the project

- What the project involves

- The results that are to be achieved by the project
- How the results are to be achieved
- The general constraints on the project.

It is also necessary to know the priorities which apply to the project, both in terms of the constraints and the results. Different priorities can be assigned to function, quality, time and costs.

Finally, it is necessary to have a clear picture of the difference between registering what has happened and planning what one wants to happen.

A plan is rarely followed without any deviations. Planning is not just drawing up a plan and recording any deviations. It also involves following up on the plan and proposing reactions to the deviations to ensure that one achieves the goals. Only when the project manager considers that reactions to deviations are *not* desirable can it be relevant to change the plan as such.

ORGANISATION OF THE SCHEDULE

Clarification of Roles

Like any other work, scheduling work must be organised. Often the detailed work in the scheduling process for minor projects will be done by the project manager. In reality, therefore, the project manager then has two functions: one as project manager and one as scheduler. In the following these two functions are dealt with separately.

During the scheduling process one gains good insight into the project and one makes choices which to a great extent influence the project. It is therefore important that the person doing the planning is competent. It is also important that both the scheduler and the project manager acknowledge the fact that the project manager has the ultimate responsibility for the plan and act accordingly. The project manager must be actively involved with and co-operate with the scheduler. It is a common source of problems that the project manager does not take the time and opportunity to participate in the scheduling work.

The detailed scheduling will normally be done in co-operation with the persons in the project organisation who are responsible for parts of the project. These people must be informed and must set aside time to take part in the scheduling work.

Plan the Scheduling Work

Part of the organisation of the work time must be set aside for the actual scheduling work. How much time the work requires depends on several factors such as the competence of the scheduler, demands for accuracy in planning and follow-up, the size and complexity of the project etc. Establishing a good detailed plan for a project on the order of half a million to a million ECUs and in otherwise "normal" conditions can take anything from a couple of days to a week's work. Reasonable follow-up on the schedule may require two or three hours a week in the project period.

Choose Simple Tools

Often the issue of the choice of scheduling tools comes up early in the process. There are a large number of more or less comprehensive computer programs in the area of scheduling. At the risk of over-simplifying, they can be grouped in two categories:

- Stand-alone PC programs which can carry out network calculations and to some extent assign resources etc. (e.g. Microsoft Project). The programs can often be used by caseworkers in a project without any special competence requirements, while at the same time they allow for relatively sophisticated use when so required and when the user has the competence.

- Stand-alone PC programs without network logic, but which are simple and easy to use for drawing up schedules, mainly in the form of Gantt diagrams. These can be drawing programs with a calendar function, or database-oriented programs with drawing and calendar functions.

One does not become a good scheduler because one uses a sophisticated computer program, but even a simple program can be useful to a good scheduler.

Scheduling tools have developed extensively in recent time. The use of such tools has changed considerably in the last 10-15 years accordingly. Today the emphasis is on using tools that are as simple as possible. One reason for this is that schedules based on network calculations have proved to be more demanding than necessary and appropriate in many situations. In particular, following up on such plans can be a big job.

One point of departure for choosing tools is to use a network program in the early phases when one has to structure and familiarise oneself with the project and study alternative implementation models (provided one masters the program and the technique). Once the schedule has been drawn up and the project is in progress, one can go over to a simpler program where one can quickly adapt the schedule without struggling with logical and other interdependencies which have a tendency to gradually become less and less relevant.

ESTABLISHING THE SCHEDULE

Get an Overview of the Project
The first thing a scheduler has to do is to get an overall impression of the project. It is an advantage if the scheduler has an insight into this type of work, although this is not always necessary. If the scheduler does not have such insight to begin with, it must be obtained in co-operation with the project manager and by interviewing anyone responsible for part of the project. In this phase the scheduler will make general notes on the content of the project.

Find the Main Structure of the Project
It is necessary to arrive at a reasonable classification or grouping of the jobs that have to be done. The starting point for such a structure is often the organisational plan of the project.

The next level of a structure will often be associated with the main physical units in each area of responsibility — for example, whole process lines, buildings/plants etc. At this stage it is rarely necessary to go into more detail with the groupings.

Think in Terms of Results

When one has to specify a project one should describe the activities that lead to results, whether it is a matter of a component, a system, a document or the like. All activities in a project can be described in this way. A decision should be available in a document, a plan should be available as a drawing or description or a specification, a contracting process should lead to a signed contract, an installation job should lead to an installed component, an inspection must lead to a report, etc.

Begin at the End

Often its is best to start with the result one wants to achieve with the project or part of the project, and ask "What is needed (to achieve the result)?" If the precondition borders on someone else's area of responsibility, this should be noted and taken up with the person responsible for that area.

Clarify the Constraints on the Schedule

It is often difficult to specify clear constraints on the schedule at an early juncture. The constraints may be related to official orders, laws and regulations, to existing physical constraints, to particular periods, to capacity limitations, etc.

Discuss Alternative Implementation Models

Once the main structure and constraints are reasonably clear, the scheduler must find alternative ways of attacking the implementation of the project and must discuss these with the project manager. This should not be a complex analysis, but a relatively simple overview of the possible implementation models so one has alternatives to draw on later, and not least so one becomes familiar with the project.

Outline a Main Schedule

By this time the scheduler will usually have enough insight into the project to outline a provisional main schedule. The aim of this is to have a basis for discussing the implementation plan and for obtaining information for the detailed scheduling of the project.

A main schedule should consist of a limited number of activities. Even for large projects, the main schedule will rarely have more than a few dozen activities. The scheduler must form a picture of the resource consumption involved in the schedule and ensure that he/she has a schedule in which the allocation of resources is reasonable at any given time. This is perhaps the hardest, most important, and most competence-demanding part of the whole scheduling process.

There is rarely any point in getting down to detailed resource studies at this stage. Instead the scheduler must exploit their own experience or obtain experience from the project manager and others. There will normally be a cost overview for the main parts of the project. The scheduler must use this to estimate a "cash-flow" and work out what this means in terms of allocation of human resources, equipment/components per week or per month. Then they must assess the results compared with the available experience of what is practical, reasonable and natural. On this basis they can estimate the time consumption for parts of the schedule and for the schedule as a whole.

A main schedule should be presented in the form of a Gantt diagram. See the model example in Figure 19.3. If the schedule concerns a physical object which is to be designed, the Gantt diagram should be followed by an overview drawing.

Figure 19.3: Outline Sketch Gantt Diagram

Activity	Start	Finish	Time	2/9	3/9	4/9	5/9	6/9
Plan the hunt	2/9	2/9	8					
Plan the feast	3/9	4/9	12					
Shoot the bear	3/9	4/9	16					
Sell the skin	5/9	5/9	4					
Have the feast	6/9	6/9	24					

Front line 4th Sept. ⟶

Inform Participants, Obtain Allies and Follow-up

At this point the scheduler and project manager will have obtained a general overview of the project and the conditions to which it is subject. This forms the basis for studying the details —

i.e. one starts working on a schedule with the final degree of detail

Before the scheduler gets down to the detailed work, it is important to inform in advance the people in the project organisation who have responsibility for the progress of the project or who will be involved in planning and follow-up on how the planning work will be implemented, how the result will look specifically, and how the schedule is to be followed up. It is also important to maintain good contacts with the parties involved during the work itself, to make sure they are motivated, and to support and help them with the job. In other words — obtain allies!

Draw-up Activity Lists

A finished, detailed schedule for the whole project period can in this context perhaps consist of 300-500 activities; with smaller projects perhaps of 100-300 activities; and for small projects of perhaps 50-100 activities.

To arrive at the detailed activities, the scheduler will normally co-operate with the people in the organisation who are responsible for the individual elements of the main structure of the project. The scheduler should meet them with a form that can be filled in as an activity list. It is often a challenge for the scheduler to arrive at a useful classification for activities. Limitation is an art, and it is easy to create too many activities. The scheduler must try to break the project down into as few activities as possible, but with allowances for the following:

- There must be a particular person in the project organisation who is responsible for implementing the activity. If the responsibility is shared, the activity should be split up.

- It must be possible for the person responsible to describe the activity reasonably unambiguously.

- The dependence of the activity on previous activities must be reasonably clear to those who are responsible for those activities.

- It must be possible to estimate time and resource consumption for the activity. Often the person responsible for the activity will hesitate to say how much time and resources an activity will require. So avoid a detailed discussion at this point. The issue is dealt with later.

- It must be possible to follow up on the progress of the activities in the form of events, milestones or fixed times.

In major projects one uses activity list forms — usually one form per activity or group of activities. The forms are often called *CTR sheets* (for Cost/Time/Resource sheets) and contain information on:

- **Title** of the activity (systematic and unambiguous)

- **Number** of the activity (according to a suitable system, which may be related to an accounting plan)

- **Duration** (days, weeks, months)

- **Resource requirements** (man-hours — can be specified by categories, in money)

- **Responsibility** for implementation

- **Assumptions** (dependence on preceding activities or basic material)

- **Goal** (the result to be produced by the activity, preferably measurable, concrete and physical)

- **Content** (if required, a description of what is to be done and how)

- **Special requirements** (unusual specifications, quality requirements etc.)

- **Reporting** (how and how often monitoring and reporting should be done)

Network or Gantt Diagram?

If the scheduler masters network techniques and otherwise considers it appropriate, they can outline the activities graphically on a network diagram. For a scheduler who masters network technique it is often useful to use it when establishing even simple plans for the first time in a project.

In some computer programs the network can be drawn directly on the screen. With smaller networks this can be very appropriate. With larger networks it can easily mean that one loses the overall view that is necessary to work up the schedule towards a good result. Overview and system are important in this context.

If the schedule is very simple it may be fine to outline it directly in the form of a Gantt diagram. This is true, for example, when one has simple, relatively independent chains of activities like budgeting — design — contracting — delivery — installation — commissioning — running-in.

Don't be Afraid to Assign a Time to Activities

One makes a point of avoiding assigning times to activities before one has formed a picture of the logical relationships among the activities in the project. Otherwise one easily ties oneself to a relationship among the activities which may not be either logical or necessary.

As mentioned before, the person responsible for an activity may hesitate to give a firm statement on the time an activity will take. It is the job of the scheduler to help them make a reasonable estimate. It often helps if the scheduler says that what they want is an estimate. It also helps to approach the timing issue gradually by narrowing down from a lower and higher limit. They can ask something like this: "This activity will probably take not less than ____ days, but surely it will not take more than ____ days either?" This is likely to get the person responsible to volunteer their own comments and estimates.

There are scientific methods of timing activities, but they fall outside the scope of this manual. Use a qualified estimate. Minor errors for individual activities balance out in the overall schedule. Adjustments can be made later when it is clear where in the schedule this is important and where they play a minor role (critical path).

Watch Out for Poor Use of Resources!

The time spent on an activity is of course related to the amount of resources allocated to it. Many scheduling programs can allow for this if one specifies the resources allocated to each activity. If the sum of the activities at any point requires more resources than are available, the program will more or less automatically re-schedule the activities so one can keep resource consumption under a given limit.

Drawing up a schedule with balanced resources can be demanding, and is often not necessary for schedules of the type covered by this manual. It is enough to be aware of resource consumption when one estimates the time for an activity, and makes the time estimate on the basis of "normal" resource consumption. At all events, the scheduler must be aware of any overlapping of activities in the schedule which may create an unreasonable strain on resources or which waste resources or are impractical for other reasons.

When a schedule has been established based on assumptions regarding the availability of resources, the project manager must ensure that these resources are in fact made available for implementation.

Do Not Plan on Too Tight a Schedule

A good schedule should be tight, but it should also have enough built-in flexibility to allow for unforeseen situations and delays. This flexibility can be obtained by preparing alternative implementation models and if necessary by building a certain margin of error into the schedule.

It Is Useful to Look at How Costs Develop

Many scheduling programs allow the user to enter costs for each individual activity in the schedule, and on that basis will calculate the development of costs. This is often easier to handle than resource consumption. Cost development in the project is a valuable support for both the scheduling work and the budgeting and control of the project.

Cost development can also be calculated extremely well with a spreadsheet. The advantage here is that is easy to do other kinds of calculation than a scheduling program allows, and one has more freedom with graphics. The disadvantage is that there is no linkage between the changes in the schedule and the spreadsheet. Many scheduling programs can export cost data to a spreadsheet.

Give the Schedule a Final "Massage"

While fine tuning the schedule one must be aware of the activities that are important for interim deadlines and for the overall schedule. If a scheduling program has been used, there will be good support for this in the critical path of activities, i.e. the sequence of activities which are determinants of the timing. If the schedule has been drawn on paper, the critical path should be marked in colour. Often it will also be appropriate to mark "quasi-critical" paths for activities.

The scheduler must look at the activities on the critical path and assess whether the time they take can be reduced, and whether the dependencies among them can be changed. When one adjusts the critical path, one or more of the noncritical paths will often now emerge as a critical one, and one will have to make a corresponding assessment of these. This way one works through the schedule in co-operation with those responsible for the different parts of the project, and gradually one arrives at a well worked-out ("massaged"), adapted, balanced schedule on the basis of which decisions on implementation can be made.

Draw-up an Easily Comprehensible Version of the Schedule

After a while, a scheduler will have a lot of data on the schedule, especially if they have used a scheduling program. Be very cautious about showing all this data to the users — exercise data discipline! This means that the users should only be given the information that is necessary and sufficient for their purposes. Distinguish carefully between "need to know" and "nice to know".

A network is the scheduler's tool. It is first and foremost the result of the network that should be shown to the users and decision-makers, and then preferably in the form of clear, manageable Gantt diagrams.

It may be appropriate to group activities for individual units or areas of responsibility on their own sheets, so that those responsible for each part have an overview of the parts of the schedule which affect themselves, without being burdened with a major plan much of which is no concern of theirs.

FOLLOW-UP AND MONITORING AGAINST THE SCHEDULE

A crucial part of the scheduling work is deciding how implementation is to be followed up. One has to decide on:

- The aim of follow-up and priorities

- How close the follow-up should be and how often

- How the information flow in data collection should run

- How the information flow in reporting should be, including how the reports are to be formed and what reactions, approvals, etc. can be expected.

With projects within the scope of this chapter it is natural to follow up on the plan at periodical meetings of those responsible for each part of the project. The frequency of meetings can vary throughout the project. Remember that one has to get things done between the meetings! During hectic periods with close follow-up, weekly meetings will be appropriate. At other times it will be sufficient to hold meetings every other week. In exceptional cases the period can be longer.

Follow-up should be well prepared and implemented efficiently. Stick to the matter in hand and the facts. Refer long discussions of conflicts or how things should be done to separate meetings among those who are concerned. The meeting should be chaired by the project manager, but the scheduler should be secretary for this part of the meeting. The meeting usually deals with activities which are relevant within a limited period. It may be appropriate for the schedule for the current period to be in rather more detail than originally. Depending somewhat on the scope and duration of the project, a relevant period could be 1-3 months ahead in the future.

Follow-up should be done by noting:

- Real progress compared with scheduled progress

- Any deviations, their consequences and how they should be treated.

As preparation for the meeting, the individual responsible should give an account of progress in their own part of the plan. At the meeting it may be practical to record real progress by marking out a progress front on a Gantt diagram. See the model example in Figure 19.3.

The minutes of the meeting must be got to the participants as quickly as possible, in a day or two at the latest. The minutes will often take the form of a "fronted" progress plan (see Figure 19.3), with specific comments on the progress and the treatment of deviations. It is particularly important to be careful with factors which cross responsibility boundaries.

When there are deviations in the progress which change the completion date (deviations from the critical path), they are just as serious when they appear at the beginning of the project as at the end. It is a common mistake to think that deviations which arise at an early stage are less serious. The reality is that these are just as difficult to catch up with as deviations that happen later. It is therefore necessary to take corrective action immediately with every deviation, irrespective of when it arises.

If there are substantial deviations from the schedule, the scheduler may have to study the effect of alternative measures in consultation with the project manager before the project manager approves such measures.

It is important to stick to a plan all the way until a project manager considers it appropriate to adopt changes. This should not happen often — all progress is reported in terms of the adopted schedule.

CHECKLIST FOR INDIVIDUAL SCHEDULES

Before starting to schedule a project one should draw up a checklist for the work. The list given on the following pages gives some keywords for this purpose. The list only forms a point of departure, and must be adapted to each individual project.

Organisation

- Role assignment
- Competence

- Resource availability
- Decision-making authority
- Reporting

Tools

- Computer program
- Planning method
- Follow-up method
- Reporting/presentation

Main Schedule

- Main goal/subgoals
- Project content
- Project structure
- External constraints
- Internal constraints
- Implementation models
- Resource consumption
- Follow-up

Detailed Schedule

- Briefing/information
- Activity classification
  ◊ responsibilities
  ◊ content/results
  ◊ preconditions/dependencies
  ◊ time and resources
  ◊ follow-up/reporting

- Activity lists/CTR sheets
- Combination/logic
- Timing
- Analysis/processing
- Presentation
- Adoption

Follow-up/Monitoring

- Aims/priorities
- Closeness
- Frequency
- Information flow
  - ◊ data collection
  - ◊ reporting
- Report(s) form
- Treatment of deviations.

PART V

GENERAL TOPICS

20

FINANCIAL MANAGEMENT AND ACCOUNTING SYSTEMS

INTRODUCTION

A business is run on the basis of the decisions made by the board of directors and by management at all levels. Given that a company must always have financial goals for its activities, financial assessments are important when decisions are being made. Financial planning and monitoring, therefore, provide an essential foundation when important decisions have to be made. Financial management, analysis and monitoring are means of ensuring that company goals are achieved.

Financial management means:

- Always making sure there is a balance between resource consumption and value creation

- Ensuring the *correct* relationships between costs, quality and time.

The problem is not to manage the company's finances, but to manage the company economically.

The need for financial management is a function of both the company's own internal structure/problems as well as the uncertainty/variations that occur in the external environment in which the company must operate. The following factors are important in this regard:

- Public policy decisions

- Technological development

- Product lifetime

- Market development/competitors

- Links with suppliers

- Investment needs.

In this chapter, a company's financial management and accounting systems are looked at under the following headings:

- Financial/Management Accounting

- Principles of Accounting

- Balance Sheet

- Profit and Loss Account

- Financing Control Systems.

FINANCIAL/MANAGEMENT ACCOUNTING

Accounting is a system for collecting, summarising, analysing, and reporting, in monetary terms, all relevant information about an organisation. In studying a company's accounting system, it is useful to make a distinction between two areas of accounting, referred to as *financial* accounting and *management* accounting. The two areas are not in fact neatly separable in practice, but the concepts and purpose related to each part are sufficiently different so that it is well to consider them separately.

Financial Accounting

Financial accounting has the primary objective of providing information to parties outside the business, that is, to shareholders, bankers, creditors, government agencies and the general public. Only in rare instances can these outside parties insist that a business furnish information that is tailor-made to their specifications. In most cases they must accept the information that the business chooses to supply. They could not conceivably understand this information without knowing the ground rules that governed its preparation. Since the typical outsider uses accounting information from many different businesses, there is a clear need for having the basic ground rules apply to all businesses, both so that the information from one business can be compared with that of another and also to obviate the necessity of learning a separate set of ground rules for each business. These ground rules are the subject matter of financial accounting.

The main documents used to show this information are the *trading and profit and loss account*, and the *balance sheet*, together with the Directors' and Auditors' reports. The preparation and presentation of these documents follows established principles which are embodied in relevant legislation in each country. Most of these principles are based on recommendations made by professional accountancy associations.

The presentation of this historical information is a necessary task. It must be remembered that the shareholders of a company are the owners of that company and the directors are managing the company on their behalf. It is essential that periodical reports of the directors' stewardship should be given to the owners. This information is conventionally given in full once a year, with interim reports being made during the course of that year.

This enables the shareholders to judge whether the performance of the company in the past twelve months has been satisfactory. From their standpoint this usually means that sufficient profits have been made to give them an adequate return on their investment. It also allows some assessment of the future prospects of the company to be formed. The taxation authorities will be equally concerned with the performance of the company for the past twelve months in order to ensure that a correct assessment is made of the tax liability of the concern on its trading activities for the period.

The whole outlook of the financial accountant will be seen to be concerned with historical information and is based on the *static* concept of yearly accounting. Thus, financial accounting is by nature limited for three reasons:

- The balance sheet presents a picture of the company on one particular day each year. It will be apparent that the whole picture presented by this statement may well have been changed the following day. New assets may have been purchased, creditors may have been paid, debtors may have been raised and stock reduced, to give but a few examples of the normal day-today activities which will affect figures shown on the balance sheet.

- The compilation of the financial accounting statements takes time. Very often, several months have elapsed before the Final Accounts, as they are called, are presented for external inspection.

- Financial accounts show the overall trading picture of the concern for a particular period. It is not possible to ascertain from such accounts whether the concern is pursuing its most profitable lines of business or what the cost of operating a department is, or whether the most effective use is being made of materials, labour and machines. Accounts usually cover a period of twelve months (the period used also for taxation calculations), but the trade cycle of the business may be more or less than twelve months. Such differences can be overcome by the use of *management* accounting techniques.

Management Accounting

In a going concern the normal state is dynamic, not static. The management accountant deals with the present and the future rather than the past. The role of the management accountant is to help management to achieve the objectives of the business.

The management accountant presents management (i.e. the decision-makers) with the best possible financial information upon which they can base their decisions, and also establishes control systems to ensure that the best use is being made of the company's resources (labour, machines, materials and money).

Management Control

An important process in which accounting information is used within a business is called management control. This is the process of assuring that resources are obtained and used effectively and efficiently in the accomplishment of the organisation's objectives. Management control has to do with the ongoing operation of the business. It consists of a more or less regularly recurring sequence of interrelated activities. For convenience, these activities may be classified as either *control* activities or *planning* activities.

Control

Control is the process by which management assures itself, in so far as is feasible, that actions taken by the members of an organisation conform to management's plans and policies. Accounting information is useful in control as a means of communication, of motivation, and of appraisal.

As a means of *communication*, accounting reports can assist in informing the organisation about management's plans and policies and, in general, the types of action that management wishes the organisation to take.

In general, it is the responsibility of management to see to it that work gets done by others. This requires, first, that personnel be hired and formed into an organisation and, second, that this organisation be motivated in such a way that it will do what management wants it to do. Accounting information can help (and also, unless properly used, can hinder) this *motivation* process.

Periodically, management needs to evaluate how well employees are doing their jobs. Such an appraisal of performance may result in a salary increase, promotion, reassignment, corrective action of various kinds, or, in extreme cases, dismissal. Accounting information can assist in this *appraisal* process, although an adequate basis for judging a person's performance cannot be obtained solely from information revealed by accounting records.

Planning

Planning is the process of deciding what action should be taken in the future. The area covered by one plan may be a tiny segment of the enterprise, or it may be the whole enterprise. The essential characteristic of a plan is that it involves a decision about action. This distinguishes *planning* from *forecasting*. A forecast is an estimate of what will happen in the future, but the forecaster makes no attempt to influence the future by his own decisions or action.

A systematic form of planning, called budgeting, occurs as part of the management control process. Budgeting is the process of planning the overall activity of the enterprise for a specified period of time, usually a year. An important objective of this process is to fit together the separate plans made for various segments of the enterprise so as to ensure that these plans are in harmony with one another and that the aggregate effect of all of them on the whole enterprise is satisfactory.

A model for financial monitoring is illustrated in Figure 20.1. In order to compare actual earnings with financial plans (i.e. budgets) made at the outset, it is necessary to decide on relevant monitoring criteria. These criteria will become key ratios that can be used at a later stage to make adjustments so as to achieve earnings that are in accordance with the plan.

Financial key ratio analysis then gives us information about the results of previous decisions in critical monitoring areas.

Figure 20.1: Financial Monitoring Model

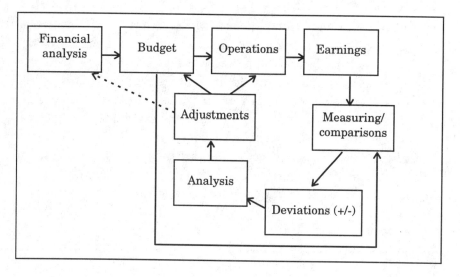

Examples of key ratios are:

- Return on investment

- Profit ratio

- Capital turnover

- Contribution margin

- Current ratio

- Acid test ratio

- Equity ratio

- Interest cover

- Stock turnover.

All of the above ratios are defined and discussed in more detail in Chapter 8 on "Financial Key Ratio Analysis".

Main Systems and Techniques
The main systems and techniques which are at present available to the management accountant include the following:

- **Historical Costing:** This is concerned with actual costs which have been incurred. Although these are of limited value (for reasons given in the section on financial accounting), they are essential in order to operate a standard costing system.

- **Standard Costing:** This involves setting up predetermined standards for costs. Actual costs are then compared with these standard costs and any differences, referred to as *variances*, are analysed and reasons sought for them.

- **Budgetary Control:** A budget is a plan specified in financial terms and relating to a future period in time. The use of budgets ensures that responsibilities for expenditure and revenues are clearly established. A continuous comparison of the actual and budgeted figures, enables any differences to be analysed. Suitable corrective action can then be taken as necessary.

- **Marginal Costing:** This involves making a distinction between fixed costs and variable costs. Only costs which vary with production are charged to the operation, fixed costs being written off against profits in the period in which they arise.

- **Cost/Profit/Volume Relationships:** It is important that management are aware of the effect of volume of output on profits. This is particularly important when a new product is being introduced or when there is a slump in the industry resulting in reduced sales. Once costs have been defined as fixed or variable, it is possible to show the relationship between sales and output, and more specifically at what output total costs equal sales. At this point there will be neither profits nor losses, and this is known as the break-even point.

- **Uniform Costing:** Uniform costing is defined as "the use by several undertakings of the same costing principles and/or practices". It is most usefully employed by large business organisations which have a number of factories spread over a wide area, manufacturing the same type of product under similar conditions or operating the same type of service. It may also be used by trade associations when processes are standardised and easily identifiable.

- **Inter-firm Comparisons:** An inter-firm comparison scheme is intended to show the management of each firm taking part how its profitability and productivity compares with that of other firms in the same industry; in what respects the firm is weaker or stronger than its competitors; and what specific questions of policy or performance should be tackled if the firm's profitability and productivity are to be raised.

- **Decision Information:** The accountant should be in a position to present management with the financial implications of alternative schemes. For example, the decision whether to "make or buy" a given component invariably requires financial appraisal.

- **Capital Investment Appraisal:** Budgeting for capital expenditure decisions is an important part of policy making. Generally, senior management assumes direct responsibility for the authorisation of all but the smallest capital investment sums. Thorough appraisal of capital investments is important for the following reasons:

1. The sums involved in capital investment are usually very substantial.

2. Once decisions have been made the resources of the firm are likely to be tied up for some considerable time in the particular project to which the capital investment relates.

3. The future of the firm may depend on a single investment decision and it may be very difficult to reverse the effects of a bad decision.

4. Capital budgeting is a long-term function and the further into the future that plans are made the more uncertain are the results.

PRINCIPLES OF ACCOUNTING

Accounting Concepts

Accounting is an art rather than an exact science, and in order to ensure some uniformity in the system of accounting it is necessary to use certain generally accepted guidelines to establish a basic framework in which the system can work. Without such guidelines the whole art of accounting would flounder and no party either internally or externally would be able to place any reliance on the results given by the accountant. Thus, in order to appreciate fully the role of management accounting in the business organisation it is necessary to have some knowledge of the basic concepts of accounting as given below.

The Entity Concept

Every business, whether it is run by one person, by a partnership or as a limited company, is regarded as a separate entity and accounts are kept for each entity. This means that in the one-person business it is necessary to distinguish between the individual as an individual and the individual as owner of the business.

The Going Concern Concept

Accounting systems are based on the assumption that every business is a continuing entity. Thus, assets are valued, for example, on the basis that they will be used to help produce further goods or that they will be sold in the normal course of trading. If the business were not treated as a going concern, the accountant would have to try to value assets on the basis of the business closing down tomorrow. Under normal circumstances this would be unrealistic, and would require many subjective decisions. Machinery, for example, which may be in good condition but is only capable of producing a certain product manufactured by the business would have little value the business were closed down the next day. When the business is viewed as a going concern, however, the machine is a valuable asset capable of earning revenue for the business in future years, and a monetary value can be assigned on it.

Measurement is in Monetary Terms

The accountant deals only in those facts which can be reduced to monetary terms. The balance sheet shows in monetary terms certain facts relating to assets of the business and the various claims, again in monetary terms, against these assets. The balance sheet will not reveal facts which may have a very important bearing on the future of the business but which are not capable of being reduced to the common denominator of money. For example, poor industrial relations, or the fact that a significant amount of plant is likely to become obsolete in the next six months due to a new invention, will be not be reflected in a company's balance sheet.

Stable Monetary Unit

It is generally accepted that the recording of accounting transactions should be based on objective evidence. This involves valuing the resources of a business at cost or market price, whichever is the lower. This in turn means that the balance sheet of a business cannot be used as a measure of the current worth of that business, when there is an unstable currency which, because of inflation, is constantly being devalued in real terms. The main reason against making up-to-date assessments of current values is, once again, the subjective nature of such assessments and the lack of reliable information about price changes on which assessments could be made. As a compromise, when it is obvious that an asset has increased in value (e.g. land), a number of companies have undertaken a revaluation of the asset and made the appropriate adjustments in the balance sheet.

Realisation Concept

Revenues should not be recorded until they are realised, but losses should be recorded even though they may not yet have occurred. This is the conservative approach which has an important influence on the accountant when transactions are being recorded. In connection with the sale of some commodity the accountant should only take account of the sale when the goods have been delivered to the buyer. No income should be shown throughout the stages necessary to get the goods into a saleable state, despite the fact that money has been spent on the processing of raw materials.

One exception to the above is in the case of long-term contracts such as shipbuilding, where it is prudent to show a proportion of the revenue each year to avoid violent fluctuations from one year to the next. In all cases, however, the recorded income should be conservatively estimated.

Expenses are Matched with Revenues

Costs should be matched with the revenue which they earn. Once the accounting period is concluded (e.g. twelve months), all costs incurred in earning the revenue received during that period should be shown. These costs may have occurred in previous years (e.g. the purchase of plant and equipment), in the present year (e.g. wages), or will occur in cash in a future year (e.g. rent which is paid in arrears).

Items which have not been fully used in earning the revenue of the period will be shown in the balance sheet as assets. In this respect they represent "stored-up" costs which will be used to produce future revenues and will be set against such revenues when they are used.

Consistency

The statements prepared by the accountant must be consistent from period to period. The same methods of valuation must be employed from year to year for the results to be meaningful and the accounts should not be manipulated to provide a desired result which is inconsistent with previous procedures adopted. This does not, of course, mean that no changes should ever take place, but changes should be infrequent and should be clearly noted on the relevant statements.

The Limitations of Accounting

Figures for a Purpose
Unlike mathematics, accounting is not an end in itself. Instead, accounting has a purpose. This may be to convey information about what has happened in a business, to provide data that is of assistance in solving a business problem, or to express future plans. The work of accountants is justified only insofar as it contributes to activity that is external to accounting. Both the beginner and the person who has long been immersed in accounting have a tendency to think of accounting as being conducted for its own sake. This attitude can be avoided by making frequent references to the purposes for which accounting data are intended.

Different Figures for Different Purposes
In mathematics, and in most of the physical sciences, there are definitions that are valid under a wide variety of circumstances. Such is not the case with most accounting definitions. Often different accounting figures can superficially resemble one another. Different figures may even be called by the same name and thus a person who is not familiar with them may easily become confused or frustrated. The most common source of confusion is the word "cost". There are many different types of "costs" including historical costs, standard costs, original costs, net costs, residual costs, variable costs, differential costs, incremental costs, marginal costs, opportunity costs, direct costs, estimated costs, full costs as well as other kinds of costs. Some of these terms are synonymous; others are almost but not quite synonymous; still others, although not synonymous at all, are used by some as if they were.

Accounting figures should always be discussed with reference to the particular problem that they are intended to help solve, rather than in any abstract sense. A statement that "the cost of an item is ECU 100" literally has no meaning unless those who hear this statement understand clearly which of the several possible concepts of cost was intended. A useful procedure to follow in approaching a specific problem is to define, as carefully as possible, the purpose for which figures are to be used in that problem and then to consider how the figures should be assembled and used for that specific purpose.

Accounting Figures are Approximations

Accounting is a system for recording and summarising measurements of business facts, and, as is the case with any measurement, an accounting figure is an approximation rather than a precisely accurate statement. Most of the data used in the physical sciences are also measurements, and like scientists and engineers, the user of accounting information must acquire an understanding of the degree of approximation that is present in the data.

There are many reasons for the inaccuracy of accounting figures. One reason is simply that a business is a complicated organism which includes vastly dissimilar elements — money, buildings, morale, machines, incentives, materials, policies, for example. There can be no precise way of adding all these diverse elements together so as to form a completely accurate picture of the whole enterprise.

The problem of obtaining reasonably accurate measurements is further complicated by management's desire to obtain information quickly. A rough approximation that is available today is often more useful to management that a more accurate figure published a year from now.

For the same reason that automobile costs cannot be precisely determined until the automobile is sold, the profit of a whole company cannot be precisely determined accurately until the company goes out of business. Nevertheless, management needs information on costs and profits for short periods of time, such as a month, and for individual divisions, products, or other segments or a business. Accounting will furnish such information, and it can be most helpful to management. The consultant must clearly understand, however, the approximations that are inherent in most accounting figures.

The degree of approximation is especially high in the case of the figures used for planning purposes. Such figures are always estimates of what will happen in the future. But businessmen are not clairvoyant and so they do not know what will happen in the future. Thus, the figures used for planning purposes can be no better than their estimates of what the future holds.

Working with Incomplete Data

When considering a business problem, one almost never has exactly the information one would like to have. In nearly every practical situation, the person who is struggling with the problem can think of additional information that would be helpful if it were available. On the other hand, there are many business situations in which page after page of figures are available, but only a small fraction of them are relevant to the problem at hand, and perhaps none of them is quite what one needs to solve the problem. It is a fact of life, however, that problems must be solved, business decisions must be made, and often the decision cannot be delayed until all the pertinent information is available. Instead, one must do the best one can with the data that is available, and then move on to the next problem.

On the other hand, a decision should not be made if a vital, obtainable piece of evidence is missing. Deciding whether or not to act on the available evidence is one of the most difficult parts of the whole decision process. It may be put as follows:

> The art of business is the art of making irrevocable decisions on the basis of inadequate information.

Figures Evidence is only Partial Evidence

Some people act as if problems can be solved completely through numerical analysis. Such people have the erroneous idea that an engineer, for example, can work out just how a bridge should look solely from their knowledge of loads, stresses, and material strengths, whilst disregarding the element of judgement completely. At the other extreme, some believe that intuition is the best guide to a sound decision, and who therefore pay no attention to numerical data. Although the correct approach is clearly somewhere between these two extremes, there is no way of describing precisely where it is. The participant must reach their own conclusion on the relative importance of numerical and nonnumerical data to arrive at the solution of a given problem.

People, Not Figures, Get Things Done

All business organisations are made up of people. Anything that the business accomplishes is the result of the actions of these people. Figures can assist people in the organisation in various ways, but the figures themselves are nothing more than marks on pieces of paper; by themselves they accomplish nothing.

Nevertheless, figures don't talk back; they give the appearance of being definite and precise, and it is a comforting illusion to imagine that the construction of a set of figures is synonymous with acting on a real problem.

An accounting system may be beautifully designed and carefully operated, but the system is of no use to management unless it results in action by people. For instance, three companies may use exactly the same system — the same chart of accounts, the same set of records and reports, the same procedure for collecting and disseminating information — with entirely different results. In one company, the system may be useless because management never acts on the information collected, and the organisation has become aware of this fact. In the second company, the system may be helpful because management uses the information as a general guide for planning and control and has educated the organisation to use it in the same spirit. In the third company, the system may be worse than useless because management over-emphasises the importance of the figures and therefore takes unwise actions.

BALANCE SHEET

A balance sheet shows the assets of a business (on one side) and the liabilities of a business (on the other side) on a particular day of the year. For each item on a balance sheet there will be a separate account. In addition there will be numerous accounts recording revenues received and expenses incurred during that period. At the end of the period, these are totalled and any balance on the account is taken to the trading and profit and loss account, which itself form part of the double-entry system.

A balance sheet when used in its proper function is not part of the double-entry system, but just shows the balances which are standing on those accounts, which have not been closed off for the period and carried to the trading and profit and loss account.

Assets are generally classified as either *fixed* or *current*.

- **Fixed Assets** include items such as land and buildings, plant and machinery, fixtures and fittings, and motor vehicles.

- **Current Assets** include items such as stocks, raw material, work in progress, debtors, cash at bank, and cash in hand.

The claims or sources of capital which relate to these assets, referred to as liabilities, are usually classified on a term basis, that is, *long-term, medium-term* and *short-term*.

- **Permanent** or **Long-term Liabilities** include items such as share capital (e.g. ordinary shares, preference shares), and retained profits.

- **Medium-term Liabilities** includes items such as loan capital, and debentures (mortgages).

- **Short-term Liabilities** include items such as bank overdraft and creditors.

In all cases, the sum of all assets will equal the sum of all liabilities. In this sense, assets and liabilities are said to "balance".

Interpretation and Use of the Balance Sheet

The first point to make is that a balance sheet is only valid for the day it refers to. Thus, the balance sheet is historical and static. Affairs and activities in a company move on and the balance sheet changes as a result.

The balance sheet can be used to indicate the following:

1. The value of assets and in particular, the value of total net assets, or *net worth*, of the company.

2. The amount of capital employed in the company. This includes shares, reserves, and profits or losses carried to the balance sheet from the profit and loss account

3. The breakdown of current assets into stocks (which includes raw materials, work in progress and finished goods), debtors (those owning the company monies) and cash (whether in the bank or in hand).

Obviously a strong balance sheet would show a high net worth. Financial management is all about increasing the net worth of a company. The current assets of a company should be carefully assessed. Too high a cash balance, for example, could mean that the company is failing to invest in future wealth producing assets. The value given for stock will indicate the amount of resources tied up in raw materials, work in progress and finished goods.

Finally, liabilities, particularly current liabilities, need to be assessed to see who are owed monies by the firm and how much. Failure to pay creditors in time may invite legal action and the ensuing troubles and bad publicity could cause a company to fail, notwithstanding its profitable operations.

PROFIT AND LOSS ACCOUNT

It is not difficult to see that profit is achieved when income exceeds expenditure. Conversely, a loss will arise when the figures show that expenditure exceeds income. In this sense, the profit and loss account is quite straightforward. It is important to be aware, however, that the profit and loss account does not record *cash* receipts and payments. Instead, it is a record of income and expenditure. In general, income is defined as sales achieved during the accounting period, and expenditure is defined as the cost of goods and services consumed during the period in producing the goods and services which generated the income. Invoiced sales may not be the only income a company receives. The profit and loss account will often show income as a result of interest received, or other exceptional items (insurance claim, government grants, for example).

One of the primary duties of all management is the creation of wealth, and profit is one measure of how effective management have been in achieving this aim. Another key criteria for business success is turnover or sales growth. The profit and loss account gives data on gross profit margins, net profit margins, increases on the previous year's turnover and the level of dividends paid to shareholders. Thus, the profit and loss account for an accounting period indicates how successful or unsuccessful the management of the company has been in conducting the business affairs of the company during that period.

FINANCIAL CONTROL SYSTEMS

Overview

The arena in which financial control operates is constantly moving. It is bounded on the one side by the workings and aspirations of the business itself. The practices of the wider business community — customers, suppliers and financiers together with the rules and regulations associated with the machinery of government — form a second boundary around the arena. If a business is unsuccessful the boundaries close in. Management has little room to manoeuvre and is subject to increasing pressure. With success comes a slackening of the boundary ropes at many points. The business is then more at liberty to enjoy the fruits of success as it moves forward to achieve further successes.

A sole proprietor can have the same problems of organisational security as a larger firm. They need to safeguard company assets from fraud and theft as does every other business. The control of assets — in particular money — can be greatly aided through the use of some relatively simple procedures. It is not suggested that every small business should set up its own internal auditing group but it is important, nevertheless, that even the smallest businesses should understand some of the generally accepted principles and practices of financial control.

Internal Control

Internal control means that the daily transactions of the business should be regularly and continuously checked either manually or by computer. It does not always suggest that each single transaction is noted and verified in the books of account. It does require, however, that the work of one person is tested independently by the work of some other person. This checking system can be effected by the matching of independently produced total sums against the relevant individual entries in the firm's ledgers.

Cash Control

Cash, money orders, drafts and cheques can be received over the counter or by post. The following simple controls are suggested:

1. Ensure that every cheque and money order is crossed for payment to the company's bank, with the instruction "to account

payee only". Further ensure that all cheques are correctly signed, are not post-dated, and that words and figures agree.

2. Each postal receipt should be immediately recorded in a register of monies received by post. Two individuals should certify the completeness and accuracy of each day's records.

3. Postal receipts may then be handed to the cashier or the manager, for depositing in the bank and for recording in the cash book. The recipient of the cash (cashier or manager) should sign the postal receipts register evidencing responsibility for those items. The cashier, or the manager alone, will have the authority for issuing receipts for monies received. Clearly the supply of receipt documents, whether in booklet form or as separate documents, should be serially numbered and retained under the control of the manager.

External Payments

Cheque books used for making payments in settlement of accounts to which a business owes money, or for making advance payments when credit terms are not available, must be safely secured in the possession of the manager. Some managers keep them at home. The manager — or an authorised representative — should sign cheques only after comparison with specific evidence of the amounts due to be paid to a supplier or other form of creditor. Extra care is needed with direct debit authorisations. Many small businesses mandate their banks to accept only the manager's signature although this can cause problems in the event of a prolonged absence from the office.

The practice of signing a number of blank cheques for a subordinate employee to utilise in the settlement of claims from creditors of other known suppliers must be completely rejected. It may save the manager's time but could result in theft or misuse of the firm's cash by that subordinate.

Payments made by cash should be supported by a receipt from the supplier. All payments should be made when they become due and neither before nor after.

In order to ensure that only goods and services genuinely required by a business are paid for, it is important that an efficient system be in place for ordering of raw materials and for the control of stocks. Again the separation of duties between various staff members can help to ensure that fraud or theft is avoided.

Wages and Salary Payments

A system of control over cash payments demands the operation of a minimum of internal check procedures. The division of duties between sections of staff can provide a measure of security against the falsification of wage and salary payments. Clearly the main objectives must be to avoid:

- The insertion of false names in wage and salary sheets, and the misappropriation (theft) of the related sums shown as payable.

- Inflation of wage and salary sheet totals which can result in cash being drawn from the bank for wage and salary payments in excess of that sum properly calculated and required with the excess amount being stolen.

A system of internal checks requires the division of duties between staff. This will give a company reasonable security against the misappropriation of cash in that, for such a misappropriation to occur collusion between two or more employees would have to take palace. Any system is effective only if it is regularly and properly operated. It is important, therefore, that the operation of the system is verified by frequent test checks carried out by management or its representative.

Conclusion

The foregoing examples of internal control systems, which operate to safeguard the firm against loss, should now lead managers of even the smallest companies to consider the work practices in operation in their own areas of responsibility. Managers should be aware that loss can arise through:

- Fraud, theft or misappropriation of cash or other documents of a monetary value.

- Theft or misuse of the firm's assets including raw materials, finished goods, office equipment, manufacturing plant and small hand tools.

- Fraudulent manipulation of a company's account books in order to conceal the true position regarding the firm's assets and its profitability.

PROJECT FINANCING

INTRODUCTION

This chapter aims to provide a brief introduction to the kinds of financing available to the business world. In general, finance will be available from both public and semi-public financial institutions as well as from private banks and credit companies.

Many projects will involve risks, and this increases the security requirements. In this case public-sector credit institutions may be particularly relevant in connection with top-mortgage financing or the financing of pilot projects.

In this chapter, the requirements for financing of projects is discussed under the following headings:

- Calculation of Capital Requirements

- Types of Loan Financing

- Equity Financing

- Drawing up the Loan Application.

CALCULATING THE CAPITAL REQUIREMENT

It is a precondition of any kind of financing that the capital requirement is accurately calculated. Both underfunding and overfunding are bad solutions. Underfunding will create cash flow problems that can have negative consequences for the company's profitability and capital structure. Overfunding is not of course a problem of the same order, but it may lead to unwise deployment of capital resources.

The profitability of the project will also be very dependent on capital costs. If the capital requirement is greatly underestimated, major assumptions for the profitability of the project may become invalid. So credit institutions are always on the alert for cost estimates that appear too low.

Here we will look in more detail at two situations where the capital requirement has to be estimated — i.e. "fixed capital requirements for investments" and "working capital requirements in connection with expansion".

Investment in Fixed Assets

For investments in buildings one should always have:

- Cost estimates from the contractor, or

- Tenders from relevant contractors, or

- A cost overview drawn up by a technical consultant.

All costs must be included, including site purchase costs, consultancy fees and construction loan interest. Any of the company's own work should also be included in the calculations — preferably assessed at the market price. This cost overview should be sent in with the loan application.

The cost overview should be itemised in detail. It must also function as the basis for calculating the construction loan requirement. It will be necessary to calculate VAT (value-added tax) or the local equivalent.

Construction loan interest can be capitalised and financed like other investment costs. It should be calculated as an average over the duration of the building period. For example, for a project involving a total investment of ECU 2,000,000, a building programme lasting eight months and with construction loan interest of 14 per cent, the calculation will be as follows:

Construction loan interest:
$(2,000,000 \times 0.14 \times 8) \div (2 \times 12) = ECU\ 93,333.$

Some credit institutions will pay out the loan in accordance with audited construction accounts, others will pay on the basis of an official valuation. Furthermore, public-sector credit institutions will often include a "tender clause" in the loan contract. This means that the bank issuing the construction loan is obliged to invite tenders before opening the construction loan.

In the case of machinery and equipment a written quotation should be obtained from the relevant suppliers. All costs including any fixtures required during construction work as well as installation and commissioning costs should be considered. Furthermore, it is important to state whether the equipment to be bought is new or second-hand.

Financing of Current Assets

The operating capital requirement can be calculated in several ways — some more exact than others. The one to use will depend on the situation and the company's financial control scheme. The best way undoubtedly is to prepare a cash flow forecast. This will indicate how the capital requirement will vary over an extended period and will provide the best basis for successful financing.

For small capacity expansions or the establishment of small companies with modest capital requirements, however, average calculations will be sufficient. In simple cases, this will involve calculating the average level of accounts receivable (debtors), and accounts payable (creditors) as well as the average value of stock. This approach is illustrated in the following example:

Assumptions	
Annual cost of goods sold (net)	ECU 1,000,000
Average stock turnover, raw materials	2 months
Total turnover (net)	ECU 3,000,000
Average stock turnover, finished goods	½ month
Average customer credit terms	60 days
Average supplier credit terms	30 days
Average work in progress	ECU 50,000

The operating capital requirement can then be calculated as follows (to the nearest ECU 1,000):

Average raw materials stocks, (1,000,000 x 2) / 12	ECU 167,000
Average work in progress	ECU 50,000
Average finished goods stocks, (3,000,000 x ½) / 12	ECU 125,000
Average customer credit, (3,000,000 x 2) / 12	ECU 500,000
Total current assets	ECU 842,000
Less average supplier credit, (1,000,000 x 1) / 12	ECU (83,000)
	ECU 759,000
+ Liquidity reserve (10%)	ECU 76,000
Operating Capital Requirement	**ECU 835,000**

To arrive at the company's operating credit requirement, we have to allow for the amount of equity available to finance part of the operating capital requirement. The following calculation can be used here:

Assumptions	
Booked fixed assets after any new investments	ECU 4,500,000
Long-term loans after financing of new investment	ECU 3,800,000
Booked equity	ECU 1,000,000

The operating credit requirement will thus be:

Long-term loans	ECU 3,800,000
+ Equity	ECU 1,000,000
Long-term capital	ECU 4,800,000
Less investment in fixed assets	ECU (4,500,000)
Equity available for operations	ECU 300,000
Operating capital requirement	ECU 835,000
Less equity available for operations	ECU (300,000)
Operating Credit Requirement	**ECU 535,000**

If we allow for the fact that the company will always have some current liabilities in the form of payable VAT, employer tax and holiday pay, this company should apply for a minimum operating credit of ECU 500,000.

These calculations assume stable operating conditions. If there are great seasonal fluctuations, a liquidity reserve of 10 per cent will be too little. In such a situation, however, it would be best to use cash budgeting to calculate the exact capital requirement.
If this company was not granted an operating credit of ECU 500,000 it would have to try to change the terms of payment used as a basis and its rate of stock turnover.

Cash Budgeting

If the company has a capital requirement that fluctuates greatly in the course of a year, it should draw up a cash flow forecast. This also applies to new companies during the start-up phase or for major capacity expansions of existing companies. Many newly-established companies run into serious cash flow problems during the initial stages through underestimating the start-up costs involved. Problems like these weigh heavily on those who have the managerial responsibility, and can inhibit profitability in the company.

In such cases, average estimates are insufficient. The company must obtain an operating credit that is high enough to accommodate peaks in the capital requirement. It must also plan measures aimed to control or reduce the amount of capital tied up in current assets. This is hard to do without a cash budget.

It is not within the scope of this chapter to discuss in detail how a cash budget should be structured. It is a complex matter and requires that cash flow forecasts for earnings have been drawn up. In our view, the following demands should be made on a cash budget:

- It should be based on a forecast of earnings.

- All planned investments and how the company intends to finance these, be it with long-term loans and/or from equity, should be itemised.

- All existing loans, interest payments and loan repayments should be itemised.

- Plans to issue new equity or to sell fixed assets should be included.

- A conscious decision should be made on how stocks are to be managed during the budget period.

- A conscious decision should be made on what credit terms are to be given when selling goods, and what credit is to be sought when buying goods and services.

- Payroll, national insurance costs, etc. should be itemised.

- As a control measure, the cash budget should be used to draw up a balance sheet budget.

A good cash budget not only provides an accurate estimate of the capital requirement. It is also a good control tool for the company. Nowadays there are data models that can be used in cash budgeting. These can make the work much easier and are very suitable for computer simulation work.

TYPES OF LOAN FINANCING

Many types of loan capital are relevant within the business world. We have chosen to divide loan capital into two groups:

- Short-term credits (maturity shorter than one year)

- Long-term credits (maturity longer than one year).

Long-term loans could have been further divided into medium-term (1 – 5 years' maturity) and long-term (more than 5 years' maturity), but in this context there is little point.

Short-term Credit

Supplier Credit
Sales of goods and services among businesses are usually based on credit. The terms might be, for example, cash within ten days less a 2 per cent cash discount, or 30 days net. This means that a supplier debt will be built up which will finance parts of the com-

pany's current assets. This credit is very flexible, and will vary with the level of activity. Its size depends on total purchases and average credit terms.

When there are fixed credit terms, supplier debt will increase in direct proportion to increases in the level of goods that are purchased.

Supplier credit is normally considered to be inexpensive credit, and thus it is exploited as much as possible. But the costs will be dependent on the time taken to pay:

- By paying quickly one can obtain very favourable cash discounts.

- Payment within the agreed credit terms means no interest will be charged.

- Late payment may mean that the company will be charged penalty interest.

Compared with the cost of ordinary operating credit, the quicker payment can be made, the more favourable for the company this will be.

Overdrafts
Overdrafts are the most common type of operating credit and are a relatively inexpensive type of financing. But this assumes that they are used in a sensible way. The costs consist of:

- Commission on the amount granted (limit)

- Interest on the amount withdrawn (balance at any time).

The effective interest will depend on how much the overdraft is used. This is illustrated in the following example:

Overdraft granted: ECU 1 million

Interest: 12 per cent per annum

Commission: 0.5 per cent interest per quarter = 2 per cent per annum on limit

Use of overdraft	25%	50%	75%	100%
12% interest:	30,000	60,000	90,000	120,000
2% commission:	20,000	20,000	20,000	20,000
Total	50,000	80,000	110,000	140,000
Effective interest	20%	16%	14.66%	14%

The above illustrates how it is expensive to have too high a limit. There must be a high enough margin to allow for fluctuations in the operating capital requirement. Because of the rules for calculating commission, even small, brief excess withdrawals would be very expensive. In general, special additional credit to cover a short-term capital requirement will also be expensive.

Confirming

This is a relatively new type of financing offered by several private finance companies. It is a rolling credit type specially developed to finance the purchase of goods.

It involves the company signing a contract with a finance company with a credit limit and a period during which the loan is to be paid back. When the credit is used, the company has to issue one or more acceptances to the finance company. After these have been redeemed, the credit can be used to purchase new goods.

The idea of this kind of credit is to enable the company to exploit cash and volume discounts. As mentioned before, this can be of great advantage to the company. The credit can also be used to tide the company over seasonal fluctuations or to exploit particularly favourable offers.

Apart from the acceptances, no special security is demanded. The payment period is generally between one and four months.

Confirming is a relatively costly form of financing with financial costs consisting of:

- Commission on the agreed credit limit (typically 1.5 per cent per annum)

- Interest on the amount borrowed at any given time (typically 16 per cent per annum)

- Confirming commission on the purchase value of the goods consignment (typically 0.3 per cent a month or 3.6 per cent per annum)

- A charge per payment to cover the finance company's handling costs (for example ECU 75).

The effective interest thus tends to be very high. When this is off-set, however, against the cash discounts that can be obtained, the savings achievable can be considerable. In such cases, confirming will be a profitable type of financing.

Factoring

Factoring means that the factoring company takes over a company's accounts receivables against cash payment. The factoring company, in other words, buys the company's invoices. This releases capital in the company that would otherwise be tied up in receivables and the company avoids having to wait on payments from its customers.

One reason why companies have a strained cash flow is that large amounts are tied up in outstanding receivables. This is particularly true of companies that are in the process of expansion.

A factoring agreement could mean that the company can release up to 70 – 80 per cent of the capital tied up in customer receivables. The remaining 20 – 30 per cent is retained as security and is released after the invoices have been paid.

Long-term Credits

Instalment Note Loans

Investments in items such as machinery, equipment, inventory and vehicles are often financed by instalment note loans. These are loans with instalments extending over 1 – 10 years (in normal practice 3 – 7 years). The interest rate varies from bank to bank, and may also depend on the object being financed. Interest plus bank charges are normally paid in advance.

Mortgage Loans

These are normally long-term loans secured by real property. A mortgage bond is issued where the borrower declares, among other things, that he pledges a certain property as security for the loan. The bond states what priority (degree of security) the lender has.

These loans are used for investments in buildings and in plant. First mortgages (mortgage loans with the top priority) have the highest degree of security and these are normally up in amounts up to 60 – 70 per cent of the value of the assets that are being mortgaged. Second mortgages can go up to 70 per cent. A few of the public-sector credit institutions may commit themselves beyond this (top-mortgage financing) and the amount of the loan may then be as high as 90 per cent of the value of the assets.

Construction Loans

Long-term loans for buildings and plant are not normally paid until construction work has been completed. Thus, companies frequently need a loan to cover financial requirements during the construction period. Construction loans are granted by private banks. Before the construction loan is granted, there must be a "promise of conversion" from the credit institutions which are to participate in the final financing. The construction loan is paid out gradually as invoices are submitted that can be attributed to the construction project. This means that the bank monitors that the loan is used for the stated purpose.

Construction loans normally have a limit in accordance with the long-term financing granted. The costs consist of commission on the amount granted and interest on the amounts withdrawn.

As security, a first mortgage is generally demanded on the building under construction.

Foreign Exchange Loans

In special situations it may be relevant in the business world to raise a loan abroad. Most banks provide assistance in obtaining such loans. This is most common in connection with export/import activities, but companies can also raise longer-term loans.

The loans are nominally in foreign exchange, so there is a risk of losses due to adverse fluctuations in exchange rates. The interest rate is normally adjusted at regular intervals (3 – 9 months). In addition there are handling charges and sometimes guarantee commission to be paid to the domestic bank.

Today so-called "basket loans" are also used. In such cases several currencies are linked so that the risk of loss on exchange is reduced. Currencies in the same "basket" normally move in opposite directions. When the rate for one currency rises, the rate for another drops thus leaves the average rate stable.

Financial Leasing

Financial leasing is a type of financing where a finance company buys the operating asset a company wants and then hires it to the company at a fixed rate. Items normally financed through leasing include transportation equipment, computers, machine tools, office machinery, printing machinery etc.

In principle, all operating assets and objects which can be considered independent units (movables) can be leased. The leasing period will often be fixed at the financial lifetime of the operating asset, typically 3 – 5 years.

The *advantages* of financial leasing are:

- Full financing of the operating asset without drawing on equity

- Leasing does not restrict the company's borrowing potential

- No security demanded (normally)

- The company can decide for itself at the end of the loan period whether it wants to carry on using the asset or not

- The rental is tax-deductible for businesses

- The debt ratio is kept lower.

The *disadvantages* of financial leasing are:

- It can be an expensive type of financing, but the differences between bank loans and financial leasing have been greatly reduced in recent years. We recommend that the effective interest per annum is used in calculations.

- Reduced flexibility, as the company is tied to the leasing contract throughout the contract period, whether it uses the asset or not (this difficulty can be overcome through *flexileasing* as described below).

- The company does not own the asset during the leasing period.

- Lease payments can be a heavy burden on cash flow. However, it is possible today to draw up a payment plan that matches the company's cash inflow.

For items which are easy to sell on the second-hand market, a new financial leasing product — *flexileasing* — has been developed. Here the lessee can in principle terminate the contract unilaterally at any time within a minimum period.

Security
For most types of loans, some form of security will be demanded, the exception being regular supplier credits (these are granted on the assumption that the company is generally capable of meeting its commitments). The security demanded varies with the financial situation of the company, confidence in company management and future risks/earning potential. The most common types of security are:

- Mortgage security

- Sureties/guarantees.

Pledges and Mortgages
This is the most common type of security. In pledging, the object offered as security is physically handed over to the pledgee. With

mortgages the owner keeps the mortgaged object and has the full use of it. For legal protection, the mortgage or pledge has to be registered with a Notary.

At the Notary's Office each property has its own page in the land register. Real property is identified by street name and number or land registry and property registration number (in rural districts). The land register has a list of all registered encumbrances, easements, debts etc. in each property. If there are several encumbrances, the date of registration determines the mortgage priorities. The mortgagees may enter into agreements on the priority of their claims — but these too must be registered in the land register.

Mortgaging Real Property

This is the most common type of security for mortgage loans. A mortgage bond is issued and is registered with a notary. There is a distinction between a "straight mortgage bond" and an "accommodation bond", where the bond only functions as security. The right to rent out real property can also be mortgaged, in which case there are certain requirements as to the formulation of the lease or rental agreement.

Security in Operating Assets

This applies to machinery, equipment and inventory which have to be mortgaged along with real property. The mortgage may apply to the operating equipment as a whole, with new investments being included automatically. This must be registered with a notary and included in the sheet in the Land Register for the property.

Security in Motor Vehicles/Plant

Motor vehicles used in business, and plant, can be offered as security individually or in their entirety. Legal protection is obtained by registering on the owner's sheet at the Notary's office.

Security in Stocks

Stocks can be offered as security for all kinds of credit. The security will consist of stocks as a whole, such as they are at any given time. Stocks can be offered as security for operating credit, supplier credit and investment loans. Legal protection is obtained by registering on the owner's page at the Notary's office.

Security in Accounts Receivable

The company's accounts receivable can also be offered as security — either individually or in their entirety. If a receivable is offered individually as security, legal protection is obtained by informing the debtor. When the entire body of receivables is offered as security, legal protection is obtained by registration on the owner's page at the Notary's office.

Security in Goods Sold

When machinery/equipment/vehicles etc. are sold, the seller may claim security in the objects sold. The security is for the credit given by the seller in connection with the sale. If the investment is financed by a third party (for example, a bank), this party too may claim security in the object — provided that the loan amount has been paid directly to the seller.

Legal protection is obtained by entering into a written contract before the goods are transferred.

EQUITY FINANCING

When the equity ratio is low, companies have high capital costs and are very susceptible to financial setbacks. A low equity ratio can be as a result of the following reasons:

- Poor profitability which prevents equity growing in line with price increases or in line with company expansion.

- Poor capital management may mean that the company ties capital up in current and fixed assets disproportionately to turnover and profitability. The result is weaker profitability and a low equity ratio.

- Inadequate retention of profits. In such cases, in the event of expansion, the equity ratio will decline.

- Poor inflow of equity. This is very common in the case of new companies. It takes very high profitability to compensate for poor initial equity.

When the capital requirement is high, one should always consider the possibility of raising equity. The equity capital we see in financing plans is often fictitious. In reality this part of "equity" is made up by short-term debt. So it is important to draw fresh equity capital into the company.

Equity and Corporate Form
The inflow of equity is closely related to the corporate form of the company. Relevant corporate forms are:

• General partnership

• Limited company

• Limited partnership.

General Partnership
Among smaller companies, this corporate form is very widespread. Few people today can initially spare substantial amounts, and in establishing a company, this type of company means a low equity ratio. Some people include both home and summer cottage in the firm to make up a satisfactory amount of equity. But this capital is unproductive and only has significance in terms of status.

Entrepreneurs often put a lot of their own work into establishing such companies. This means there is a hidden reserve in fixed assets that can be of great value. It is difficult to inject new capital into this kind of company. The owner can only do so by transferring values from other areas into the company.

In general, in partnerships where several people join forces as partners, the potential for raising equity capital is rather higher. Here the number of partnership interests can be increased when there is a need for more equity. The problem is that if one of the partners wants to withdraw, they will take a considerable share of the equity capital with them. This means that the company's equity will be greatly reduced. To secure the equity capital in such companies, agreements should be reached beforehand that regulate things like the allocation of profits and the liquidation of the partnership.

Limited Company

The limited company is the most common type of company today. There are usually tax-related and/or liability-related reasons for this. In a limited company the liability of the owners is limited to the share capital — unlike private companies, where the owners are liable with all of their capital. In family limited companies the bank often asks for security from the shareholders, and then the limitation of liability is of less value.

The limited company form is better for raising equity than the private company. This is particularly true of the establishment of bigger companies. In small companies very often one individual or one family wants to control the majority of shares, and this imposes limitations on the amount of share capital. In comparison with a private company, though, the equity can be doubled without reducing controlling rights.

In special situations it is also possible for public-sector institutions to subscribe for shares. Industrial and regional development funds, for example, can do this though, in practice, this approach is rarely used. It is more common for local authorities or county development companies to subscribe for shares. This can be done in situations where the establishment of the company is of great importance in regional policy and there is a shortage of equity.

A limited company can raise equity by floating shares — that is, issuing new shares. This enables the company to maintain its equity ratio through major investments or expansion.

Limited Partnership

The partners in a limited partnership consist of one or more general partners and one or more limited partners.

The distinctive aspect of this corporate form is that the limited partnership is not a taxpayer as such. Profit and loss are taxed for the individual partners separately. Many of these companies run at a loss for the first few years, which makes this type of company interesting for people with high marginal tax rates.

The general partner and limited partners have different liabilities:

- **The general partner**. The general partner is liable for the whole debt of the limited partnership with all his capital.

- **Limited partners**. The limited partners are only liable for the partnership capital they have subscribed. Usually payment for only one unit in a limited partnership is demanded on the establishment of the company. Payment for the remaining shares may be demanded later if there is a need for it. How much the limited partners can deduct in tax returns from their part of the partnership deficit is limited by the partnership capital they have subscribed.

This corporate form has proved very favourable in terms of raising equity. The reason for this is, as mentioned above, the tax consequences of the form.

The disadvantage of this corporate form is that if a general partner has little capital to inject in the partnership, they will have a correspondingly small share of the profits. Furthermore, the general meeting of the limited partnership can "freely" dispose of the profits of the company. If these are pulled out of the company, the capital situation can deteriorate in the longer term (although this can be limited by the terms of the articles of association).

In capital expansions, the same principles are observed as in limited companies.

Venture Capital Companies

The concept of venture capital first arose in the USA in 1958, when the establishment of industrial companies with tax benefits and access to public-sector loans was permitted. The intention was to help small companies starting up.

Venture Capital — What Is It?

Venture capital is a way of financing small and medium-sized enterprises. It is a way of financing equity where the inflow of capital is conditional on the use of qualified advisers. The investment company almost always becomes a minority partner.

The added value that a venture capital company can contribute can be attributed as much to its specialised competence as to the capital injection. The investment company often makes competent staff available as discussion partners for management or as board members.

Forms of Equity Financing

The most common forms of venture capital financing are:

1. **Injection of New Capital (Growth Financing)**. New capital is required in many cases including:

   - The establishment of new companies

   - Over-fast expansion ("expansionitis")

   - Major capacity expansion

   - Takeovers of competitors

   - Expansion of the product range

   - Marketing new products.

   For companies with a poor financing structure, high financial costs will be a problem. In such cases an injection of new capital can improve the company's cash flow.

2. **Share Purchases**. The investment company buys out some or all of the existing shareholders. This does not add a lot of equity to the company.

3. **Financing a Change of Ownership**. In this type of financing the investment company will help the owner of the company or will finance a management buy-out. The capital from the new owners and loan financing are then used, together with capital from the financing company, to buy out the original owners of the company.

What Does Venture Capital Cost?

The investment company does not want returns in the form of dividends or other cash payment. Returns are expected through a rise in the company's share price.

Share Issues

There are several ways of increasing a company's share capital. It can be done without injecting new capital (by a bonus issue) or by injecting new capital into the company (by a new issue of shares).

In a *bonus issue* (or *scrip issue*) the share capital is increased, but some of the rest of the equity — statutory reserve, revaluation reserve and free reserve — are capitalised and thus reduced. Another alternative is to re-evaluate fixed assets and issue new shares. Bonus issues are always carried out either by appreciating properties or capitalising the "bonus" of previous years (i.e. profits allocated to reserves).

In *new issues* limited companies raise more capital by inviting people to subscribe for new shares. The share capital is then increased by the nominal value of the new shares. If the new subscribers pay more for the shares than the nominal value — they pay a "premium" — this is allocated to the statutory reserve.

Bonus Issues

In bonus issues the capital in the company is split into more units. The company does *not* gain any outside capital. In principle a bonus issue can be compared with a large cake formerly cut in two, but now cut into more slices. The cake does not get any bigger. It just has more pieces.

The transfer to share capital can be done both by transferring distributable equity and nondistributable equity to share capital. Distributable equity consists of the free reserve and other distributable reserves. Nondistributable equity that can be capitalised includes the statutory reserve and revaluation reserve. The issue means a redistribution of equity so that the share capital increases while other equity capital is correspondingly reduced.

The other way of holding a bonus issue is to write up the value of fixed assets and issue new shares (bonus shares).

A fixed asset may have a real value that is higher than its book value. The book value can then be written up to the real value. The precondition for such a write-up is that the extra value is substantial and permanent. The revaluation reserve arises in connection with the revaluation of the fixed assets.

New Issues

A new issue, unlike a bonus issue or share split, is a method of financing. The company gains new outside capital by issuing and selling shares.

New shares are often issued at a price lower than the quoted share price. So existing shareholders are granted preferential rights to subscribe for new shares. Rights are issued which can, within a given period, be negotiated and quoted on a Stock Exchange (a "rights issue").

A new issue may be regarded as an unfortunate move by some people, as it involves asking for extra capital from existing shareholders.

In some cases the company can hold a special (non-public) issue. The company then approaches particular groups and sells the shares directly to them. In such cases the company's own shareholders may have first option or the company may approach investors outside the company, bypassing the existing shareholders. In the latter case the general meeting must have approved this way of doing it.

The payment for a new share, the issue price, may not be less than the nominal value of the share. Normally shares are issued at a premium. Surplus capital is then allocated to the statutory reserve so that the share capital is not affected.

The aim of a new issue is that the company gains new capital. This may be because it wishes, for example, to:

- Remedy cash flow problems

- Carry out a planned expansion

- Improve the debt-to-equity ratio

- Take over another company

- Meet requirements for quotation on a Stock Exchange.

Mixed Issues

We also see examples of mixed issues. A bonus issue and new issue can be held at the same time. The aim of the bonus issue is then, for example, to make it easier to carry out a new issue. The combination of a new issue and a split also occurs.

Public Issues / Private Issues

The ways in which shares are issued can also be classified into public and private issues.

A *public share issue* is open to all who want to invest. One subscribes to public issues at stockbrokers' offices and the stockbroking departments of banks.

A *private share issue* is more in the nature of a private investment scheme where a number of named investors commit themselves in advance to subscribe shares. New shareholders may then subscribe in advance before the general meeting has adopted an expansion of the share capital. Another approach is for one or more major investors (such as a bank) to subscribe for all of the share capital expansion with a view to selling the shares again later. If the issue is a private one, only a restricted group of people is permitted to participate in the issue.

DRAWING UP THE LOAN APPLICATION

Most credit institutions require some kind of formal loan application. Some have standard application forms and others have drawn up guidelines. The extent to which a full loan application is required will normally depend on the following factors:

The Size of the Loan

This is true both in absolute terms and in terms of the company's size. If a company with a staff of 40 wants to borrow ECU 50,000 for a new machine, it is unlikely that much effort will have to be given to filling in the loan application. Normally the company's own contacts within a bank will be able to finance such investments.

Local Bank /Other Credit Institutions

The company's own bank, through its long familiarity with the customer, will know enough about the company to be able to grant small loans without any special examination of the company's situation. With larger loans, information on the project will be sufficient. Matters are different with other credit institutions. They have neither personal familiarity with the loan applicant nor knowledge of the company. To assess the project they therefore need a more comprehensive loan application.

Degree of Expansion

If the reason for the loan is a major expansion or the establishment of a new company, the need for more in-depth analysis of the project arises. The risk is then normally higher and the profitability and liquidity consequences and market potential must be assessed in more detail. This means that the formulation of the loan application must always be adapted to the situation in hand. If a more formal loan application has to be drawn up, though, it will be an advantage to apply some sort of systematic approach. This will ensure that all the relevant information is included and will make presentation of the case at the credit institution much easier.

Requirements

Many credit institutions, as mentioned above, have their own requirements for the way in which a loan application should be set out. The requirements of most credit institutions will be satisfied if the following areas are addressed in the application:

1. **General information about the company**. This should include:

   - Name, address, phone number

   - When the company was founded

   - Owners, major shareholders, chief executive, organisational structure

   - Bank references, insurance company, any auditors and accountants

   - Number of staff

   - Industry and main products

   - Main market for products.

   When establishing a new company, it is important to give an account of the background of the owners and of key management personnel.

2. **Financial position of the company**. When an existing company applies for a loan, the financial statements and any auditors' reports for the last three years should always be submitted with the application. If the financial statements present an incorrect picture of the profitability and financial situation of the company, this should be mentioned in the application. This may be a matter of hidden stock reserves, high training costs, investments over operations etc.

   In addition to the financial statements for recent years, there should also be an assessment of future profitability. When a new company is being established or substantial expansion is planned, this is a must. The simplest way of doing this is to draw up an operating budget.

3. **Project description**. This should be an account of what the loan is to be used for. This becomes particularly important for larger loans. Information to be given should include:

   • What the project is all about?

   • Why do you want to realise the project?

   • Plans for the future

   • Consequences for the number of employees.

   If the application is for a loan to be used for product development projects, co-operative projects etc., this fact should be emphasised. In such cases the company should find out what information the credit institution in question requires.

4. **Market assessment**. For market expansion plans and the establishment of new companies, this is perhaps the most important item of all. The documentation of market conditions should be as specific as possible — especially if there is a lot of competition and the products have no particular advantage. Important information here will be:

   • Any market analyses that have been conducted. The bigger the share of the market the company wants to gain, the more important will this kind of survey be. Here the company should exploit any potential for obtaining financing of the cost of consultancy fees.

- The names of any relevant customers who have been contacted, and the annual quantities they are likely to buy

- An account of how the company plans to market its products.

This is not just a matter of providing information. If the application shows that the company has done thorough groundwork on these issues, this will in itself create a positive picture.

5. **Estimate of capital requirement**. For ways of estimating the fixed capital requirement and company capital requirement, see "Calculating the Capital Required" at the beginning of the chapter. The estimate of capital requirements and any drawings and other documentation can be included as a special appendix.

In the case of special projects (product development, "research", co-operative projects) and applications for various kinds of subsidies from public authorities, it is important to give a clear picture of the types of costs that have to be considered.

Otherwise, we can only stress once more the importance of including all the costs that can be attributed to the project. This is important both for the profitability assessment and for the structure of company financing. Any deliberate playing-down of the capital requirement will in the last analysis only hurt the company.

6. **Financing plan**. The last item will be to draw up a financing plan. This should include the fixed capital requirement, the operating capital requirement and any other more specialised capital needs.

In the case of investments in buildings, the equity ratio should be at least between 10 per cent and 20 per cent. One should specify how the equity is to be raised. This is simple enough when establishing new companies or if fresh equity is to be raised. If not, the equity must be obtained from the company's own work in the project or by releasing capital within the company. This can be done by:

- Reducing stocks or accounts receivable
- Increasing current liabilities.

The latter approach can only be recommended if this debt is lower than normal terms of payment would require.

22

MARKETING

INTRODUCTION

Poor understanding of the market and weak marketing are a typical problem in many SMEs throughout Europe. This is not only a problem of marketing new products or exports, but also of marketing established products in the markets where the company has long experience. Many SMEs have considerable potential for improvement through serving their present markets better, and the aim of this section is to help companies to identify the most important improvement measures.

In this chapter marketing is discussed under the following headings:

- Market Strategy
- Resources of Marketing
- Personal Sales.

MARKET STRATEGY

Market strategy starts with the company's business plan, and the aim is to draw up the operative marketing plan (see Figure 22.1). Market strategy gives an account of the way the company will use the means and resources it has available for marketing to achieve the main aims defined in its business plan. Market strategy is the basis of a marketing budget and the related marketing activities related to sales and advertising activity. Market strategy also forms the basis of company pricing and terms of payment.

Figure 22.1: From Business Plan to Marketing Plan

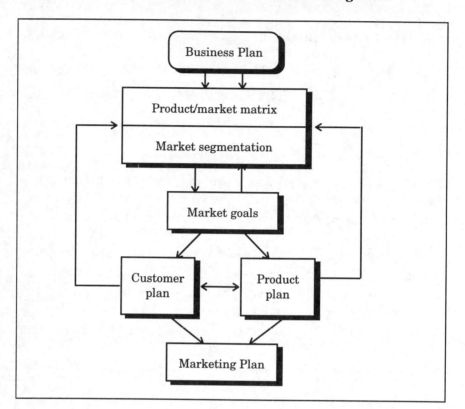

The Product/Market Matrix

We take our point of departure in the product/market matrix shown in Figure 22.2. This simple matrix identifies the products and customers that make up the markets in which we work. The products must be described in the matrix as they are perceived by the customers, not as they are defined by the company. A manufacturer, for example, might define their products on the basis of technologies like laminated wood, aluminium and the like. But the customers do not buy a piece of laminated wood. They buy a door, a window and so forth. The products cover different needs among the customers, so in practice we will set up product groups. A wooden goods manufacturer of doors and windows would, for example, set up Outside Doors, Inside Doors, Patio Doors and Windows as the four product groups.

In the same way we must draw up systematic customer groups. The point of dividing customers into different groups is to highlight the fact that we have sets of customers with very different needs both in terms of the products they want and the way they want to buy and use our products. Analysis of the end-users will often reveal important factors which the company can use in its marketing. For the wooden goods producer it would perhaps be appropriate to distinguish between Corporate Construction, Corporate Maintenance, Private Construction and Private Maintenance. These four main groups will have very different needs. For example, a private individual building a new house would probably need 10 – 15 windows of different sizes from basement to roof, and will often want to buy all the windows in one order. This means that the window supplier must be able to offer a wide selection of windows. If the customer wants to replace windows in connection with maintenance, the important thing will probably be to find a window that has the right size and appearance for the rest of the house. This makes demands on the manufacturer in terms of the ability to supply "customised" goods. Similarly, we can imagine that there would be a big difference between these customers in terms of the importance of price, distribution, functionality and so on.

Figure 22.2: Product/Market Matrix

Market/ Customer Groups	Product Groups				Total Market Groups
	Outside Doors	*Inside Doors*	*Patio Doors*	*Windows*	
Corporate Construction					
Corporate Maintenance					
Private Construction					
Private Maintenance					
Total Product Groups					

Once the product/market matrix has been set up it will be very useful in several ways for assessing:

- Market size and development — product by product, market by market

- The company's present competitive advantage and profitability — product by product, market by market

- Different strategic potential of the individual products and markets.

Market Segmenting

The product/market matrix is a way of dividing the total market up into sub-markets. Next, each sub-market can be broken down into smaller segments. In the example above we have identified the sub-market "Corporate Maintenance". However there may be several types of companies in this one category. We could, for example, distinguish between industrial companies and service companies, the point being that these two segments of the sub-market "Corporate Maintenance" may have very different needs and should therefore be handled differently.

A market segment is a group of customers with relatively uniform demands and needs compared with the rest of the market. The total market may be large and composed of many groups with different demands and needs — that is, many segments. The aim of segmenting is to arrive at a customer group, a segment, which is suitable for the company, meaning that the company has a better background for competing in the selected segment than in other parts of the market. In other words, it is a matter of arriving at a segment where the company's strengths can be exploited, and its weaknesses become less important. One can then develop products and services which are better targeted at that segment, and the segment can moreover be worked on with a relatively uniform approach. By specialising in a segment the company gets increasingly better at supplying good products and services, while its marketing and the rest of its value-creating activities become increasingly cost-effective.

In practice there are some important problems one runs into when one has to segment and work on the segment in a goal-oriented way. Segmentation is a two-stage process: in the first stage one identifies the segments; in the second, one describes them.

- The first problem is thus to arrive at segments which have different needs and which are meaningful in the sense that the company can orient its work towards one or more of them. The point is to find groups of potential customers with different needs and to pick out the segment or segments where the company can emphasise its strengths. One can find such segments by asking one's own and one's competitors' customers about the purchasing criteria to which they attach most importance when they choose a product.

- Once we have identified the segments (on the basis of needs) the next job is to describe them in a way which is practically useful. In the corporate market one often describes the segments on the basis of industry, company size and/or geographical location. A good description of the segments helps us to calculate their size. Furthermore, it is easier to work deliberately with the segments when we know the industry, size and/or geographical location.

The wooden goods producer, for example, may have carried out a market analysis and found out that the companies which buy doors in connection with maintenance (the sub-market "Corporate maintenance") have two important buying criteria: functionality and the size of the doors.

- The first criterion, functionality, might on the one hand be functionality in the form of soundproofing and fireproofing; on the other hand it might be the special design of the door in terms of style and colour.

- The second buying criterion was size. This can have the opposite poles "customised" and "standard sizes". In Figure 22.3 we show how these two criteria are used to identify four segments, A-D. Segment A has most customers, as illustrated by the size of the circle. Segment B is typified by the fact that the customers here want soundproofed and/or fireproof doors in standard sizes. So this is a segment of the market which has different

needs from the rest of the market. It is a very interesting segment for the wooden goods manufacturer, because it is an area
where the firm can exploit its specialised competence. Moreover, none of the competition have specialised in this area. Further investigations show that Segment B can be described as
consisting of small and medium-sized manufacturing companies.

Figure 22.3: Segmentation of Market for Doors

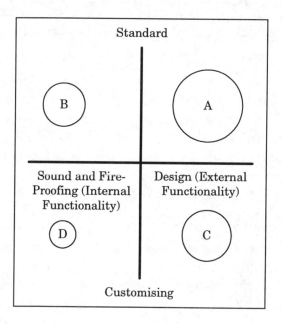

When the market segment has been identified and described, we
must calculate the size or market potential. It goes without saying that there is little point working in a segment that is micro-
scopic in size, or a market which is big, but without the payment
potential. The wooden goods producer found out that there were
about 30,000 manufacturing companies. Of these, only 5,000
needed specialised doors (soundproof and fireproof in standard
sizes), and on average they replaced their doors once every ten
years — when they would replace five doors on average. The size
of the market was thus (5,000/10) × 5, i.e. 2,500 doors a year. To
this one can add growth through new construction. The company's

market share in this segment will depend on how attractive the products are compared with those of the competitors.

One will often discover segments where the competitors have not been particularly systematic in their efforts, so there is a possibility of becoming big in those segments. For many companies, *it is better to be big and dominant in one segment rather than small in the total market*. When one is dominant in one segment one has the following advantages:

- The company can concentrate its product development and does not have to spread its resources too much.

- There are special advantages to be gained when purchasing special goods in larger volumes.

- By being dominant in one segment one can also be at the cutting edge in product development and pull the market in the desired direction.

- The company that dominates a segment or a market can often charge higher prices because it has better products and more credibility as a specialist supplier.

Another major problem in segmenting is putting together a product range and working on the segment in a way that is consistent. Product, additional services, price, terms of payment, sales arguments, advertising and distribution all have to be co-ordinated towards the segment. Obviously, if one sells a high quality product to a segment which appreciates this, the product must truly be high-quality. The sales arguments must build up the quality point and the advertising material must have an exclusive effect and not look cheap. If one tries to sell high quality with a mediocre product at a high price and with "cheap" advertising material, one will probably "bomb" on the market and will not be taken seriously by the customers.

If the company works on several segments, it is often a practical and financial problem to draw up a marketing approach that is consistent within each segment and differentiated between the segments. The thinking behind segmentation is attractive, but it has its price. The more segments the company has to work with, the more it must expect to spend on marketing, since it cannot benefit from economies of scale. Not only will the marketing costs increase, but often the purchasing, production and distribution costs will too. Several segments involve more specially designed products that are produced in smaller series, and are often distributed in different ways. Smallish companies should therefore focus on one or two segments. Segmenting thus involves a choice of specialisations oriented towards certain customer groups. At the same time it means that one chooses not to focus on others. There is no point being a specialist and at the same time trying to please everyone!

Market Goals

We distinguish between two types of market goals, i.e. profitability and market position.

1. The first goal is a matter of profitability for the company and customer groups (cf. the product/market matrix). It is important to break down costs by product and market. All costs must be distributed over products and customers in terms of real consumption of resources. Distribution of costs by turnover is usually quite meaningless, and as a rule gives a quite wrong picture of profitability.

2. The other goal is market position. The most important thing in the manufacturing industry is to satisfy the customer! Satisfied customers become loyal, regular customers. In addition, satisfied customers are decidedly the best advertisement we can have in terms of positive "grapevine advertising".

Other goals in marketing are:

- **Familiarity.** The company must be known as a supplier, and the market must know about the company's products.

- **Profile** (perception). The market must also perceive what we are good at (or want to be good at).

- **Preference.** It is important that the customers not only know us and our products and think they are good, but that they also prefer our products and choose them.

- **Accessibility** (distribution). A precondition of the customers buying our products is that they are available where the customer wants to buy them.

The wooden goods producer could, for example, set a goal that customers' answers to questions about their overall satisfaction with the products will increase from 6.5 to 7.5 on a scale from one to ten. Familiarity with the company's name should increase from 20 per cent to 40 per cent when the corporate customers are asked which door manufacturers they know. The company should have the best doors when it comes to soundproofing and fireproofing, and the goal should be that the corporate customers who say that the company is the best should increase from 10 per cent to 40 per cent in the course of next year. The percentage who say that they prefer the company as a supplier must rise from the present level of 5 per cent to 10 per cent. The point is that the market goals must be specific so that they can be measured. Market goals which are vaguely formulated and cannot be measured have minimal value. Market analyses are a useful aid in the work of market positioning.

Competition Analysis

In a competitive situation a company needs to offer products and services that are more attractive than those of the competition, and must at the same time do this more effectively than the competition, so that the company will earn money. The problem is that both the market and the competitors are in constant flux, so the company must constantly think ahead. The "strategic triangle" shown earlier in Figure 1.1 on page 20 expresses the essence of this situation.

It is important that a company should know its own and its competitors' positions relative to the market. The company must further understand the factors that drive developments forward in the competitive situation, and the positions that competitors and the market are likely to have in a few years. This is what we call competition analysis.

A competition analysis reveals both threats and opportunities in the company's environment. These are compared with the company's own strengths and weaknesses. In the strategy context it is precisely the strengths and weaknesses that are significant in relation to those of the environment that are interesting and important.

The competition analysis is divided into an analysis of the industry and an analysis of the competition. Our aim is to arrive at a strategy that strengthens the company's present competitive advantages, reduces the relative strength of the competitors and prepares the company for the demands of tomorrow.

The Industry

As noted previously in Chapter 1, the competition in a market, in terms of both type and intensity, depends on five competitive forces (see Figure 1.3 on page 24).

A strategy for tackling these forces and taking the offensive must define the forces in relation to the industry in which the company works and the company's own position in the industry.

New Entrants

The intensity of competition and profitability in an industry is often related to how easy it is for others to break into the market. This is often called the industry's entry barriers. The key questions concern whether things will happen in the industry in the next few years which will affect:

- Economies of scale

- Product differentiation

- Capital requirements

- What it would cost the customer to change suppliers

- Access to distribution channels

- Official regulations (concessions etc.)

and which will make the entry barriers for new actors higher or lower.

Customers

A trading relationship will normally be such that the party with most bargaining power will also have the advantage in the transaction. A company bargains both with customers and suppliers, and profitability is directly dependent on the margins it can obtain in both directions. In this context, the customers may be big companies, dealers, agents, private consumers, etc. It is important to find out whether there will be significant changes in the next few years which will affect the bargaining power of these customers. This balance of power is often dependent on the following factors:

- Few, but large purchases

- Standardised and differentiated products

- Relative importance of purchases to the customers

- The customers themselves have small margins

- The customers can "integrate backwards" and produce their own goods.

Suppliers

Just as we analyse the bargaining power of the customers, we can also analyse changes in the company's relationship with its suppliers. There are four main sources of the supplier's bargaining power:

- Scarcity of suppliers

- Supply of unique and differentiated products

- Can "integrate forward" and take over the company's functions

- The relative importance of the industry to the supplier.

Substitute Products

One can in reality say that all the companies in a given industry compete with other industries that make substitute products. These generally create the price ceiling in an industry. The substitute products that are most important to watch out for in the strategic context are:

- Substitute products which have a favourable price/performance development

- Substitute products made in industries with high profitability.

Rivalry

The intensity of competition or degree of rivalry among competitors will also be a determinant of the level of profitability. In competition analysis we should find out whether we can expect changes which will affect the intensity of competition. The degree of rivalry tends to increase with the following factors:

- Many competitors

- Competitors of the same size

- Little growth in the industry

- Low degree of differentiation

- The temptation to "dump" prices (high fixed costs)

- High exit barriers (tied investments).

In the industry analysis it is important to identify the features of development that can be significant for the industry in general. In the strategy work these must be interpreted so they become meaningful to the company. The things that should be considered in relation to the identified factors or events are, first, the timing and probability; then at the next stage one should consider what implications this will have for the competitive situation in the industry. The consequences in which we are particularly interested are changes in the buying criteria, whether there will be new entrants, and whether the changes will significantly affect the general level of profitability in the industry. The table in Figure 22.4 shows how this can be represented formally.

Competitors

In the strategy context we analyse competitors for two reasons:

- To find out what their plans are and

- To find out how they will react to our measures, and what consequences this will have.

A competition analysis should be focused on the few most important competitors. In practice it emerges that the number of significant competitors is rarely more than five.

Of course we cannot simply obtain this information directly from our competitors. Instead we must interpret data and impressions we have gathered. A survey of a competitor should include information on:

- Goals and business strategy

- Finances

- Marketing

- Production

- Organisational structure.

Figure 22.4: Table for Industry Analysis

Important changes	Time	Probability	New Buying Criteria	New Entrants	Profitability
Entry barriers					
Customer power					
Supplier power					
Substitutes					
Intensity of competition					

In such a survey we must find out about both *resources* and *competence*. Resources in the marketing context, for example, will be a matter of whether they spend relatively large sums on product/market development. The effect of the investment also depends, however, on how good they are at this work. Competence can then, for example, be measured in terms of how many successful campaigns they have had in the last five years compared to ourselves and the industry in general.

By analysing the competitors systematically, we can come a long way without any kind of espionage. By simply collating the items of information one can find in annual reports, interviews, articles and the like, we can elicit very clear pictures of what we are actually looking for. Often a systematic arrangement of what the company itself already knows will be just what we need. The US intelligence service during the Second World War based 96 per cent of its data on material that was publicly available in the form of newspapers, radio programmes and the like!

- Annual reports
- Articles
- Job advertisements
- The company's own apparatus (sales)
- Advertising material
- Dealers/customers
- Suppliers.

The competitors' measures or expected countermeasures can be assessed on the basis of:

- Probability
- Risk
- Timing.

In the strategy work we often come up with several alternative plans for approaches to competition. By systematically reviewing the countermeasures with which competitors are likely to meet each of these alternatives, we will often discover which strategies are best. If the competitors do not react to our measures, and at the same time we manage to take a substantial market share while maintaining profitability, then we have identified a successful strategy.

Positioning

The interpretation of information on changes in the industry and among competitors can be arranged in an importance/capability matrix. Such a matrix illustrates the company's current position and its strengths and weaknesses. The figure can also be used to illustrate changes in the industry and changes affecting a competitor.

Consider the matrix illustrated in Figure 22.5. The two dimensions in the matrix represent the importance of buying criteria, and relative position with respect to each criterion in relation to the competitors. The example illustrates the position of a furniture manufacturer vis-à-vis a foreign competitor. The most important buying criteria at the time were price, colour/design, seating qualities and dealer support. The company was relatively strong on price and dealer support, but weak in colour/design and seating qualities. The company should give high priority to the criteria that are most important and those where it has a relatively weak position. So in this example the company should give priority to doing something about colour/design.

Figure 22.5: Example of Priority Matrix

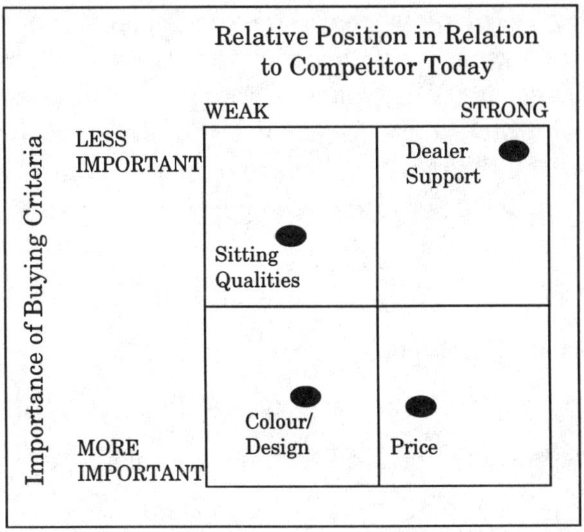

When analysing the competition the company should ask the following questions:

- How are the competitors planning to change their positions?
- How will the competitors react?

- Will the importance of the buying criteria change in the near future (will there be any new factors)?

The first two questions will be answered through competition analysis. The last question will be answered from the industry analysis.

Customer Plan

The company must draw up a plan for how it is to reach the individual customer groups in the product/market matrix. Each customer group should have its own budget specifying expected sales and planned market investment.

There will often be a need to identify key individuals who must be worked on in each customer group. These key individuals, often called the target group, are the people who influence and make decisions on the choice of products and suppliers. These people (influencers and decision-makers) as a rule have different needs and motives for making purchases, and will often have very different degrees of knowledge of the product.

The wooden goods manufacturer who sells soundproof doors to manufacturing companies must relate to the buying committee or executive who makes the decision, the architect who influences the decision and the personnel who will be using the premises.

For each customer group the company draws up a plan specifying:

- Number of sales visits and telephone calls per customer

- Recruitment of new customers

- Timing of sales visits and telephone calls

- Sales arguments to be used with decision-makers

- Sales arguments to be used with influencers

- Prices and terms of payment

- Trade fair activities

- Advertising and brochure material.

Product Plan

The company must draw up a plan for the way each product group is to be developed. Each product group should have its own budget indicating anticipated sales and planned market investment.

By "product" we mean what the customer buys — that is, the actual product plus the related services. Both packaging and technical service are included in what the customer buys. One of the most important things is to profile the product's competitive advantage. There must be a clear plan for why the customer should choose this particular product rather than a competitor's (cf. the prioritised buying criteria). The wooden goods manufacturer who sells soundproof doors should emphasise their excellence in the field of soundproofing. In addition, factors like design, maintenance and fireproofing may also be important. This must of course be based on facts, not wishful thinking about what should be emphasised on the market.

For each product group the firm should draw up a plan specifying:

- Competitive advantage
- Quality level of core product
- Quality level of secondary services
- Sales arguments
- Prices and terms of delivery
- Trade fair activities
- Advertising — brochure material.

If the company serves more than one customer group (or segment) with a product, it must draw up a product strategy for each customer group.

Buying Criteria

Buying criteria are the primary factors that a customer takes into consideration when buying goods or services. Examples of buying criteria include price, "quality" (which can mean many different things), delivery times, proximity to the supplier, the supplier's reputation, etc. Some typical buying criteria were listed previously in Figure 9.1 on page 228 — not necessarily in order of priority. For a fuller discussion of buying criteria, see Chapter 9 on "Product/Market Priorities".

Marketing Plan

Important reporting on the market strategy can be found in the marketing plan. The plan can consist of an "analysis" part and a "strategy" part as shown below.

Market Analysis

Total market. This should give an overview of the total market for the products and services offered by the company. The overview should list the most important competitors and their respective market shares. It should also show the customer structure in the form of turnover pattern.

Comments should include remarks on:

- Changes in laws, public policies, technology and society in general which will affect our market in the form of turnover, buying criteria or the purchasing process.

- Probable development of turnover in the total market and the industry for the individual products.

- Probable development of distribution factors in terms of changed conditions and power structure.

Position. This describes the position the company's products have on the market compared with the competition's products. Position is also relative to important segments of the market. Market position can be described in terms of the degree of customer satisfaction (of current customers), familiarity on the market, perception/profile, preference and physical availability/accessibility.

The comments will include remarks on:

- Probable development of segments in terms of preferences (buying criteria) and expected total sales.

- Probable development of competitors' positions.

Market segments. In this part one goes into more depth about the various segments the company has identified. Each segment is described in terms of who the customers are, what and how much they buy. It is also important to give an account of buying criteria and the purchasing process. The satisfaction of the segments with our company, and their perception of it (profile) should also be commented on.

The comments will include remarks on:

- Profitability of the segments for our company.

- The measures that would be relevant for our company.

- The measures we can expect from our competitors.

Competition analysis. This part reviews the most important competitors. We must obtain information that describes their turnover, product advantages, cost profile and the like.

The comments include remarks on:

- The strategy the competitor is likely to use for the next year. This means which segments the competitor will prioritise and what resources are likely to be used.

Current marketing. This is about the productivity of the company's present marketing. The company should focus on certain key figures such as:

- Turnover per sales rep

- Percentage of deliveries which are 100 per cent correct

- Time from order to delivery.

In addition to productivity, the company should give an account of profitability in terms of products and customers. Not least, the company should have a deliberate approach to:

- Customer satisfaction, and preferably a systematic measurement over time.

The comments will include remarks on:

- Historical development of key figures in the last few years

- Comparison of key figures with those of competitors (if available)

- Suggestions on how to improve key figures.

Conclusions. In this part the analysis is summarised in terms of the most important challenges facing the company — both threats and opportunities. It is essential that these conclusions are operative and unambiguous. Each conclusion must be succinctly formulated in an underlined sentence.

It is not the aim of this part to give an account of goals and strategies. Here we must only present a basis for decision-making.

Market Strategy

Market goals. This part deals with both profitability figures and market position. The comments deal in particular with:

- What profitability we expect on an overall basis and for the individual product and market groups.

- What effect an improvement in the market position is expected to have on profitability.

Customer plan. This part should specify the company's plan in relation to the individual customers. This means priorities, extent of focus and anticipated sales per customer or customer group. In addition to a relatively detailed plan for influencing the market, and sales work in particular, there should also be an account of product range, prices and terms of payment and any distribution factors.

The comments deal in particular with:

- The reasons why we think the plan will work, in other words we should say why the anticipated effect is likely.

Product plan. This part should be about the company's plan for the individual products. This involves priorities, extent of focus and expected sales per product or product group. In addition to a relatively detailed plan for influencing the market and in particular the sales work, there should also be an account of product range, prices and terms of payment, and any distribution factors.

Marketing budget. The market and product plan should also be expressed as a financial budget. Here we should indicate the anticipated turnover and profitability as a whole and for the respective product/market combinations. The marketing costs must also appear and be distributed over products and customers. The budget should cover not only the year for which we are planning, but the likely development in the subsequent two years, such that the horizon for the marketing plan is about three years.

Activity plan. For each customer group and product group there should be a more detailed plan for the measures and activities to be implemented. The activity plan specifies what is to be done, who is responsible, budgeted costs and when the measure is to be implemented. In marketing the *timing of an activity is often crucial to its effect*. The customer's purchasing process may follow certain cycles so that important decisions are made, for example, in a particular month. As a rule, it is just before these decisions are made that the companies should concentrate the main thrust of their marketing effort.

In addition to activity plans for customers and products there will often be some general activities that apply to the marketing work as a whole — for example the implementation of major campaigns, trade fair activities, product development, competence-raising and the like.

RESOURCES OF MARKETING

The Target Group
In marketing one talks about resources as the "Four Ps". These are product, price, promotion and placing (distribution). The resources are chosen and combined to increase the attractiveness of the products to the target group on which the company wants to focus. This is illustrated in Figure 22.6.

The target group is a detailed specification of who is to be worked on in the selected segments. The target group will consist of those who make the decisions on the choice of supplier and product, those who influence these decisions, and often those who use the product. The probability of succeeding with marketing is directly dependent on the company's knowledge of the target group. The most important thing is that we really understand the needs and problems of the customers. It is also important to know the customer's motives, since they are rarely rational in the business economy or socio-economic sense. If the wooden goods manufacturer who sells soundproofed doors emphasises that they are maintenance-free to a purchasing group that consists of the company's doorkeepers and maintenance workers, these people will see the doors as a threat, not as an advantage, because their own jobs could easily become superfluous.

Figure 22.6: Resources in Marketing

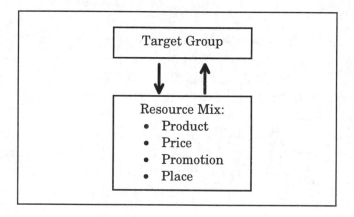

The product competence of the target group is often an important factor to take into account. Some customers know a great deal about the technology of the products and understand the relationships between technology and product advantages. But most customers have a low level of knowledge, and are often little interested in the product group as such. A survey of the target group's level of knowledge will often be critical to success with sales arguments, advertising and other influencing work.

It will also be useful to know who the people in the target group actually are: what is their educational background, their financial situation, where they live etc. Important information on the target group includes:

- Problems and needs of the customers

- Motives of the customers

- Decision-making processes of the customers

- Composition of purchasing groups

- The customer's position and background (corporate)

- The customer's financial situation, lifestyle, family situation etc. (consumers)

- The customer's knowledge of technology and product

- The customer's interest in the product

- The customer's media habits.

Product

We can distinguish three levels of the product concept, the core product, the concrete product and the extended product, as shown in Figure 22.7.

The core product is what the customer actually buys to meet their needs. A woman who buys lipstick actually buys "hope" (the core product). When a craftsman or others buy a drill they are actually buying "a hole" (core product). The window manufacturer is actually selling "light and heat".

The core product must be made available and concrete. The concrete product has up to five characteristics: quality level, features, design, brand and packaging.

The extended product includes installation, delivery and payment terms, guarantee and various types of after sales service. *The potential for finding competitive advantages is often in the extended product.* The window producer may, for example, differentiate by offering suggestions and solutions for curtains in bay windows.

The company can make its products and services more attractive to the target group by improving one or more features of the product or service. To satisfy segments with different needs, the company will have several product variants or service elements adapted to the needs of the segment.

Figure 22.7: The Three Levels of the Product Concept

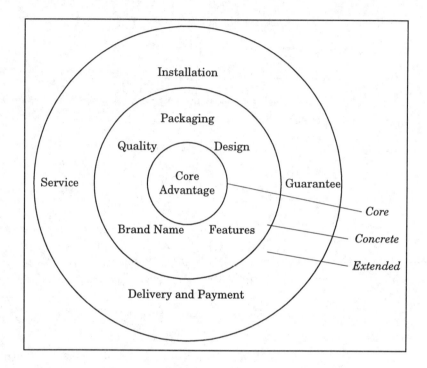

Price

Price is one of the most important strategic variables. The level of prices should be established on the basis of the value the product or service has for the customer, compared with other suppliers. *In other words, the price should first and foremost reflect the value of the products, not the company's costs.*

The price must be presented in combination with the product features, since the customer buys advantages and solutions, not products. A product with a high price may have features which mean that the customer in the overall view gets a cheaper solution. A low price means little if the product does not satisfy the customer's specifications. With up-market segments price and performance can be set higher than with segments with lower demands and less willingness to pay. Many factors play a role in pricing, and in Figure 22.8 we have listed the most central ones that the company should take into account.

The key question is:

- Are we maintaining the optimum price level? Or would a price increase or reduction lead to positive/desirable results in terms of turnover volume and profitability?

Figure 22.8: Factors Influencing Company Pricing Decisions

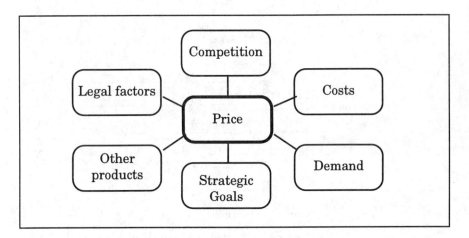

As a rule, the company can increase prices without affecting sales significantly (i.e. giving the company an overall higher turnover) when:

- There are few competitors

- The customers do not notice the price differences

- The customers would have a lot of trouble changing suppliers

- The customers think the products are more expensive because the quality is better.

Companies with well known brand names will often take a higher price because in most cases the customers are willing to pay for the security and any symbolic prestige inherent in the brand name.

If the wooden goods producer is alone in supplying soundproof doors to manufacturing companies, they will be able to command a higher price, since the customer will then have no other good options. If the wooden goods manufacturer also has a well-known brand name and a good reputation, they will be able to command an even higher price.

Promotion

Promotion includes several types of measures that the company can use to influence the market. The relative importance of these measures is illustrated in Figure 22.9.

Figure 22.9: Relative Importance of Marketing Measures

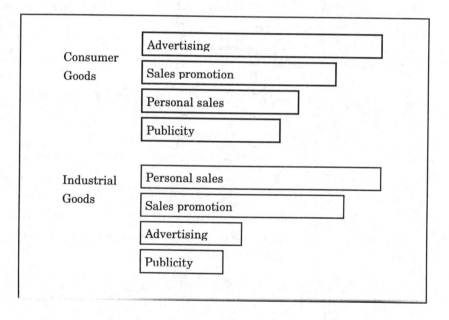

On the corporate market personal sales are often the most important resource. In connection with sales, the salesperson must have professional aids in the form of catalogues, presentation material and demonstration aids. If the aim is to become known by the target group, promotional activities in the form of advertisements, sales letters and brochures may be the right approach.

The wooden goods producer could, for example, send a brochure to everyone who has recently bought a site, since as a rule these will be the people who build new houses and will need information on doors and windows. In addition, the company may work systematically to place editorial copy in newspapers and magazines, i.e. publicity or PR. This is a cheap form of promotion which is of great value because editorial comment is perceived as neutral and thus more convincing. The company will find this kind of publicity easier to get if it is launching a new product, has been awarded a new export contract, a new co-operation agreement, or has similar news.

Distribution

Distribution as a resource in marketing is used to make the product or service physically available at the right place and time, and in the amount that the target group wants. On the consumer market, the company will as a rule use local distributors who stock the products close to the customers. On the corporate market, the company will normally keep central stocks from which it can dispatch goods on order. The wooden goods manufacturer will probably try to gain a foothold in the big building goods centres to present their products there. The distributor will also contribute advice so the customers' needs can be met. When the distributor has taken an order, this goes to the manufacturer, who supplies directly to the customer, but is paid through the distributor. So distribution involves a number of important functions such as information, ordering, payment and delivery.

An important competitive resource is the ability to reduce the time between order and delivery — in other words to make the products available quicker. Another requirement of companies is that they deliver what the customer ordered — i.e. 100 per cent filing of the order. The satisfaction of the customers depends on the company, in every delivery, supplying exactly what the customer ordered in the right amount and at the right time.

PERSONAL SALES

Experienced managers, sales managers and sales reps know that when many different people with different roles are involved in the buying/selling process, the sales become very complex. If one allows for the duration of the sales cycle and the uncertainty this can lead to for the result of the sale, personal sales becomes a profession that requires professional practitioners. Able salespeople succeed because they know when, why and what they must do at each stage of the sales cycle to move the prospective customer towards a final agreement. Such salespeople have systematically built up trust and respect among their customers because they have never regarded the customer as an enemy. At the same time all the customers have the feeling that they have achieved a favourable, fair deal. Common to all able sales reps is the fact that they have a good plan for every sales situation. The salespeople work to obtain:

- Orders or sales

- Satisfied customers

- Long-term customer relations

- Strong references and a positive "grapevine"

The Purchasing Process

One normally divides the purchasing process of customers up into five phases as shown in Figure 22.10. The purchasing process, from the customer's point of view, starts with the identification of a problem. The customers experience that they have a problem and lack a product or a service, and therefore want to take action to solve this problem. The first thing that happens in the purchasing process is that the customers think through their needs and the buying criteria that are important.

Once the problem has been identified the customers proceed to an active searching phase to find relevant alternative products that can solve their problem. First they will search their own memory to find options. If the customers have a good option stored away in their memory, there is often little reason to search any further. It is therefore important in many contexts that the company is among the options the customers have stored in their memory. The customer will as a rule actively seek information on the market. Important sources of information are colleagues, friends, distributors, consultancy firms and suppliers. The information may be in the form of experience, good advice and advertising in the form of brochures and the like.

Figure 22.10: The Purchasing Process from the Customer Perspective

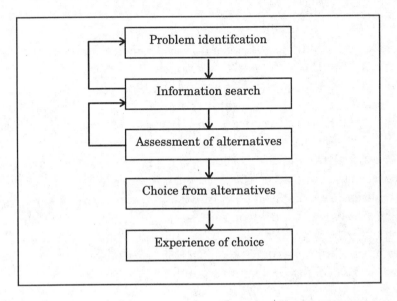

Gradually, as the customers collect information on the various alternative products that are available on the market, they will also evaluate strengths and weaknesses of each. Products which do not satisfy certain minimum requirements will automatically be excluded from further consideration. So for the selling company it is important that the customer has the right information or impression of what it has to offer, so that it is not precluded because of misunderstandings.

In their evaluation, the customers will try to rank the alternative offers according to how they appear in terms of the most important buying criteria. If a customer places most emphasis on soundproofing, the products which are best in that respect will be ranked first. If the relevant products then vary in price, and the "best" is most expensive, the customer must form an idea of what value (price/performance) the various products have. It is important to be aware that most evaluations are not rational in the sense that the objectively best product according to the customer's own criteria comes out as the product the customer prefers. A good sales rep will, for example, be able to influence the evaluation simply because they give a pleasant and professionally able impression. In this phase certain expectations are created as regards the various alternatives, and the expectations of the product which is selected are very crucial to the customer's perceived experience of the product or service.

After the customers have made their choice and received the new product, the customer's experience of the product or service begins. If their expectations are fulfilled, the customers will on the whole be satisfied with their choice, and the likelihood of their buying again or buying more will increase. Satisfied customers are in addition the best ambassadors for our products.

A complicating factor in the purchasing process is the fact that several people are involved. On the corporate market, most major purchases are organised in purchasing groups. This means that there are several people who take part, and they all have different kinds of experience, knowledge, motives and buying criteria. The purchasing process then becomes very unmanageable and very hard for the selling companies to relate to.

Who is Involved in the Purchase?

A sale often involves several types of buyers in the purchasing process, each playing their own unique role. The roles may be played by a person, a group or people or by the board of the company. The critical point is to identify who the real decision-maker is. Usually it is the person who has the formal authority to make the decision, but almost as often we find that the real and the formal decision-maker are not the same. If the seller is to increase the probability of success, they must be able to identify all types of buyers, and to understand their unique roles and functions in the sales/purchasing process. An able salesperson will "cover" all these persons in terms of calling on them, talking to them, and discovering their individual "hobby horses".

"The Economic Buyer"

The economic buyer gives final acceptance of the purchase. This person or role is very important, as they:

- Have direct access to the budget resources
- Can release budget resources
- Can exercise discretion in the disposition of the resources
- Have veto powers.

This person's focus, on which they will base their assessment of the purchase, is:

- What will the net effect of this be on the final result of the company (increased turnover, reduced costs, increased profitability, etc.)?
- What influence will the decision have on the organisation (increased productivity, increased motivation, etc.)?

"The User-Buyer"

The user or users make statements on the effects or changes the purchase will mean in their everyday life or working goals. These will typically be people who want to use, or advise on the use, of your product. Such a person's statements will be personal, since they are the ones who have to live with your product. For this reason there will often be a direct link between the person's improvement or success and the success of your offer.

The focus of this person's decision-making criteria will naturally be:

- How will this affect me?

"The Technical Buyer"

Technical buyers make statements on whether the product or service will meet predefined requirements for solutions. As such they function as "doorkeepers". Typically, they will assess the quantitative aspects of your offer or solution. On the basis of their objective evaluations of the relevant alternative solutions or offers, they will make their recommendations. They cannot say yes (they do not have the final say), but they *can* say no — and often do. The focus of their decision or recommendation is:

- Does the product and/or service fulfil the specifications?

"The Helper"

The helper will function as support for the seller. Such a person can be identified in the purchasing company, in the seller's company or outside both companies. The focus and motivation for behaviour in this role will be that you succeed with your offer — this will of course be because this person will also have personal motives and advantages associated with the success of the seller. The seller must identify these motives to establish the most realistic co-operation possible with the helper. This person or persons gives you and interprets information on:

- The situation

- Purchaser roles

- Personal motives of each purchaser.

The following criteria can be useful to look for when identifying a "helper" in a sale:

- The seller should have the confidence and respect of the helper

- The helper should have the confidence and trust of the purchasers involved in the sale

- The helper wants your (i.e. the seller's) solution.

In practice, all three conditions must be fulfilled to work with a helper in a sales situation.

Customer Profile

On the basis of the company's definition of its customer group(s), sales management will assign each sales rep a sales area. It is within the framework of the opportunities and threats of this area that the salesperson can meet their budget and periodical quotas. The first thing the sales rep must do is describe a conceivable ideal customer and a conceivable nightmare customer. An example of an ideal customer profile is one who:

- Has confidence in your company

- Has innovative and decisive management

- Is loyal to suppliers

- Has established projects and budget resources
- Is able to pay.

An example of a profile of a nightmare customer is one who:

- Has a slow-moving and unmanageable decision-making process
- Is not interested in long-term relations; focused on prices
- Has an authoritarian management structure
- Has had bad past experiences with your company
- Buys rarely
- Is financially weak.

In preparing for a sale, the sales rep can compare each potential customer with the above profiles and "see" how far from or close to the ideal customer profile they are.

Sales Plan
The aim of a good sales plan is that the company and its sales rep are in the right place with the right people at the right time — so they can make the right presentation. This means they must analyse each individual situation. On the basis of the analysis the sales rep draws up a realistic action plan which can fulfil the sales objective. Before doing this, they will have acquired a thorough understanding of their sales territory, their customers, their current purchasing situation and the real purchasers. The sales rep will maintain a high level of market cultivation which they will administrate within a systematic working methodology.

Purchasing Situations
As part of the sales rep's qualification work (e.g. comparisons with the ideal customer profile) they must clarify the purchasing company's so-called purchasing situation. To begin with, the salesperson must be convinced that a successful sale will lead to changes in the company in question. As a consequence of this, it is natural to assume that the people affected will react to the changes in different ways. It is important to distinguish among

four main types of purchasing situation called "growth", "problems", "steady boat" and "utopia". To increase the likelihood of success, and to distribute the selling time available as well as possible, the sales rep must be familiar with the various purchasing situations and the approach to each of them.

"Growth"

The purchaser and/or the purchaser's company is in a growth phase. The company is experiencing discrepancies between the situation today, as a consequence of growth, and the way they would like things to be. They key concepts in the sales rep's priorities are higher capacity, increased productivity and higher quality. If your solution will deal with or solve any of these problems, you are a relevant supplier. The probability of a sale is high in such situations.

"Problems"

The purchaser and/or the purchaser's company is experiencing problems. The company is experiencing discrepancies between the present situation and the way things were before the problem arose. If your products or services will remove the problem and bring the purchaser back to normal, you will be a relevant supplier. The probability of a sale is high in such situations. Because problems take priority over everything else, this is the strongest purchasing situation a company can be in.

Both "growth" and "problems" as purchasing situations can be described by saying that companies will buy because there is a discrepancy between their experience of reality today and what is necessary to win on the market in the long and short terms.

"Steady Boat"

The purchaser and/or the purchaser's company is experiencing no problems. They are in harmony with the way they want reality to be and with what is necessary to get ahead. They have no motive to introduce the changes that a purchase would necessarily involve. Why rock the boat now when we have (at last) got it under control? The probability of a sale in such a situation is slight.

"Utopia"

The purchaser and/or the purchaser's company has never had it so good as now. This is despite many signs of problems. The purchaser will not or cannot see them, but everyone else outside can. The sales rep's efforts to convince the purchaser otherwise will be perceived as an attempt to prove the purchaser wrong. The probability of a sale in this situation is very close to zero.

Common to "steady boat" and "utopia" as purchasing situations is the fact that the sales rep can use their time more productively elsewhere. Such companies have a perception of reality that is identical to their wish for the way it should be. When and if the purchaser experiences a discrepancy between the experienced and wished situation, they will contact the sales rep.

The Sales Cycle

Every sale has its sales cycle. This can vary in time and complexity, but in principle all sales have a common sequence of phases as illustrated in Figure 22.11. Each phase is typified by its own unique characteristics and the salesperson must know where in the cycle they are. At the same time they must have a clear strategy for how to move the prospective customer to the next phase. Running too quickly through the phases or attempting to "skip" a phase may lead to discomfort and trigger defence mechanisms in the purchaser. This can endanger the whole sale. It is therefore a golden rule that "the buyer needs time". It will be the sales rep's job to ensure that it does not take an unnecessarily long time.

A sales rep's most important resource is time. How the sales reps manage their time therefore becomes critical to their own and their company's success. The distribution of time will depend on a number of factors:

- The number of jobs that have to be done to move the potential customers to the next phase in the sales cycle

- The amount of work to be done

- The amount of money involved in each sales situation

- Planning of drives targeted at new customers

- Administration of sales cycles.

Figure 22.11: Phases of the Sales Cycle

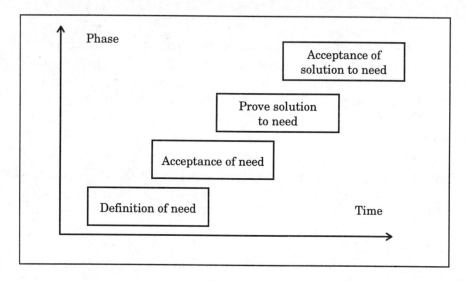

In purely visual terms, one can regard a sales cycle as a kind of funnel. One is either above/outside the funnel (prospecting); in the funnel (in the middle of the sales work), or in the neck of the funnel (the final spurt of the sales work).

A good sales rep will spread their time over these areas — 40 per cent, 20 per cent and 40 per cent respectively. One allows just about as much time to beginning as to finishing. Depending on the product, market and competition, a rough rule of thumb is that every tenth approach to a potential customer results in an actual customer. For the sales rep this means that each time they finalise a sale, they should have ten new potential customers in or on the way into the funnel. The percentage of customer approaches that lead to actual customers can easily be calculated, and the sales rep should use this ratio actively. If they are not aware of this, the flow of customers could easily dry up.

Customer Database

The customer database is another resource which has great potential in marketing, depending on how one builds it up and exploits it. Today there are many good computer systems for this purpose. The customer database can be used for mass mail shots of standard letters, "personalised" standard letters and for planning sales and calls. The database should also include sufficient information on consumption of resources (costs) on each customer, so that the profitability of customers can easily be calculated. A customer database can include information on:

- Name, address, phone, fax
- Names of decision-makers, influencers and users
- What purchases are made, how often, and turnover per year
- Last contact with the customer
- Stage of the purchasing process
- Information on the customer's market development.

23

INTEGRATED CUSTOMER-BASED PRODUCT DEVELOPMENT

INTRODUCTION

Costs are high in Europe, so European firms must offer products which have qualities and incorporate skills for which the customer is willing to pay. This means that product development is particularly important for European manufacturers.

Product development often involves the improvement of products a company sells to existing customers. To exploit the potential better it is important to consider the whole range of product development — from improved documentation of existing products to the development of new products based on new technology and competence.

The main challenge facing most European SMEs with regard to product development is:

- Establishing a clearer product development strategy — with greater differentiation

- Better organisation of the development projects.

Companies must carry out ongoing evaluations of the impact of the forces of competition on their own situation, including whether there are other solutions, or whether other solutions can be developed which can replace the company's own product or render it superfluous.

The degree of risk increases with increasing complexity. The development of new products or a new product generation may take a long time, may be risky, and may be very costly. Uncertainty is further increased if one aims to break into new markets with new products.

This chapter describes a product development process which increases the likelihood of commercial success on the market and reduces costs and risk exposure.

The term *increased value* is used throughout this section. By increased value creation we mean improved productivity through:

- More efficient use of resources

- Increasing sales/volume by

  ◊ taking market shares (the competitive factor is usually price)

  ◊ offering new and better products (product development).

The subject material in this chapter is discussed under the following headings:

- Product Development Strategy

- Integrated Customer-Based Product Development

- Product Safety

- Examples.

PRODUCT DEVELOPMENT STRATEGY

By product development strategy we mean the decisions made with a view to controlling the company's product development activities.

Product development is carried out in cross-functional project work. In project work on new products one does not follow the ordinary control structures in the firm. Unpredictable issues may put productive co-operation to the test, and good project management may be crucial to achievement of the goal.

To ensure that the product development projects move in the right direction and that the project staff work efficiently and effectively together, the product development work of the company must be based on a specific product development strategy. This must be logically compatible with the business idea of the company.

In the product development work, *quality* is of major importance as well as *strategy*. This means that as well as doing the right things, one must do them properly.

The product development strategy must be the company's guide to the product development work, and must therefore be understood and accepted by all those involved. In order to function well from day to day it must be brief and concise, with specific instructions, for example:

> "The distinctiveness of our product is tied to the use of turntables, and this must be maintained."

> "The products must be adapted to the EC machinery directive and all relevant EN or DIN standards."

One can continue this way to provide instructions in important issues of principle for product development.

Analysis and the Formulation of Strategy

As with all strategy work, the process must begin with:

- Identifying internal strengths and weaknesses to find out "what we *can* do".

- Identifying external opportunities and threats to find out "what we *should* do".

- Identifying the owners' intentions — "what they/we *want* to do".

The fact that we have "strengths" and "weaknesses" compared with competitors means that the product development strategy must be different for the different markets in which the company operates.

The need for more cross-functionality means that a far wider group of the company staff must be involved in the product development work than is usual in strategy work. The chief executive officer of the company must of course be an active team player. The product development strategy must be decided by the board of the company.

Time must be spent on assessing whether the company can "live with" the consequences of any alternative product development strategy. Will it function as the guiding principle it is supposed to be? In such a process it will be natural to adjust the formulation to ensure, among other things, that it is understood in the same way by everyone.

In view of the demanding tasks ahead in the product development work, the benefit of *consensus* cannot be overstated.

A product development strategy which is based on solid knowledge of customer conditions and customer preferences, and which is at the same time founded on the strengths of the company, increases the likelihood of developing the right products.

It is often asserted that Japanese companies are good at developing exactly the products that a majority of the customers need. In this context, seven points are often emphasised as important in the product development process:

1. Effective monitoring of competitors

2. Good knowledge of the market's requirements and wishes (can be understood as the requirements of authorities and the wishes of the customers!)

3. Quick adoption of new technology

4. Short implementation time

5. Systematic working methods

6. Constant quality improvements

7. Ability to co-operate and adapt.

Product Development Goals

The product development goals must come as a natural consequence of the strategy process. The goals have been achieved when customers have shown that there is enough demand for the product at the price the company asks, and when the company's profit on the product is satisfactory. There will normally be goals for the product and the project:

- Money — financing and profitability

- Time

- Quantity

- Quality — detailed specifications and functional requirements which are later turned into selling points.

A good product development strategy can increase the efficiency of the product development, especially as it helps one to avoid a number of "dead ends".

Improved planning reduces the need for changes after production has been started. This way one also improves the overall economy of the project. It is a fact that making an effort in the planning phase costs less than in the implementation phase.

The product development process involves trial-and-error. Correct strategy and planning will therefore give even greater returns than in other areas.

The product development strategy also affects other substrategies. The interplay of factors must be so clear that the substrategies reinforce one another — only then do they have the optimum impact. If the product and marketing strategies require niche products with great flexibility in design and short delivery times, for example, the production strategy cannot work towards long series and few variants.

Some would say that too detailed a strategy will prevent innovation. This is a risk that must be evaluated in relation to the tasks to be dealt with. There are many examples of product development failures due to poor strategies. It can happen, for example, that the production cost framework is not observed, which means that the competition picture changes radically.

Remember:

Compatibility with the customer's requirements, compatibility with the company's internal strengths.

Alternative Product Development Strategies

Product development is not synonymous with innovation or the invention of new products, although, of course, it also includes these.

Product development may be:

1. Testing, certification and documentation of existing products.

2. Adaptations to obtain added value.

3. New applications for existing products.

4. Further product development.

5. New products based on the company's own competence.

6. New products based on available competence.

Certification and documentation may be necessary to break into new markets with existing products.

Adaptations to obtain added value function well in a market with little growth and may be a way of extending the lifetime of the product.

In practice, it has often proved difficult to find new applications for existing products unless the product can become much cheaper — as has been the case for example with PCs, car phones and high-pressure washers.

Further product development is the most common form of product development. We are surrounded with successful examples of this every day: cars, cycles and ball-point pens. Note that the "Car of the Year" has rarely been a best-seller. Meeting the customer's expectations is a different matter from listening to salesmen and specialists!

The development of new products is necessary for everyone. It is important that the management of the company has its "feelers" in good working condition so that the development work can begin in time. Some people will presumably still remember what happened with the move from wooden skis to plastic skis, or from mechanical to electronic calculators. The companies that dared to take the leap to new technology early won a better position, and several of those that hesitated too long have disappeared or have been weakened.

Taking the leap from one's own familiar technology to the new one may be the right action for many companies. But apart from good strategies, it takes competence, motivated staff and solid resources in general.

Figure 23.1: Alternative Product Development Strategies

Copying	Innovation

• Customer demand is relatively familiar and predictable
• Customer recognition and approval takes place quickly
• Fits in with current marketing/sales and distribution
• Fits in with current goals of the company.
	• Potential large, but unpredictable demand. Risk of failure also great.
	• Customer approval may be slow in coming at first, but the competitors' attempts at imitation can also be slowed down.
	• May require new, customised marketing/sales and distribution
	• May clash with current:
	  ◊ company structure
	  ◊ distribution of responsibilities
	  ◊ products (which are threatened).

INTEGRATED CUSTOMER-BASED PRODUCT DEVELOPMENT

Whichever of the six alternative product development strategies the project group takes as the basis of its work, the following requirements must be observed in the product development work:

- The development work must constantly be rooted in *the customer's needs* and *the company's strategy*.

- The process must involve co-operation between group work and specialist work where the professional groups (Marketing — Development and design/Engineering — Production) work in parallel to reduce overall time consumption.

- The project management must play a major role, inasmuch as co-ordination and efficient communication are essential to achieving the goals.

- The phases of the project from acknowledging a need to realisation must be played out on a narrow path where the results are continuously co-ordinated by the professional groups involved.

- The customer and sub-suppliers must be involved as natural partners in the process.

- The process must continue throughout the lifetime of the product.

- The customer's needs, wishes and requirements must be directly acknowledged and approached with systematic working methods.

Project Management

> *Question:* "What are the characteristic of companies with successful product development?"

> *Answer:* "Good management in general — and good project management in particular."

Product development should be organised as a project. The following concepts are normally used in project organisation:

- **Head of Project.** One should appoint someone from the top management of the company as the person with overall responsibility for the project — in small companies this should be the chief executive officer, in larger companies it could be the technical director. The Head of the Project is the immediate superior of the Project Manager and is responsible for ensuring that the project goals are laid down.

- **Steering Committee.** It is a matter of discretion whether there should be a steering committee. It may be useful in certain cases — for example if several companies are co-operating on product development, if it is a development contract for the public sector, a sub-contract, or if several people from the top management of the firm apart from the Head of the Project want to have an influence on the selected project.

- **Project Manager.** The Project Manager is responsible for managing and implementing the project within the given framework, and for ensuring that the goal is achieved. A person may be Project Manager full-time or part-time — it depends on the nature and size of the project.

- **Project Group.** The project staff may be picked from the organisational structure of the company, from line or staff functions, or from external sources. In the project they are accountable to the Project Manager. The Project Group and the Project Manager deal with the cross-functional co-ordination of the project. The members of the Project Group can work full-time or part-time on the project.

- **Project Secretary.** This function will be necessary for large projects, or in companies where the same Project Manager has many projects, or needs assistance because of other duties.

Choice of Project Manager

The Project Manager for product development must be chosen with care, and must:

- Have a good knowledge and understanding of the company's strategy and plans.

- Be able to manage development and interrelationships between departments and the external environment.

- Have sufficient knowledge, experience and capabilities — in relation to the project.

- Be able to manage, plan and follow up.

- Be able to administrate, structure and optimise.

- Have decision-making authority.

It is also important that the person appointed has the free time to do the work. The person directly responsible for ongoing production or maintenance will perhaps have difficulties when the everyday work has to be give priority. In small companies it will often be the chief executive or perhaps the sales manager who is both Head of the Project and Project Manager.

In many development projects it may be a disadvantage to have a member of the regular product development staff as Project Manager. A company manager in a company with wide experience of product development put it as follows:

> "The developers must not be let loose! With all due respect for their work and their abilities, they are in almost every case far too tied up in the development process, not in getting *finished* with a product."

In the following, project management in product development is discussed as being the combined responsibility of the Head of Project and Project Manager.

Economy and Profitability

The first thing one does is to get an economic overview of the finished product — by using simulations, for example.

The project management must both have financial control of the project costs and deal with the verification of product profitability after all stages of the development project.

In the early stages of product development it is possible to influence the costs of the product, but the opportunity to exert this influence is quickly reduced. In the organisation of product development it is important to allow for this and to obtain and exploit the necessary market and production information right from the start. Figure 23.2 shows that development costs only constitute 5 per cent of the product costs, but *determine* a whole 70 per cent of the product costs. The material costs make up an average 50 per cent of the product costs, and in the later phases after design/engineering 20 per cent of the product costs can be affected by issues related to materials — for example, by material administration and price negotiations. Work and administration costs make up a total of about 45 per cent of the cost of the product, but in this case only a total of 10 per cent of the product costs can be affected.

Figure 23.2: Influence on Production Costs

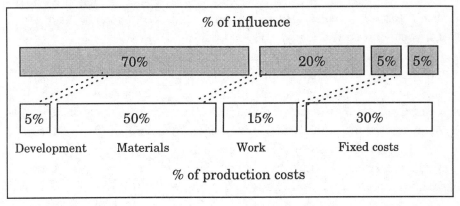

The costs of the actual product development work, on the other hand, are often highest in the last stage of product development. The first phases of product development are relatively cheap, but the costs increase greatly as product development progresses. It is therefore important, as early as possible in the product development process, that one rejects the product ideas that do not hold out any prospects of a good business result. Prototype production, trial production, test series and the like are usually the most costly procedures. Before one gets that far, one should have arrived at the "80 per cent right" product, so that one only has to test variants for which one cannot just as easily obtain the information in other ways.

However, there are exceptions to every rule. In special cases, to save time for example, one may make several prototypes early in the product development work and test them even though this is a relatively expensive product development method.

Time
Time is an important factor for generating earnings from product development. McKinsey & Co. claim that a 50 per cent overrun on development costs reduces the profit by 4 per cent, while a six-month delay in a new product reduces profits by 33 per cent.

Integrated Customer-based Product Development (see Figure 23.3) is a variant of "Integrated Product Development", and has proved particularly useful in shortening product development time frames. In the USA, integrated product development is called "concurrent engineering", and Figure 23.4, which is taken from *Business Week*, shows among other things that "time to market" can be reduced by 20 – 90 per cent.

As an aid to controlling the project work it may be useful even for small product development projects to use *network planning*; for large projects it is absolutely essential. Time management and co-ordination of the activities can be improved greatly by using such a system — for example, Critical Path or PERT. The latter was launched during a very large product development project — for the Polaris submarines — and is said to have contributed greatly to the success of the project.

In product development one must be prepared to make quite a few changes in the time schedule originally set out. This is a natural consequence of the fact that there are many unknown factors in a product development project. With a PC-based system one has a relatively good chance of updating network plans quickly. This can be used for better planning of the work so one does not waste too much time. It may be useful to have a general plan for the whole project and a more detailed plan for the work in the period of the project immediately ahead. The Project Manager must incorporate suitable milestones and must define clearly the tasks that must be finished before others can be started. In order to reduce time consumption it may be necessary to abandon predetermined ideas of the sequence of product development — for example, by having a job worked out in two or more alternative versions, with the resultant increased costs for the analytical work — while waiting for the results of another job to determine the choice among the alternatives. Cases like this require solid project management competence.

Figure 23.3: Integrated Customer-based Product Development

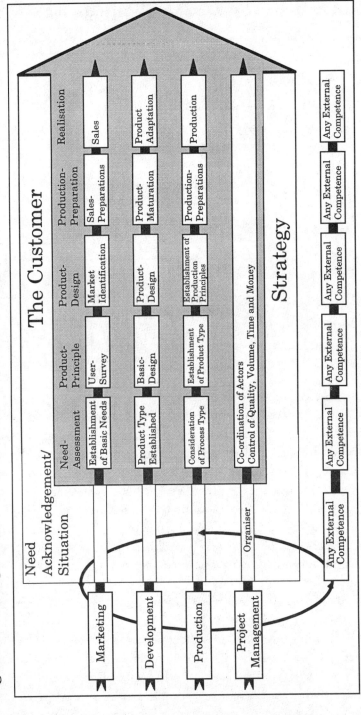

Figure 23.4: Results of "Concurrent Engineering"

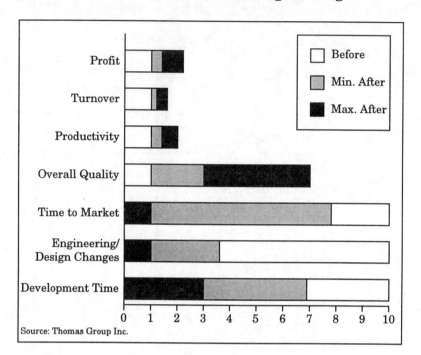

Source: Thomas Group Inc.

Co-ordination of Actors Involved

The most important function of project management in product development is to get the participants to work together to develop the project in the right direction. This also means that the work must follow the strategy of the company. Project management must control efficiency, make sure that the necessary issues are clarified and that the work is done to a suitable level of detail.

The starting-point for the co-ordination work is the description of the goals, organisation and available resources of the project, including the requirements and goals set for the product.

The project management must create motivation for the project. This task is also to a great extent passed on to the top management of the company. It is motivating for the staff to know that the top management is interested in the project. If the management openly transfers its interest from a project which has not yet been completed to a new project, this often means that the concluding work in the old project goes more slowly. With its example, the management can affect the success of the project.

The project management must also be open to input which brings valuable alternative views into the project. It should be possible to change or stop a project if one sees that it will not lead to the desired result.

Strategic Underpinning

In the planning and starting phase of a project it is necessary for the tasks of the project to be reviewed and discussed thoroughly in terms of the company's strategies. The Project Manager will often report to the chief executive of the company and will have the main responsibility for ensuring that the work of the group moves in the same direction as the company's strategies. Any doubts and uncertainties about the strategic underpinning of the project must be submitted to the chief executive of the company for final decision.

It is the job of the management of a company to look for new business opportunities and to ensure that the product portfolio is renewed. If the company fails to start on this work in time and to make it into an ongoing task, a crisis situation which the company is unable to control may arise. In smaller companies it will be the chief executive who has this responsibility. This is probably the chief executive's most important function. It includes the job of ensuring that the company has the skills necessary to exploit the opportunities that do exist.

Competence

The company must invest time in acquiring specialist knowledge so as to keep up to date in its critical technology areas and their alternatives.

The forces of competition (shown previously in Figure 1.3 on page 24) also represent sources of competence and information. These can be exploited by systematically:

- Building up and cultivating contacts with suppliers, customers and resource environments which possess the relevant skills and knowledge — including those outside the company's own industry.

- Keeping oneself informed about competitors, potential new actors and substitute products:

◊ through exhibitions and trade fairs;

◊ by reading relevant periodicals and annual reports;

◊ and by keeping up with material technology, production technology and information technology.

Among other resources and sources of advice on which the company can draw, we can mention consultants, research institutions, design councils, licensing agreements, patent registries, databases, R&D co-operation agreements, marketing contracts and strategic alliances. Using a suitable range of these types of services is essential to any company today, large or small.

The work of keeping the company informed by drawing on external sources of competence which can be used for product innovation must be dealt with by allocating specific responsibilities and describing specific tasks.

The kind of external competence which deserves closest attention, and which can be invaluable, is contact with a customer during development work. Co-operation on product development between customer and supplier is usually something which creates productive progress. This is the main point of the following section, which describes a method for such co-operation.

Customer-based Analysis Using QFD

No one is likely to deny that it is important that the company's product meets the need of the customer as fully as possible. However, clarifying that need so that the information can be used in the design of the product is not always a simple task.

One method for product development work which makes systematic use of customer information is the Quality Function Deployment method (QFD). The method is particularly suitable in the early phases of the product development for carrying out a customer-based need assessment which leads to technical specifications for the product and to further development and improvement of the product. The method originated in Japan and has since become popular in the USA. Figure 23.5 shows the working method in a simplified version of the *product planning matrix,* which is the central working document for the QFD method.

Figure 23.5: Simplified Version of Customer-based Analysis Using QFD

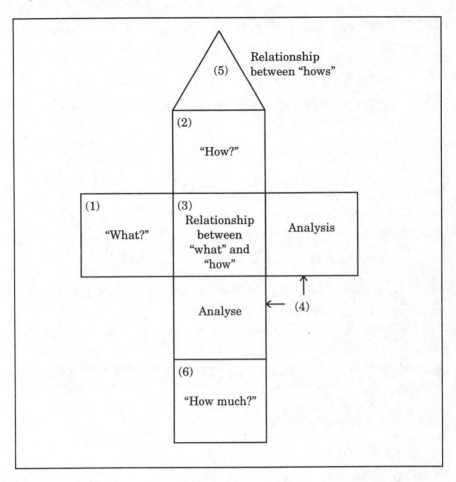

The work is best done in a project group, the composition of which covers the different, but equally necessary, kinds of competence required by the product and its development. As a starting-point the group needs enough basic specifications to define, among other things, the purpose of the project and who the customer is. This includes, for example, whether it is a new product, or an existing product which is to be improved or modified.

Often there are several sources of demand which together make up "the customer". This may be the case with sales to companies. Then it is not unusual for purchasing, financial, operating, maintenance and other staff to be included. With groceries on the other hand, the buyer and the user are often the same person and this is who one primarily has to include. But, as pointed out below, one must also take other sources of demand into consideration.

Stage 1: The Customer's Requirements and Wishes

Once one has clarified which customers one has to accommodate, the work begins on Stage 1, the field on the left in Figure 23.6. One draws up a systematic list of the customer's requirements and wishes. It is important that the information on this is obtained such that it really reflects the customer's wishes, needs and buying criteria.

Matters of the product's function for the user belong here, for example. The question is:

"What should the product do, be and achieve?"

As pointed out previously, official requirements and regulations must also be considered.

The requirements of the customer must be grouped appropriately — for example in general groups and sub-groups. Below we give examples of general groups for customer requirements where one of the general groups is subdivided into two sub-groups. In reality there will often be more general groups, and in each general group there will usually be more sub-groups.

- Utility functions

- Reliability

- Safety/security

- Price

- User-friendliness:

  ◊ ergonomic features

  ◊ comprehensibility

- Aesthetic requirements.

Figure 23.6: **Example of Customer-based Analysis Using QFD**

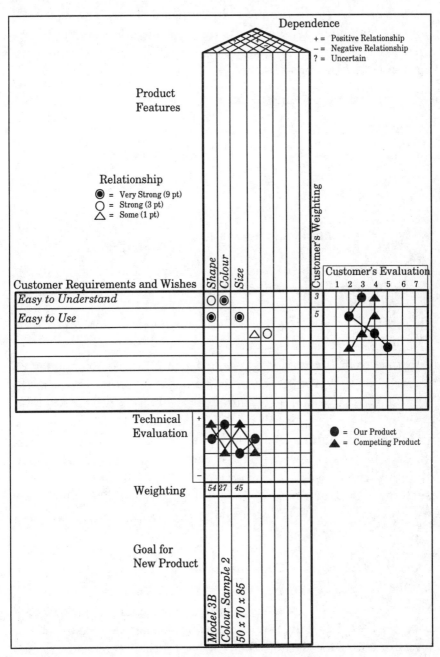

Stage 2: Technical Product Features

In Stage 2, second from the top in the middle of the figure, the technical features of the product are listed. These are structured like the customer requirements and one includes whichever features are important to the customer or in terms of official requirements. The question here is:

"What is the product like?"

Examples of technical product features:

- Shape

- Colour

- Size

- Power consumption for operation.

These features must be quantified. "Shape", for example, should be graded by a customer panel.

Stage 3: Relationship between Customer Requirements and Product Features

At Stage 3, in the middle, the relationship between customer requirements and product features is analysed. The closeness of the relationship is graded on a suitable scale. One could, for example, use a scale from 0 – 9, where "0" (no relationship) is not entered in the matrix. Figure 23.6 indicates that there is a close relationship (9) between the colours used and ease of understanding how the product is used — for example, that the opening button of a seat belt has a red colour so that it is easy to see. The shape may also be important in understanding use, and is indicated as a close relationship (3 points).

Stage 4: Evaluation of Your Product against that of Your Competitor

Stage 4 consists of evaluating your product against your competitor's product. This falls into two parts: the customer's assessment, on the right of the figure, and your own technical measurements, in the middle below Stage 3. In Figure 23.6 the customer's assessment is shown as a grading of a competitor's product and your own product on an evaluation scale from 1 – 7. To obtain the customer's evaluation one may have to conduct a special survey. One can also ask for information on how customers weight their different requirements in relation to one another.

The example in the figure shows that the customer gives the competitor's product four points for both "easy to use" and "easy to understand", while your own product only gets two points for "easy to use" and three points for "easy to understand". Of these two criteria the customer considers "easy to use" to be most important — this is weighted at 5, while "easy to understand" is weighted at 3.

In Stage 4B the results of the evaluation of the technical features of the company's own product and the competing product are entered. The features may be the kind that are quantifiable, or may be gradable — for example, by an evaluation panel.

In the figure a graphical representation is sketched in under 4A and 4B. This gives a faster visual overview than if one only uses a numerical presentation. The original numerical values should of course be included as documentation.

Next to the bottom in the middle field of the figure we see a weighting of the product features. This is to obtain a measure of the importance that each of the technical features has for the customer's requirements and wishes. In the example, the shape of the product is quite important (three points) for whether it is "easy to understand", and very important indeed (nine points) for whether it is "easy to use". The customer has weighted "easy to understand" with 3, while "easy to use" has been given a weight of 5. Shape as a technical feature thus gets the total weight of 3 x 3 + 9 x 5 = 54.

This weighting must be *used with some caution,* as it depends greatly on whether the assessment of the relationship between customer requirements and technical product features is correct.

Stage 5: Interdependence of Product Features

One should also investigate whether some of the product features influence one another. This is done in Stage 5 — at the top as "the attic of the house", where a positive relationship with the product features is marked with "+" and any conflicting features are marked with "-". If you are uncertain whether there is a relationship or not, this can be marked with a "?".

The example in the figure indicates that there is a positive relationship between the shape and size of the product. However, there is a negative relationship between the colour of the product and another unspecified feature of the product. This means that the unspecified feature is changed in an undesired direction when the colour is improved. One cannot improve both features at the same time.

Stage 6: Concluding Analysis of the Matrix and Formulation of Goals for Technical Features of Your New Product

One should go through the matrix to see, among other things, whether there are empty rows — this may mean that customer requirements have been forgotten. Empty columns may mean that the product has "superfluous" features, but these may be customer requirements of which the customer himself is not aware, so that he has not formulated any requirements. If there are rows or columns where there are only weak relationships, this may mean uncertainty in areas where one should be cautious about focusing attention. You should also look for any discrepancies between the customer assessment and the technical evaluation of the competing product. If there are any such discrepancies, it may be that the customer's requirements have been misunderstood, or there may be errors in the survey.

It may be necessary to supplement the matrix with more features and functions.

Finally, at the bottom of the figure, one formulates the objectives for the technical features of the new product. This specification of technical requirements is linked to the customer's requirements and is used as documentation for the product development work.

In formulating the objectives one can consider, among other things:

- The weighting

- Studies of the competition

- Any clashes with what is technically feasible
- The company's product strategy
- The company's limitations.

Other Ways of Using the QFD Method

The QFD method can also be used, if necessary along with other methods and aids, for the analysis and verification of subsystems and components and for production planning. One disadvantage is that the method may at first seem excessively long-winded compared with the benefit.

Marketing

Marketing knowledge must be exploited throughout the product development process. The marketing department must obtain information on unmet product needs for the company and must participate in the work of *defining the need*. It is also an important task to clarify what kind of product will satisfy the need — or how one of the company's existing products must be changed to meet the need.

With *acknowledgement of needs* as the basis, the market work continues in the next phase with "use" surveys. This is done to obtain information on the customer's use of the product and on competing products. The work in this phase can best be described by reference to the previous section on "Customer-based analysis using QFD". Market work means obtaining detailed information on the customer's use needs and buying criteria, and on how the competitors meet these requirements. The QFD method is particularly useful in this phase and the market work is important if the product is to be a success.

At a sufficiently early point in the product formulation phase one must obtain information from the market on the kind of market volume the product could achieve:

- First, for a rough economic analysis of whether the product has the right to life
- Later, so that production plant can be planned appropriately.

The work of the marketing staff will probably increase greatly throughout the next phase, when the production preparations are made. This is also when the sales preparations are made, the sales system is established and sales and market launching are planned. Depending on the industry one is in, one often produces a "zero series" here, or a test product for trials with the customers.

When everything is ready for normal production, sales begin and one has real proof of whether the plans were right and the product is marketable. Product development continues its marketing work by obtaining information on the use of the product by the customers, on any faults that should be remedied, and any information on possible improvements for later product variants.

Development/Design and Engineering

Roughly speaking, the development/design and engineering work consists of the following processes after the requirement situation has been clarified and acknowledged:

- Establishment of the product type with which one will try to meet the requirement

- Schematic design or, in some industries, establishment of a schematic method or process — often with a prototype or laboratory product

- Product design — where one hopefully gets the proof that the product works

- Product maturation — with design details in accordance with sales volume and production

- Product adaptation.

Engineering design has been defined as:

> "Transferring a set of specified *functions* to a set of product specifications."

This definition can also be used for other kinds of product development work than in the engineering industry. One possible aid in the early stages of this process is QFD, as described in a previous section. This tool can also be used to assess alternative solutions against one another.

A technically and economically sound choice of materials is one of the most important preconditions for the development of successful products at the lowest possible cost. The choice of materials affects both the design and production methods.

It is during the development/design and engineering work that the important decisions are made on how the product is to be produced. It is during this work that there is the greatest potential for influencing the cost of the product. In Figure 23.2 it was suggested that a whole 70 per cent of the cost of the product was fixed at this stage.

Production

In many cases the production department is not really involved in the product development work until after the product design has been fixed and a prototype of a laboratory product is available. And when one then fails to get the product ready at the desired time for launching on the market, or the product turns out to be more expensive than anticipated, there is great dissatisfaction. If the ICPD model is used, this problem can be avoided; but with the strong focus on the marketing aspect, there may still be a risk that the marketing and development departments will dominate the process, and that important aspects of production will be suppressed. In that case it is the responsibility of project management to see that the production aspect is involved — that the project development is integrated and balanced.

Production costs, as pointed out earlier, are to a great extent influenced by the design of the product — but they are also influenced by production quantities. With a larger quantity production can be arranged so that the payroll costs per unit produced are lower, and the cost of the goods can also be affected.

In order to calculate cost factors, production must be planned right from the start of product development. It is a matter of course that production costs are calculated along with the engineering design. One should also calculate how much the market quantity must be to make the production costs low enough to make the product competitive. If this quantity cannot be achieved, the project must be reassessed.

If production requires new production plant or changes in the existing plant, one can at least obtain information early in the project on how this can be done. Some — perhaps all — of the planning can begin before the product has been fully designed, and this can shorten the time until the product is launched.

PRODUCT SAFETY
(in the light of product development work for the EU Single Market)

Product safety:

• Is part of the quality of the product

• Ensures that goods do not cause personal injuries or damage to property.

This is how the "General Product Safety Directive", 92/59/EEC, states that product safety is to be understood as an active feature of the product for which the producer is responsible. This is how damage and injuries are to be avoided.

Technical Obstacles
One of the big tasks in realising the EU Single Market is the removal of "technical trade barriers". Technical trade barriers often arise in the form of product safety requirements. In order to remove these national requirements, new common EU requirements have been established to replace them. These new product safety regulations often have a tendency to appear tighter than the requirements that the various countries had previously.

The tools that the EU has chosen to ensure a common high level of safety for products freely traded within the EU Single Market are directives based on "the New Approach".

What these have in common is that they:

• Have all been issued after 1985

• Assign more importance to European, international and national standards

- Require the use of a common identification system (the CE label).

Another aim has been to serve the interests of the consumers by ensuring that product liability can be legally enforced across national boundaries, all the way to the producer (see next section).

The Product Safety Directives
At present the following have been issued:

- General product safety Directive 92/59/EEC

- Eleven "New Approach" product safety directives, e.g. the Machinery Directive, Construction Goods Directive, Toys Directive, etc.

The rules of the General Product Safety Directive are used when there is no specific safety directive for a product. One main rule is that:

- The producer must be able to place safe products on the market

It is important to be aware that in this context:

- The producer may be the company that has really manufactured the product (including a sub-supplier), if that company is based within the EU

- The "producer" may be the importer or company claiming to be the producer, for example, by placing its product on the market

- The directive also gives several other possibilities in the chain leading to the user.

A *safe product* means:

- Any product which, within its expected service life, poses no risks, or only such risks as are compatible with the use of the product, and which, with due consideration for a high level of protection of people's health and safety, can be considered acceptable:

◊ because of the composition, design, packaging, presentation and labelling, assembly, maintenance, disposal and applications of the product, or because of its direct or indirect effect on other products or its combination with other products.

◊ when it is used as intended or in a way which can reasonably be expected, among other things with due observance of the information on its use given by the producer or the producer's representative, and especially with due consideration for the normal behaviour of children.

The possibility of creating greater safety or of obtaining other less dangerous products is not a sufficient reason for regarding a product as "unsafe" or "dangerous" (Def. from *Journal of the European Communities*, 27.6.90.).

The CE label

One important factor in the product liability directives is that they state that "safe products" must be identified by a CE label. This is meant to indicate that the product meets the requirements of the product safety directives (for example that a machine observes the requirements of the Machinery Directive) and that it can be sold freely within the EU Single Market.

Figure 23.7: The CE Label

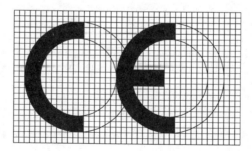

The product safety directives require their terms to be observed if a product conforms to a "harmonised standard". "Harmonised" in this context means that the standard has been drawn up by CEN,

CENELEC or ETSI and that it is stated in *OJ, the Official Journal* (see the explanation of abbreviations on page 556).

All this may seem very tidy, but in practice it may be disturbed somewhat by the fact that an individual country is allowed to stipulate stricter environmental requirements than those provided for in the EU rules.

Product Development

The "New Approach" directives are general in nature and therefore give few direct instructions that are useful to those who work with product development. It is anticipated that a set of harmonised standards will give the rules which ensure that the minimum level of safety is achieved. The production of these standards is proceeding more slowly than expected, and for many products they will not be available for a long time to come. In some areas, however, many standards are ready (for example EN 292 — Machine Safety). These can give us a good indication of how requirements will be formulated in other product areas. For example, EN292 – 1 Item 3.11, Design of a Machine, states that this work involves a series of activities:

(a) The study of the machine itself throughout its life cycle:

   ◊ design/construction

   ◊ transport and preparation

   ◊ use

   ◊ dismantling and disposal.

(b) Instructions relating to all phases (except design).

As a last example we can include what EN292 says about machine safety, i.e. it is the ability of the machine to do the following *without causing personal injury*:

- Perform its function

- Be transported

- Be installed

- Be adjusted

- Be maintained
- Be dismantled
- Be disposed of.

Abbreviations

Abbreviations of European standardisation organisations:

CEN: Comité Européen de Normalisation. The CEN draws up standards in most technical areas except electrical engineering and electronics (CENELEC) and IT and communication matters (CENELEC and ETSI)

CENELEC: Comité Européen de Normalisation Électrotechnique

ETSI: European Telecommunications Standards Institute.

EXAMPLES

An Example for Reflection

Roofing tile manufacturer: Market leader, well-established brand name, distinctively sanded, coloured surface. Regardless of surface colour, all tiles are produced in grey concrete.

Problem: After acid rain became common in the 1970s and 1980s, the coloured, sanded surface was washed away after a few years and all roofs appeared as grey concrete regardless of their previous colour.

Result: Complaints increased to an extent that was threatening to the company — both financially and in terms of the reputation of the brand name.

Suggested solutions: Sales staff and distributors exerted pressure on the company to choose its competitor's solution with a smooth surface and through-coloured tiles. It emerged that for the competitors, because of the through-coloured concrete, the washing-off of the surface did not produce results dramatic enough to pose a major problem. (This on the whole was how the company's licensers abroad had solved the problem). In other words, the simple solution was close at hand, until the company asked the customers (the house owners in its own market) why they chose the company's products — and even in most cases paid higher prices than for tiles from the competitors mentioned.

The message was clear: The sanded surface — among other reasons because snow settled on the roof. If you took this away, there was nothing but the name to distinguish the product from those of all the competitors.

The solution was just as clear, but not as simple: Keep the sanded surface, but make it absolutely resistant to acid rain for at least 20 – 30 years. With the aid of a large, expensive project the new product was developed, and some of the other product features were also improved.

The leading position of the company was maintained (at the last moment) and today it is stronger than ever.

An Example to Follow

In developing its kitchen appliances Høyang Polaris used the following methods of need assessment according to Jostein Refsnes:

1. Literature searches in a database (NSI).

2. Study of patents.

3. Trips (Japan, USA).

4. Visits to trade fairs.

5. Contacts with dealers.

6. Contact with users/Tests in a hotel kitchen.

7. Co-operation with a research institute.

8. Simulation with special equipment (induction cooker).

9. Accelerated testing.

10. Market surveys.

11. User panel.

12. "Opinion Leaders".

13. Development of society (scenario).

Scenario: The "Kitchen of the Future" (initiative: Høyang Polaris AS.)

Goal: Insight into the way the kitchen environment could conceivably develop.

Method: Gather together Norwegian companies with a shared interest in kitchen development.

Working approach:

1. Lectures/studies of

   - Sociological development

   - Architectural development

   - Technical development.

2. Exchanges of ideas as regards the company's own product development.

3. Demonstration of prototypes to a panel of critics.

Companies participating:

- Siemens A/S (cookers, electrical household appliances)

- Intra A/S (kitchen sinks)

- Stabburet A/S (food)

- Figgjo A/S (dishes)

- Høyang Polaris AS (cooking vessels)

- Sivesind Møbelfabr. kitchen furnishings.

24

PRODUCTION TECHNOLOGY OVERVIEW

INTRODUCTION

Production technology has become as much a part of business strategy as marketing and finance. Whether you are using straightforward manual techniques or different levels of automation, the effectiveness of your production operation will, at the end of the day, be a major factor in your survival and prosperity. If you look at the range of manufacturing technologies available, it might be tempting for, particularly a smaller company, to say "this is not relevant to my company" or "this would be too difficult to implement".

In practice, however, many SMEs are already involved to a greater or lesser extent in using advanced manufacturing techniques in the following areas:

- Some companies have progressed part of the way already towards achieving Computer Integrated Manufacturing (CIM), or Just-in-Time (JIT) manufacture.

- Most companies have made reasonable progress at using modern production engineering techniques and have some Computer Numerically Controlled (CNC) equipment.

- Many will have installed production management systems and Computer-aided Design/Manufacture (CAD/CAM) systems are becoming more common.

- Materials handling can vary from conveyor to a robot to an automatic guided vehicle and shouldn't really present much problem.

Obviously, integrating all these islands of automation into CIM operation is a major step and one which most companies are not ready to tackle just yet. However, consultants who are working on assignments in SMEs should try to identify opportunities for that company which will advance their technology base a little further along the track and perhaps persuade them that automation is not an impossible goal.

The subject material of this chapter is looked at under the following headings:

- Production Engineering
- Computer Numerical Control
- Design for Manufacture
- Computer-aided Design
- Computer-aided Manufacture
- Automated Assembly
- Materials Handling
- Electronic Data Interchange
- Just-in-Time Manufacture
- Computer-integrated Manufacture.

PRODUCTION ENGINEERING

Many companies have an outdated attitude to production engineering which costs much more than they would be prepared to admit. Any new product that is developed is put into production without much thought as to how it is to be manufactured, how many people will be required or what tooling and handling aids are needed.

Consequently they miss delivery dates, end up with excessive work in progress and scrap and find that profit margins are much lower than they would have expected. The main problem is that they do not apply logic to the organisation of production or new technology to the manufacture of new products.

Most small to medium sized manufacturing companies need a production management system (PMS) put in place as part of their strategic business plan, with a view to introducing some form of group technology to the work place to enable them to respond more appropriately to today's manufacturing demands.

COMPUTER NUMERICAL CONTROL (CNC)

It is noticeable how little CNC is used in manufacturing companies who do production for their own products as opposed to those sub-contract manufacturers who do production for others. The sub-contractor has recognised how important it is to apply modern production methods and technology to their processes to remain competitive in the face of increased competition from other sub-contractors.

So why does the in-house manufacturer not invest in new technology as much as the sub-contractors? We must remember that the small- to medium-sized manufacturer probably has product development budgets, market development budgets and production engineering costs that the sub-contractor may not have. Typically, product and market development costs can be very high, taking up a large percentage of available capital and it may be that new equipment is quite far down the list for or priorities for investment. Even if new equipment is purchased it will be basic and will replace old worn equipment. The company may even want to acquire new technology but does not know how to get information on it or what is available for its requirements.

One quick way to obtain new technology which will increase machining accuracy is the addition of Digital Read-Out (DRO) to existing machinery. In most cases a DRO can be retrofitted directly to the slides of milling machines, lathes, etc. The immediate result is an increase in the accuracy of machined parts, an introduction of relatively simple new technology to the workforce and an opportunity for the company to enter into a new phase of manufacturing practice.

The next major step for the company will be the introduction of CNC equipment. This also can be done at various levels but most companies, depending on the processes being employed, will start by replacing largely manual machines with numerically controlled (NC) machines. Typical machines in this range include:

- **Cut-Off Saw.** Previously a horizontal hacksaw or bandsaw with a manual vice, NC saws will have automatic start and stop, bar feed to a predetermined length, automatic grip and release and proximity sensing for diameter of stock. They can run unattended.

- **Shear.** Previously manual feed with hand or foot operation and a manual backstop, the NC shear can be hand or magazine fed with predetermined automatic motorised backstop. The shear blade can operate on short cuts to reduce operation cycles. Automatic front stop for cutting "Y" dimension after 90° turns.

- **Brakepress.** As with the shear, material handling and operation were manual. Now NC brakepresses are available that offer automatic motorised backstops and NC down stroke to give a predetermined bend angle along with thickness compensation. Flat sheets may be magazine fed but bent sheets may require additional handling equipment for removal. Hydraulic tool clamping is become more important for quick top and bottom tool changing.

- **Turret Press.** This equipment is uniquely NC in that there was no serious manual alternative. This equipment will replace a range of low tonnage manual power presses using die-sets. The NC turret press is a single hit power press with a magazine of up to 50 pierce, blank and form tools, some of which can rotate. The flat material blank is hydraulically clamped to an X-Y co-ordinate movable table which places the material under the tool head, the tool is selected automatically from the carousel and the operation on the metal completed. The pattern of holes, forms and outline is usually programmed directly into the machine or on magnetic tape or floppy disc. The turret press is most suitable in small volume processes because of its ability to change tools very rapidly and accept an infinite number of blank sizes.

- **Sheet Rolls.** Used for the production of tubular products it is usually manually fed and operated. The NC tools act similarly to the NC brakepress in that it can be pre-programmed to assess plate thickness and roll to an exact diameter. Additional automatic plate handling equipment and tube removal equipment is available.

- **Machining Centres.** Previously lathes and milling machines were manual or semiautomatic but were separate entities. The machining centre has combined many of the operations of both machines so that with bar feed or blank magazine it is possible to perform many machining operations on one machine that previously required several, and to do it unattended. There are, of course, NC milling machines with tool magazines and blank holders, and NC turning centres with bar feed and tool changers all of which work unattended. Programming may be directly to machine or remote via tape or disc.

- **Cells.** This is a relatively new concept in automated manufacture which consists of a group of machine tools linked by automated material handling systems. A common cell layout for the sheet metal industries would be a shear feeding a turret press feeding a brakepress, all pre-programmed and numerically controlled and completely unattended. This type of set-up can be seen in companies producing computer cabinets and white goods. The material handling aspects of the cell would include conveyors, pick and place units and robots with customised grippers. The cell can be expanded to include riveting stations, welding stations and feed to surface finishing plants such as plating or painting.

- Other automated cells can be seen in the plastic processing industries, leather goods industries and timber processing industries among others.

In all cases the common thread running through companies with automation is high productivity, low labour costs and increased profits. Smaller companies may find automation hard to justify in the short term but should consider it as part of their long-term business plan.

DESIGN FOR MANUFACTURE (DFM)

One area of business that receives very little attention is design for manufacture, yet this advanced manufacturing technique has been around for many years in other guises such as *value analysis* or *cost reduction systems.*

A condition on many contracts with suppliers is that there be a price reduction of perhaps 10 per cent per year over the term of the contract. The supplier can achieve this in two ways:

- Reduce costs in his manufacturing operation, and/or

- Introduce design changes in the product with the approval of the customer.

Design for manufacture normally applies to the initial design of a new product where a methodology is followed to ensure that the product is easy to manufacture at an economic cost and is built to the required quality and reliability etc. Design for manufacture requires collaboration between design engineers, manufacturing engineers, materials people, supplier and the end user. Various rule based systems have been developed for DFM, notably a US one from Boothroyd & Dewhurst and a system from Lucas Engineering & Systems in the UK.

The two main aspects of DFM are:

- Parts standardisation, and

- Parts reduction.

From the suppliers' point of view, if they can achieve either of these on behalf of their customer, then there is going to be a saving on material. Typically, savings are made in areas such as:

- Standardising hole sizes so as to avoid excessive tool changes

- Rationalisation of production operations such as folding

- Standardising fastener sizes

- Using lighter materials in non-structural parts.

Obviously, any such changes must be made in collaboration with the customer's engineers, but you will usually find that they will be keen to help you affect savings, provided their plant has the local autonomy to do this.

COMPUTER-AIDED DESIGN (CAD)

When computer-aided design was originally introduced into industry it was very basic and essentially consisted of computer-aided drawing only. Very few small companies thought it worthwhile because it was very expensive, required large computers and the drawing board was more capable of interaction with others.

A modern CAD system, however, running on a personal computer (PC) with other business and engineering software is now truly an interactive design aid, combining design, drawing, bills of material, solid modelling, finite element analysis and real-time simulation of production.

Small companies involved in product development will find that the price tag, equivalent to one year's salary for a designer, can be fully justified on perhaps one project when they consider the quantity of time and repeat work that can be saved using a basic PC-based CAD system. Follow-up projects if they are similar to one existing on file can be completed in nearly half the time. It is also true to say that the quality of the output, that is, the hard paper copies, is sometimes so good that the services of industrial design consultants or visual artists can be reduced considerably.

COMPUTER-AIDED MANUFACTURE (CAM)

The term "Computer-aided Manufacture" usually refers to the output of a CAD program when applied to a machine tool such as a lathe, milling machine or turret press. The designer produces a component design on the computer and uses this to programme a NC machine tool directly which will run unmanned, possibly even at night.

There are other new CAM applications now coming on the market in the area of model making. One process, known as "Stereo Lithography", takes the 3D design program and uses a laser to build a solid model in a resin which is later cured in an oven. The main advantage of this technology is that during the model-making stage of product development the model can be available in a number of hours instead of days or weeks, thus giving the marketing group or the customer the opportunity of commenting much earlier than previously.

CAM is also used in the textiles industry for both sample cutting and mass production of clothing components directly from the designers computer, allowing very quick style and size changes on the production floor.

Most toolmakers using CAD/CAM will do the rough machining and drilling of cavities and waterways on a NC machining centre overnight, thus taking advantage of cheap electricity and reduced labour requirements.

The signage industry uses CAD/CAM extensively for cutting metal or plastic letters for use on shop and office signs. The equipment in use here is a laser profile cutter which is programmed directly from the design computer. The process is practically like plotting a drawing except that the result is a finished product. A laser profile cutter can be used for almost any material in any industry.

AUTOMATED ASSEMBLY

Most small manufacturing companies are afraid of automated assembly and will not even consider it. Yet when broken down to its basic form automated assembly is simply the fitting together of two components by mechanical means.

That may be a very simplistic statement, but when considering automated assembly as a potential recommendation the consultant must always look at appropriate technology for the company and not drop them into high technology before they are ready for it.

Most small or medium sized manufacturing companies with an assembly process would probably welcome a reasonable recommendation for low cost automation if it could be financially justified. Most automation can be justified if appropriate volumes are available.

The consultant should consider what opportunities are available for the company. Assemblies which are easiest to automate are those involving the fastening of components with screws. It is acceptable in the short term to have an operator place the components of the assembly into a fixture which is connected to self-feed automatic screwdrivers, one per fastener. These screwdrivers may be pneumatic or electric, will have fast advance followed by controlled screw feed, may be supplied with screws from a common or individual bowl feed unit and can be interchanged rapidly if a design change specifies a different screw. The component in the fixture will also be clamped automatically at the start of the cycle. The advantage of this small automatic set-up is that it will place multiple screws in an assembly at the correct torque in the same time as the fixing of one screw, and the quality will be consistent. It is also an introduction to automation which is easy and low cost.

The company may follow-up later with pick and place units which assemble the components of the assembly into multiple fixtures on an indexing conveyor which feeds the screw driving unit. Later on an automatic packaging machine may be added to the line. It can therefore be seen that by phasing in a program of low cost automation elements it is possible to have a fully automatic production line in a time frame which suits the company's financial and production situation.

Other examples of automated assembly which can be put in place on a phased basis include:

- Robotic welding with manual component placement which can be further automated with pick and place assembly followed by robotic removal and stacking

- Automatic spot welding with multiple heads such as on heating radiators, with similar follow-on automation.

When considering automation it is also necessary to return to the concept of design for manufacture (DFM). One of the main problems found by companies that install automatic assembly systems is the inability of the equipment to handle the components effectively. Problems occur in such areas as the assembly of round objects or screws into holes, the tolerances may be too wide or the object may need lead-in chambers. In welding by robot it may be necessary to reduce tolerances to enable the welding head to produce an accurate weld. The reduction of tolerance on components may lead to an increase in component cost which must be taken into account when considering automation.

A DFM analysis will take all the facts and requirements of the system into account and will provide a positive or negative justification for automation at that particular time.

MATERIALS HANDLING

When considering the phased implementation of automation modules which do work or assembly it is sometimes convenient to include human labour at low wage levels to perform the mundane tasks of feeding components into the system or taking finished assemblies away to the next operation. There comes a time, however, when it is justifiable to also automate the material handling aspects of the system and to integrate all modules into a full automatic production line.

There are many ways to automate the transport of material from A to B:

- Vibratory bowl feeders are used to transport small parts from a mass stock to the assembly end of pick and place units of automatic screwdrivers. As the component is transported from the bowl it is oriented into the correct attitude for use.

- Indexing conveyors, usually with component fixtures spaced at an exact pitch, are used to transport assemblies from one work station to another or from an automation cell to a packaging or finishing unit.

- Robots are used to move components from one machine to another or to load and unload moulding or pressing tools. Other applications for robots include palletising, handling hot castings or forgings and loading blanks into machine tools.

- Automatic Guided Vehicles (AGV) are mostly used for long distance transport, typically between buildings or between work station within a large factory building. They would be loaded and unloaded by robot at each end. Most AGVs are battery operated and are guided by a signal wire or tape on the ground. They are pre-programmed to a specific route with specific stops and can park themselves at the end of their cycle for battery recharging. Another application for AGVs is the transport of raw material from an automated stores to the required production machine.

ELECTRONIC DATA INTERCHANGE (EDI)

The next area of factory automation we must look at is not as tangible as those on the factory floor, and is not likely to be seen so often in the smaller company. It also assists with the integration of vendor/company/customer which has become more common in recent years. It is electronic data interchange (EDI).

Sir John Harvey Jones, former Chairman of ICI and now a successful management consultant, once said:

> "The man who is really close to his customer, who is really inside his mind and whose operations are linked to his in the most intimate way possible, will stand the best chance of survival, both for him and the customer".

EDI provides the means to link the two parties in such a way that the supplier is, to all intents and purposes part of the customer's operations.

Trading between companies has traditionally been done by paper, moving in the 1980s to documents produced by computer, posted to another company and re-entered into another computer. This is all quite an expensive process where the cost of paper-based trading can be anything up to 15 per cent of the value of merchandise involved. Quite apart from the physical costs involved, the delay can also be a problem. Communication times are compared below:

- Letter: .... 1 to 2 days
- Telex:.................... 5 minutes
- Computer:............. 13 seconds

Added to this is the likelihood of key punch errors, lost or delayed orders and misinterpretation or translation errors.

EDI employs only one entry of data i.e. at the customer's terminal — all purchase orders invoices and payments being made automatically between the customer's and supplier's computers and between their bank accounts. A definition of EDI would be:

> "The electronic transfer from computer of commercial or administrative transactions using an agreed standard to structure the transaction or message data."

The idea of all this is that there is an electronic route for data between partners while the goods produced travel by road or rail in the normal way. Specifically, EDI is being used to transfer:

- Office information

- Graphical information

- Payments through electronic funds transfer

- Product information such as bar-code data

- Business transactions such as purchase orders and invoices.

The costs involved to the supplier are fairly small — a PC, a modem and some software. This will at least allow them to receive and transmit messages and formatted files from purchase orders and invoices. Obviously, they must invest in a production management system to take it further.

Small companies often find themselves reacting to a demand from a major customer to adopt EDI. To a small company use of EDI is often a requirement for maintaining important trading relationships and thereby EDI can sometimes become a survival issue.

JUST-IN-TIME MANUFACTURE (JIT)

As with most new technologies, Just-in-Time is being driven by the multinationals. This is to be expected as they would be the first to feel global and corporate pressures. Obviously, a multinational would apply Just-in-Time to their own operation first and suppliers would over time be asked to adapt to the new delivery schedules. Suppliers have in the main adapted extremely well and many are now supplying on a daily or twice-daily basis to the larger multinationals.

What we are interested in, however, is ensuring that the supplier benefits from Just-in-Time manufacture as well. There is no reason why his operation should not parallel that of the multi-nationals and benefit from shorter set-up times, reduced inventories and shorter lead-times. So we are going to focus in on a review of a theoretical supplier's shop floor and where they can make improvements and savings without too much heartache and investment.

The ultimate aim of JIT is to eliminate all waste associated with making a product and in this context, waste is anything which does not directly add value to the product.

The main areas in which waste occurs are:

1. **Transportation**. The palletising of parts and subsequent handling around the shop floor, particularly in batches.

2. **Delay**. Because of batching, discrete lots of work in progress build up in pallets around the shop. These batches wait between operations for periods of time which are far in excess of the time it actually takes to make them on the various machines.

3. **Over-production by volume**. This involves the situation whereby a lot of 100 items entails actually making 105 items. The extra five are made to cover scrap and setting up. However, these extra five have not been ordered, may not be paid for and drag the profit margin down.

4. **Over-production by time**. This involves the situation where items are made early on the principle that large batches are made to cover set up times. Typically, for a weekly call-off of 50 items, a monthly batch of 200 is made in week 1. Demand is satisfied from stock for the remainder of the month. However, 150 items are made one week too early, 100 items two weeks too early and 50 items three weeks too early. Items made early must be batched, handled and delayed tying up floor space, labour and finance.

5. **Stocks**. Stocking adds no value to items and ties up capital without any return. Storage is inherently wasteful.

6. **Scrap**. JIT adopts the concept of inspection to prevent defects, to inspection to identify the causes of defects, so as to eliminate them. The traditional approach of inspection to find defects after production is not used.

JIT attacks these wastes in the following manner:

1. **Transportation**. Change the layout of the shop so that items are not batched and transported about. Put machines in a cell so that work flows from one machine to the next.

2. **Delay**. Use continuous flow production whereby batching is eliminated in favour of passing on individual items to the next machine in line as soon as that item is ready. Much work on faster set-up is needed.

3. **Over-production by volume**. Pay great attention to set-ups and right-first-time to make only what has been ordered.

4. **Over-production by time**. Do not make items until just before they are needed.

5. **Stocks**. If finished product lead time is one day then only one day's worth of stock is permitted.

6. **Scrap**. Shift responsibility for quality onto the person who makes the item and away from the inspectors.

Typical benefits of a successful JIT implementation are better customer service, large reduction in delivery times and lead time, quality improvements, reduction in working capital requirements due to lower stocks, better use of facilities and improved competitiveness. Furthermore, the lead times on products can be reduced from weeks to days and stocks reduced by 75 per cent or more.

A comprehensive training programme is needed for both direct and indirect staff from the shop floor right up to senior management. The issue of employee involvement cannot be stressed too strongly and a project will only be successful provided there is a strong senior management commitment. The training stresses the issues of team work to identify and resolve problems and this is a technique which is carried on from the implementation stage right through to the months and years of subsequent operation.

Finally, it is vital to begin JIT implementation in an area where you know you are going to be successful. So the choice of the pilot project is critical. The pilot project will demonstrate the idea and theory, will boost morale and gain support and it will train operatives on JIT techniques.

COMPUTER-INTEGRATED MANUFACTURING (CIM)

CIM is essentially the linking of JIT and EDI on the supplier's side with the production management system of the customer.

As the relationship between the customer and the supplier develops, so the linking of their operations will increase. In a Just-in-Time situation, the supplier will require a reasonably accurate forecast over the first 30 days, although with JIT in operation, they will be flexible enough to respond quickly to changes in orders without finding that they have excess work in progress already made. Their JIT system will enable them to fill the orders without tying up excessive working capital in stocks of finished or part finished goods.

The supplier's production management system (PMS) is an information planning and management tool enabling them to run the business efficiently, handling sales orders, works orders and material requirements. The basic features of the PMS are:

- Sales planning and control

- Production planning and control

- Stock planning and control

- Manufacturing database

- Integrated financial package.

Sales planning and control will handle cost and delivery estimates, sales order entry and works order entry.

Production planning and control will handle master production planning, capacity planning, scheduling and work in progress.

Stock planning and control will cover inventory control and materials requirements planning.

Each of these elements is linked to the manufacturing database and ideally all should be integrated back to accounts.

For really effective JIT operation, an EDI link is essential to ensure that the lead time reductions achieved are not cancelled by delays in the administration system.

25

ORGANISATION OF THE PRODUCTION PROCESS

STRUCTURAL ORGANISATION

Targets

The organisation of lean enterprises is based on simple hierarchical structures with a high degree of personal participation. In such companies, the job of management does not consist of the issuing of formal instructions and of the exercising of control, but instead, the emphasis is on setting targets and preparing guidelines as well as rigid requirements concerning quality and productivity and in making use of the internal company competition. Figure 25.1 shows the characteristics of Lean Production.

Measures to Reach the Targets

One method that can be used to "flatten" the structural organisation (i.e. reduce the number of different layers of management within the organisation) is the introduction of teamwork as a principle of the organisation of work. Teamwork aims at making use of the experience, the capability and the skills of employees, for the benefit of productivity.

The control of output and performance by a superior can be replaced by mutual control between team members whose status is equal. After all, no other employee knows individual strong and weak points, preferences and dislikes, strategies to avoid some tasks and capabilities better than a worker's immediate colleagues. So teamwork can be planned, shared and controlled precisely and effectively. The team members check the productivity of their own colleagues by means of discussions based on solidarity (or — negatively — by exerting pressure on others).

Figure 25.1: Characteristics of Lean Production

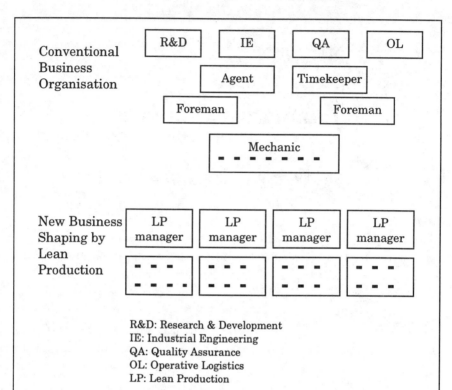

The introduction of Lean Production modifies all positions in the company: on the shop floor, the indirect areas are reduced. All control and operational tasks are assigned to the teams that are orientated to high quality and costs.

Several types of job rotation, job enlargement and job enrichment and, in consequence, the possibility to qualify oneself for superior tasks, require teamwork. Furthermore, the individual considers co-operation in a team as being something positive. This leads to greater contentment and thus employees' productive potentials are used extensively.

The introduction of teamwork presupposes a modified organisation of production processes: from the orientation of functions to the orientation of objectives. In all functional areas (research & development, order management, production), production processes should be structured according to organisational principals of group technology, i.e. with orientation to products (division of quantities instead of division of work). Co-operation in teams with integrated tasks and a high grade of autonomy takes the place of complex hierarchical structures with bureaucratic and formalistic decision-making and with many points of intersection.

FUNDAMENTAL PRINCIPLES OF THE OPERATIONAL ORGANISATION: PROCESS ORIENTATION

Targets

According to the fundamental philosophy of lean enterprises, only the employees involved in the process contribute directly to the increase in value of a product. Every other employee is an "indirect" one.

Measures to Reach the Targets

All work can be described as a process (or as part of a process) made up of a sequence of tasks that are carried out within a defined and limited system and produce results. *Process orientation* (see Figure 25.2) means focusing on the sequence of operations. The work process is characterised by the dynamics that occur when working through several tasks one after the other. The tasks within a process (or part of a process) can be done by employees whose functions in the enterprise are totally different.

Every process results in an output which must be in line with customer demands (of quality). The same demands go for the inputs to a work process.

The concept of "organisation of process-chains" is characterised by its modular structure. The modules are linked together through their respective inputs and outputs as illustrated in Figure 25.3. The main emphasis is directed to input and output, the cross-functional co-operation between organisation units: a description of the points of intersection replaces a job description.

Figure 25.2: Process Orientation

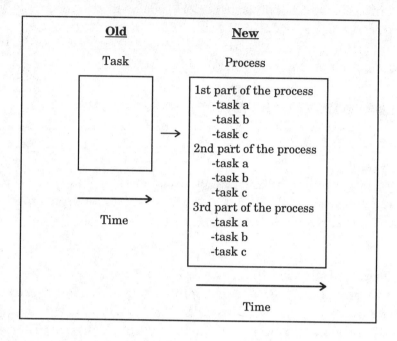

Figure 25.3: Organisation of Process Chains: Cross-Functional

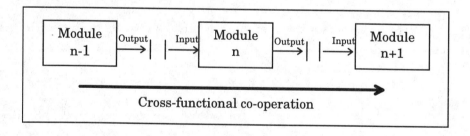

The process that deals with the management of incoming orders, for example, is made up of sub-processes including sales, marketing, purchasing and production. Each of these sub-processes is typically carried out by the employees of different functional areas including sales/marketing, logistics, production and assembly.

All processes have different focuses and targets as shown in Figure 25.4.

Figure 25.4: Focuses and Targets

Name of the Process:	Target:
Process of productivity	To manufacture a product just in time
Personnel planning process	To provide personnel just in time
Production planning process	To provide just in time all necessary resources for working on the order
Production process	To produce a shaft

When building up a process-oriented operational structure it is important to realise that every employee is both a customer and a supplier: a customer from the view of the preceding process, and a supplier for the one that follows. This is illustrated in Figure 25.5.

Figure 25.5: Elements of the Process Chain: Customer/Supplier Relationships

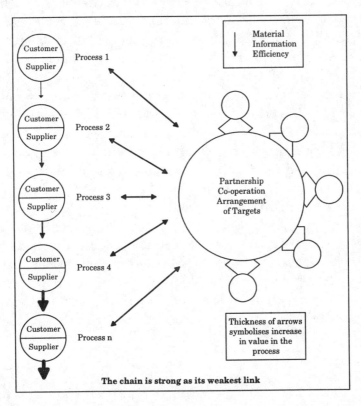

The chain is strong as its weakest link

RELEVANT PROCESS-CHAINS IN PRODUCTION

Targets

The process of productivity can be divided into several cross-functional processes that are linked together.

Measures to Reach the Targets

The design of the process of productivity in production starts at the process-chain of development that covers the period between the idea for a product and its introduction to the market. Consequently, there are interfaces with the market and the production area.

The process-chain of purchasing — involving a flow of information and materials between different companies — covers the period it takes for transfer of information between customer and supplier as well as the delivery time for replacement materials. The latter is made up of the ordering time, the delivery time from the suppliers and, if necessary, the time that is needed to receive material and to carry out any incoming inspection that might be required. This process-chain has interfaces in common with the market and the production area.

The process-chain of production covers the period between the provision of all necessary materials and the handing-over of the finished product. In the course of information processing, the information flow runs opposite to the material flow, precedes it and runs parallel to it up to order management and production planning and control. These two process-chains have interfaces with the manufacturing area and the market.

The process of productivity is concluded by the process-chain of sales which covers the period between the time the finished product is handed over from production (for example, from the assembly area) and the time it is delivered to the customer. Accordingly, the process-chain of sales has interfaces with the production/assembly area and the market This is illustrated in Figure 25.6.

Figure 25.6: The Process of Productivity in Lean Production

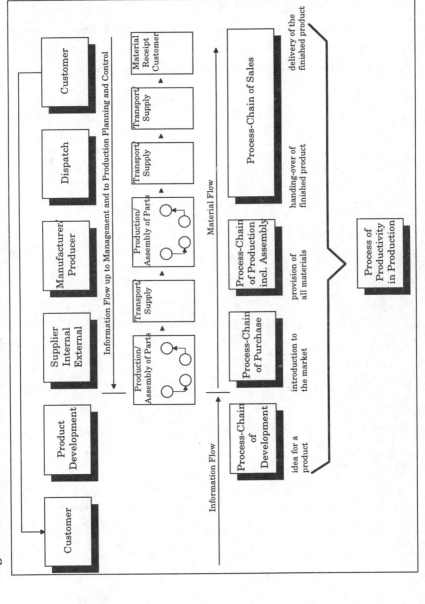

When designing a Lean Production system, the following essential characteristics must be taken into account: diversity of product range, the way of releasing orders, the volume of production orders, the type of organisation used for production and the production depth. This is illustrated in Figure 25.7.

Figure 25.7: Characteristics for the Design of Lean Production

product structure	one-piece products			multi-piece products		
grade of typifying a product	products being different for each customer		standardised products with variants specific for each customers	standardised products with variants specific for the supplier		standardised products without variants
way of releasing orders	single customer orders			customer orders based on skeleton agreements		stock orders
type of organisation of the product	shop floor production	production in groups	flow production without the pressure of time	flow production with the pressure of time		systems of single unit production
production depth	single-stage production			multi-stage production		

Based on these characteristics, the following concepts and tools have been developed and are typical of a lean organisation:

Just-in-time (JIT)
The right product/information in the right quantity and quality, at the right time and the right place.

Kaizen

Gradual and continuous improvement of situations and conditions by following up every fault, every deviation to the original cause and by eliminating it.

Total Quality Control (TQC)

This concept prevents a fault accumulating by being carried through the whole process.

Total Productive Maintenance (TPM)

A concept of efficient maintenance that is practised not only by the maintenance crew but by everybody.

THE JIT PHILOSOPHY WITHIN THE LEAN PRODUCTION PHILOSOPHY

The philosophy of JIT is an integral part of Lean Production as a method of shaping a business. JIT rigorously supports a production strategy that is oriented to market/customer's demands.

The principles of the JIT philosophy are:

- Delivery in accordance with due dates and demand

- Production in accordance with due dates and demand.

The realisation of this philosophy demands:

- Integrated information processing

- That materials are procured synchronously with the production process

- Multi-functional personnel

- A transparent flow of material, information and energy.

Targets

The targets of JIT are as follows:

- Avoidance of unnecessary stocks (aim for zero stock)

- A reduction of interim storage inventories and buffer stocks to the smallest possible extent

- A reduction of the in-process inventories (material, parts, products)

- A reduction of throughput-times (related to the total process and to single functions)

- Improvement in the standard of service in delivery.

Measures to Reach the Targets

From the Point of View of the Customer

- Precise purchase planning

- Precise control of due dates

- Co-operation based on partnership with the suppliers and arrangements concerning short-term and detailed planning

- Delivery of goods precisely on time to within a day of agreed delivery

- Delivery of goods from suppliers who are near to the factory precisely on time to within hours of agreed delivery

- Joint inventory control in stores of suppliers/haulage contractors.

From the Point of View of Suppliers

- Processes in control and process capability in production

- Precise production planning

- Flexibly employable production planning and control systems

- Production processes that are well-suited to each other (reduction of set-up times, storage times, types of transport)

- Design of departments, workshops, production centres and machine rooms well-suited to each other

- High-quality processes (TQC)

- Preventive maintenance of machines (TPM).

JIT Affects All Areas of Responsibility

- Factory planning and design, including decisions concerning locational factors

- Production methods (flexible processing equipment, automatic systems)

- Systems to handle the material flow

- Methods of quality assurance

- Selection of means of transport and of carriage systems

- Relationships with suppliers.

JIT Demands the Synchronisation of:

- The material and production planning of the enterprises or functional areas which are in contact with each other.

- The technical details of transport of goods from supplier production to recipient production (means of transport, packing drums, lot sizes, time and distance).

REGIONAL HEADQUARTERS FOR ORDER MANAGEMENT AS ONE TOOL TO LEAN PRODUCTION

Targets

Market conditions and competition make enterprises reduce production times on the one hand and product cost on the other hand while product quality has to be increased.

With regard to the management of incoming orders, the adherence to delivery dates often gives rise to problems. Apart from this, other problems arise because:

- Many functional areas are involved in the management of orders

- There are long throughput times in the functional areas that precede the production

- Products become more and more complex

- At the beginning of the order, necessary information is still missing

- More recently, bills of needed materials have become longer

- Due to a reduced production depth, the dependence on external suppliers is increased

- Needed capacities for new orders become known too late

- Much shorter delivery times are requested

- All in all, masses of data and quantities have to be managed.

These problems cannot be solved in meetings only, however often they take place. The total throughput time of order management is illustrated in Figure 25.8.

Figure 25.8: Total Throughput Time in Order Management

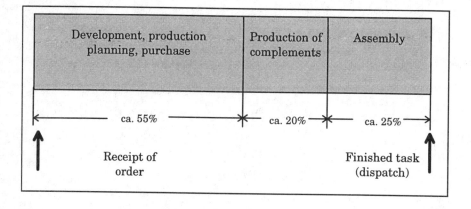

Measures to Reach the Targets

The introduction of the so-called regional headquarters may help to bring about an order management system which is better oriented to customer demands. The functional modules shown in Figure 25.9 are assigned to these regional headquarters for order management. A model of a decentralised system of order management is illustrated in Figure 25.10.

Figure 25.9: Functional Modules of the Regional Headquarters for Order Management

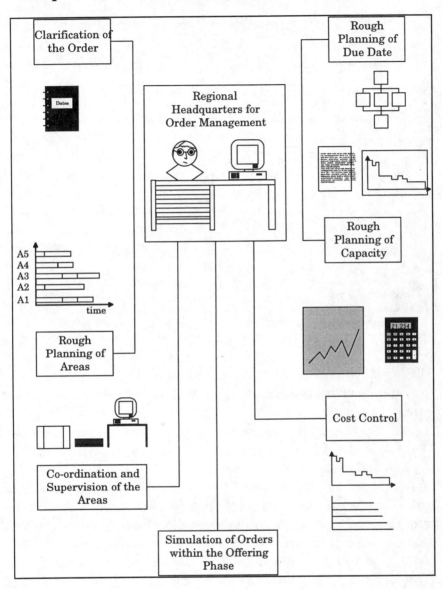

Figure 25.10: Model of a Decentralised Order Management System

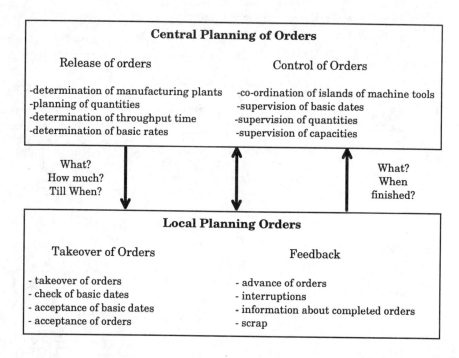

The organisational structure of the regional headquarters makes the interdependencies and combinations of process chains transparent.

The establishment of regional headquarters for order management is aimed at the reunion of functional areas whose operational functions have been separated.

Quantities, capabilities and due dates of the different functional areas like sales, marketing, research and development, purchase and production are roughly planned and co-ordinated. The essential functions for planning and control are centrally concentrated in the regional headquarters for order management. By this, different functional areas are much better co-ordinated or concentrated, but process chains related to one order which are connected immediately with each other are not created. Only a rigorously objective-oriented integration of tasks (e.g. into production segments) may really solve the prevailing problems.

SEGMENTATION OF PRODUCTION

The concept of "segmentation of production" can be distinguished by five definable characteristics.

Orientation towards Market

Segmentation of production is aimed at setting up product/market/production combinations. The individual products of a company, with their different strategies of competition, are no longer worked on in one workshop, but in fabrication areas that are built up in view of the specific strategy of competition.

Product Orientation

One result of the orientation of the organisational units towards specific strategies of competition (group-technology) is a small spectrum of products. At the same time a high work-content (fabrication depth) can be reached, resulting from complete treatment. Product orientation reduces expenses for co-ordination. In this regard synergetic and specialisational advantages should be reached and only a few capacity-interlinks should exist. Typical characteristics of product orientation are:

- Disentanglement of capacity units with the same kind of technology (tuning, milling, etc.) on the objective principle

- Spatial concentration of different working funds, criterion: product and runoff

- Complete treatment of a group of similar products and parts

- Co-ordination of installation capacity

- Universal use of employees.

Integration of Various Process Parts from the Total Logistic Process

Process parts of the total logistic process, such as marketing, purchasing, manufacturing, assembling and dispatch, should be integrated into the units of organisation; in this way the whole job management is treated as one unit. This avoids co-ordination problems and conflicts of interest because of organisational points of intersection (to improve identification of employees with their product, continuous chains of process).

Transfer of Indirect Functions

Tayloristic processes of work resulted in many cases in numerous points of intersection because of the separation between planning and production and between direct and indirect functions. These points of intersection result in long throughput times, high general costs and often in too many, and sometimes conflicting, targets. The transfer of indirect work to the workers on the shop floor should help to avoid these negative consequences. The level of autonomy of these decentralised units of organisation should be as high as possible in order to:

- Transfer maintenance functions partly into fabrication

- Integrate quality-production and responsibility for quality into the process

- Introduce workers within a section to self-management

- Transfer external jobs to the operating workers within the process.

Responsibility for Capacity and Costs

The organisational units are built up as cost centres and assessed by a defined system of targets as shown in Figure 25.11. The organisational principle of segmentation of production supports the success of a project much more than for example the performance production arrangement.

Figure 25.11: Target Systems and Characteristic Values

Target System	Examples of Characteristic Values
Capacity target	Rentability
Quality target	Defective work quota
Cost target	Productivity
Value-keeping target	Organisation of stock, range, turn over ratio
Flexibility target	Job sizes, product standards
Personnel target	Quota of personnel expenses in the produce, labour turn over, down times
Technical know-how	Capacity and use

INTRODUCTION OF TEAMWORK

A further fundamentally essential element of Lean Production is the purposeful involvement of the employees into problem solving processes. Competence and problem-solving capacities are expected from the personnel. Operational structures are created according to the principle of a useful combination of "self-organisation and organisational work" in order to reunite planning and operational functions and to replace the rigid planning of activities by a responsible planning of results.

Practical experiences have shown that extremely poor job contents have effects impeding productivity. Job enlargement and the personnel's self-organisation within a team produce promising solutions for the introduction of business shaping according to the Lean Production philosophy.

These teams assume several tasks for their own fields of activity: planning, control, organisation and maintenance. They also are responsible for quality and productivity as well as for the continuous improvement of production processes and the rigorous elimination of unnecessary tasks and jobs. In addition, they play an important part by permanently qualifying the staff in a training on the job.

The target of teamwork is to transfer a maximum of tasks and responsibilities to those employees who really work in value-adding processes. This new way of thinking is illustrated in Figure 25.12. In the previous way of thinking, targets were set at the top and given to the bottom. In the new way of thinking there is bilateral communication about targets and proceedings to reach targets.

That means the establishment of a simple but comprehensive information system which enables everybody to quickly react on problems and to understand the situation of the factory as a whole. The most important aspects of information management are illustrated in the table in Figure 25.13.

Figure 25.12: New Ways of Thinking: Extension of Communication

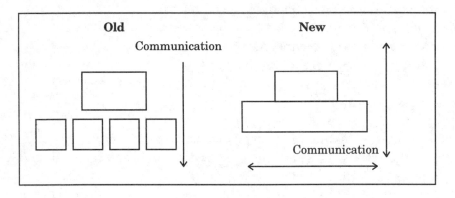

Figure 25.13: Information Management

Wishes of the Personnel
• To be informed about all changes in time • To understand the sense of one's own tasks • To be asked and to be taken seriously.
Practical Example
• First information about introduction of new products and types • Information about annual projects ("kick-off meeting") (generally: enterprise; particularly: department) • Monthly information about business management data (turnover, profit, cost situation, scrap, comparison with neighbouring departments) • Daily "morning meeting" concerning production requirements, output, matters of quality and personnel, feedback.

The transmission of relevant information and the readiness to discuss with the employees of all hierarchical levels guarantee a broad agreement with the business policy, intensify the communal spirit as well as the identification with business targets.

This does not only include the information which is necessary to do one's daily job, but also that which supports the personnel's understanding for the enterprise and its significance.

In particular, the poorly-qualified workers on the assembly line should get a general view of the relationship between their own special task and the total job, so that they can appreciate the reason for their work within the whole industrial process and, in consequence, remain interested in their work.

Teamwork results from an operating methods process in which the structure of the tasks is determined and by free organisation of the working hours and partial autonomy for many groups.

It is necessary to prepare the introduction of teamwork in a company carefully. During the initial stages, everyone must be involved. All staff and top management are responsible for the working atmosphere — they must completely support the group activities and identify themselves with their work and their results. Employees who do not participate actively in a team should be informed about the teamwork in order to feel involved in the results.

In addition, the establishment of organisational "promotion units" — clearly perceptible for everybody — is to be recommended, i.e. committees which are settled on a higher hierarchical level and are presided over by a member of the top management, if possible.

It is important that a special representative (i.e. a coordinator) for the team is nominated whose position in the business hierarchy is sufficiently prestigious, so that they are able to verify the relevance of the new "teamwork introduction" project.

Depending on its special markedness, teamwork in production is characterised by the following features:

1. Organisation:

   - Group discussions take place at least once per week

   - The discussion does not go on for more than two hours

   - Discussions take place during working hours

   - On the basis of given tasks and targets the team has free choice of subject

   - Handicapped and less efficient persons have to be involved into the organisation of teamwork

- Group speaker is elected in secret ballots for a defined period.

2. Extended job contents:

- Determination of machine utilisation within the scope of a fine-tune in production

- Determination of sequences to achieve the order within the scope of a fine control

- Autonomous planning of holidays and of shift organisation

- Continuous improvement of products and processes (Kaizen).

When teamwork is introduced, it must be examined how far job enrichment may reach without causing negative effects regarding productivity and costs, e.g. as a result of a drop in productivity because of decreasing routine work or as a result of increased costs for jobs that are put into a higher wage category. Figures 25.14 and 25.15 illustrate some of the main aspects of introducing teamwork into an enterprise.

Figure 25.14: Teamwork

Composition
5-8 persons of a team 1-2 hours/week (paid)
Examples of Tasks
• To find causes of faults • To improve productivity • To reduce the scrap • To propose how to save energy • To improve the internal company transport • To reduce personnel, material or general costs.

Figure 25.4 (continued)

Ten Prerequisites
• Voluntary participation (paid)
• To find the optimal quantity of group members
• Selection and training of the group leaders
• Training of the group members
• Free choice of the problems
• To inform the factory committee in good time
• Payment for proposals of the group members
• To realise the proposals to solve the problems by oneself
• No constraint for success
• Acceptance, financial aid and motivation by the management: Awards, certificates

Advantages of Teamwork	
For the employee	*For the enterprise*
• More knowledge about composition and function of the products	• Improved co-operation between the functional areas
• Intensified use of personal capacities and experiences	• Improved communication and management by co-operation
• Improved co-operation, also with superiors	• Improved work flow and reduction of causes of faults
• Less monotony	• Reduction of costs
• More responsibility	• Reduction of throughput times
• More freedom of decision-making	• More customer satisfaction
• More contentedness	• Increased competitiveness
	• Improved working atmosphere

Figure 25.15: Operational Concept for the Introduction of Teamwork

1. Presentation/elaboration of the business strategy including the targets of the introduction of teamwork.

   Target: well-suited model to design teamwork in the enterprise

   Method: discussion with executives within the scope of a workshop

2. Examination of the current structural and operational organisation regarding its suitability for the introduction of teamwork

   Target: description of the organisational environment where teamwork shall be introduced

   Method: discussion within the scope of projects

3. Qualifying of employees for teamwork

   - Information about strategy, targets, organisational environment

   - Training in groups

   Target: acceptance for teamwork among the personnel

   Method: training in groups including problem-solving tasks as well as the preparation to the process of teamwork in the company.

4. Introduction of teamwork into practice

   Target: rigorous and persistent realisation of the principles of teamwork

   Method: management coaching within the scope of the presentation of teamwork (practice-oriented and oriented to the solutions of problems)

5. Control of the results

   Target: permanent control of the success of realisation

   Method: management consultation regarding elaboration and application of indicator control systems.

26

HUMAN RESOURCES

INTRODUCTION

It has become trite to say the most significant development of the next decade will take place not in the physical but in the social sciences, that industry — the economic organ of society — has the fundamental know-how to utilise physical science and technology for the material benefit of mankind, and that we must now learn how to utilise the social sciences to make our human organisations truly effective.

Many people agree in principle with such statements; but so far they represent a pious hope — and little else.

Let us begin with an analogy. A half century ago basic conceptions of the nature of matter and energy had changed profoundly from what they had been since Newton's time. The physical scientists were persuaded that under proper conditions new and hitherto unimagined sources of energy could be made available to mankind.

We know what has happened since then. First came the bomb. Then, during the past quarter century have come many other attempts to exploit these scientific discoveries — some successful, some not, but nevertheless considerable progress has been achieved.

The point of this analogy, however, is that the application of theory in this field is a slow and costly matter. We expect it always to be so. Few are impatient with the scientists because they cannot tell industry how to build a simple, cheap, all-purpose source of atomic energy today. That it will take at least another quarter century and the investment of huge amounts of money to achieve results which are economically competitive with present sources of power is understood and accepted.

It is transparently pretentious to suggest any direct similarity between the developments in the physical sciences leading to the harnessing of atomic energy and potential developments in the social sciences. Nevertheless, the analogy is not as absurd as it might appear to be at first glance.

To a lesser degree, and in a much more tentative fashion, we are in a position in the social sciences today like that of the physical sciences with respect to atomic energy in the 1930s. We know that past conceptions of the nature of man are inadequate and in many ways incorrect.

> We are becoming quite certain that, under proper conditions, unimagined resources of creative human energy could become available within the organisational setting.

CHANGING SOCIETY

Some of the greatest changes in social structure in the history of the human race have taken place this century. These changes have been non-violent, which is perhaps why few people pay them any attention. Yet had any of the great economists or sociologists of the last century been appraised of them, they would have laughed in disbelief. Consider the cases of the domestic servant and the farmer and compare it to what is happening to the industrial worker:

- **The domestic servant.** The first scientific census, the British Census of 1910, famously defined lower middle class as the family that could not afford more than three servants. How many people have seen even one servant lately? Servants antedate history by millennia, and in 1913 they were the largest single employee group in any developed country — 30 per cent of all wage earners were domestic servants. They are almost all gone.

- **The farmer.** So, almost, are farmers. There is now no developed country in the world in which farmers form more than 8 per cent of the population. The political power of the farmer has evaporated. In the 1988 US presidential election the farmer became a non-person. Both candidates went to Iowa for two hours, but that was all. They could not care less how the 3 per cent of the US population who are still farmers cast their votes. Politicians have good antennae.

- **The worker.** The blue-collar industrial worker is going the same way. No century has seen anything like the rise and fall of the industrial worker. A very short time ago it seemed that this group was controlling society, politics and markets. By the end of the century, however, in every developed country blue-collar workers will be no more important or numerous than farmers. Their numbers have declined by a full third in the past 20 years.

  It is not only the numbers that have fallen, however. There are now few manufacturing companies where blue-collar labour costs rise above 15 per cent. A country such as Spain has 5-7 years during which its reservoir of highly trained, cheap labour will remain an asset. By the end of the century if its manufacturing has not evolved to the point where labour costs are below 15 per cent, that labour force will have become a liability. No western country can compete with Shanghai, where $1.00 a day is an excellent wage, and only the top 10 per cent of the work force makes even $1.00.

The answer for Western manufacturing is not necessarily automation. Information is not the same as automation, or even information technology, and no firm should start by buying a machine. Rather, the first step is to *rationalise the process* in order to identify what machines are necessary.

A company which begins by buying robots or automating its existing process will almost certainly waste huge amounts of money and become less productive in the process. General Motors proves the point: GM spent the not inconsiderable sum of $30 billion on robots, with the result that labour costs went up, not down. GM's blue-collar labour costs are now 28 per cent (in the USA). At the new Honda plant, built in a high-wage area, the figure will come down to 11.5 per cent. Cars, remember, are a relatively ancient industry. In the new industries, costs should be even lower.

Most people believe that the favourite child of capitalism was the owner of capital: the capitalist. A better candidate is blue-collar industrial workers. In 1850 they were still labourers hired by the hour, paid a few pennies, without social standing or political power. They were neglected and despised. By 1950, however, they belonged to the dominant social class. They enjoyed health insurance, pensions, job security and political power that would have seemed unthinkable only two generations before. They still have the benefits, of course. But the brief moment of dominance is suddenly over. And all this without real social convulsions.

THE LEARNING SOCIETY

In the place of the blue-collar world is a society in which access to good jobs no longer depends on the union card, but on the school certificate. Between, say, 1950 and 1980 it was economically irrational for young American males to stay at school. Sixteen-year old school leavers employed at a unionised steel plant could be taking home much more money than their university-educated contemporaries. Those days are over. From now on the key is knowledge.

> The world is becoming not labour-intensive, not materials-intensive, not energy-intensive, but *knowledge*-intensive.

Japan today produces two and a half times the quantity of manufactured goods as 25 years ago with the same amount of energy and less raw material. In large part this is due to the shift to knowledge-intensive work. The representative product of the 1920s, the automobile, at the time had a raw material and energy content of 60 per cent. The representative product of the 1980s is the semiconductor chip, which has a raw material and energy content of less than 2 per cent.

The 1990s equivalent will be biotechnology, also with a content of about 2 per cent in materials and energy, but with a much higher knowledge content. Assembling microchips is still fairly labour-intensive (10 per cent). Biotechnology will have practically no labour content at all. Moreover, fermentation plants generate energy rather than consume it. The world is becoming knowledge-intensive not just in the labour force, but in process.

Knowledge is Always Specialised

The oboist in the London Philharmonic Orchestra has no ambition to become first violinist, or at least no realistic one. In the last 100 years only one instrumentalist, Toscanini, has become a conductor of the first rank. Specialists remain specialists, becoming ever more skilful at interpreting the score. Yet specialism carried dangers, too. Truly knowledgeable people tend by themselves to over-specialise, because there is always so much more to know. As part of the orchestra, that oboist alone does not make music. He or she makes noise. Only the orchestra playing a joint score makes music. For both soloist and conductor, getting music from an orchestra means not only knowing the score, but learning how to manage knowledge. And knowledge carries with it powerful responsibility, too. In the past, the holders of knowledge have often used (abused) it to curb thinking and dissent, and to inculcate blind obedience to authority. Knowledge and knowledge people have to assume their responsibilities.

Managing Work and the Employee

In hiring a worker one always hires the whole person. It is evident in that one cannot "hire a hand", its owner always comes with it.

That one can hire only a whole person rather than any part thereof explains why the improvement of human effectiveness in work is the greatest opportunity for the improvement of performance and results. The human resource — the whole person — is, of all resources entrusted to man, the most productive, the most versatile, the most resourceful.

Many stories demonstrate that when we talk about the management of worker and work, we are talking about a complex subject:

- First, we are dealing with the worker as the human resource. We have to ask what the specific properties of this resource are. And we get entirely different answers accruing to whether we put stress on the word "resource" or on the word "human".

- Second, we must ask what demands the enterprise makes on the worker in its capacity as the organ of society responsible for getting the work done, and what demands the workers makes on the enterprise in their capacity as human beings, as individuals and as citizens?

- Finally, there is an economic dimension grounded in the fact that the enterprise is both the wealth-producing organ of society and the source of the worker's livelihood. This means that in managing workers and work we must reconcile two different economic systems. There is a conflict between wage as cost and wage as income which must be harmonised. And there is the problem of the worker's relation to the enterprise's fundamental requirement of profitability.

EMPLOYEE RESOURCES

If we look at employees as a resource, comparable to all other resources but for the fact that they are human, we have to find out how best to utilise them in the same way in which we look at copper or at water-power as specific resources. This is an engineering approach. It considers what the human being is best and least capable of. Its result will be the organisation of work so as to fit best the qualities and the limitations of this specific resource, the human being at work.

But human beings have one set of qualities possessed by no other resource: they have the ability to co-ordinate, to integrate, to judge and to imagine. In fact, this is their only specific superiority. In every other respect — whether it be physical strength, manual skill or sensory perception — machines can do a much better job.

But we must also consider the person at work as a human being. We must, in other words, also put the emphasis on "human". This approach focuses on the person as a moral and a social creature, and asks how work should be organised to fit their qualities as a person. As a resource, man can be "utilised". People, however, can only utilise themselves. This is the great and ultimate distinction.

Motivation

The qualities of the person are specific and unique. Human beings, unlike any other resource, have absolute control over whether they work at all. Dictatorships tend to forget this; but shooting people does not get the work done.

The human resource must therefore always be motivated to work.

In other words, it is workers' motivation that controls workers' output. This is particularly important in industry today. For fear, the traditional motivation of the industrial worker, has largely disappeared in the modern West. To eliminate it has been the main result of the increased wealth produced by industrialisation. In a society rich enough to provide subsistence even to the unemployed, fear has lost its motivating power. And to deprive management of the weapon of fear has also been the main aim of unionism. Indeed, the worker's rebellion against this weapon and its use is among the main driving forces behind the union movement.

But, contrary to what some human-relations experts assert, to remove fear does not by itself motivate. All it creates is a vacuum. We cannot sit back and expect worker motivation to arise spontaneously, now that fear is gone. We must create a positive motivation to take its place. This is one of the central, one of the most difficult, one of the most urgent tasks facing management.

People — Not Machines — Are in Control

Human beings also have control over how well they work and how much they work, over the equality and quantity of production. They participate in the process actively — unlike all other resources which participate only passively by giving a preconditioned response to predetermined impulse.

In the most completely machine-paced operation, the speed and quality of which appear to be completely determined by the machine, the worker still retains decisive control. It may be almost impossible to find out how they manage to beat the machine; but, as the old Latin proverb has it, human nature asserts itself even if thrown out with a pitchfork — or with a conveyor belt. And in any operation which is not the tending of semi-automatic machinery by semi-skilled operators — that is, in all work of a

clerical, skilled, technical, professional or managerial nature —
this control is practically absolute.

Groups

The human being works in groups and forms groups to work, and
a group, no matter how formed or why, soon focuses on a task.
Group relationships influence the task; the task in turn influences personal relationships within the group. At the same time
the human being remains an individual.

> Group and individual must therefore be brought into har-
> mony in the organisation of work.

This means specifically that work must always be organised in
such a manner that whatever strength, initiative, responsibility
and competence there is an individual, becomes a source of
strength and performance for the entire group. This is the first
principle of organisation; indeed, it is practically a definition of
the purpose of organisation. That this is not the case on the traditional automobile assembly line is in itself sufficient evidence
that we do not as yet know how to manage worker and work.

Individual Growth

Finally, people are distinguished from all other resources in that
their "development" is not something that is done to them; it is
not another or better way of using existing properties. It is
growth; and growth is always from within. The work therefore
must encourage the growth of the individual and must direct it —
otherwise it fails to take full advantage of the specific properties
of the human resource.

> This means that the job must always *challenge* the worker.

Nothing is more contrary to the nature of the human resource
than the common attempt to find the "average work load" for the
"average worker". This whole idea is based on a disproven psychology which equated learning speed with learning ability. It is
also based on the belief that the individual worker is the more
productive the less control they have, the less they participate —
and that is a complete misunderstanding of the human resource.

Above all, the concept of the average work to be performed is inevitably one which considers average what any but a physical or mentally handicapped person could do. The person who is just barely normal but who has neither aptitude not liking for the job becomes the measure of all things, their performance the norm. And human work becomes something that requires neither skill, effort, nor thought, presents no challenge, allows for no differentiation between the highly skilled and highly motivated and the near-moron.

This whole concept, as many stories show, is poor engineering. It results in constantly lowering performance norms rather than in raising the performance levels of the entire work group. It destroys the productivity of the human resource. The nature of man demands that the performance of the best, not of the poorest, worker should become the goal for all.

THE DEMANDS OF THE ENTERPRISE ON THE EMPLOYEE

If we turn to the demands of enterprise and employee on each other, the first question is: What must the enterprise demand in order to get the work done?

A Fair Day's Labour for a Fair Day's Pay?

The standard answer to this is the catch phrase "a fair day's labour for a fair day's pay". Unfortunately, no one has ever been able to figure out what is fair in terms of either labour or pay. The real trouble with the phrase is, however, that it demands too little, and demands the wrong thing.

What the enterprise must demand of workers is that they willingly direct their efforts towards the goals of the enterprise. If one could "hire a hand", one could indeed demand delivery of fair value for a fair price. If one could buy labour, one could buy it by whatever unit applies to it; but labour is not an "article of commerce", as the law knows. Precisely because labour is provided by human beings, a fair day's labour is unobtainable. For it implies passive acquiescence — the one thing this peculiar being is not capable of giving.

The enterprise, if it wants to get anything at all, must demand something much bigger than a fair day's labour. It must demand, over and above fairness, willing dedication. It cannot aim at acquiescence. It must aim at building aggressive *esprit de corps*.

This will be particularly important under mass production of uniform parts and their assembly into diversified products, under process production, under automation. For these systems of production require that almost every worker take responsibility for actions, for the simple reason that almost every worker controls and determines the output of the whole through the way in which they perform their jobs, run their operations, maintain their equipment. A fair day's labour for a fair day's pay, consciously or unconsciously, assumes a system of production under which workers do nothing but what they are being told to do.

The enterprise must expect of the worker not the passive acceptance of a physical chore, but the active assumption of responsibility for the enterprise's results. And precisely because this is so much bigger a demand, we are likely to be able to realise it — where we have never obtained the fair day's labour. For it is a peculiarity of human beings that they yield best to high demands, that, indeed, their capacity to produce is largely determined by the level of the demands made on them.

Acceptance of Change

There is a second demand the enterprise must make on workers; that they be willing to accept change. *Innovation* is a necessary function of business enterprise; it is one of its major social responsibilities. It requires, however, that people change — their work, their habits, their group relations.

The human being has a capacity to change beyond all other animals, but it is not unlimited. In the first place, while people can learn amazingly fast, their unlearning capacity is much slower (fortunately for the race). We know today that learning capacity does not disappear with age. But the more one has learned the more difficult is unlearning. Experience rather than age, in other words, is the bar to easy unlearning and with it to easy or fast learning of new things. The only way to get around this is by making ability to unlearn itself part of what a man learns. This requires that one learn by acquiring knowledge rather than simply experience. It requires, "teaching" rather than "training" programmes — many of the typical programmes of today make a person rigid, rather than flexible, teach tricks of the trade rather than understanding. And the need to train workers in the ability to unlearn and to learn will become greater as the skill and knowledge level of the worker increases.

Change is not only an intellectual process but a psychological one as well. It is not true, as a good many industrial psychologists assert, that human nature resists change. On the contrary, no being in heaven or earth is greedier for new things. But there are conditions for man's psychological readiness to change. The change must appear rational — people always present to themselves as rational even their most irrational, most erratic changes.

It must appear to be an improvement. And it must not be so rapid nor so great as to obliterate the psychological landmarks which make people feel at home; their understanding of their work, their relations to their fellow-workers, their concepts of skill, prestige and social standing in certain jobs and so forth. Change will meet resistance unless it clearly and visibly strengthens a person's psychological security; and people being mortal, frail and limited, their security is always precarious. The enterprise's demand for the worker's ability to change therefore requires positive action to make it possible for them to change.

THE EMPLOYEES' DEMANDS ON THE ENTERPRISE

The demands of the employee on the enterprise are also misdefined in the phrase of the "fair day's pay". Workers in making their demands on the enterprise are whole people, not an economic sub-section thereof. They demand over and above economic returns, returns as individuals, as people, as citizens. They demand the fulfilment of status and function in their jobs and through their work. They demand the realisation of the promises to the individual on which our society rests; among them the promise of justice through equal opportunities for advancement. They demand that their work be meaningful and that it be serious.

High standards of performance, a high degree of competence in the way the work is organised and managed, and visible signs of management's concern for good work are among the most important things demanded of an enterprise and of its management by the worker.

As a human being and citizen, especially in a free society, the employee also imposes limitations on the business enterprise. The enterprise hires the whole person, but it has no right to take delivery of the whole person. Serving only partial needs of society, it must never control more than a part of society's members, its citizens. Business enterprise must not become the "welfare corporation" and attempt to embrace all phases of the individual's life. It must, both in its demands and in the satisfactions it offers, confine itself to its proper sphere as one, though a basic, organ of society. A claim for absolute allegiance of workers is as impermissible as a premise of absolute responsibility for them.

THE ECONOMIC DIMENSION

Finally there is a big group of problems that have their origin in the economic sphere.

External and Internal Environments

The enterprise lives in two economic systems, an external and an internal one. The total amount available for the internal economy (and that means, above all, for wages to the employee) is determined by what the business enterprise receives for its product in the external economy. It is externally and market-determined.

Internally, however, the enterprise is not a market economy. It is a "redistributive" one in which the product of the whole is distributed among the members of the enterprise according to a predetermined formula. Both market and redistributed economy are basic patterns, but the business enterprise is the only human institution known to us in which the two have ever become indissolubly linked. While the effort of management must be directed towards receiving more, that is, towards making the total product greater, the attention of the worker within the enterprise is directed towards receiving a larger share of whatever the total product may be. Some are interested in an ever-increasing share of an ever-shrinking pie.

While extreme, their attitude is typical — indeed, it is almost inevitable. Outside the enterprise the considerations are economic. Inside the enterprise they are based on power balance and power relationships.

To the enterprise, wage — that is, the financial reward of labour — must necessarily be a cost. To the recipient, however — to the employee — wage is income, the source of their livelihood and that of their families. Wage to the enterprise must always be wage per unit of production. Wage to the recipient must always be the economic basis for their and their family's existence which is before and beyond the units or production turned out. There is thus a basic divergence. The enterprise needs flexibility of the wage burden. The individual values, above all, a steady, stable and predictable income based upon a person's willingness to work rather than upon economic conditions.

Profit

Finally, there is the two-fold meaning of profit. To the enterprise profit is a necessity of survival. To the worker profit is somebody else's income. That profitability should determine their employment, their livelihood, their income, is to them subjection to an alien domination. It is arbitrary, if not "exploitation".

It is a common belief that opposition to profit is a phenomenon of modern industrial society. Nothing could be farther from the truth. It goes back hundreds of years to the dawn of modern society. The roots of the European worker's bitterness against "capitalist exploiter" and "profiteer" lie, for instance, in the bitter hostility to profit of the Flemish or Florentine weaver of the fifteenth century. And modern industry, far from aggravating this hostility, has greatly eased it. It is no accident that the more industrialised an area the less radical its workers, the less bitterly hostile to management, enterprise and profits.

But it is still true that the worker's hostility to profits is a serious threat in an industrial society. Such a society depends for its existence on the adequate profitability of its enterprises. In such a society, moreover, the bulk of the citizens and voters are employees. This makes hostility to profit such a serious threat that it would indeed be a powerful argument for nationalisation of industry if it resulted in the disappearance of the hostility to profit. And some believe that the real death blow to the socialist dream came when the nationalisation of industries in Britain and France after World War II proved that workers resist and resent the profits of nationalised enterprises fully as much as those of "capitalist" ones (perhaps more).

The enterprise must operate at adequate profit — this is its first social responsibility as well as its first duty towards itself and its workers. Management must therefore find some way to persuade workers to accept profit as necessary, if not as beneficial and in their own interest.

THE ORGANISATION'S ROLE

Finally for the first time in human history it really matters whether or not people learn. The knowledge society requires that all its members be literate, not just in reading, writing and arithmetic, but also in (for example) basic computer skills and political, social and historical systems.

Every employing institution will have to become a teacher. Large numbers of Japanese employers and some European already recognise this. But what kind of learning? In the orchestra the score tells the musicians what to do; all orchestra playing is team playing. In the information-based business, what is the equivalent of this reciprocal learning and teaching process?

One way of educating people to a view of the whole, of course, is through work in cross-functional task forces. But to what extent do we rotate specialists out of their specialities and into new ones? And who will the managers, particularly top managers, of the information-based organisation be? Brilliant oboists, or people who have been in enough positions to be able to understand the team, or even young conductors from smaller orchestras? We do not yet know. Above all, how do we make this terribly expensive knowledge, this new capital, productive?

The world's largest bank reports that it has deployed $1.15 billion in information and communications systems. Banks are now more capital intensive than ICI. So are hospitals. Only 50 years ago a hospital consisted of a bed and a sister. Today a fair sized hospital of 400 beds has several hundred attending physicians and a staff of up to 1,500 paramedics divided among some 60 specialists, with specialised equipment and labs to match. None, or very few, of these specialisations even existed 50 years ago. But we do not yet know how to get productivity out of them; we do not yet know in this context what productivity means. In knowledge-intensive areas we are pretty much where we were in manufacturing in the early nineteenth century.

When Robert Owen built his cotton mills at New Lanark, he tried to measure their productivity. He never managed it. It took 50 more years until productivity as we understand it could be satisfactorily defined. We are currently at about the Robert Owen stage in relation to the new organisations. We are beginning to ask about productivity, output and performance in relation to knowledge. We cannot measure it. We cannot yet even judge it, although we do have an idea of some of the things that are needed.

How, for instance, do famous conductors build a first-rate orchestra? They say that the first job is to get the clarinettist to keep on improving as a clarinettist. They must have pride in the instrument. The players must be craftsmen first. The second task is to create in the individuals a pride in their common enterprise, the orchestra: "I play for the Vienna, or Chicago, or the London Philharmonic, and it is one of the best orchestras in the world". Third, and this is what distinguishes a competent conductor from a great one, is to get the orchestra to hear and play that Haydn symphony in exactly the way the conductor hears it. In other words, there must be a clear vision at the top. This orchestrating focus is the model for the leader of any knowledge-based organisation within leading industries.

THE CHANGING NATURE OF THE PERSONNEL FUNCTION

Personnel management, one of the traditional areas of management consulting, has undergone many changes over the last 20 to 30 years. The main changes that currently affect the nature and role of the personnel function occur in the following areas:

- First, the subjects of personnel management — people working in organisations — have changed in very many respects. People have become better educated and prepared for their jobs, more aware of their rights, better informed and more interested in many issues that used to be the exclusive domain of politicians or government officials. Their value systems have changed; their employment and life aspirations have increased.

- Secondly, an increasing number of personnel issues, including conditions of employment, work and remuneration, are regulated by legislation or have become the subject of collective agreements between workers' and employers' organisations. When dealing with these questions the consultant must be fully aware of the existing legal and labour relations frameworks, of the role of the trade unions and of the need to inform or consult them (in conformity with local practice).

- Thirdly, many new approaches to the "human element" in organisations have emerged. The title "Personnel Manager" has being replaced with "Human Resource Manager" in many organisations. People began to be viewed as the most valuable resource of an organisation, and a number of conclusions were drawn from this basic premise as to ways of treating people and motivating them for higher performance, the role of leadership, the investment in training and development, or the choice of staff development systems. This has been linked with advances in the behavioural sciences, in particular in psychology and sociology, applied to the functioning of organisations and to the relations between individuals and groups within organisations. A wide range of "organisational development" theories and concepts emerged and began to be applied to the analysis of human problems in organisations, and to methods likely to increase the effectiveness of individuals and groups in achieving organisational goals.

- Fourthly, it has been increasingly recognised that the management of people is more culture-bound and value-laden than any other area of management. Practices regarded as standard in one country or organisation may be unthinkable in another environment (e.g. flexible working hours, open-plan offices, dining-rooms common to all staff irrespective of position and grade, direct access to top managers, or the use of confidential personnel files). Both personnel practitioners and management consultants have become more cautious and more selective in transferring personnel practices from one environment to another when dealing with people of different ethnic, social, cultural, religious and educational backgrounds. Sensitivity to these differences has increased with the growth of international business, the advent of modern enterprises and organisations in developing countries, the expanding employment of foreign workers and managers, and the improvements in management education.

LABOUR/MANAGEMENT RELATIONS

We have already referred to the need for consultants to take into account industrial relations practices and implications generally, and particularly when dealing with responsibilities within the personnel management function. This section looks briefly at various points relevant to labour/management relations.

Any consultant called upon should be well informed about the legal, political, social and economic circumstances of labour/management relations in a given country, sector and particular organisation. The consultant may be called in because problems already exist in labour/management relations, because there are internal or external forces that are likely to lead to problems, or because advice is needed in the initial formulation or reformulation of labour/management relations policies.

In each case a key issue will be the presence or absence of workers' representatives, in particular of a trade union in or for the enterprise, and, where trade union or another form of workers representation does exist, the nature and role of that representation.

The essential questions in labour/management relations which the consultant may be called upon to deal with could include one or more of the following:

1. Advice on dealing with workers' representatives on a day-to-day basis. These may be trade union representatives, or representatives directly elected by all the workers with none, or with only indirect, links with a trade union.

2. The mechanics of handling workers' grievances, including advice on the setting up of grievance procedures, together with advice regarding other conflict resolution procedures.

3. Collective bargaining and, in particular, management organisation for collective bargaining. The significance of this question will depend to some extend on the level at which bargaining takes place (for the industry as a whole; for the industry in a particular region or locality; for a group of enterprises; or at the enterprise level). But in most cases where there is a trade union presence in the workplace, a certain degree of collective bargaining, possibly of an informal character, will take place in the enterprise even if more formal or official bargaining takes place at a higher level. Consultants are sometimes called upon to participate in the management bargaining team or even to act as management spokesmen in negotiation.

4. Machinery and procedures for management/worker consultation and co-operation on issues of common interest such as productivity, welfare facilities, etc. (as opposed to issues of an antagonistic nature such as grievances or bargaining demands).

5. Dismissal and redundancy principles and procedures (whether within or outside the context of collective bargaining).

6. The position to be taken by employers' associations in tripartite (government, employers, trade unions) or bipartite (either with government or with trade unions) consultation at the national level.

This is not necessarily an exhaustive list of possible areas with which the consultant may have to deal, but it covers the major areas in which advice will be sought.

Some factors that a consultant should be aware of when providing advice on labour/management relations include the following:

- **Legal framework.** The relevant legal framework, which is highly individual to particular countries, might reflect rules on trade union recognition, workplace workers' representation, collective bargaining procedures, dispute settlement (including work stoppages), forms of workers' participation in decisions within the enterprise, formation and content of individual contracts of employment, and so on. In charting courses of action to be recommended to the client, consultants must of necessity take account of existing legal rules. It is obvious that individual company rules on conditions of employment must also be taken into consideration. And where particularly complex legal problems have to be resolved with the aid of the consultant, they may have to suggest recourse to the services of a qualified lawyer specialising in labour law (if they themselves do not have such training).

- **Existing collective bargaining agreements.** The consultant must also be fully aware of the relevant provisions of any existing collective agreement that applies to the enterprise concerned (whether such agreement be for the industry, the region, or the enterprise itself). The consultant must be aware not only of the provisions of the agreements but also of possible interpretations of those provisions which may have been subject to scrutiny by labour courts, arbitrators, or other decision-making bodies.

- **Existing custom and practice.** In virtually all established enterprises, organisations or industries there will be labour/management relations customs, usages and practices which often demand the same respect that is accorded to legal regulations. At times these customs, usages and practices are common to a specific region or locality. It is essential that the consultant should be fully aware of them. This does not mean that the consultant may not be in a position to influence changes in established industrial relations practices. However, the consultant must recognise that in doing so extreme care should be taken and consideration given to possible unforeseen consequences of breaking with traditional practices.

- **Worker representatives.** It is also very important that consultants should make themselves familiar with the position, outlook and concerns of the workers' representatives who will be involved in any course of action that they might recommend, since possible reactions from the workers' side must be a determinant in such recommendations. However, before considering personal contacts with such representatives, consultants should, in agreement with the client, consider what contacts would be appropriate before and during the framing of their recommendations. Dealings with workers' representatives can be very delicate, and consultants should discuss with management just which areas they may touch on in such contacts as well as the limits of their authority to commit to management should the contacts be of a nature where commitments may be made or inferred.

UNION/MANAGEMENT RELATIONS AS A PROCESS OF PSYCHOLOGICAL GROWTH

It has frequently been noted that union/management relations follow a fairly typical course of change over time. When a union is first organised in a plant, the relationship is likely to involve a high degree of suspicion and conflict. Usually this "fighting stage" gradually disappears and is followed by a relatively neutral stage characterised by a decrease of suspicion, a growth in mutual understanding, and in general a mildly friendly atmosphere. This is the stage of successful collective bargaining. Where circumstances have been favourable, a third stage in union/management relations emerges. This is a stage in which suspicion and conflict have disappeared, and in which the atmosphere is one not only of acceptance but of constructive joint efforts to solve common problems. The term union/management co-operation has been applied to this third stage of the process.

This transition from stage to stage becomes more meaningful if is viewed not merely as a process of change, but as a process of psychological growth and development. The transition becomes even more meaningful if the emphasis is laid on the emotional aspects of the developmental process rather than on the intellectual aspects alone.

There are four important characteristics of psychological growth that apply equally to the individual and to union/management relations:

1. In the first place, psychological growth is a slow and arduous process. It involves a myriad of small changes in thinking and behaviour which normally occur imperceptibly day by day. Although the rate of growth may vary somewhat, depending upon circumstances, sudden jumps occur rarely and then only as a consequence of rather severe crises. Co-operative plans that emerge suddenly as a result of the very real threat of the complete bankruptcy of the company, for example. This is not normal growth, but an abnormal "spurt" brought about by a crisis.

2. In the second place, psychological growth is not an all-or-nothing process. Even the emotionally mature adult retains some childish habits. On the other hand, the child can in some ways be startlingly mature. The same thing is true of union/management relations. The growth process is uneven; maturity is achieved in one small way today and in another tomorrow. Many "childish" habits and ways of thinking are retained long after their usefulness has apparently disappeared. The differences between one stage of union/management relations and another can be viewed only in the overall sense. Detailed analysis reveals elements of every stage at any given time. Each individual participant possesses some habits and attitudes that are childish and others that are mature, and the interacting individuals differ among themselves in this over-all maturity.

3. The third characteristic of growth is that it may be arrested at any stage. Just as some individuals of 40 are still at an adolescent level of emotional development, so do some union/management relationships remain in the fighting stage for long periods of time. This characteristic of being arrested in the course of development is so common that real emotional

maturity is rare among individuals. Likewise, genuine co-operation between union and management is rare. When one recognises how complex are the necessary emotional adjustments between individuals and groups in union/management relations, it is not surprising that only a small proportion of union/management combinations have succeeded in reaching a fair degree of maturity.

4. Finally, psychological growth, unlike physical growth, is a two-way process. Retrogression is not at all unusual. Occasionally, in a critical situation, mature habits and ways of thinking that have been acquired painfully and slowly will suddenly disappear, to be supplanted by childish ones that have been presumed to be long since dead.

In the end, the psychological growth of union/management relations is no more than the growth of the participating individuals. The situation in any given organisation is exceedingly complex because of the varying extent to which one individual or another dominates the picture, and because a number of different individuals are participating in the relationship.

The process of psychological growth in labour/management relations takes place through the interaction of the participants. The interaction occurs in face-to-face meetings between representatives of the two groups, and in the day-to-day contacts between individuals on the job. A change in management's ways of acting or thinking influences the union, and results in a change (not necessarily the same one) on the part of the union. This alteration in the union's thought or action in turn reacts upon management, and through this circular interaction the relationship develops.

The key factors which can influence this psychological growth are:

- The difference between collective bargaining and co-operation

- Basic differences in union and management organisation

- The influence of the personalities of management

- The influence of the personalities of union leaders

- The quality of foremanship

- A recognition of the ability of the average worker

- A willingness to share equitably the gains from co-operation

- Union security

- Mutual understanding.

CONDITIONS OF EFFECTIVE LEADERSHIP IN THE INDUSTRIAL ORGANISATION

The relationships among people at work is looked at from the point of view of dynamic psychology which, because of its origin in the clinic, directs attention to the whole individual living and interacting within a world of other individuals. Life, from the point of view of dynamic psychology, is a continuous striving to satisfy ever-changing needs in the face of obstacles. The work life is but a segment — although a large one — of the whole.

The Setting

Within this framework we shall examine some of the important forces and events in the work situation that aid or hinder an individual as they strive to satisfy their needs. First of all, we must recognise a fundamental fact: the direct impact of almost all these forces upon the individual is through the behaviour of other people. This is obvious when we speak of an order from the boss, or pressures exerted by fellow workers to get the individual to join a union. It is perhaps less obvious when we speak of the impact of the business cycle, or the consequences of a fundamental technological change. Nevertheless, the direct influence of these forces on the individual — whether they are a worker or a plant manager — occurs through the medium of the actions of other people. We must include not only the easily observed actions of others, but the subtle, fleeting manifestations of attitude and emotion to which the individual reacts almost unconsciously.

For purposes of discussion we may arbitrarily divide the actions of other people that influence the individual in the work situation into three classes: actions of superiors, of subordinates, and of associates. We shall limit our attention mainly to the actions of superiors as they affect the subordinate in their striving to satisfy their needs. This relationship is logically prior to the others, and it is in many ways the most important human relationship in industry.

The Dependence of the Subordinate

The outstanding characteristic of the relationship between subordinates and their superiors is their dependence upon them for the satisfaction of their needs. Industry in our civilisation is organised along authoritative lines. In a fundamental and pervasive sense, subordinates are dependent upon their superiors for their job, for the continuity of their employment, for promotion with its accompanying satisfactions in the form of increased pay, responsibility and prestige, and for a host of other personal and social satisfactions to be obtained in the work situation.

Among workers, surveys of attitudes invariably place "fair treatment by superiors" toward the top of the list of factors influencing job satisfaction. And the extent to which unions have attempted to place restrictions upon management's authority reflects not only a desire for power but a conscious attempt to reduce the dependence of workers upon their bosses.

There are certain inevitable consequences of the dependence of subordinates upon their superiors. The success or failure of the relationship depends on the way in which these consequences are handled. An understanding of them provides a more useful basis than the usual "rules of thumb" for considering problems relating to industrial relations. These consequences of the dependence of the subordinate will be discussed under two main headings:

- The necessity for security in the work situation, and

- The necessity for self realisation.

The Necessity for Security

Subordinates will struggle to protect themselves against real or imagined threats to the satisfaction of their needs in the work situation. Analysis of this protective behaviour suggests that actions of superiors are frequency perceived as the source of threats. Before subordinates can believe that it is possible to satisfy their wants in the work situation, they must acquire a convincing sense of security in their dependent relationship to their superiors.

Management has recognised the financial aspects of this need for security, and has attempted to provide for it by means of employee retirement plans, health and accident insurance, the encouragement of employee credit unions, and even guaranteed annual wages. However, this recognition does not get at the heart of the problem: *the personal dependence of the subordinate upon the judgements and decisions of his superior.*

Labour unions have attacked the problem more directly in their attempts to obtain rules governing promotions and layoffs, grievance procedures, arbitration provisions, and protection against arbitrary changes in work loads and rates. One important purpose of such "protective" features in union contracts is to restrict superiors in the making of decisions that, from the worker's point of view, are arbitrary and threatening. They help to provide subordinates with a measure of security despite their dependence on their superiors.

The Conditions of Security: An Atmosphere of Approval
There are three major aspects of the subordinate-superior relationship — at any level of the organisation — that affect the security of the subordinate. The most important of these is what we may term the "atmosphere" created by the superior. This atmosphere is revealed not by what the superior does, but by the manner in which they do it and by their underlying attitude toward their subordinates. It is relatively independent of the strictness of the superior's discipline or the standards of performance that they demand.

Security for subordinates is possible only when they know they have the genuine approval of their superior. If the atmosphere is equivocal, or one of disapproval, they can have no assurance that their needs will be satisfied, regardless of what they do. In the absence of a genuine attitude of approval, subordinates feel threatened, fearful, insecure, Even neutral and innocuous actions of the superior are regarded with suspicion. Effective discipline is impossible, high standards of performance cannot be maintained, "sabotage" of the superior's efforts is almost inevitable. Resistance, antagonism, and ultimately open rebellion are the consequences.

The Conditions of Security: Knowledge

The second requirement for the subordinates security is knowledge. They must know what is expected of them. Otherwise they may, through errors of commission or omission, interfere with the satisfaction of their own needs. There are several kinds of knowledge that the subordinate required.

Knowledge of Overall Company Policy and Management Philosophy

Security is impossible in a world of shifting foundations. This fact is convincingly demonstrated when we hear the cry for a national labour policy frequently. "Without it we don't know how to act". Likewise, subordinates in the individual company require a knowledge of the broad policy and philosophy of top management.

Knowledge of Procedures, Rules and Regulations

Without this knowledge, the subordinate can only learn by trial and error, and the threat of punishment because of innocent infractions hangs always over his head.

Knowledge of the Requirements of the Subordinate's Own Job — Their Duties, Responsibilities and Place in the Organisation

It is surprising how often subordinates (particularly within the management organisation) are unable to obtain this essential knowledge. Lacking it, one can never be sure when to make a decision, or when to refer the matter to someone else: when to act or when to "pass the buck". The potential dangers in this kind of insecurity are apparent upon the most casual consideration.

Knowledge of the Personal Peculiarities of the Subordinate's Immediate Superior

The good salesman never approaches a new prospect without learning all that they can about their interests, habits, prejudices, and opinions. Subordinates must sell themselves to their superior, and consequently such knowledge is indispensable to them. Do their bosses demand initiative and originality, or do they want to make all the decisions themselves? What are the unpardonable sins, the things this superior never forgives or forgets? What are their soft spots, and what are their blind spots? There can be no security for subordinates until they have discovered the answers to these questions.

Knowledge by Subordinates of the Superior's Opinion of Their Performance
Where do I stand? How am I doing? To know where you stand in the eyes of your superiors is to know what you must do in order to satisfy your needs. Lacking this knowledge, the subordinate can have, at best only a false sense of security.

Advance Knowledge of Changes that May Affect the Subordinate
Resistance to change is a common phenomenon among employees in industry. One of the fundamental reasons is the effect of unpredictable changes upon security. If subordinates know that they will always be given adequate warning of changes, and understand the reasons for them, they do not fear them half so much. Conversely, the normal inertia of human habits is tremendously reinforced when one must be forever prepared against unforeseen changes in policy, rules, methods of work, or even in the continuity of employment and wages.

It is not necessary to turn to industry for evidence in support of the principles outlined above. Everywhere in our world today we see the consequences of the insecurity caused by our inability to know what we need to know in order to ensure, even partially, the satisfaction of our needs.

> Knowledge is power, primarily because it decreases dependence upon the unknown and unpredictable.

The Conditions of Security: Consistent Discipline
The third requirement for the subordinates' security in their relationship of dependence on their superiors is that of consistent discipline. It is a fact often unrecognised that discipline may take the form of positive support for "right" actions as well as criticism and punishment for "wrong" ones. Subordinates, in order to be secure, requires consistent discipline in both senses.

They require, first of all, the strong and willing backing of their superiors for those actions that are in accord with what is expected of them. There is much talk among some managements about supervisors who fail to "back up" their subordinates. The insecurity that arises when a subordinate does not know under what conditions they will be backed up leads them to "keep their necks pulled in" at all times. Buck passing and its consequent frictions and resentment are inevitable under such circumstances.

Given a clear knowledge of what is expected of them, subordinates require, in addition, definite assurance that they will have the unqualified support of their superiors so long as their actions are consistent with those policies and are taken within the limits of their responsibility. Only then can they have the security and confidence that will enable them to do their job well.

At the same time subordinates must know that failure to live up to their responsibilities, or to observe the rules that are established, will result in punishment. Every individual has many wants that conflict with the demands of their job. If they know that breaking the rules to satisfy these wants will almost inevitably result in the frustration of their vital long-term needs, self-discipline will be less difficult. If, on the other hand, discipline is inconsistent and uncertain, they may be unnecessarily denying themselves satisfaction by obeying the rules. The insecurity born of uncertainty and of guilt, which is inevitably a consequence of lax discipline, is unpleasant and painful for the subordinate.

Every subordinate, then, requires the security of knowing that they can count on the firm support of their superiors for doing what is "right", and firm pressure (even punishment) to prevent doing what is "wrong". But this discipline must be established and maintained in an atmosphere of approval. Otherwise, the subordinates' suspicion and resentment of their superiors will lead to the opposite reaction from the desired one. A mild degree of discipline is sufficient in an atmosphere of approval; even the most severe discipline will in the end be unsuccessful in an atmosphere of disapproval.

The Necessity for Independence

When subordinates have achieved a reasonable degree of genuine security in their relationship with their superiors, they will begin to seek ways of utilising more fully their capacities and skills, of achieving through their own efforts a larger degree of satisfaction from their work. Given security, subordinates seek to develop themselves. This active search for independence is constructive and healthy. It is collaborative and friendly, yet genuinely self assertive.

If, on the other hand, subordinates feel that their dependence on their superiors is extreme, and if they lack security, they will fight blindly for freedom. This reactive struggle of independence is founded on fear and hatred. It leads to friction and strife and it tends to perpetuate itself, because it interferes with the development of an atmosphere of approval that is essential to security.

These two fundamentally opposite ways in which subordinates seek to acquire independence have entirely different consequences. Since we are concerned with the conditions of the successful subordinate/superior relationship, we shall emphasise the active rather than the reactive striving for independence.

The Conditions of Active Independence: Participation

One of the most important conditions of the subordinates' growth and development centres around their opportunities to express their ideas and to contribute their suggestions *before* their superiors take action on matters that involve them. Through participation of this kind they become more and more aware of their superiors' problems, and they obtain genuine satisfaction in knowing that their opinions and ideas are given consideration in the search for solutions.

Participation of this kind is fairly prevalent in the upper levels of industrial organisations. It is often entirely lacking further down the line. Some people insist that the proponents of participation at the lower levels of industry are unrealistic idealists. However, there are highly successful instances in existence of "consultative supervision", "multiple management" and "union/ management co-operation".

The important point is that participation cannot be successful unless the conditions of security are adequately met.

Many failures among the currently popular Labour/management Production Drive Committees can be traced directly to this fundamental fact that active independence cannot be achieved in the absence of adequate security. There is a real challenge and a deep satisfaction for the subordinate who is given the opportunity to aid in the solution of the difficult but fascinating problems that arise daily in any industrial organisation. The superior who, having provided security for this subordinates, encourages them to accept this challenge and to strive with them to obtain this satisfaction, is almost invariably surprised at the fruitfulness of the results.

The Conditions of Active Independence: Responsibility

A corollary of the desire for participation is a desire for responsibility. It is another manifestation of the active search for independence. Insecure or rebellious subordinates — seeking independence in the reactive sense — do not accept responsibility. They are seeking freedom, not the opportunity for self-realisation and development.

The willingness to assume responsibility is a genuine maturational phenomenon. However, subordinates cannot accept responsibility until they have achieved a certain degree of emotional security in their relationship to their superiors. Then they want it. They accept it with obvious pleasure and pride. And if it is given to them gradually, so that they are not suddenly made insecure again by too great a load of it, they will continue to accept more and more.

The process of granting responsibility to subordinates is a delicate one. There are vast individual differences in tolerance for the inevitable pressures and insecurities attendant upon the acceptance of responsibility. Some subordinates seem to be content to achieve a high degree of security without independence. Others thrive on the risks and the dangers of being "on their own". However, there are few subordinates whose capabilities in this direction are fully realised.

The Conditions of Active Independence: The Right of Appeal

There are occasions when subordinates differ radically but sincerely with their superiors on important questions. Unless the superior follows an "appeasement" policy (which in the end will cost them the subordinates' respect), there exists in such disagreement the possibility of an exaggerated feeling of dependence and helplessness in the minds of the subordinates. They disagree for reasons that seem to them sound; yet they must defer to the judgement of a person whom they know to be fallible.

If these occasions are too frequent, the subordinates will be blocked in their search for independence, and they may readily revert to a reactive struggle. The way out of the dilemma is to provide subordinates with a mechanism for appealing their superior's decisions to a higher level of the organisation. Subordinates can then have at hand a check upon the correctness and fairness of their superior's actions. Their feeling of independence is thereby increased.

This is one of the justifications for an adequate grievance procedure for workers. All too often, however, there is no similar mechanism provided for members of management. Indeed, in the absence of a union it is difficult to safeguard the individual against measures by their immediate superior, but it is possible to guarantee a reasonable degree of protection.

If the relationship between subordinate and superior is a successful one, the right of appeal may rarely be exercised. Nevertheless, the awareness that it is there to be used when needed provides the subordinate with a feeling of independence which is not otherwise possible.

SUMMARY

Subordinates in the industrial organisation are dependent for the satisfaction of many of their vital needs upon the behaviour and attitudes of their superiors. They require, therefore, a feeling of confidence that they can satisfy their needs if they do what is expected of them. Given this security, they require opportunities for self-realisation and development.

Among the conditions influencing the subordinate's feelings of security are:

- An "atmosphere" of approval

- Knowledge of what is expected of them and of how well they are measuring up to these expectations

- Forewarning of changes that may affect them, and

- Consistent discipline in the form both of backing when "right" and punishment when "wrong".

The conditions under which subordinates can realise their own potential include:

- An adequate sense of security in relation to their superiors

- Opportunities to participate in the solution of problems and in discussion of actions that may affect them

- The opportunity to assume responsibility as they become ready for it, and

- The right of appeal over the head of their immediate superior.

These conditions are minimal. The success or failure of the subordinate/superior relationship at every level of the industrial organisation, from that of the vice president to that of the worker, rests to some degree upon their fulfilment.

> Union-management relations, and ultimately industrial relations, must in the final analysis be proactive and responsive rather than reactive and static.

27

THE NEED FOR COMPETENCE-BUILDING

INTRODUCTION

When changes are being introduced in a company, attention is more often than not centred on the actual purchasing of new equipment. The consequences this new equipment may have for personnel and the organisational structure are often seen as being of secondary importance. The effect of this may well be that the project as a whole gets off to a sluggish start and results are slow in coming. At the very worst the whole project may fail, and in-house conflicts may become the order of the day in the company.

Care must be taken, therefore, in making sure employees have both a positive attitude to the new technology and the necessary training in the use of it.

In this chapter, we look at the importance of employee competence and training when changes are being planned. The consequences of the introduction of new equipment and new methods of working are also discussed.

The need for competence-building is looked at under the following headings:

- Analysis of Organisational Structure

- Competence-building and Training

- Organisational and Personnel-related Consequences.

ANALYSIS OF ORGANISATIONAL STRUCTURE

Many companies have invested large sums of money in modern technology without reaping the expected benefits. The reasons for this can be complex, but one of the most important is that management "delegates" responsibility for the implementation of technological projects to technological experts.

Technologists are important as team players in their specialised areas, but the result of a successful project is dependent upon many factors which are not related to technological feasibility.

Any changes must start with an overview of the organisation's present situation. In particular, the following aspects of the organisation must be taken into account:

- Activities/responsibility/management

- Organisation/structure/division of labour

- Competence

- Attitudes

- Systems/routines.

These factors are discussed in more detail below.

Activities/Responsibility/Management

A company's activities can be represented by the value chain as shown previously in Figure 10.1 (see page 243). In the figure, activities are shown to be either "primary" activities or "support" activities:

- Primary activities are aspects of the direct product manufacturing process and customer contact (e.g. logistics, operations (manufacturing), marketing and sales, and service)

- Support activities support the primary activities, typically as "support functions" (e.g. finance and administration, human resource management, purchasing and technology development).

One issue that often arises during activity and information analysis is that the actual division of responsibility and functions in the company fits badly with the value chain that has been outlined. A simple matrix can be used to shed light on this issue, to find the greatest discrepancies if any, and identify options and measures for dealing with them (Figure 27.1).

Figure 27.1: Matching Responsibility and Activities

Responsibility/Function Activities	Administration	Finance	Technical	Market
Primary Activities				
1. Inbound logistics				
_____	X	X	X	
_____	X			
2. Production and operations				
_____			X	
_____			X	
3. _____				X
Support Activities				
1. Resource management and development				
_____	X	X		
_____	X		X	
2. Purchasing				
_____	X	X	X	
_____		X		
3. _____	X			

Organisation/Structure/Division of Labour

Every company has a formal organisational structure, drawn up in accordance with the company's main functions and activities. This structure shows the division of responsibility in the company and should be person-oriented, inasmuch as various persons (managers) are given the responsibility for achieving subgoals. Different organisational structures include:

- **Functionally-oriented** (purchasing, production, sales, human resource management, finance)

- **Product-oriented** (Product A, Product B, etc.)

- **Market-oriented** (regions, industries, customer groups)

- **Matrix-oriented** (where the above-mentioned division of responsibility forms part of a multi-dimensional organisational model as outlined in Figure 27.2).

Figure 27.2: Multi-dimensional (Matrix) Organisation

	Product A Respons.	Product B Respons.	Product C Respons.
Region A Respons.			
Region B Respons.			
Region C Respons.			

In practice, a company's organisational structure will generally be made up of a mix of the above models.

Each division can also be divided into its respective functions, along with an assigning of responsibility or partial responsibility for them. As with the main activities/responsibilities (Figure 27.1), it is a good idea to compile an overview (Figure 27.3) that shows:

- Which functions are this division's responsibility

- Who has the responsibility/partial responsibility

- Estimated resources required.

We have just described a company's *formal* organisational structure. Every company will in addition have a more *informal* structure that can be defined as "how it works in practice". These two structures are seldom identical, and do not have to be, but the gap between the two (this can usually be identified by chatting with employees and following your own "gut feeling" and experience) may well be the source of important problems when changes are being introduced.

- Will the informal organisational structure create problems for measures even though "on paper" everything is as it should be (in the formal structure)?

- Do management and those sections of the organisation most affected by the changes agree with the structural differences?

Figure 27.3: Functions, Responsibilities and Resources

Purchasing Division Functions	Mary Smith	John Taylor	Dorothy Jones	Peter Baker
Production plans	40%	10%		
Purchasing plans				
—quotes/tenders	40%	10%		
—cost estimates		20%		
—ordering		30%		
—follow-up		30%		40%
Invoice control				
—registration			60%	20%
—control			20%	40%
—entry			20%	
—remittances				
Human resource management	20%			

Competence/Attitudes

A simple form that can be used to list the competences necessary for the successful introduction of a change is given in Figure 27.4. Using this form, one can build up a picture of the present situation and the competence situation the new method of working requires. The form thereby constitutes the basis for planning to raise the level of competence in the company.

This section also has to do with organisational psychology. An understanding of what forces/factors (cultures) there are in the company can help to keep ambitions for the proposed changes at a level that is "acceptable", both with regard to the actual speed at which the changes are introduced and the whole training aspect of the changes.

Those directly affected by the measures must be given the time and opportunity to understand and learn how this new equipment/system functions, and what consequences its introduction will have for them and the company. All too often solutions are imposed on employees, creating a conflict situation at the outset, just when members of staff should be standing "shoulder to shoulder" in their efforts to develop a more productive, competitive company.

Figure 27.4: Competence Requirements

Area — examples	Present situation*					Req* 1-5	Measure — examples
	1	2	3	4	5		
Computer competence		X				4	Course
Project management							Employment
Material control							Job rotation
Finance competence							Networking — competence exchange
Production control							Engage consultant
etc.							Project organisation
							External expert
							Internal transfer
							etc.

* 1 = no/poor 2 = fair 3 = OK 4 = very good 5 = expert competence

Some companies compile two sets of requirement specifications when planning to introducing new measures:

- The first specifies the technical requirements, and functions as basic material for tenders from potential suppliers.

- The second is aimed at the company itself, and lists the in house measures that need to be implemented if the new technology is to be introduced successfully and contribute to the goals set for it.

We would like to emphasise that all projects must pay due attention to open communication with all the organisational units affected by the changes, and that the projects should be implemented and developed in a way that allows those affected by them to influence the solutions and the actual pace of implementation.

Key Questions

The following key questions will help to concentrate work on the most important issues regarding organisational structure and competence:

- How does the organisational structure (organisation chart) look? Is it oriented towards functions, operations (manufacturing), marketing, or is it matrix-based?

- How many people are employed (annually) in the company (per year for the last three years), and how are they divided among the various functions in the organisation?

- To what extent does this match the distribution of the activities in the company's value chain? Can changes in the organisational structure improve this match and increase the chance of successfully introducing new measures and changes?

- What about the informal organisational structure? Will this create problems for the proposed measures that appear to be trouble-free in the formal organisation?

- How does the present level of competence compare with the technology measures that are to be implemented?

- Will attitudes among the employees create problems with competence-building?

- Does the company have the ability to hold on to key personnel that have to be trained?

- Could the use of technology provide opportunities for developing the organisational structure by:

   ◊ creating better linkages between different parts of the organisation?

   ◊ supporting decentralisation?

   ◊ providing more job satisfaction for employees?

   ◊ automating dangerous/unpleasant jobs?

COMPETENCE-BUILDING AND TRAINING

Think in Terms of Training Early

Planning information and training should be a part of the project right from the start. This is necessary if enough time and money are to be allocated to this aspect of the project and a training programme is to be started early enough for the company to be capable of using the technology as soon as it has been set up.

Planning a Training Programme

The following points are central to a company training programme:

- What is the goal of the training?

- Who needs training and at what level?

- Need analysis

- Who is to be responsible for the training?

- Where is the training to take place?

- Implementation plan

- Evaluating the results.

Planning the amount of training made necessary by technical changes demands that the company must be capable of surveying the actual need for training. This then allows the company to plan and implement a training programme on the basis of rational considerations. The company must also have a good overview of the skills it needs in this respect.

Finally, it has to ask what kind of skills individuals should acquire. What types of training will guarantee that employees get the proper reward for their efforts in the form of personal development and stimulation?

Goal of the Training Programme

Is the goal short-term — aimed first and foremost at offsetting a lack of knowledge, in this case training in the use of equipment for those who will be affected in some way by it in the near future?

If the goal is more long term and dynamic, and aimed at making the company more flexible, then the natural goal would be to achieve maximum utilisation of the technology by employees. They should not only learn to use the equipment, but should also be made capable of controlling the technology by a comprehensive training programme. If doing this means savings in one or more areas in the company, then the resources allocated to training are quickly recovered. Should the company also aim to raise the general level of competence, it will be significantly strengthened in the event of future reorganisation and restructuring.

Who Needs Training and at What Level?

The next step is to consider who needs to be trained and what the purpose of the training should be. Each of the following groups will need different types of training:

- Users/operators (in operating the equipment)

- Service personnel (in maintenance and repairs)

- Management (insight in the technology and its potential applications)

- Project Managers (project management, insight into the technology, applications and use of the equipment)

- Sales reps (to utilise the positive effect it has on customers)

- Employee representatives (for use in collective bargaining contexts)

- All employees (briefings).

Do not forget the need for overlapping either.

Need Analysis

The final effect of any training programme is dependent on just how well the actual need is understood. The effect also depends on the extent of agreement between the company's and each employee's goals and needs.

The need analysis can be divided into three steps:

- Step 1: A need survey. There are many methods for surveying needs, among which employee interviews and data collection, or preferably a combination of both, are well-suited for this purpose.

- Step 2: Interpretation and analysis of the collected data in the light of the demands of the new technology, knowledge of the company and the various professional groups.

- Step 3: The overall picture of need, adjusted after Step 2, will form a good basis for deciding the goal, content, and form of training.

All too often companies "leap-frog" over the last two steps, and the result is that the impact of the training is poor, less meaningful, and falls short of the desired effect.

Who Is to Be Responsible for the Training?
At an early stage in the proceedings it is necessary to decide whether the training should be carried out with help and expertise from outside the company, or by building up an in-house capability for the purpose, or whether there should be a combination of the two.

When considering this point, attention should be paid to:

- The level of complexity and the gap between the new and present technology and competence.

- Whether the company has suitable employees (technical and "good with people") who can be released sufficiently from their present work and can be trained to a level where they can then take responsibility for all or part of the training programme for other members of staff.

- Whether it is desirable to have competence in the company for training new personnel.

- Whether all training should be done in advance, or the new technology should be introduced one level or division at a time.

Where Should the Training Be Done?

Generally speaking, the further from the practical situation the training is done, the greater the transfer problems can be. There are the following alternatives:

- Training in the working situation as part of the normal working day.

- Training connected to the daily working situation, though clearly separated from the daily work.

- Training under the company's own auspices, but physically removed from the normal place of work. This training can be done with the company's own resources or with outside help and schemes specially adapted to the needs of the company.

- Training bought on the open market. This type of training is difficult to adapt exactly to some of the participants, since they do not all have the same needs and frames of reference. So each participant must try to transfer the new knowledge to his or her own working situation. If this method is chosen, it is important to set aside time for working with the new knowledge just after the course.

The various alternatives ought to be considered carefully in terms of topic, number of persons involved and the goals to be achieved.

Implementation Plan

A fundamental principle of adult education is that the content and design of any training programme should match the needs of the participants. Among "needs" we can include the demands of the company and society in general for professional competence as well as the more personal wishes of individual participants for additional skills.

It is also important to take the following points into consideration in the planning stage:

- Adults learn easier when they participate actively and can influence their own teaching process.

- Adults have insight and experience that can be utilised and so can facilitate the learning process. So the level of learning must be adapted to the expectations and needs of the participants.

- Adults learn best when theory and practice are not taught separately, but combined in the learning process.

When implementing a course of training it is important to take into account the capabilities of each participant, and create a secure, stimulating teaching atmosphere where trial and error are permissible, and the trainee has time to feel comfortable with the new skills.

It will also be necessary to set up a schedule for training that fits in with the other schedules for the introduction of technology, and to co-ordinate and follow it up throughout the course of the implementation period.

The important factors that need to be considered when planning a course of training were shown previously in Figure 16.3 on page 392.

Evaluating the Results

Follow-up and evaluation of the training must not only be done at the conclusion of the project, but also during the course of the programme in accordance with the schedule and the goal. It is more than likely that unforeseen obstacles will arise that make it necessary to carry out adjustments if the desired effect of the training is to be attained.

- What is the purpose of the evaluation?
- What questions need to be answered?
- What is the most suitable evaluation technique?
- When is the evaluation to take place and who is to do it?

It is important that the purpose of the evaluation is clear so that the level and criteria of evaluation suit the purpose. Company training has three main purposes:

- **An educational evaluation** should establish whether participants have absorbed the course material. Here one can restrict oneself to measuring the end product, or can instead evaluate the whole process. Measuring the end product alone is often too narrow an approach. Process evaluation, on the other hand, provides ongoing evaluation of the educational methods, the learning process, the beneficial value in the working situation, and social factors. This then provides those running the course and the participants themselves with beneficial feedback and possibilities for adjusting the course framework along the way.

- **A financial evaluation** measures whether the results gained from the course in financial terms measure up to the cost of the course. This is a comprehensive and difficult evaluation to carry out.

- **A sociological evaluation** aims to investigate how the material learnt during the course is transferred to and utilised in the working situation. This evaluation is done at a "job behaviour" level. A sociological evaluation can expose any transfer barriers in the company, and may lead to changes in the company's training policy.

The choice of evaluation technique depends on the evaluation level. In company training the following four levels are most relevant:

- **The response level** measures participants' reaction to the training; whether they are satisfied, got anything out of it, etc. Evaluation at this level is normally done at the end of a course.

- **The learning level** measures what participants have learnt, i.e. knowledge, proficiency, and to some extent also attitudes. An examination is an example of this type of evaluation.

- **The "job behaviour" level** measures what participants have learnt in the working situation. This evaluation consists of investigating whether the training process has led to the desired results in practical job performance.

- **The organisational level** measures any consequences the course may have had for changes in the company's organisation — for example cost-benefit evaluations, changes in forms of co-operation and so on.

Figure 27.5 provides an overview of the various evaluation methods.

Figure 27.5: Various Evaluation Methods

Evaluation Technique	Evaluation Level			
	Response	Learning	Job Behaviour	Organi- sation
Measuring satisfaction	X			
Measuring expectations	X			
Evaluation on the basis of a scale (1-5, good-bad, etc.)	X			
Verifying knowledge (test, exam)		X		
Observing changes in job behaviour (how)			X	
Activity studies (what)			X	
Measuring effect on organisa- tional level (consequences)				X

ORGANISATIONAL AND PERSONNEL-RELATED CONSEQUENCES

The purpose of this section is to focus on the possible consequences of the introduction of change in a company. Both consultant and company should start the work by considering all the negative effects, thus grounding the project on a more secure basis. If this work is to have the necessary structure it should take the form of a consequence analysis: a systematic survey of the consequences, both direct and indirect, of introducing the proposed change.

Personnel May Be Made Redundant

As early as possible the company must clarify and make known within the organisation what is to happen to people whose present work functions will disappear. The various alternatives are: reassignment, natural attrition, early retirement, and, as a final resort, notice of termination. If the company is in a situation where personnel have to be dismissed, it will be crucial for the further progress of the project that the step is seen as being an acceptable one.

"Reduced" Competence for Line Managers

In situations where production responsibility for the new, advanced equipment is moved downwards in the organisation, line managers will often lose some of their professional advisory role. It is necessary to get their acceptance of this new situation, and even to consider whether they too should be trained in the use of the new equipment.

Confusion about Existing Functional Areas

An organisation's structure must always be adaptable to changes in the world around it. New technology can demand a great deal of such flexibility, and may also demand a great deal from those affected by it. A typical situation is where the company's support functions can become much more integrated, which in turn leads to a certain amount of confusion among the previous functions and areas of responsibility (e.g. financial and stock overviews may be available to everyone, not just the finance and store managers; and the gap between technical data equipment and administrative systems may disappear). It will often be necessary for the company's chief executive to be involved in the conflicts that can arise from these processes.

Establishing/Closing Down Whole Units

A situation may also arise where complete office environments and divisions need to be broken up. Changes of this dimension must be carried out with a clear goal as to why it is necessary, and in close co-operation with the people affected by it.

Transfer of Personnel Not Open to the New Technology

A few people often refuse to co-operate in the introduction of new technology. This is usually due to their own feeling of insecurity as to whether they can learn to operate the new system. Active motivation and working together with these members of staff is very necessary; the process may well show that it is a myth to say that "older people" are not interested in participating.

Increased Dependence on Key Personnel Leading to Increased Vulnerability

New technical equipment is often complicated and demands special competence in order to be able to utilise it, keep it operational, and expand and tie it in with existing equipment. This competence is normally restricted to a few people, so the company is vulnerable if one of these decides to leave.

The company must therefore be clear about whether this competence should be secured by using its own resources or by obtaining outside professional help. It will often be a good idea to keep a sensible balance between one's own and outside competence. The company must see that such considerations are taken into account, and that any necessary agreement is reached with the supplier during contract negotiations.

Resistance from the Informal Company Organisation

In every organisation, enormous influence is wielded by informal leaders or trend-setters, whose importance is not always reflected by the official company structure. Successful implementation is dependent on their being brought into the project at an early stage.

Establishing New Jobs

New jobs established in connection with new investments are often seen as being prestigious within the company. These positions are of strategic importance for the company's future, and will demand both professional ability and an ability to motivate other staff around the person concerned. Top management will also be very aware of these people. The relationship with others in the organisation must be carefully considered, both where salary levels and placement in the organisation are concerned.

Long-term Human Effect

An ability to readjust its organisation is probably one of the most important elements if a company is to survive in the future. Many feel insecure when faced with change, and creating a belief that security lies in change must be seen as a clear goal for the company.

In the implementation and following-up of a technology project it is therefore crucial that results can be measured and then communicated to employees. This allows the company to create an environment where not only the executive management but also the rest of the organisation continually search for areas of improvement.

28

INFORMATION TECHNOLOGY

INTRODUCTION

Information flow diagrams are a general technique for obtaining an overview of the information flow among activities in a company's value chain. This section shows how the diagram should be used to indicate critical activities and barriers in the flow of information.

Techniques are presented which can help the consultant to identify important issues in connection with *goal-orientation* and IT *system coverage*. The analysis is also a first step towards the introduction of new control systems.

Information technology has developed (and still is developing) at a fast rate in recent times. Thus, an analysis of how information is used must include an analysis of the technology that is being used to deal with it. The aim of the technology analysis is to reveal issues and options in the company's existing use of technology. An issues/options assessment like this will help the consultant to find the technologies that should respectively be prioritised, phased out or changed.

Information technology is discussed in this chapter under the following headings:

- Information Analysis

- Analysis of Existing Systems

- Data Processing Technology Platform

- Information Required by Operational Management.

INFORMATION ANALYSIS

Information analysis is primarily meant to answer key questions concerning:

- Which information is used in which of the company's business activities, and for what kind of decisions (the information requirement) in terms of goal-orientation requirements.

- How the information is structured today, and how it should be structured in future.

- What issues and options are associated with the current and future use of information.

As well as being an important method for revealing issues and options, information analysis is a fundamental requirement for the establishment of:

- A future information structure, including organisational demarcation of responsibilities for different types of information.

- A future system architecture and classification of subsystems, i.e. of how the organisation's information systems "hang together".

These two points are particularly important during the establishment of decision support systems, where the focus is on obtaining and integrating information from many sources to support the management's decision-making requirements. In such cases the information analysis is carried out in parallel with an analysis of the company's goals and critical success factors, or perhaps as a direct extension of this type of analysis.

Key Techniques

The key techniques that can be used in information analysis are:

- **Information flow or data flow diagrams**, which show how information is transferred among the business activities of the company.

- **Data models**, which show the organisation's information structure, regardless of organisational structure, technology and system.

- **Information matrices**, which show the relationships among information types and several other factors (e.g. existing systems, functions, organisational units etc.).

- **Goal hierarchies**, which "link" the company's goals at various levels.

- **Issues/options lists**, where the issues are formulated on the basis of information analysis.

Data Models and Information Matrices

The basic idea behind this kind of information analysis is to identify issues and options by looking at the data model from different perspectives. The idea of this "cross-linkage" is best gained from some examples:

- Cross-linking the entities in the data model with existing information systems reveals which types of information are not covered by any system, and which have "double coverage" (redundant information in different systems). The perspective is also used to determine a "conversion strategy" for the transition to a new system (which information is to be converted from which "old" system, and in what order).

- Cross-linking the data model with the company's goals and critical success factors reveals which information must be obtained to follow up on goals. If this information (entities) is again cross-linked with existing systems, we can reveal how information can be retrieved from different systems (MIS) to establish integrated management information systems etc.

- Cross-linking the data model with organisational levels and/or geographical sites reveals how the information can be distributed in a *distributed information system*.

The cross-linkages must be adapted to the needs of the project. In connection with the establishment of a management information system, for example, the first two variants above are most important.

The approach described below identifies primary types of "cross-linkage".

Procedure

The overall approach to information analysis is:

1. Establish a general data model

2. Determine perspectives for "cross-linkages" in the data model

3. Reveal issues and options through cross-linkage.

Establishing a General Data Model

A data model (or "entity-relationship" (E/R) diagram) shows the concepts that concern the company and the relationships among them.

Customers, suppliers, customer orders and products are examples of such concepts. In a data model these are called entities. The links between entities are called relations. The most "normal" relations in a data model are "has" relations and "consists-of" relations. A customer "has" one or more orders, and an order "consists of" one or more order lines etc.

Figure 28.1 shows a simplified data model for a typical orders-stocks-purchases application. This will be used as an example in what follows. The numbering in the figure is explained below.

A customer (1) is identified by a unique ID concept, and belongs to an industry (2) and a customer type (3). The customer has no orders, one order or several orders (4). Each order consists of a number of order lines (5) which again belong to a certain product (6).

Customer types may be entitled to certain product terms (7) when they order different types of product. The product terms determine the price, terms of payment, delivery time etc. The company has classified customers into customer types such that "key customers" get the best terms. Special terms may also have been agreed with individual customers. This is marked by a facultative relation (i.e. a non-obligatory relation).

When an order has been placed, one first checks whether special terms have been agreed for this product with the customer in question, then whether there are special terms for the customer type. If none of these tests are "passed", the "standard price" registered for the product is used.

Figure 28.1: Basic Data Model

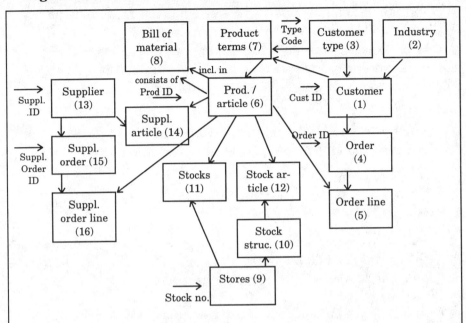

The data model does not distinguish between "saleable products" and the input materials of which the product consists. But the bill of materials structure (8) shows how products/articles consist of other products/articles.

The company has several stores (9) which are in turn divided into store structures (10) — for example, shelves. The stocks (11) shows stocks of a given product or articles in a particular storage unit. Similarly, stock article (12) shows where in the stores (which shelf etc.) the article or product is physically located.

The company uses a number of suppliers (13) of goods. The linkage with supplier article (14) shows which suppliers can supply which products and articles. Each supplier may have one or more supplier orders (15), which in turn consist of supplier order lines (16) each associated with a particular product/article.

Although we will not review general principles for designing a data model here, there are a few guidelines which should be observed in establishing a basis for this kind of information analysis. The most important are:

- Keep the model as simple as possible, without "losing" any essential information. As a general rule, the model should be easy to read and should fit on a normal A4 page. If necessary, it is better to establish more than one model than to try to make one model "exhaustive". A rule of thumb is that there should be a maximum of 25-30 entities in one and the same model.

- Limit the number of relations. Only include those that are critical for understanding (typically "has" and "consists-of" relations).

- ID concepts for the most important entities are essential information.

- Establish an ideal data model — that is, a model that shows "how things should be" irrespective of whether the present system and databases in fact realise the model.

With this as a point of departure, we are ready to consider "cross-linkages".

Determine Perspectives for "Cross-linkages" in the Data Model
As mentioned above, the need for "perspectives" varies with the project in question. Three fundamental perspectives consist of looking at the data model in terms of:

- Existing and planned information systems

- Goals and key ratios

- Technology boundaries.

These perspectives can be explained as follows:

Existing and planned information systems. This perspective is almost obligatory in connection with the establishment of a system architecture, subsystem classification, management information systems and conversion strategy.

Goals and key ratios. With reference to the model in Figure 28.1, control of profitability for different customer groups probably at least requires access to information on customer types, industries, customers and orders, in addition to budgeting and accounting information. This perspective is critical for the establishment of management information systems.

Technology boundaries. In companies with a lot of different types of technology (especially in hardware and database systems) this is an important perspective for establishing an overall system architecture. Normally a distinction is made between "main classes" of technology — for example, "IBM mainframe/CICS/IMS" and "IBM mainframe/IDMS-DC/IDMS" as opposed to "Unix machine/ORACLE" and "PC/dBase". Where information has to "cross technology boundaries" separate subsystems are normally established "on each side".

Identify issues and options through cross-linkages. Issues and possible solutions (options) are revealed by cross-linking the data model with a single perspective, or with several perspectives at once. To decide on a future system architecture (among several alternative options) several perspectives must usually be used at once. There are two main ways of documenting cross-linkages:

- "Labelling" in the actual data model

- Setting up information matrices.

Figure 28.2 shows the data model from Figure 28.1 with cross-linkages with four existing information systems shown by "labelling". The area of coverage for each system is indicated by "ringing", shading or colouring the entities affected. If the four systems made up the company's whole system portfolio, this "ringing" would have revealed important shortcomings, including a lack of system support for purchasing and stock control. In addition, several entities have "double coverage" — for example, customer information is covered wholly or partially in three parallel systems.

At the same time the figure reveals clear options. For example, it might be an idea to set up/maintain a joint product/article reg-

ister and change the order system so that the product information
is retrieved from this register.

Figure 28.2: Cross-referencing Data Model and Systems

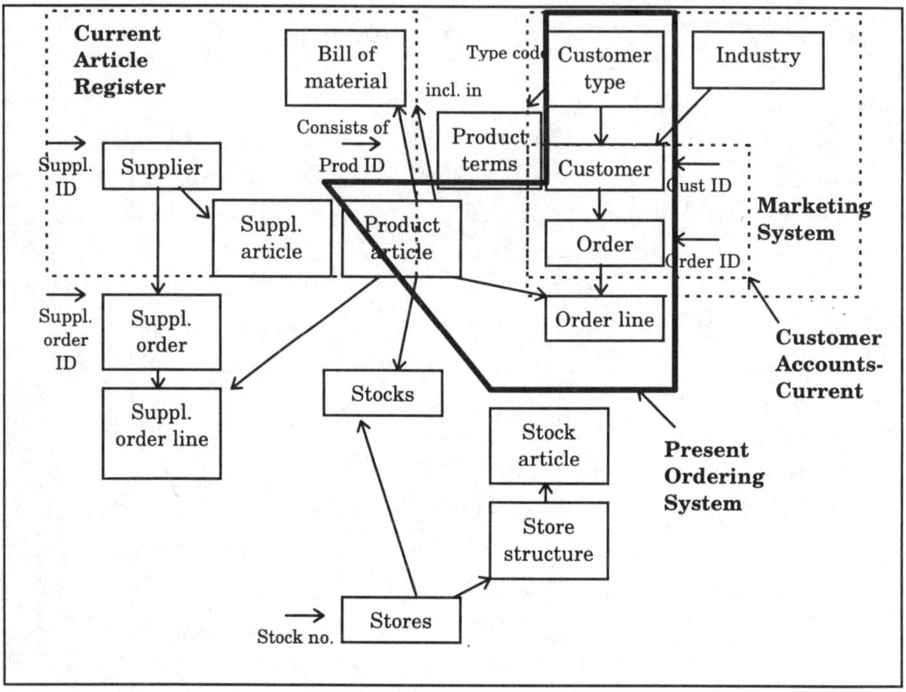

Figure 28.3 in principle shows the same "exercise", but we are
now using an information matrix. The entities of the data model
(or groups of these) are placed along one axis, and the relevant
"perspective" (in this case the existing systems) along the other
axis. In the simplest form of matrix, one simply puts a "cross" in
the cells — for example a cross for the entities which are (wholly
or partly) covered by the systems.

In Figure 28.3 there is more information in the cells. In particular, the degree of "coverage" is indicated ("covered", "partly
covered" or "needs covering") along with key words for issues.

The matrices provide an opportunity for better documentation
of additional information, but on the other hand setting them up
is a more laborious process.

Figure 28.3: Information System Matrix

Entity System	Customer Type	Industry	Customer	Order/ order line	Product/ article	Bill of material
Order system	*Covered* Differs from customer type in marketing system	*Needs covering* Necessary for profit-ability control by industry	*Covered* Needs different shipping and in-voicing addresses	*Covered*	*Partly covered* Different ID con-cept from product register	
Article register					*Covered* Different ID con-cept from order system	*Covered*
Customer accounts			*Covered* Problem with accounts —current ID versus cust. ID	*Partly Covered* (only at order level)		
Market system	*Covered*	*Covered*	*Covered*			

Experience has shown that some special type of "labelling" in the data model is most useful:

- The data model is drawn on an A4 sheet which is marked with two crosses — for example in the lower left and lower right corners.

- Each "perspective" is drawn with a felt pen on transparent plastic (for example an overhead pocket). Before labelling the perspective, the same two crosses are drawn on the pocket.

- Using transparent plastic means that the data model can be seen from a random number of perspectives at the same time, when the crosses are "laid over" one another.

We have only dealt with the most general level of the potential of this kind of information analysis. The technique is also excellent for revealing — for example — inconsistencies and lack of system support.

ANALYSIS OF EXISTING SYSTEMS

To assess how the company's data systems function and what potential for better exploitation there is in the systems, we must draw up an overview of the systems. This overview should first and foremost include information on main functions, users, hardware and costs, as well as problem areas, frequency of errors and potential for expansion and improvement.

Analysis of existing and planned information systems forms part of most planning processes as an element in the assessment of company-internal strengths and weaknesses (internal analysis).

Descriptive Techniques

Existing and planned systems can be described in many ways. The most important are:

- **System descriptions** in forms which document the most important features of the system.

- **System overviews**, which extract the most important information from the system descriptions and document them in tables.

- **System architecture**, which shows how the systems "hang together", and in particular which information can be transferred.

- **Issues/options lists**, which describe issues in terms of the system analysis, and possible solutions (strategies and measures) for addressing these problems.

Figure 28.4 shows the relationship between the first three of these techniques.

Issues and options are revealed by assessing the system portfolio from different perspectives, usually by asking key questions. This means that we deal with the whole body of system documentation (system descriptions, overviews and architecture). Critical questions should be asked to reveal both "where the shoes pinches" and what can be done to address these problems. The issues/options list can thus serve as a "clearing house" for key information gleaned from the use of the other three techniques. The ability to identify issues and options directly (without formal use of the other techniques) will increase with experience.

Figure 28.4: Relationships between Techniques

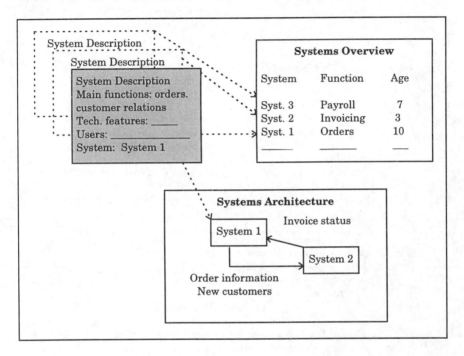

Key questions are listed in the next section. Figure 28.5 shows an extract from an issues/options list that can be set up on the basis of the answers to the key questions and by using the system descriptions.

Key Questions

Primarily, we are looking for systems that stand out in some particularly positive or negative respect. The most important questions are:

- Which systems stand out as being strategically important for the company?

- Are there systems with particularly discontented users? This could for example be because of low functionality, long response times and running times, low operational stability etc.

Figure 28.5: Example of an Issues/Options List

Priority	Issue	Possible Solutions	Status
	No decision-making support for production planning	Expand present order system ("Toss") with a seasonally-adjusted forecast for the next two months	Possible
	Invoicing is held up by an average of x days because of manual error correction in connection with the interface between the order system and customer accounts. Potential cost reduction of ECU x by establishing correct transfer (no delays)	Change customer identification in the accounts-current system to corresponding "Toss" IDs. Move registration of new customers to "Toss" with daily electronic transfer to accounts-current system.	Possible
		Establish joint customer database for all system incl. "Toss" and accounts-current.	Possible
	Errors in stock information are causing delivery problems for product X because of a shortage of components Z and Y. There is a shortage every ___ days on average. In addition, it is possible that capital tied in non-critical components is far too high.	Carry out ABC analysis for all art.	Possible
		Increase safety margin for components Z and Y by 100% immediately.	Adopted
		Expand present order system ("Toss") with seasonally-adjusted forecasts for the next two months. Generate purchase orders for critical components automatically on the basis of forecasts.	Possible
		Integrate the order system and stock system to ensure consistent stock information.	Possible

- Are there systems without clear user groups and system responsibility? In large organisations it is in fact quite common to find existing systems that "no one has a claim on any more".

- Which systems are relatively old? Development methods, principles and tools have changed a lot in recent years. High age might indicate poor quality. Average age is typically 6 – 7 years. One should be particularly wary of systems that are more than 9 – 10 years old.

- Are there systems with particularly low operational stability? If so, this could indicate poor technical quality with a high risk of error and stoppages.

- Are there systems with old-fashioned or atypical technology? One is often forced to phase out such systems (even if they functionally "hold their own") because the people with the key competence have left or because the technology has been phased out by the supplier.

- Which systems have particularly high development costs? This is most interesting in the case of new systems or systems under development. With older systems, the quality of statistical material can be too poor to give clear indications.

- Which systems have high operating costs, especially as regards the volume of data processed? High unit costs may mean doubtful system structure and technical quality.

- Which systems have particularly high maintenance costs? In many cases a complete replacement may be cheaper than extensive troubleshooting and modifications.

- Are there systems with particularly high backlogs? This may indicate poor functional quality and/or the use of ineffectual development tools.

- Are there systems which use technology that does not match the company's technological strategies? This may be true of both hardware and system software (for example the operating system and database system).

- Are there systems that seem particularly inflexible or have inappropriate data structures?

- Are there in-house-developed systems which should have been bought in as standard systems? It is very common for companies to sink great resources in in-house development of systems that could have been bought at a tenth of the price and with better functionality. The argument ". . . but we have special needs" is typical in such cases.

- Are there systems that stand out because of poor security in terms of protection against misuse, errors and/or loss of data? Often, one also finds a number of systems which do not meet the requirements of the authorities as regards security and monitoring (for example the Data Security Act, regulations concerning registration of personal data).

- How do the systems interrelate? Are there over-complicated interfaces with "traffic problems" in information transfer?

- Is the same important information stored in many different systems? This could lead to a high risk of inconsistency. In some cases double storage can be a direct threat to business activities. A classic example is companies which are prevented from making organisational changes because parts of the accounting plan are "hard-coded" and stored in parallel in many systems.

- Is there a clear shortage of automatic interfaces among important systems?

- Is there a recurring problem with lack of system support for decision-making in the present system portfolio? In such cases, important decision-making information is typically missing, or is hidden deep in bulky reports that arrive too late.

- Are there business or functional areas that do not have their fair share of system support? Often, good system support is missing for strategically important business areas, while there is good coverage of purely internal functions and business areas with limited earnings.

- Are there systems with an unnatural mix of business and/or functional areas? Poorly-controlled in-house development often leads to attempts to cover all possible functional areas in the same system, which in the end fail to provide satisfactory coverage for any of them.

- Does the system portfolio match the company's business and competition strategies? One often finds exclusively rationalisation-oriented "bread-and-butter systems", even in companies which do not compete on price.

DATA PROCESSING TECHNOLOGY PLATFORM

The technology analysis generally concentrates on the main lines in three primary areas:

- Computers

- Communication systems

- System software.

Other peripheral equipment (for example disc drives and tape streamers) is of limited interest.

The technology analysis is important because the choice of technology gives the company a strong lead in the realisation of system requirements. Old-fashioned and incompatible technology generally means long development periods, low changeover rates and thus poor support for business needs.

Key Techniques

The most important descriptive techniques are:

- **Hardware architecture**, which shows in diagrammatic form how existing hardware, communication networks and peripherals "hang together"

- **Hardware descriptions and overviews**, which document important parameters for different hardware and communication solutions

- **Software overviews**, which document the basic software for the various computers

- **Issues/options lists**, which describe the issues arising from the technology analysis and possible ways of dealing with these (options).

As Figure 28.6 shows, the technology analysis is closely related to the analysis of existing (and planned) information systems, since the technical infrastructure makes up the *platform* on which the systems "run".

Any technological changes — especially in hardware and basic software — may have considerable consequences for the company's information systems.

Figure 28.6: Relationship - Technology and System Analysis

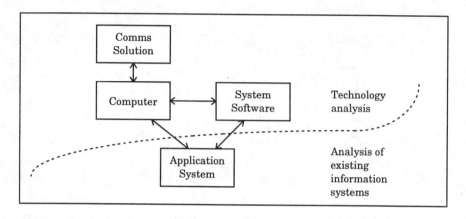

Procedure

The general procedure for analysing existing technology is:

- Document the company's hardware architecture. Stress the types of hardware — not, for example, the exact number of each type.

- Identify issues and options on the basis of the key questions in the last paragraphs of this note (exclusively software questions). Set up an issues/options list (Figure 28.7).

- Draw up a software overview for the software used by the most important information systems on the most important hardware platforms. Identify issues and options on the basis of the key questions for software, and update the issues/options list.

It is important to avoid unnecessary detail in the analysis. Keep a firm focus on finding issues and options, not on the survey work as such.

General Key Questions

Issues and options are revealed by assessing the technological situation of the company from various perspectives, often by using key questions.

Figure 28.7: Issues/Options List for Technology Analysis

Priority	Issue	Possible Solutions	Status
2	We lack a company strategy for minicomputers and PCs. At present we have six different, incompatible technologies and are unable to transfer critical information. What can be done?	Establish absolute company standards. Phase out technology x and technology y before 199x. Establish purchase schemes (discount agreements and site licenses). This will give us a "mild" form of standardisation (without compulsion) as divisions will gain clear cost reductions by following company policy.	Rejected Possible Possible
2	No general management of network monitoring. Errors are not detected as they arise. No monitoring for unauthorised link-ups or information-tapping.	---	---
1	Hardware x forces us to develop bread-and-butter routines in-house. Eight million ECU spent on in-house development of new accounting and payroll system in last two years.	---	---

We are primarily looking for technology which stands out in some particularly positive or negative respect. Key questions are:

- Are there clear technological goals and strategies? If so, is there existing technology which is clearly at cross-purposes with these?

- Does the company have a conscious approach to experimentation with new technology and general technology management, as opposed to only using well-tried technology?

- Which technology is relatively old? Four or five years is "two generations", and must be regarded as a high age for computer equipment — inasmuch as old equipment often means expensive maintenance contracts.

- Does the company have a lot of different and incompatible technology in areas where this could be avoided? Typical examples are many different minicomputer technologies, many operating systems, many database systems etc. What are the reasons for this?

- What technology has strikingly high running and/or service/maintenance costs?

- Is there technology which causes undesirable and unintentional ties with suppliers, and thus higher costs?

- Is there little-used, "odd" technology which requires expensive maintenance of special competence?

- What is the general situation as regards protection against misuse and data destruction?

Assessment of Existing Computer and Terminal Equipment

- What is the potential for using standard applications on the platform?

- What is the potential for using industry standard tools on the platform?

- What are the annual investment and operating costs for the hardware? Are they particularly high or low in relation to comparable hardware? Why?

- Does the company have a lot of different and incompatible hardware at the same "level" (for example, many minicomputer technologies, many PC types)? Why? What are the potential cost savings from cutting down the number of variants?

- How does the hardware architecture match up with the company's organisational structure? Typical examples are highly centralised hardware in a highly decentralised organisation — and vice versa.

- How is the running of the hardware managed in general, and the running of local equipment in particular? How professionally is the operational work done?

- Are there clear strategies for which software and what types of applications should run on different categories of computers? How does the present situation measure up to these guidelines? Are there examples of software running on an unsuitable hardware platform — in both cost terms and functional terms (for example word processing and spreadsheet on a mainframe)?

- What sort of networking potential can the hardware manage? Can the hardware be effectively linked up with the communications networks relevant to the company?

- How operationally stable and accessible is the hardware?

- Load/degree of utilisation

- Response times

- Normal up-time per 24 hours

- Availability as percentage of normal up-time

- Are the company's communication linkages good enough?

- Are all the necessary resources available from one and the same workplace?

- How do the selected networks measure up to trends in technological development? Have systems been chosen with high "survivability"?

- How are network operations and monitoring managed in general?

- How do the selected networks match up with the company's hardware? Are many mutually incompatible networks used because of hardware incompatibilities? Has this led to undesirable "locking-in" to suppliers?

- Are the networks adequately secured against tapping, misuse of information, physical damage etc.?

- How would you rate the network systems in terms of overcapacity/undercapacity? Is there expansion potential?

Assessment of Basic Software

Operating Systems and On-line Monitors

- Are there different operating systems on the same hardware platform? Why?

- To what extent do the operating systems entail undesirably close ties with suppliers?

- What is the potential for using standard applications and tools with the selected operating system platforms?

Database and Filing Systems

- To what extent are database and filing systems tied to particular hardware platforms and/or operating systems?

- Are many database/filing systems used on the same hardware platform? Why?

- To what extent are industry standard database/filing systems and/or international standards used in user interfaces?

INFORMATION REQUIRED BY OPERATIONAL MANAGEMENT

"If you don't know the score, you don't know if you are winning"

Experience has shown that only a small proportion of managers really know how well their departments and companies are actually performing and therefore many plans are made and decisions are taken without the support of factual information. As well as this, there are no means of measuring the benefit or otherwise that results from those decisions.

It is essential therefore that systems are set up to continuously monitor performance, and this section will attempt to address three questions:

- What information does a manager need?

- How should the information be collected and collated.

- What are the best means of presentation to be easily understandable and cause maximum impact?

In this section, we concentrate on the information required by operational managers and front line supervision to run day-to-day business operations effectively. *Financial* information obtained through ratio analysis is also essential — this is discussed in some detail in Chapter 8.

Accounts

Most companies have a fairly well established accounting system and more and more of these are now being computerised. However, there still seems to be a basic mistrust of the computer systems, and it is surprising how much duplication of effort takes place with manual systems being continued for months and even years after the computer systems have been installed and running satisfactorily.

These computer systems make the production of monthly trading accounts very simple and straightforward and therefore the trading account should be available very soon after the end of the month. However unless firm deadlines are set, there often are inordinate delays in producing the figures, many companies not being able to complete the accounts until weeks after the end of the month, and really too late to be of significant value. There seems to be a preoccupation by accountants for absolute accuracy, whereas from a management information point of view, speed is of the essence. One or two per cent inaccuracy is of no significance and can easily be corrected in the next month's figures.

The presentation of monthly accounts should be kept as simple as possible. It is often very difficult, especially for the non-accountant to assimilate pages and pages of tightly packed computerised printouts. Naturally there has to be detailed backup of the figures presented that can be referred to if necessary, but for maximum impact and ease of understanding, there should be a one page summary showing Sales, Direct Costs of Sales, Indirect Costs for the main departments in the company, and of course the most important bottom line "Trading Profit".

In order to answer the question "Are we winning?" it is essential to have some targets against which the performance is measured, therefore targets or budgets are an essential part of the management information system.

Budgets and Budgetary Control

Budgets are frequently viewed as exercises that are carried out at the beginning of the year (or very often after the beginning of the year) and then, because they require so much time and hassle to prepare, they are then fixed until the next year. This was particularly true before the advent of the computer spreadsheet.

Budgets should be looked upon as plans and immediately those plans become unrealistic, they should be reviewed.

The computer spreadsheet is a very powerful tool for many management information systems and especially for the preparation of budgets. If they are properly designed, all the calculations are automatic and changes to any figure can be instantly reflected throughout the spreadsheet so that they can also be extremely useful for carrying out "What if?" analyses.

The most difficult area in the preparation of a budget is that of sales forecasting and therefore both for budgeting purposes and for production planning when a company is making for stock rather than against customer order, it is absolutely essential to get forecasts as accurate as is possible.

Sales Forecasts

Because of the difficulty in accurately forecasting sales, it is important to gather as much information as possible, and not to rely on one source. It is suggested that the following can give useful indications:

- **Order Book.** Obviously if firm orders have been received for product, this must give the most reliable indication for future sales in the short term, however in the longer term, very few companies, particularly when the production cycle time is relatively short, have the luxury of order books extending further forward than a month or two. Nevertheless, if records are maintained of order book value, then trends can be picked up as to whether the rate of order intake is increasing or decreasing.

- **Enquiry Rate.** A good indication of order receipts in the future should be the rate of enquiries or quotations that are being processed, records of level of enquiries or quotations should be kept.

- **Conversion Rate.** If the conversion rate of enquiries into firm orders is calculated and recorded on an ongoing basis then a more reliable sales figure should be capable of being predicted from the enquiry rate.

- **Historical Sales Information.** If accurate historical records are kept of actual sales, then underlying trends can be picked up, particularly if moving averages are used to smooth month to month variations. Moving twelve month averages are especially useful if sales are of a seasonal nature.

- **Sales Projections from representatives and agents.** Sales forecasts tend to be particularly unreliable when they are supplied by representatives and agents who invariably overestimate their capabilities and make wildly optimistic forecasts.

If there are a range of products it is not good enough to forecast overall sales values, each product should be forecast separately in terms of quantities and selling price. It is no good to forecast to sell 1,000 apples and actually receive orders for 1,000 oranges. You will not be able to supply the oranges, and you will be left with a stock of 1,000 apples!

Using all the above information in a balanced and unprejudiced manner should allow reasonably accurate sales forecasts to be made, especially if these forecasts are reviewed and updated at regular intervals and past forecasts and actual performance are compared.

The importance of the accuracy of the sales forecast cannot be too highly stressed as it affects the whole operation of a manufacturing company:

- The procurement of materials

- The labour requirements

- The ability to minimise delivery lead times

- Reduction of stock holdings

- Improve cash flow.

The forecasting of cash flow is notoriously difficult because not only is it entirely dependent upon sales, it is also affected by the amount of credit taken and given as well as interest rates, capital expenditure etc.

A company than can accurately forecast its cash flow is usually a company that has good management information systems and is well controlled.

Materials

In most manufacturing companies, materials make up the largest proportion of actual costs, so that if materials can be accurately controlled then the largest expenditure is controlled and potentially the greatest savings can be made.

In order to monitor the performance of materials control, the following measurements might be made:

- **Stocks.** These can be divided into Raw Materials, Work in Progress, and Finished Stocks. Continuous monitoring of these must be maintained.

- **Materials price variance.** If standard costings are used then this can be defined as:

$$\frac{\text{Value of materials purchased at standard price}}{\text{Value of materials purchased at Actual cost}} x 100\%$$

- **Materials usage variance.** This should be a measurement of the materials wastage factor.

- **Service Ratio.** This will monitor the performance of the stock control system and is particularly important in the electronics industry where a product may have many hundred different components and if one of them is not available then not only the product cannot be made, but also all the other stocks will be held and cannot be sold.

- **Purchasing Commitment.** Stock holding and cash flow control are very dependent on the rate of flow of raw materials into a company. If the value of outstanding purchase orders for materials is monitored, then prior warning can be received of potential increases in stocks and cash flow problems.

Labour

- **Labour Efficiency.** This is best measured by the following simple formula:

$$\text{Product efficiency} = \frac{\text{Standard hours produced}}{\text{Hours paid for}} \times 100\%$$

Once the overall efficiency has been established then this can be utilised for production loading and budgeting purposes.

- **Absence.** A measurement of the average absence rate will give a measure of the number of employees required to produce a given number of hours work. This can be defined as:

$$\text{Absence rate} = \frac{\text{Hours lost}}{\text{Nominal working hours}} \times 100\%$$

- **Labour Turnover.** A measure of the effectiveness of personnel policies, wage rates etc. in relation to other companies in the area is very useful information, particularly bearing in mind the time and cost of training new personnel. It is surprising that many managers feel that their labour turnover is low but when the actual turnover is measure, it can be found to be well over 30 per cent.

Credit

Most computerised accounting systems can produce aged schedules of creditors and debtors, but as well as this, a measurement of average days credit taken and given in relation to total purchases and sales will give a good indication of the effectiveness of credit control within the company.

Presentation

"A picture is worth a thousand words". To this well known saying, perhaps the following could be added "A picture is worth ten thousand numbers".

It is impossible for managers to assimilate all the figures that can be produced by computer systems and to pick out trends and variances.

The spreadsheet is an ideal tool for collecting, collating and presenting information and the following are some examples of how information can be presented in order to produce the best understanding and impact of vital management information.

Product Record

As previously stated, sales forecasting is probably the most difficult area of planning and budgeting, so that a full understanding of the pattern of sales of every product is very helpful in accomplishing accurate sales forecasts and production planning.

The example of a product record illustrated in Figures 28.8 and 28.9 shows how a spreadsheet can be used.

Figure 28.8: Product Record Illustrated by Spreadsheet

Product Record   Product   Product 1

Sales 199x-199x	May	Jun	July	Aug	Sept	Oct	Nov	Dec	Jan	Feb	Mar	Apr	Total
Sales forecast	650	650	650	600	550	500	400	100	250	300	350	500	5,500
Sales forecast cum.	650	1,300	1,950	2,550	3,100	3,600	4,000	4,100	4,350	4,650	5,000	5,500	
Forecast MMA	432	412	392	393	410	426	438	444	432	433	451	458	
Sales actual	708	525	958	420	573	657	371	72	178				4,462
Variance	58	(125)	308	(180)	23	157	(29)	(28)	(72)				
Sales actual cum.	708	1,233	2,191	2,611	3,184	3,841	4,212	4,284	4,462	4,462	4,462	4,462	
Cumulative variance	58	(67)	241	61	84	241	212	184	112				
Sales MMA	436	407	412	398	417	446	455	460	441				
Budget sales value	6,500	6,500	6,500	6,000	5,500	5,000	4,000	1,000	2,500	3,000	3,500	5,000	
Actual sales value	6,716	4,985	9,116	4,139	5,507	6,130	3,810	718	1,841				
Budget unit sales value	10.00	10.00	10.00	10.00	10.00	10.00	10.00	10.00	10.00	10.00	10.00	10.00	10
Actual unit sales value	9.49	9.50	9.52	9.85	9.61	9.33	10.27	9.97	9.25				
Variance %	-5.1%	-5.0%	-4.8%	-1.5%	-3.9%	-6.7%	2.7%	-0.3%	-7.5%				
Sales qty. last year	1,102	880	898	589	343	304	264	20	398	284	136	412	5,630
Sales value last year	8,869	6,986	6,679	4,974	3,028	2,512	2,354	201	3,402	2,212	1,147	3,827	46,191
Average unit price	8.05	7.94	7.44	8.44	8.83	8.26	8.92	10.05	8.55	7.79	8.43	9.29	8.20
Production													
Production programme	360	360	1,080	720	36-0	360	360	0	360	360	360	360	5,040
Production prog. cum.	360	720	1,800	2,520	2,880	3,240	3,600	3,600	3,960	4,320	4,680	5,040	
Production actual	360	360	1,080	720	360	360	360	3,600	3,600	3,600	3,600	3,600	
Production actual cum.	360	720	1,800	2,520	2,880	3,240	3,600	3,600	3,600	3,600	3,600	3,600	
Stock	200	25	157	457	239	96	186	74	184	244	254	114	
Forecast stock													

Figure 28.9: Product Record Bar Graph

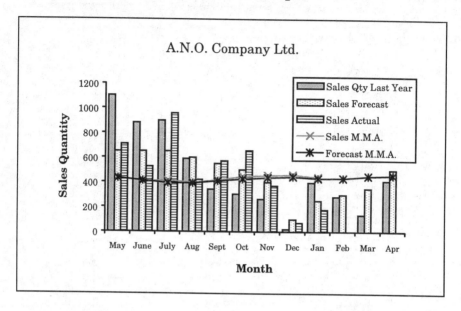

The monthly and cumulative sales forecast can be compared with the sales in the pervious year and current year. Moving Monthly Averages (MMA) are automatically calculated over a twelve month period to smooth out seasonal variations. It can be seen how the forecast of future sales will affect this moving monthly average. Therefore, the forecast can be adjusted to give a realistic projection.

A record of the production plan is compared with the sales forecast to compute a forecast of the stock that will result from these projections.

Overall Sales

The individual product records can be consolidated into an overall sales record that can be presented in the form shown in Figure 28.10, the three-dimensional effect allowing easier comparison between the two years.

Figure 28.10: Overall Sales Record

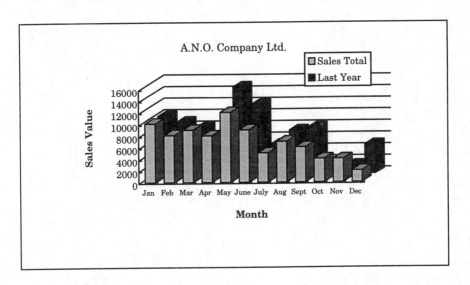

Bar Graphs

Figures 28.11 and 28.12 show how different presentations of the same information can make the information easier to assimilate.

Figure 28.11: Production Output — Bar Chart Type 1

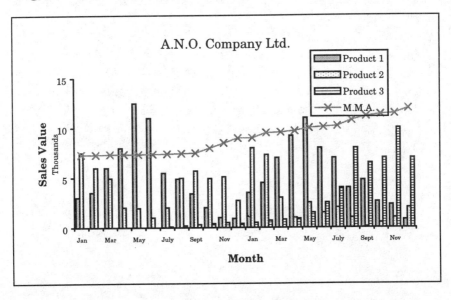

Figure 28.12: Production Output — Bar Chart Type 2

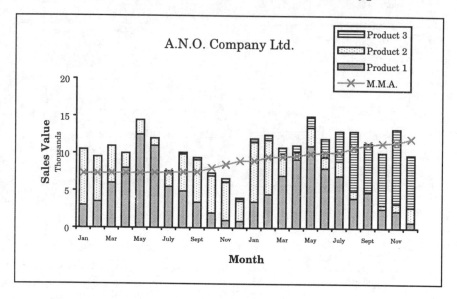

Figure 28.11 shows the sales of the individual products in bar format, but the impact on overall sales is much more clearly shown in the stacked bar format of Figure 28.12. It can also be clearly seen how using a twelve month moving average smoothes out both the individual monthly and seasonal variations to give a clear trend.

Pie Charts

These are useful for illustrating percentages of a total. The example illustrated in Figure 28.13 not only shows how the magnitudes of costs has varied from year to year but also are proportional in size to the total.

Figure 28.13: Pie Charts

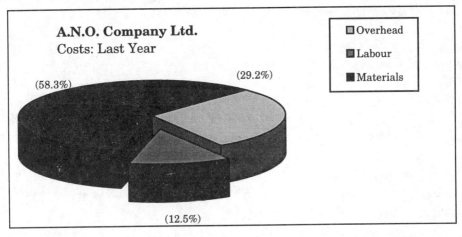

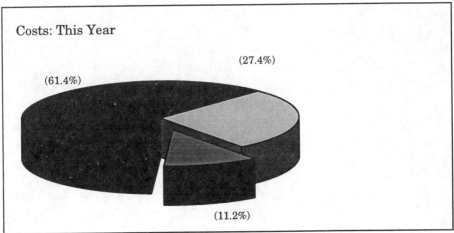

29

INDUSTRIAL CO-OPERATION/ NETWORKING/CLUSTERS

INTRODUCTION

In recent years, there have been fast and unfortunately rather unpredictable changes in the pattern of needs and general constraints.

- The growth in demand for "material satisfaction" is subsiding, with increasing competition and demands for specialisation as a consequence.

- The use of new technologies has lead to increased development costs and reduced product lifetimes with stricter demands on product development and commercialisation time as a result.

Specialisation has meant focusing on a smaller part of the value chain, and at the same time "defocusing" on other priorities. "Defocusing" means that parts of the value chain must be covered by others.

High development costs have meant increasing volume (to reduce unit costs) or cost-sharing with others — in other words, economies of scale which can be achieved through co-operation in product development and production.

Reduced product lifetimes have meant there have to be creative approaches to fast commercialisation — often through marketing co-operation.

Thus co-operation is a fundamental business trend that goes to the heart of the most important challenges for European industry: low competitiveness, high costs, poor capacity utilisation and low marketing competence. This is illustrated in Figure 29.1.

Figure 29.1: The Need for Co-operation

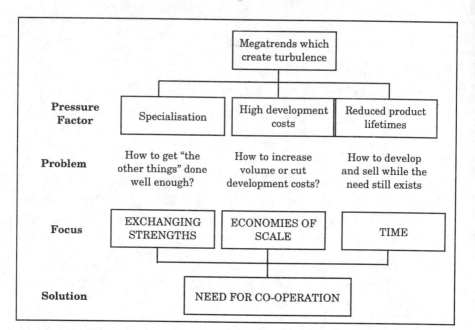

By industrial co-operation we mean a binding commitment to co-operation between two or more parties where at least one of the parties is a manufacturing company.

WHEN ARE INDUSTRIAL CO-OPERATION PROJECTS THE RIGHT APPROACH?

Industrial co-operation projects are only the right approach when the following conditions have been met:

- The co-operation strengthens the general strategic direction of each party, and

- The co-operation means substantial cost reductions.

In addition, co-operation may:

- Permit price stabilisation, or

- Lead to a clear improvement in the strategic advantages of the parties.

The over-riding principle in all cases is that:

A co-operative project must always strengthen the company's general strategy, and must always be tied to the realisation of short-term profitability potential. The long-term effects should come as an extra bonus.

Companies which have worked in co-operative processes know that it takes a long time, that the negotiators gradually get to know one another, and that through time one may find oneself wanting to find co-operative options which in practice do not exist. They also know that the resistance that a co-operative project will always encounter in an organisation must be balanced off against short-term, quantifiable financial results.

But very many industry co-operation projects are not grounded in the above principles, so the percentage of failed co-operation projects is high.

This chapter focuses on how successful industrial co-operation can be ensured by treating the development of co-operation as a strategic process.

PHASES OF THE CO-OPERATION PROCESS

A process of co-operation can be divided into three phases as shown in Figure 29.2:

1. **Establishment of a co-operation strategy**. This phase results in an explicitly formulated co-operation strategy, with clear business arguments, requirements as regards financial and strategic bonuses, and identification of the characteristics of the partner one is looking for.

2. **Assessment and selection of a co-operative partner**, which, on the basis of the co-operation strategy, will result in prioritised candidates and an analysis of their possible motives for wishing to co-operate.

3. **Negotiations and implementation**, which covers the negotiation process in two stages and the subsequent implementation of the agreement and action plans established.

Figure 29.2: Phases of the Co-operative Process

1   Establishment of a Co-operation Strategy

2   Assessment and Selection of a Co-operative Partner

3   Negotiations and Implementation

The three phases are further subdivided into eleven steps as illustrated in Figure 29.3.

Each step is dealt with in turn below. A sample case is used to illustrate the process.

Step 1: Develop an Understanding of the Company's Own Situation

An industrial co-operation project is by nature irreversible (for a period), because the background of any co-operative arrangement is the use of another party's advantages in an area rather than one's own, poorer alternative. A dependency is created; competence is replaced; people leave; new investments must be made; new owners may take over. In our experience it is very difficult to predict all the effects of an industrial co-operation project. So there is a high risk involved in initiating such projects without rooting them in a thoroughly worked-out strategy.

A solid understanding of the company's own situation is also often essential to the implementation of successful negotiations. The negotiations are a kind of game where one's own high priorities are linked with the other party's low priorities. It takes thorough strategic understanding to do this in a way that maximises the company's bargaining power.

Main rule:

> The co-operation process must begin with a thorough identification of the company's own situation (i.e. carry out a general strategic analysis of the business).

Figure 29.3: Phases and Steps in the Co-operation Process

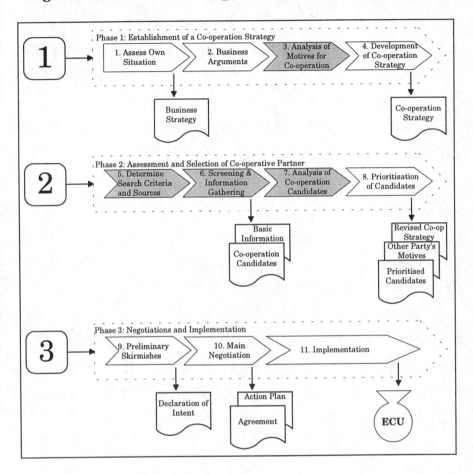

The Case

A manufacturing company — "S" — in the plastics industry with a turnover of about ECU 40 million has achieved a position of market leadership in a domestic application area. However, in recent years a competing industry has begun to make an impact on the market. This new competitor has consistently used lower pricing to take market share. This has led to a loss of market position in all areas other than the one in which the company is the market leader. Within this primary area the company can offer product advantages which to some extent balance the price disadvantages, but this may be a temporary situation, and the risk seems high. Profitability has become poorer, although turnover has remained stable. Weak profitability and low equity have meant that the company does not have the resources to fight off the attacks with more product development or marketing. In addition, the economic trough in the company's country of location since 1988 has led to increasing price pressure which has further weakened profitability. The export share is about 20 per cent, but the company itself does not have the resources to increase this.

Step 2: Formulate the Business Arguments

Step 2 in the co-operation process is to sum up the company's general business strategy in a formulation of the business arguments for co-operation:

- Identification of general strategic direction

- Selection of prioritised analysis areas.

The Case

The chief executive ("*L*") of the company seeks external assistance from a consultant, *B,* who carries out an analysis of the situation, and outlines the company's main strategic challenges as follows:

- *S*'s variable costs are abnormally high, and the contribution ratio can be improved by changing the product design to one that can use other, less expensive raw materials.

- *S*'s production system has a considerable amount of under-utilised capacity, so that unit costs could be reduced by higher production volumes. Furthermore, parts of production could be automated, especially the stacking of products when they come off the machines, which is a labour intensive job.

- *S* has a very solid, but exposed position in its primary market. The product has export potential.

The consultant, *B*, decides in consultation with the chief executive *L* to focus on the following analysis areas:

- The potential for reducing variable costs

- The potential for reducing unit costs in production through utilisation of idle capacity and rationalisation

- On the basis of the above, an analysis of the potential for price reductions in the face of the price pressure on the market

Step 3: Analysis of Motives for Co-operation
As mentioned earlier, the primary motives for co-operation are (a) cost reduction (b) price stabilisation and (c) strategic advantages. There are many techniques available to the consultant to determine the potential for realising these motives. These are discussed in detail later in this chapter.

The Case
The consultant *B* develops the following co-operation motives for *S*:

1. Cost reductions:

   - Purchasing co-operation to reduce variable costs. The potential here seems to be a reduction of about 7 per cent.

   - Added volume in production. There is potential for a reduction of about 40 per cent in unit costs in production, corresponding to a reduction of about 6 per cent in the overall cost position (production costs account for about 15 per cent).

   - Injection of competence to automate production, since this is a new area for the company. The potential is about five man-years, corresponding to about 17 per cent of fixed production costs and 2.5 per cent of the overall cost position.

2. Price stabilisation:

   - An inflow of new product variants which can help to win back market shares outside the primary applications.

3. Strategic advantages:

   - The business portfolio suggests the desirability of marketing co-operation with the market-leading product on the international scale, both to remedy the volume problem in production and to reduce dependence on domestic demand.

- *S* needs a supply of product development competence to secure its market-leading position at home.

- *S* should strengthen its balance sheet result to reduce its financial risk, and to ward off the attacks of its competitors.

Step 4: Development of a Co-operation Strategy

At this stage the development of a co-operation strategy is a matter of a rough prioritisation of the company's needs, as well as a critical review of what the company can offer a co-operation partner.

On this basis a consequence analysis is conducted to help find a company to co-operate with. This systematic need/offer/consequence breakdown will form the basis for the choice of information sources and searching criteria.

The Case:
Figure 29.4 shows the company's outline of a co-operation strategy. The consultant, in consultation with *L*, has classified the company's primary needs as follows:

- *Cost reduction.* Here the company can offer about 25 million ECU in annual purchasing volume. Purchasing co-operation is a possible form of co-operation. However, if *S* could find a potential partner which also produced the raw materials, *S* would really have something interesting to offer.

- *Volume expansion.* The company needs to exploit its production capacity, so it is natural to assume that a partner should be someone in the opposite situation. What *S* can offer is a strong position on the domestic market, which may represent an interesting distribution channel for a co-operation partner.

- *Capital.* *S* needs to strengthen its balance sheet result by an estimated ECU 4 million. The partner must be strong in capital.

Figure 29.4: Outline of Co-operation Strategy for Company "*S*"

Co-operation Strategy		
Our Needs	*What We have to Offer*	*Consequences for Selection*
Primary Motive — Cost reductions	ECU 25 million in purchases a year	Particularly favourable if partner produces our raw materials
		Partner has production competence and "knows about" automation
Volume	Strong domestic market position (market share 40%)	Partner has product portfolio that needs distribution in Norway
		Partner has high capacity utilisation
Capital		Capital-strong partner
Secondary Motive — International sales	Interesting niche product	Partner has international sales organisation outside Scandinavia
	-	
Product development competence	--	Partner has product development competence which can safeguard our primary market

As secondary needs, the consultant specifies international distribution of the products with which *S* has been successful on the domestic market. One consequence of this will be that the partner should have an international distribution apparatus suitable for *S*. Finally, *B* adds product development competence to the "shopping list".

Step 5: Determination of Search Criteria and Sources

It is necessary to translate the company's co-operation strategy into criteria that will form a basis for selecting information sources and searching techniques.

The Case:

B decides to concentrate the search on the following specific criteria:

- A plastics raw materials producer

- Headquarters outside the company's home location

- Without its own distribution channel in the company home location

- Share capital in excess ECU 20 million.

In addition, *B* wants to keep an eyes out for "experience data" on a co-operative partner of the following type:

- Strong domestic market position

- Experience of the type of competition that *S* has faced from other industries in its home market

- Good international profile, and well known for having expertise in advanced production technology.

B quickly realises that it will be necessary to combine modern search techniques with industry interviews to find candidates that satisfy these criteria.

Step 6: Screening and Information Gathering about Candidates

The Case:

The search for a possible partner identifies three interesting foreign candidates — *F3* (German), *F4* (Finnish) and *F6* (Swedish). Two of these satisfy the wishes *S* has as regards experience. In addition, *B*'s interviews have revealed three local firms (*F1*, *F2* and *F5*) which may be relevant candidates. None of these produces the company's raw material, but they may have other motives. One firm has the potential of becoming an important customer for *S*, and *B* wonders whether backward integration may be a motive. The two other Norwegian firms are competitors with *S* in the secondary market areas where *S* has lost market share. The question is whether the strategies of these companies are compatible with intercompany co-operation.

It is most important in the co-operation processes to have enough alternatives — thus the consultant, *B*, decides to obtain information on all six alternatives.

Step 7: Analysis of Co-operation Candidates

In co-operation projects, the analysis of the potential co-operation partners cannot be carried out without conducting interviews with the various candidates. This is because one needs knowledge of the other parties' strategies to understand their motives. This kind of information is sensitive, and can normally only be obtained in personal meetings.

Once one has understood the strategic situation of the various co-operation candidates, the alternatives are analysed on the basis of the company's co-operation strategy — but now as if the roles had been exchanged.

Figure 29.5 is an overview of the characteristics of the candidates in relation to the co-operation strategy.

The Case:

The consultant, *B*, gets the Chairman of the Board of *S* to send a short fax to the chief executive of each of the companies, and within a week *B* follows up on the phone. From one of the local and one of the foreign firms, *B* "gets the cold shoulder", and so these are temporarily disregarded.

B conducts interviews with the remaining four candidates. The results are mixed. One of the local firms (*F1*) expresses very strong feelings about focusing strategically in the area that competes with *S*. This fits badly with B's idea of future production co-operation. The other local firm (*F2*) which has the potential of becoming a customer, shows keen interest, but the chief executive exhibits an attitude that makes a bad impression on *B*. *B* thinks that *F2* might easily have the motive of wanting to "slaughter" *S* and dismiss the management. The two foreign candidates both show great interest. *F3* is a German firm, but during the conversation it emerges that the company is in the process of being taken over by a US company. *B* thinks this might mean distractions in the negotiation phase, because the managers will be more occupied with thinking about their own future than about *S*. The fourth firm, *F4*, is Finnish. *B* notes that the chief executive says that he is familiar with the challenge facing *S* in the other market segments, and that *F4* has managed to contain this competition on its Finnish home market.

B sums up the information as presented in Figure 29.5.

Figure 29.5: Analysis of Co-operation Candidates

Criteria	F1	F2	F3	F4
Primary motive:				
Producer of raw materials	no	no	yes	yes
Automation competence	high	medium	high	high
Distribution motive / Norway	no	yes	yes	yes
Capacity utilisation	---	high	high	?
Investment capacity	medium	high	medium	high
Secondary motive:				
International distribution	none	limited	strong	strong
Product develop. competence	not relevant	strong	medium	strong
Our assessment of economic potential for partner	medium	limited (except takeover)	strong	strong
Expressed motivation	some	strong	strong	strong
Our objection	wrong strategy	high risk (mgmt)	being taken over	OK!
Priority		3	2	1

Step 8: Prioritisation of Candidates

The essential thing in prioritising co-operation candidates is not to focus on the interests expressed by the interviewees in the initial interviews. Company co-operation is a complex process in which motives often lie hidden and may be difficult to identify. The surest guide when prioritising will, for experienced consultants, be the financial motive of the other party or their apparent lack of one: "Follow the money!".

Only when the financial motivation is genuine and "rings true" should other qualitative factors — for example, the expressed motivation — be assigned crucial importance. The financial situation of the candidates is of less importance as long as it is acceptable, but means much more if it is under a minimum level.

Timing is much more important in co-operation processes than most people think. Bad timing must not be confused with a lack of motivation — in six months' time the company may be the prime candidate. Important examples of situations which should be given a low priority as far as timing is concerned are:

- Change of management (defocusing)

- Strategy changes (indecision)

- Budget periods (lack of time for follow-up).

The Case:
B critically reviews the analysis of the co-operation candidates. What would make one of the firms seriously consider investing about ECU 4 million in S? Since B has eliminated $F1$ to begin with because of its strategic focus, there are three candidates remaining. In B's experience this is too low a number to have at the start of a negotiation process — ideally their should have been five realistic alternatives. B quickly realises that company S has more to ask for than to offer. The only really strategically valuable thing the company has is its distribution channels on the domestic market; but this is long-term in nature. So B thinks that it would be unrealistic to obtain a co-operation partner who could not quickly establish a supplier relationship with the company in return for an investment. B therefore decides to give $F4$ the highest priority, followed by $F3$ and $F2$. Also, as quickly as possible, the consultant will "reactivate" the two remaining candidates, because it appears that the local firm $F2$'s main motive is a possible takeover of S. The company, therefore, needs more alternatives.

The bottom line in Figure 29.5 shows the priorities.

Step 9: Preliminary Skirmishes

Contrary to what many people believe, it is rarely difficult to set up a first meeting for negotiations; but the possibility of arranging the second meeting may depend on how the first was set up. Most chief executives will go for a co-operative arrangement that benefits their company, as long as their own position will not suffer. In cases where this might happen (for example mergers), the Chairman of the Board should therefore be present at the first meeting. In co-operative arrangements in which the elimination of lower-level joint functions is a possibility, the Managing Director should also be present.

The crucial things in the first meeting are to:

- Prepare a set of working hypotheses for the financial interests of the parties, and try these out

- Create and consolidate strategic motivation in the parties

- Establish selected areas for further analysis

- Draw up a schedule.

The consultant must adopt the role of being an important catalyst in the co-operation process, and gain the necessary trust from the parties to be given the role of the person responsible for the project. This rarely proves a problem, even though the consultant originally represents only one of the parties.

At the second or third meeting one of the most important jobs of the consultant is to motivate the parties to make a declaration of intent. Such an agreement, which is often no more than one or two pages, will typically safeguard the parties' interest in confidentiality — this is an objection that may emerge after the initial meeting. However, the declaration of intent may also have the following process-related effects:

- It requires an active decision from the parties, since it is a document that has to be signed.

- It typically establishes an official schedule which commits the parties to ensuring that there is some progress.

An experienced co-operation consultant knows when the time is ripe for the declaration of intent, and how much pressure to exert. Now and then it may be best to avoid such an agreement, but only in a decided minority of cases.

Before establishing the declaration of intent, one of the consultant's most important jobs is to keep more co-operation options open. By signing the declaration the company selects one alternative for further discussion — probably for a minimum period of three or four months. But it is still very important not to close off any the other options, because in our experience many co-operation negotiations are broken off at a later stage.

The Case:
B holds meetings with *F4* and *F3*, but at present avoids *F2*. It seems to be "full speed ahead" with both the Finnish *F4* and the German *F3* alternatives.

In the course of the first meetings *B* is convinced that the potential for increased sales of raw materials is the main motive of the Finnish firm, although this is never said openly. *B* considers it critical to establish a ceiling for these purchases early in the negotiations, so that the other party will not set its sights too high. The board of *S* decides that 30 per cent is acceptable and does not represent too high a supplier risk. *B* plays this card out early, and 30 per cent purchases from the Finns is established as a "norm" for the further work.

The progress with *F4* is fine, but the pace drops dramatically when the time for signing the declaration of intent approaches. *F4* involves its own lawyers, and the agreement also "suddenly" has to be approved by other bodies. *B* notes that *F4* is being bureaucratic about the signature and revises his schedule for the conclusion of the main negotiation phase.

Step 10: Main Negotiations
The consultant's role in the main negotiating phase is critical, and it is of crucial importance that the consultant is aware of their own limitations. Any negotiating process needs a person who is able to "talk about something else" and yet also has the ability to "get to the point". Such process qualities can be learnt,

but competence can also be brought in by reinforcing the negotiating team with a suitable person — for example from the board.

In the main negotiating phase one will experience much use of tactics:

- Delaying of deadlines — for example by blaming internal factors that mean postponements will be necessary

- Sudden gambits cutting across previous agreements, to "test" the firmness of the opposite party's views

- The use of third parties to "tighten up" demands — for example lawyers or the company's own board.

An experienced co-operation consultant will be able to navigate their way through these complications, which always arise, because they will base their philosophy of co-operation on the following factors:

- Because the consultant has a strategic attitude to their own and the opposite party's motives, they have a basis for understanding when negotiation gambits are purely tactical and can be rejected.

- Because they always have alternatives, they can control the process in terms of the schedule and the level of the company's own requirements.

- Because they understand negotiation psychology, they understand that all parties need to show their bosses "how good they are", and that the opposite side, therefore, has to win out in some areas.

An important issue in the negotiation phase is when support functions like lawyers and accountants should be brought in. This can be a delicate problem that needs a lot of thought. Too early may mean that the business negotiations are "thrown off course" by overemphasis on details. Too late may mean that the process is delayed by up to two months because the experts have to demonstrate their specialised skills and tell the negotiators how much better they could have been. In general, therefore, outside resources should only be brought in after the fundamental business

matters have been fully negotiated, but before getting down to the
negotiations on detail.

The Case:
B achieves most of what he wants. But B is not "dazzled" by this:
he sees that the reason is probably that he was right about $F4$'s
main motive — short-term profits from sales of raw materials to
S. B "gives" something by agreeing that the capital injection will
be in the form of an irredeemable loan rather than pure equity
capital. This in fact does not play a major role for S, since the liquidity effects are the most important thing. S also accepts a
"fine" if the purchases from $F4$ have not reached the 30 per cent
ceiling within a specified number of years. With this, the negotiation team from $F4$ has been given something to show back in their
company over and above the actual purchasing agreement, and S
gets its other points through.

Step 11: Implementation
The implementation phase begins with the drawing up and approval of an implementation plan. The consultant's role in follow-
up may be:

- To make sure the parties keep their promises, and document
  any failures to do so

- To make sure the short-term financial bonuses are documented, understood and distributed

- To ensure steady progress.

Getting married should not mean one ends up thinking about the
advantages of being a bachelor. The parties must be reminded of
the strategic foundation of co-operation and the joint long-term
goals.

The Case:
A project organisation has been set up to implement the co-operative strategy, where B is the prime mover.
      To realise short-term profit potential, B sets up a working
group in production technology to take a closer look at the ra-

tionalisation potential in the company, and how *F4* can help to solve this problem.

It is too early to say whether the co-operative arrangement will work, but the board and the chief executive of *S* are very satisfied with the results of the process. Above all, the company's basis for a successful future has been strengthened, and the financial risk has been greatly reduced.

SCHEDULING A CO-OPERATION PROCESS

The time it takes to develop company co-operation can easily be underestimated. Experience shows that it can take six months before the main negotiations have been concluded, and meticulous legal advisers can easily delay the final stages by another two or three months. Unforeseen circumstances emerge as a rule and represent further delays: reorganisations, new strategies, replacements of legal advisers, the budget for the next year.

In addition, time is very often used as a tactical negotiation ploy by one of the parties — somebody suddenly has all the time in the world. In practice, it is impossible to respond to this without having alternatives which mean one can make demands for progress, and this is one of the reasons why alternatives are one of the best negotiation cards to have.

HANDLING THE RELATIONSHIP WITH THE BOARD AND MANAGEMENT

In recent years several international studies of the survivability of co-operative agreements have been done. Most of these studies, whether they focus on co-operation of the merger type, joint ventures or for example development co-operation, conclude that there is over a 50 per cent chance that a co-operative agreement will fail.

It is important, therefore, that the consultant understands why co-operative projects traditionally fail. There are two main causes:

- Too little focus on short-term financial gains
- Too little emphasis on organisational grounding.

An industrial co-operation project creates turbulence in an organisation: reporting channels change, the future of divisions becomes uncertain, some people get new bosses. Although these things will not necessarily happen in a co-operative project, the organisation, right up to the level of the Managing Director, will in time develop a view that these things can happen. This creates insecurity and uncertainty about what the future will bring. If the consultant does not take an active approach to counteract this insecurity, the consequence over time is often that people, consciously or unconsciously, begin to work against the co-operative arrangement.

Briefly, we can say that the co-operative process must be accompanied by a certain amount of external pressure (for example from the Board of Directors) and so much built-in motivation and safety nets that the effect of these factors weighs heavier than the organisation's natural unwillingness to see the co-operative arrangement becoming permanent. Some of the implications of this are that the financial effects of co-operation must be easily visible, easily quantifiable and quick in coming (to counteract any tendency to work against co-operation); and that the co-operative arrangement must be well grounded at a high level of the organisation — often at board level (especially if the Managing Director's job or role could be endangered).

PITFALLS IN THE CO-OPERATION PROCESS

Effective co-operation processes are base on avoiding the following blunders:

- Failure to analyse and assign one's own strategic priorities
- Too few candidates
- Not enough allowance for the opposite party's financial motive
- Forgetting that everyone has to gain something
- Forgetting the importance of short-term profit potential
- Insufficient organisational grounding.

ANALYSIS OF MOTIVES FOR CO-OPERATION

The analysis of the motives for co-operation is meant to determine the potential for *realising* the necessary conditions for entering into industrial co-operation:

- Cost reductions

- Price stabilisation

- Strategic advantages.

An overview of recommended analytical techniques is given in Figure 29.6. How much emphasis to give to the use of these techniques will be determined in Step 2 of the co-operation process. In our "case company", S, for example, an improvement of the cost position will be the bearing element.

Figure 29.6: Overview of Recommended Analytical Techniques

Cost Reductions	Price Stabilisation	Strategic Advantages
Trend analysis	Industry structure analysis	Boston matrix
Cost allocation	Life cycle analysis	Product/market analysis
Value chain analysis	"S" curve analysis	Customer structure analysis
Capacity analysis		Buying criteria analysis
Sensitivity analysis		Strengths/weaknesses analysis
Phased cost reduction programmes		Risk analysis

Tool: Trend Analysis

An analysis of the company's cost position begins with a trend analysis for the most important cost categories. Experience indicates that a comparison of three different years over a six-to-ten-year period will give the best results — for example, 1982, 1986 and 1990; but two reference points over a five-year period, for example, will also as a rule give a clear frame of reference.

Figure 29.7 shows the developments between 1985 and 1990 in the case of company *S*. During this relatively short period the company's contribution margin as a percentage of sales has been reduced from 45 per cent to 37 per cent. This immediately provides a basis for attacking the company's primary problem: price pressure and the increase in variable costs. Consequently, the consultant must do the necessary analytical work to draw conclusions on how much of the margin reduction is due to price reductions and cost growth respectively.

Figure 29.7: Trend Analysis of Cost Structure

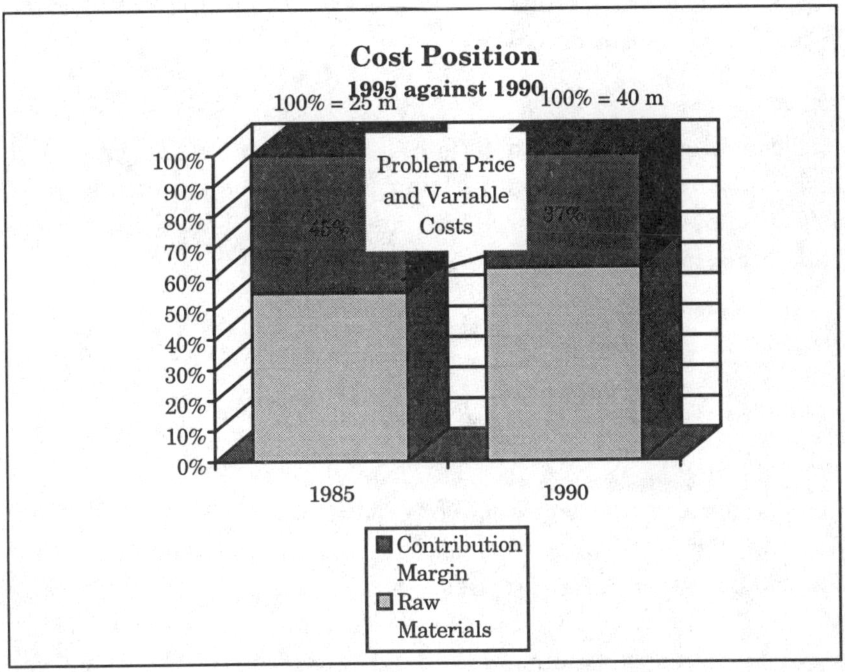

Cost Position
1995 against 1990
100% = 25 m   100% = 40 m

Problem Price and Variable Costs

45%   37%

100%
90%
80%
70%
60%
50%
40%
30%
20%
10%
0%

1985   1990

■ Contribution Margin
▨ Raw Materials

Tool: Cost Allocation

After an analysis of past trends, the analytical work continues with the allocation of the company's fixed costs — with the special aim of identifying reduction potential through intercompany co-operation. Ordinary costing requires one type of cost distribution, and marginal analysis of incremental volume requires another. Similarly, co-operation projects require their own approach.

The costs of each step of the process and activities must be allocated such that the direct costs disappear when the process step or activity is eliminated.

This costing concept, called "causal costing", is particularly important for industrial companies where the company must choose between producing for itself rather than purchasing from others.

The causal costing method is fundamentally different from the traditional "direct costing" concept. For a machine line at the start of a production system, direct costs will normally include a percentage of the division's maintenance costs, interest and depreciation on the machines etc. From the co-operation perspective, the question is, however, what costs can be eliminated by an industrial co-operation project?

The Case:

The consultant looks into *S's* production system, and examines the first part of the manufacturing process. The consultant asks for the company's own cost allocations for this stage of production, and obtains the following information:

Variable costs:	1,000
Direct costs:	2.0 mill.
Volume (units):	2,000

The costs up to the next stage of production are thus ECU 2,000 per unit. The company management informs the consultant that the company can purchase ready-made semi-manufactured components in bulk at ECU 1,900, so they are considering closing down this stage of production and perhaps co-operating with their sub-supplier.

B wants to examine this more closely and subsequently finds out that the company has included a percentage of maintenance and production management costs, and interest and depreciation on the ECU 2.0 million in direct costs. *B* thinks the machinery has no second-hand value of any significance. Using the causal costing concept, *B* allocates the costs as follows:

Direct costs:	1.25 mill.
Allocated costs:	0.75 mill.

B also finds out that with small changes in shift scheduling and organisation the speed of the machines can be increased by 25 per cent and thus produce 2,500 units without increasing costs.

B reasons as follows: The relevant costs that are eliminated by the phasing-out of the production stage are only ECU 1.25 million. At full capacity utilisation these costs would amount to ECU 500 per unit. *B* goes to the management of *S* with these conclusions and tells them that co-operation with the sub-suppliers may be interesting, but only if they can offer a permanent price level of less than ECU 1,500 per unit. The decision is shelved!

The causal costs concept is also relevant to staff divisions like production management, purchasing, finance and marketing. Here too divisional costs will as a rule be fundamentally different from the costs which in fact disappear in intercompany co-operation — examples are percentages of other divisions' costs, data processing costs, rent, etc.

Tool: Linkage of the Company's Cost Structure with the Value Chain

After the various divisions' costs have been allocated in accordance with the above guidelines, they are filled in in the company's value chain (shown earlier in Figure 7.2 on page 181) as shown in Figure 29.8. The direct relative importance of causal costs in the value chain thus provides a very effective focusing tool for finding where the emphasis should be placed in finding interesting co-operation options. Understanding the relationship between direct causal costs and overhead (allocated costs) is important because:

- In co-operation in which the company's own production is taken over by others, only the direct costs (in the short and medium term) of one's own company are eliminated.

- In co-operation in which volume or activity is added, only the direct costs are normally increased (and not even these if the activity has idle capacity — see the next point).

- In co-operation where one staff division is to replace the corresponding functions in two different companies, it is similarly true that the one party's direct staff costs are eliminated (in the short and medium term).

Figure 29.8: Cost Allocation over the Value Chain

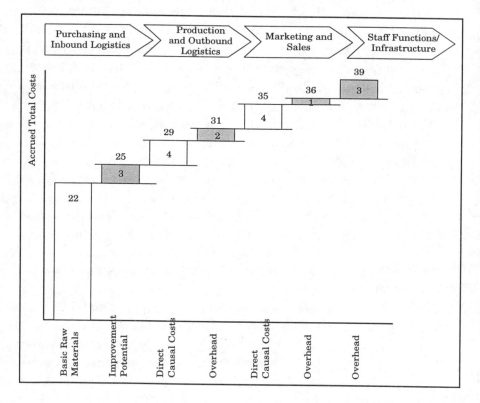

The Case:

B concludes that costs can be influenced most in purchasing and production.

Tool: Capacity Analysis

An important tool in planning co-operation projects is an analysis of the capacity of the various divisions. The identification of capacity potential is an activity traditionally associated with production. But is may be just as important to develop an understanding of the capacity inherent in the company's infrastructure — for example in finance/accounting, stocks and marketing/sales.

The essence of capacity planning is:

> Understanding when the cost "leaps" come, and how the company can be given added volume to optimise capacity utilisation in all its divisions, so the company's value chain will be "capacity-balanced".

The Case:

B finds that by reorganising production capacity can be increased from the current 40 million to 56 million (i.e. by 40 per cent) without increasing "overhead" functions in production. The company has recently invested in a new computerised control system, and with this, turnover can grow to about 100 million. *B* also examines the capacity of the other divisions, and finds out that they can all handle a 40 per cent volume increase without substantial cost leaps. True, another two sales reps must be engaged, but in marginal terms this is insignificant because the 16 million in extra turnover will give the company a gross incremental contribution margin of about ECU 6 million. So *B* decides to let the capacity ceiling of production determine the volume strategy in relation to a co-operative partner.

Tool: Sensitivity Analysis

A potentially effective tool for understanding the effects of a co-operation strategy is drawing up sensitivity analyses for the most important cost elements and plotting these on a diagram indicating the potential for improvement with, for example, a plus or minus 5 – 10 per cent change in these cost factors.

With this approach the search for co-operation partners can be focused on relations which could reduce those costs where the effect of an improvement would be greatest.

An example of such an analysis is shown in Figure 29.9.

Figure 29.9: Sensitivity Analysis

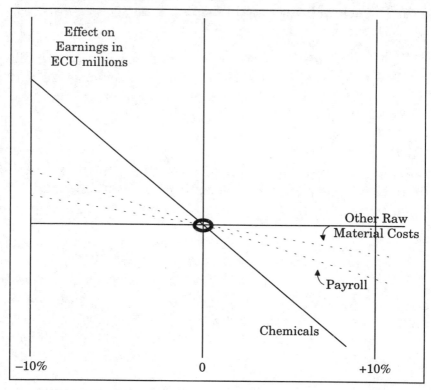

Tool: Phased Cost Reduction Programmes

Phased cost reduction programmes are a process technique that helps the organisation itself to identify reduction potential and prioritise relevant measures. The technique is that management, working with a consultant, gives the various divisions the job of drawing up planned measures for a 5 per cent cost reduction which will not harm the performance of the organisation. After the programme has been processed and approved, the same is done again, but this time with a 15 per cent reduction as the target — that is, a further cut of 10 per cent. Finally the process is repeated with a 25 per cent reduction.

If properly done, this technique produces very well-processed plans for ways in which cost reductions can be carried out and which will affect the organisation's performance as little as possible. In relation to the issue of potential co-operation partners this is a useful aid in realising short-term gains.

Potential for Realising Price Stabilisation

The target of this activity is the identification of how co-operation can bring about price stabilisation — that is, the maintenance of a price level, or an extended lifetime for a price level, which would otherwise be reduced. This area of focus is especially important for companies in the following situations:

- When the company has an efficient production system, but lacks market position and profile.

- When the company's products are nearing the end of their life cycle, and there is a need for new product variants.

- When the company's product lifetime is facing considerable challenges due to new technology or manufacturing processes.

- When the industry structure is on the move, and strategic alliances are concentrating market power among fewer actors.

Tool: Industry Structure Analysis

All studies of the influence of industry structure on price levels indicate that firms with high market shares are more price-leading — that is, that concentration of market power increases the potential for bringing about price stabilisation.

In situations of declining prices — for example due to trade cycles, market stagnation, changes in technology etc. — market alliances will be a sensible priority for intercompany co-operation.

Tool: Life Cycle Graphs

The position of a product in a life cycle graph is crucial for predicting market maturation and stagnation. But at the same time the life cycle curve provides information about the necessity of renewing the product spectrum to counteract future price drops. In the co-operation context this can mean:

- Access to new product variants

- Access to new technology

- Access to product development competence.

Tool: "S" Curves

The "S" curve concept was developed in the seventies to illustrate how new technologies cause turbulence because of completely new assumptions for the improvement potential of products. Figure 29.10 illustrates the "S" curve concept.

Figure 29.10: "S" Curve Analysis

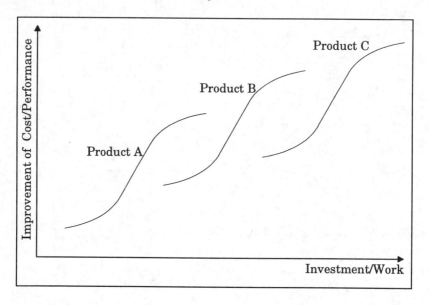

If we apply it to our industrial co-operation model, it is important that the company understands where on the "S" curve the product currently is. If the position is far down, there will probably be room for future improvement in the price/performance ratio, and the product lifetime is hardly a key issue. However, if the placing on the "S" curve is higher up, so that it is in practice costly and difficult to improve price/performance, this may indicate that the company is facing considerable market challenges, and an expansion in the company's product range and/or manufacturing technology will be far more important.

The Case:

For company S the situation is that there is much to suggest that the product is high on the "S" curve. The price pressure from other industries offering substitutes indicates that other production concepts have better conditions for reducing costs. So it is important for S to procure product development competence from someone who has experience of a corresponding competitive situation.

Potential for Improving Strategic Advantage

The aim of this activity is to identify how co-operation can improve the company's strategic advantages or position. This area of focus is especially important for companies in the following situations:

- When the company's business portfolio is in a state of imbalance.

- When the company's customer structure is fragmented or shows signs of weakness.

- When the company has a competence gap in relation to the buying criteria on the market.

- When the company's risk profile is one of high exposure and should be improved.

Tool: The Boston Matrix

Figure 29.11 shows the traditional BCG (Boston Consulting Group) matrix, which is a tool for long-term planning of the balance among product lines or business areas.

Tool: Product/Market Matrix

A typical product/market (P/M) matrix is reproduced in Figure 29.12. While the BCG matrix is a "macro" tool for planning the long-term business profile, the P/M matrix is a "micro" tool for analysing production line possibilities in various application areas. Two co-operation alternatives plotted on the same P/M matrix will provide considerable understanding of market synergies in product lines and the sales apparatus.

Figure 29.11: The Boston Matrix

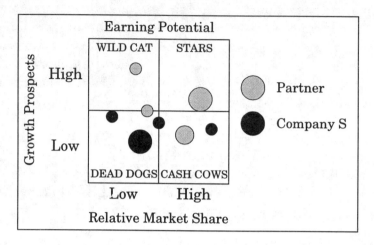

Figure 29.12: Product/Market Matrix

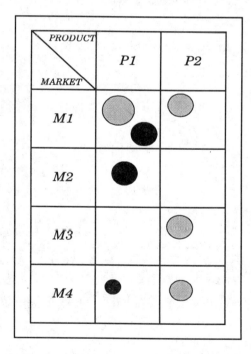

Tool: Customer Structure Analysis

For many companies it is not difficult to demonstrate inconsistencies between the company's goals and strategies on the one hand, and its customer portfolio on the other. The most common gaps take the form of:

- Too many small customers (fragmentation)

- Emphasis on the wrong industry

- Customers with insufficient potential

- Markets with low barriers against competitors.

A comparison of the customer portfolios of co-operation candidates with one's own customer structure will thus be an important prioritising tool. However, this is typically an activity that the parties carry out at the later stages of the co-operation process because of the sensitive nature of the information.

Tool: Improving Satisfaction of Buying Criteria

Figure 29.13 shows the transition from a product/market matrix to an analysis of the importance of the buying criteria for this P/M segment. Our own company is facing competence challenges, and a co-operative partner should be able to inject the resources necessary for better satisfaction of the critical buying criteria that determine the customer's decision to buy.

Tool: Fill In Strengths against Weaknesses

Figure 29.14 shows the company's and the co-operation candidate's strengths and weaknesses placed on the value chain. The over-riding principle is that co-operation should be based on the parties' strengths. This means that co-operation alternatives where one party is pressurised into actions which reduce that company's strengths should be avoided. But this can be far more difficult to implement in practice than one might think at first glance. In company mergers, for example, location often turns out to be a burning issue, despite the fact that one of the parties may have a substantially better point of departure in terms of storage functions and logistics associated with an effective location.

Figure 29.13: Buying Criteria Analysis

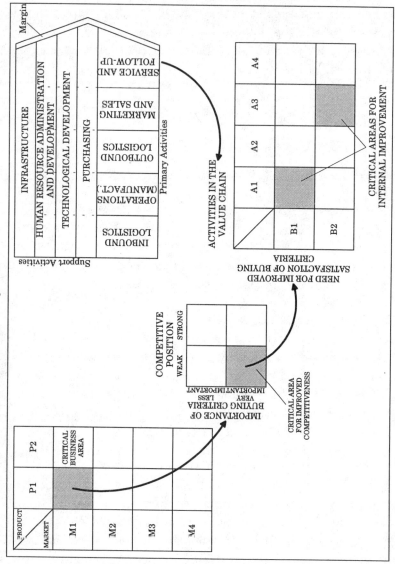

Figure 29.14: Filling in Strengths and Weaknesses

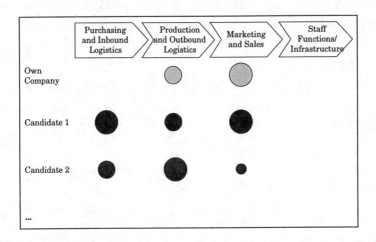

Tool: Risk reduction

An important — and often underestimated — motive for co-operation is the reduction of risks — financial, market-related, technological, process-related or organisational (for example with the injection of new management competence).

Figure 29.15 shows a model for the consequence analysis of risk. Our case company *S* has identified injection of capital as an important motive for the reduction of market risk. The background of this is that the company does not currently have enough resources to respond to its competitors' attacks with a market or product development effort.

Figure 29.15: Risk Analysis

Risk Factor	Probability	Consequences	Action
Lack of market resources	Already exists	Loss of market share	Capital injection
Market stagnation	High	Reduced earnings	International sales through co-operation

SEARCHING FOR CO-OPERATION PARTNERS

This section describes how one gets from a co-operation strategy to clearly identified candidates for industrial co-operation. The searching process covers two steps of the co-operative process outlined earlier in this paper:

- **Step 5**: Determining searching criteria and sources, in other words deciding where to search and what to look for.

- **Step 6**: Screening and information gathering, where one identifies co-operation candidates and gathers in fundamental information about these on the basis of defined sources and criteria.

As a rule of thumb one should have three real co-operation candidates at the start of the negotiation and implementation phase (Step 9 in the model given in Figure 29.3). This is necessary to ensure real bargaining power. Experience indicates that half the identified candidates will be "dropped" as a result of more thorough analysis and prioritisation (Steps 7 and 8 in the model). This means that the actual searching process should result in the identification of and information gathering on five or six candidates.

The techniques are based on looking directly or indirectly for companies. However, the general principles are about the same for other types of searches (for example for relevant material technologies, laws/regulations etc.).

Difficulties in Searching

The identification of co-operation partners is simple once one has identified accurate and "neutral" qualities that the selected organisations or companies have to exhibit. Identifying, for example, local plastic producers with at least 150 employees is not much harder than looking someone up in a telephone book.

Features which normally lead to very simple identification would include:

- Industry classification

- Product groups

- Address/geography

- Number of staff

- Turnover and profits.

What these have in common is that the information is freely available and is included in most supplier and product catalogues/databases. On the other hand, such catalogues and databases often require accurate specification of the search criteria as in the figure. The use of the Yellow Pages, for example, requires the specification of a geographical area and industry/product classification.

The difficulties arise when exact criteria cannot easily be determined. Examples are searching for potential co-operation partners who:

- Exploit a particular type of technology or competence in the product, production process or production control

- Have idle production capacity of a certain type available

- Have access to a well-developed sales, marketing and distribution apparatus for target markets and customer groups.

These are typical formulations from a co-operation strategy, which is precisely the point of departure for the searching process.

Figure 29.4, presented earlier, gives an outline of a co-operation strategy for the case company S. The form lists the company's wishes, what it can offer a potential partner, and the consequences for the choice of a co-operation partner, all based on the company's strategy and business motives for co-operation.

The right side of Figure 29.4 in reality lists provisional search criteria, but in a relatively imprecise form. The problem is to get from this level to criteria, searching techniques and sources which enable us to identify co-operation candidates.

The working form in Figure 29.16 simplifies and structures this process considerably. Using the form, one is "forced" to decide on the co-operative partner's probable features in a number of areas — first at the general textual level, then by specifying the search criteria, and finally by selecting information sources. It should be stressed that the form can be "used manually" and is not particularly tied to database searching.

Thus, the first step of the searching process is filling in the form in Figure 29.16, and the next step is the use of this information to identify co-operation candidates.

Figure 29.16: Form for Determining Criteria and Sources

Area	General Description	Search Criteria	Information Sources
Strategic Position			
Type of company/ industry	Production company in plastics industry. Possible producer of raw material X (?)		
Products	Product portfolio which could exploit S's market apparatus in Norway		
Markets and customer groups			
Competitors/ Competitive situation			
Supplier factors			
Value Chain			
Product development	Product development competence in S's area of focus		
Production and logistics	High capacity utilisation on own production equipment		
Sales and marketing	International sales organisation outside Scandinavia (?)		
Finance	Strong in capital		
Internal Resources			
Organisation and management			
Personnel and competence	Competence in automation and production technology		
Resources			
Other factors			

Main Types of Information Source

The choice of information source is wholly dependent on how precise one's knowledge is of the features of the partner one is looking for.

In general, various information sources are used to obtain four main types of information:

1. **Information on information sources** — in other words, help with where to search

2. Probable **features of possible co-operation partners** — in other words, information that supplements the form in Figure 29.16 and/or adjusts the co-operation strategy in itself

3. **Identification of co-operation partners** — that is, finding company registration numbers, addresses etc. of companies that satisfy certain criteria

4. **Basic information about named companies** (for example, financial statements for the last three years), after these have been identified.

It cannot simply be assumed that the same information source is suitable for obtaining all these main types of information. The most important information sources are:

- Employees of the company and their "informal networks"

- Customers, suppliers and competitors

- Industry associations and interest groups

- Research institutions and competence centres

- Periodicals, newspapers and article collections

- Product and supplier catalogues/databases

- The co-operation candidate itself (!).

Employees of the Company and Their "Informal Networks"
The most important contribution of employees is often to identify information sources (Information Type 1), and probable features of the partner (Type 2). It is important to exploit the professional skills of staff to detail and specify the features in Figure 29.4 (an

example: what does "automation competence" mean in practice in terms of technologies/search concepts/key words for automation of plastic production?). If there are possible co-operation candidates among the company's present competitors, suppliers or customers, then the staff are also a critical source for collecting basic information (Type 4) of a non-official nature ("gossip").

Customers, Suppliers and Competitors
Current customers, suppliers, distribution channels and competitors may be candidates for co-operation. A systematic review of the company's own information about the surrounding value system may thus help to identify candidates (information of Type 3). A competition analysis of the target industry on the domestic market may also bring out the "winner" features (Type 2) one wants any foreign partner to exhibit on its own domestic market.

Industry Associations and Interest Groups
Industry associations, trade unions and interest groups for various functional areas, job categories etc. are first and foremost suitable for identifying information sources (Type 1) of various categories: periodicals, databases, similar organisations in other countries, key personnel in research/development etc. Industry associations can then be used to identify features of the desired partners (Type 2), typically by means of indirect and direct profession/industry-oriented questions (for example about the state of automated production control in the industry). In overview situations the industry associations may directly be able to provide lists of co-operation candidates (Type 3) from their own membership files etc.

Research Institutions and Competence Centres
These are used in the same way as industry associations and interest groups — that is, especially to identify information sources (Type 1) and features (Type 2) of partners. The main libraries of institutions like the universities, engineering colleges etc. are some good starting points for identifying relevant information databases for electronic searches. Specialised staff in certain product, production and control technologies often have a good informal network with similar competence centres elsewhere.

Periodicals, Newspapers and Clippings Libraries
Databases of clippings from business-oriented newspapers and periodicals can be a help in all four main types of information gathering. The most important area where these can be used, however, is often to identify sources (Type 1) and retrieve basic information (Type 4). In source identification, for example, one can search for newspaper articles about "market developments in plastic production in Europe", or the combination of "production automation" and the key words "plastic or rubber". This type of search is in practice impossible to do manually. Once candidates have been identified, such business databases are typically used to retrieve basic information of the type "find everything written about Company X in the last three years". Business databases normally have free-text search features as well as fixed indices like firm, person, subject etc. Some variants of such databases are "bibliographical" and subject-oriented databases — for example databases combining the business world, technology, research results etc. in the general area of "welding".

Product and Supplier Catalogues / Databases
These are first and foremost suitable for the identification of candidates (Type 3 information) when simple search criteria can be given. Typical examples are the telephone book's "Yellow Pages" and private variants of this — "Kompass Norge" etc. A few databases allow free-text searches for information in product and production technology, product/market focuses etc. These can often be used both to identify features (Type 2) and to retrieve basic information (Type 4).

The Co-operation Candidate Itself
Information retrieval from the candidate itself should not be underestimated as a possibility. If the candidates have been identified, at least all "freely available" information (annual reports, brochures, product sheets, customer-oriented "newsletters" etc.) should be collected.

Figure 29.17 sums up the use of the various types of information sources.

Figure 29.17: Information Types and Sources

Type of Information Information Source	1. Sources	2. Probable Features	3. ID of Possible Companies	4. Information on Companies
Company employees' informal networks	X	X		(X)
Customers, suppliers, distribution, competitors		X	X	
Industry and interest groups	X	X	(X)	
Research institutions/ competence centres	X	X		
Periodicals, newspapers, clippings libraries	X	X	X	X
Product/supplier catalogues/databases		(X)	X	(X)
Co-operation candidate itself				X

Step 5 of the Process: Determining Searching Criteria and Sources

This step consists of the following activities:

- A provisional description of the potential co-operation partner

- Selection of a procedure and information sources for supplementing information on features

- Drawing up key questions

- Supplementation of information on features

- Definition of searching criteria and sources for identification of candidates.

The activities can best be illustrated by working through them for the case company *S*:

Provisional Description of the Co-operation Partner
The consultant *B* sets up the matrix in Figure 29.16 on the basis of the outlined co-operation strategy (Figure 29.4). The features

described are so far relatively imprecise. The management group in *S* meets. They go back to the basis for the co-operation strategy — that is, Steps 1-4 — to find whether information on important features can be supplemented. The motive of purchasing co-operation requires the partner itself to be a producer of plastic raw materials used by *S* in production. In other words, the product type and/or international industry code (the so-called ISIC code) will have been indirectly determined. However, the company wants to be careful about restricting the search to raw materials producers alone.

In discussions, the requirements as regards the partner's readiness to invest (a minimum of ECU 4 million) are tied to a stated minimum turnover and share capital. It is further agreed that they are primarily looking for a company with its head office outside their own country of location, and with a strong position on the domestic market (among the three leading companies on its market). Indirectly, one can also make assumptions about the partner's markets/customer groups. If the partner is to be able to exploit *S's* market apparatus in their home country, parts of the partner's domestic market should have the same structure as *S's*. After the meeting, the description of the co-operation partner looks as in Figure 29.18.

Selection of Procedure and Information Sources for
Supplementing Information on Features
On the basis of the form in Figure 29.16, Consultant *B* phones the main library at the local College of Technology, enquiring where one can find more information on plastics producers, producers of raw materials for plastics, and production automation in the plastic-producing industry. The consultant is told of a special bibliographical database, RAPRA, as well as more ordinary types of database. In the library's register of articles the consultant also finds the names of two key persons with special expertise in plastic production and automation, a professor at the College of Technology and a group leader at the Centre for Industrial Research. These seem to be important starting points for gaining a better understanding of the industry and international actors.

Figure 29.18: Revised Features and Search Criteria

Area	General Description	Search Criteria	Information Sources
Strategic Position			
Type of company/ industry	Production company in plastics industry. Possible producer of raw material X	ISIC = 356 ISIC = 3513	
Products	Product portfolio which could exploit *S's* market apparatus in Norway		
Markets and customer groups	Large industrial companies . . . (?) Market areas where *S* has lost market share		
Competitors/ Competitive situation	Among three leaders on domestic market		
Supplier factors	Self-supplied with raw materials in . . .		
Value Chain			
Product development	Product development competence in *S's* area of focus		
Production and logistics	High capacity utilisation in own production. High degree of production automation		
Sales and marketing	International sales organisation outside Scandinavia (?)		
Finance	Share capital at least = ECU 20 million		
Internal Resources			
Organisation and management	Head office outside Norway		
Personnel and competence	Competence in automation and production technology		
Resources			
Other factors			

B now has the following list of important information sources:

- *S's* production division
- The plastics industry association
- The local College of Technology, Professor *NN*

- The Centre for Industrial Research, Group Supervisor *XX*.

The starting material thus only includes "manual" sources.

Drawing Up Key Questions
The consultant now prepares for interviews with selected information sources. He critically assesses how "open" the identified sources are likely to be and adjusts the questions accordingly. Besides the company's own production division, it is assumed that the college professor *NN*, because of his academic interest, is likely to be most open, and so forms a natural starting point. *B* sets up key questions that indirectly deal with:

- Developments in plastic raw materials and related material technologies

- Industry associations and interest groups outside Norway

- Trends in the automation of plastic production

- The most important challenges facing the industry

- The most important international actors

- Possible sources of more detailed information.

Supplementation of Information on Features
S's production division stresses that *B* should play down the focus on automated production in favour of a more efficient logistical flow. The manager of the division also points out that the firm *F1* has come a long way in both robotised plastic production and JIT ("just-in-time") logistics concepts. *F1* is a competitor to *S* in one of the areas where *S* has lost market share. *B* adds logistical competence as a possible feature of the partner, and decides to include questions about local competitors in the coming interviews.

   In the main, *S's* understanding of the competition is confirmed in the subsequent interviews. The local companies *F2* and *F5* are alternatives to *F1*. Professor *NN* at the College of Technology points out minimum requirements for R&D efforts in plastic technology, and suggests England, Germany, Sweden and Finland as the most likely countries for advanced raw materials production. The German firm *F3* is also mentioned explicitly as a candidate.

Definition of Search Criteria and Sources for Identification of Candidates

The identities of potential Norwegian candidates have already been sufficiently clarified in interviews. For searching internationally the starting point is also good. Figure 29.19 sums up the situation. *B* draws up the following three-point plan for database searching:

1. A search in "European Kompass Online" for "plastic producers" or "plastic raw materials producers" with turnovers at least equivalent to ECU 300 million.

2. Selected companies found in the first search broken down by country. Germany, England, Sweden and Finland are given special attention.

3. A "parallel" search in the "plastics database" RAPRA. Alternative search key words provisionally "automation" and "logistics" in combination with the word "plastic".

The results from Item 3 are compared with the results from 1 and 2 before any further action is considered.

Step 6 of the Process: Screening and Information Gathering

In the last step of the process the candidates are actually identified, on the basis of defined search criteria and sources from the previous step. It should be emphasised that this is a matter of "screening": some selected candidates will certainly turn out to be irrelevant after closer analysis and prioritisation have been carried out. The step consists of the following activities:

- Searching

- Consideration and documentation of the identified candidates

- Supplementation of basic information about the candidates.

Figure 29.19: Criteria at Start of Screening

Area	General Description	Search Criteria	Information Sources
Strategic Position			
Type of company/ industry	Production company in plastics industry. Possible producer of raw material X.	ISIC = 356 ISIC = 3513	European Kompass On-line or other catalogue
Products	Product portfolio which could exploit *S's* market apparatus in Norway.		
Markets and customer groups	Large industrial companies . . . (?) Market areas where *S* has lost market share		
Competitors/ Competitive situation	Among three leaders on domestic market. Experi-ence of competition in . . .		
Supplier factors	Self-supplied with raw materials in . . .		
Value Chain			
Product development	Product development competence in *S's* area of focus.	Keywords: Polymers, Composites	RAPRA?? (Check with Inst. of Tech.)
Production and logistics	High capacity utilisation in own production. High de-gree of production auto-mation. Advanced logistics.	Keywords: Automation, Logistics	RAPRA?? (Check with Inst. of Tech.)
Sales and marketing	International sales organisation outside Scandinavia (?)		
Finance	Share capital at least = ECU 20 million. R&D budget at least = ... million. Turnover at least = ... million.	Turnover > ECU 300 million	European Kompass On-line or other catalogue
Internal Resources			
Organisation and management	Head office outside Norway.	Countries: Germany, England, Finland, Sweden	
Personnel and competence	Competence in automation and production technology. Competence in logistics.	Keywords: Logistics, JIT (?)	
Resources			
Other factors			

Searching

Searching in international databases requires professional competence in setting up the "right" search criteria for the database in question. *B* personally contacts the library service of the nearest Institute of Technology. The librarian goes through B's overview of features, asks questions and comments on the selections. Although *B* has done thorough spadework, the librarian has ideas for improvements. In particular, the librarian thinks that Item 3 of the plan should be changed to searching in an international business database — for example, PTS PROMPT — because *S* is more concerned with market and competitive position than with material technology. In addition, more alternative search words should be added — tentatively, "just-in-time", "robotisation" and "CIM".

Consideration and Documentation of Identified Candidates

Items 1 and 2 of the search produce a total of 17 candidates, ten of them in the four high-priority countries. Item 3 turns up several hundred articles. Skimming the titles removes a number of irrelevant ones. For the remaining articles abstracts are retrieved and reviewed by *B*. Several of the articles point to the companies *F3* (German), *F4* (Finnish) and *F6* (Swedish), all of which were in the selection from Item 2, are raw materials producers with international distribution and have a high degree of automated logistics and production. *B* notes in particular that *F3* was also mentioned by Professor *NN* as early as the survey of features.

B arranges the data gathered in the following folders:

- A folder for each of the three local companies that emerged from the industry interviews

- A folder for each of the foreign companies *F3*, *F4* and *F6*

- A folder for the "second-string candidates", mainly those that emerged from Items 1 and 2 of the search

- A folder for "general industry information", with articles that do not refer directly to individual firms.

The search has produced enough candidates for a meaningful analysis, and a repeated search with "extended" criteria is unnecessary.

Supplementation of Basic Information about the Candidates
For the companies *F3*, *F4* and *F6*, *B* orders the full articles from the business database (not only abstracts), and puts them in the folders. The material is comprehensive and *B* considers that further searching in databases would bear very little fruit at present.

The search is thus in all essentials over. *B* has identified six possible candidates for co-operation, and has collected all the basic information about them. As a last check, *B* phones Professor *NN* at the College of Technology for some more informal information about the foreign candidates.

Summing-up and Tips
The procedure described, and especially the form in Figures 29.16 -29.19, permit a structured transition from a general co-operation strategy to clearly identified candidates. The following factors should be stressed:

- Attach considerable importance to the informal and "manual" network: employees and contacts at customers, suppliers, research institutions etc. These are critical for finding a starting point for the search, and often know about information which never ends up in a database. Don't underestimate gossip!

- To exploit the informal network, plan the questioning in advance, on the basis of what you already know (or think you know) about features of the co-operation candidates and the knowledge of the person to be interviewed. People like to talk about what concerns them if they are asked the right way. Avoid questions which can be perceived as touching on confidential information (for example ask about the number of personnel rather than turnover).

- If you use the database search technique, get experienced help with setting up the search criteria. Set up stepwise and/or "parallel" searches with "manual adjustments" along the way rather than giving too many criteria at once. Never believe 100 per cent in what comes out.

CONCLUSION

Industrial co-operation is necessary, and will become increasingly so if European countries are to face the challenges ahead. At the same time, the development of co-operative projects is a difficult process which makes great demands on the consultant's across-the-board competence and talent for organisational psychology. The foundation of success is to treat company co-operation as a strategic process, where correct understanding of the parties' real financial motives is the most important element.

A co-operation project should always strengthen the general strategies of the companies, and should always be associated with the realisation of short-term profitability potential. The long-term effects should be an extra bonus.

Short-term profitability in practice means a reduction in the cost structure of the parties. Thus the identification of areas for cost savings are crucial in the development of motives for co-operation.

Only once the cost reduction potential has been clarified does it become interesting to look at analyses which reveal longer-term strategic priorities for price stabilisation and improvement of the companies' strategic advantages.

30

PURCHASING

INTRODUCTION

Purchasing in today's industrial environment is no longer a case of shopping around for the best price and delivery for the products or services required by the production unit. It is quite common to find that the cost of purchased raw materials and services amounts to more than 50 per cent of manufacturing costs. Consequently, the company's influence must extend beyond the factory to the vendors from whom purchases are made. It is important that companies today form a strong relationship with their vendors in all areas of operation, including quality control, engineering, production and accounts. It follows that companies should seek to work with their vendors so as they become an integrated part of the overall strategic business plan.

In this chapter, the relationship between company and vendor is looked at under the following headings:

- Specifications

- Purchase Orders

- Purchasing Management

- Vendor Assessment

- Vendor Rating.

SPECIFICATIONS

In general, it is the responsibility of the vendor to ensure that the purchased product conforms to specified requirements.

Specifications can take several forms, including those specifications that are supplied by the vendor as part of their advertised business and those specifications that are supplied by the customer, in written form, as a statement of their requirements. Both vendor and customer must agree that the specification is acceptable and that the material or service that is supplied shall conform to it.

Vendor specifications are generally not negotiable since the material is supplied to a wide range of customers and is standardised to a particular requirement. The customer must therefore satisfy himself that the part or material is suitable for the use to which it is to be put.

A described service, however, is often open to negotiation and can be tailored to suit the application which requires the service. In such cases, it is the responsibility of the customer to specify any changes or deviations in the service required, in written form, prior to commencement. In the case of a service such as printing or cutting, the customer will have to supply artwork or dimensions to the vendor. The agreement will then include elements of both vendor and customer specifications.

Customer specifications — that is, the requirements that are particular to the company — are generated to suit the products and processes in the customer's factory. They are generally unique and not available to anyone else. These specifications should contain data which clearly describes the requirements for the product being purchased and must include all dimensions, tolerances for permissible deviation, inspection procedures, finish, service conditions and any other technical data required. Specifications will be comprised of drawings or of written notes or a combination of both. In general, each component, material or assembly should have its own separate specification in order to avoid confusion.

A service specification supplied by the customer will contain information and technical data on the type of service to be supplied, the frequency or quantity, inspection criteria and any other requirements that have been agreed in advance with the vendor. In some cases, material will be supplied to the vendor to have a service such as plating, painting, printing or cutting, performed on it. It is then the responsibility of the vendor to ensure that the material is in good condition when it arrives and is capable of accepting the service that is to be performed. The vendor must also ensure that the customer-issued material is not damaged during the time it spends in the vendor's factory. In such cases, the service specification should include data on the handling of customer supplied material and its subsequent return.

Written contracts between vendor and customer can be any written document which agrees the purchase of a combination of material, labour and services. Written contracts will usually apply to products or services that have a large monetary value or to projects which will be spread over a long time scale. The purchase price will often be based on phased payments against results or targets achieved. The price will sometimes be negotiable between phases. With a written contract it is important for both parties to agree on the many aspects of the contract that could give rise to conflict. It is also important that both parties recognise each other's rights and requirements. For large contracts, it is advisable for both parties to take legal advice on the wording of the document before agreement.

PURCHASE ORDERS

It is not acceptable for any company to attempt to purchase any material or service without providing a written document describing the requirements of the company and giving an identification number for the vendor to invoice against. Indeed, it is foolish for any vendor to accept a verbal request without written confirmation.

Many small to medium-sized companies do not have adequate ordering procedures which causes confusion, delays and vendor dissatisfaction which ultimately damages the business.

A purchase order must contain several items of basic information:

1. The **name and address of the vendor** and possibly a contact name, to ensure that the document actually gets to the correct person within the vendor's organisation.

2. The **purchaser's name and address** and a contact name so that the vendor knows where to deliver the material and who pays him. It may also be necessary to provide an additional address if delivery is to a different factory location.

3. The **identification of the material or service** to be purchased in a form of words that will be understood by the vendor.

4. The **specification of the material or service**. This may be the vendor's identification number or the customer's specification or drawing which has been previously agreed.

5. The **quantity required**. This may seem quite obvious but it may be that the material is sold by weight, length, volume, multiples of a quantity or perhaps in fractions of the total quantity delivered on a timed basis.

6. **Delivery date or period**. The customer must take into account the vendor's time scale for manufacture and place the order early enough to give the vendor time to deliver so as the customer's own production process is not compromised. On the other hand, the customer should not arrange to get the delivery too early as this may give rise to problems with storage space and cashflow.

7. **Price**. This is the most important item on the purchase order and the one that historically causes most problems for both parties. In most cases, the basic purchase price has been agreed by all parties in advance and is stated clearly on the purchase order. However, there may be other costs associated with the transaction, such as local or national taxes, delivery costs, special packaging costs or installation costs. There may also be discounts for quantity or time which must also be shown on the purchase order. All of these should be identified on the purchase order so that when the invoice arrives at the customer's premises, the accounts department can match both sets of costs and not cause delays and potential conflict.

Finally, the purchase order must arrive at the vendor's premises on time, preferably before the goods leave and certainly before the goods are invoiced. A copy must be kept by the customer so that it can be matched up with the invoice and so that stores personnel can check deliveries that are received against the relevant order.

PURCHASING MANAGEMENT

Purchasing management is an administrative task. The purchasing manager does not have to be an engineer or a financier but does have to be a skilled negotiator. Most small and medium-sized industries may not have a person dedicated solely to purchasing. Nevertheless, the person who carries out this task must be aware of the importance of the purchasing function for the well-being of the company.

One of the most important tasks associated with purchasing management is the creation and maintenance of a supplier database. The latter should be treated as a strategic business document and should be kept up-to-date. The database will contain all the information relating to company purchases across the full spectrum of manufacturing and administration, and will enable the company to find out how much it costs to operate the business.

A supplier database will contain the following basic information:

1. A list of all products and services purchased, identified by product number, specification, company code number, etc.

2. A list of approved current vendors and alternative suppliers, with addresses and contact names.

3. A historical price range for the products and services purchased with an indication of possible trends for future purchases.

4. Identification of any specialised tooling owned by the company but kept in vendors' premises, or any specialised equipment used by the vendor.

5. A list of services available from each vendor even if all are not currently in use by the customer.

6. A record of the vendor's ability to meet the company's quality and delivery requirements. This is generally referred to as a vendor rating.

7. Any other information which will enable the company to obtain a clear picture of their relationship with their vendors.

Purchasing management should have a knowledge of basic raw material costs and labour costs in the industries that they are purchasing from, including a knowledge of future trends for these costs. This information will enable management to assess quotations more effectively by breaking them down into their constituent parts and by knowing where the vendors may be able to give better prices or services. This information can be most useful to the company's marketing management when they are deciding on future price changes for the company's products.

One issue that is common to purchasing management in all industries is the question of the number of different vendors per component. The well-known quality consultant, W. Edwards Deming, once said that "no manufacturer that I know of possesses enough knowledge and manpower to work effectively with more than one vendor on any one item". Nevertheless, it is sometimes astonishing how many individual components are purchased from a multiplicity of vendors by even a small manufacturing company. When it is established, however, how many man-hours are devoted to negotiating price, delivery, specification, vendor assessment, etc. for each component or service purchased, the rationale behind the Deming statement becomes evident.

The one factor which prevents a company from using only a single vendor for a given component is price. Most purchasing managers are of the opinion that their main task is to obtain the best price for each component and to do this continually with every purchase order. They consequently seek quotations from several different vendors for each purchase order written and then place the order with the vendor who gives the lowest price. Many other factors should be taken into account, however, such as delivery, quality, service, and the maintenance of good relationships. All of these factors also cost money, not to the customer directly, but as a component of the quoted price. In some cases, the vendor who bids at the lowest price has done so at the expense of some other factor. The low price vendor may, for example, compromise on quality so as to maintain acceptable margins. Even if a vendor has reduced the price through reducing their own margins, this can prove to be unsatisfactory in that it may threaten the long-term viability of the vendor's operation. If the vendor ultimately goes out of business as a result, the customer will have lost, forever, what may have been a good vendor.

There will be instances when it is necessary to have approved alternative vendors for the same component. This will occur, for example, when a large increase in volume cannot be met in time by the primary vendor or when an item of strategic importance is required and quantity cannot be guaranteed by only one vendor. In these cases, the customer must be able to operate just as effectively with the secondary vendor as with the primary vendor and must treat them both as equals.

The purchasing manager's job should be totally integrated with all other management and administration within the company. The relationship between purchasing management and quality control, finance, production and marketing can be critical to the smooth operation of the business. The purchasing manager should sit at policy making meetings, engineering change order meetings, and contribute to marketing plans. The purchasing manager's knowledge of the cost of manufacture can be invaluable.

VENDOR ASSESSMENT

Very few manufacturing companies assess their vendor's ability to meet their requirements on a continual basis. In most cases, a component is identified by engineering and is incorporated into the product or process that is under development. The purchasing manager is informed, and subsequently obtains quotations for volume plus alternative sources and there the process ends. All too often, there is no investigation into the chosen vendor's ability to maintain the initial quality, or to deliver subsequent orders on time, or even whether the vendor is financially sound.

Some vendor assessments are based on the vendor's historical record of supply. Such assessment is sufficient in many cases, but is not possible for new vendors. Furthermore, as a company develops and expands its product base, it will also expand its vendor base and thus, the smooth running of the company will be subjected to more outside influences. For this reason a vendor assessment programme should be introduced.

Apart from the historical record method of vendor assessment, there are two other methods of assessment which can be used separately or in conjunction with each other. The methods are the use of a vendor questionnaire and a vendor audit.

The questionnaire can be as simple or as complex as is necessary to obtain the information required. The questionnaires used by large corporations which are purchasing from other large companies are generally many pages in length. Even small companies, however, need to know some basic facts about their vendors. The questionnaire will consequently ask the following questions:

- Has the company a quality manual?

- Has the company a quality system?

- Is the company registered to ISO 9000?

- Are the following items addressed?

  ◊ management responsibility

  ◊ contract review

  ◊ document control

  ◊ purchasing

  ◊ product identification

  ◊ process control

  ◊ incoming goods inspection

  ◊ in-process inspection

  ◊ final inspection

  ◊ calibration

  ◊ control of non-conforming product

  ◊ corrective action

  ◊ handling, storage, dispatch

  ◊ internal quality audits

  ◊ training

  ◊ quality records

- Are staff quality conscious?

- Is quality information readily available?

- Is there a planned maintenance system?

- Is there a housekeeping policy?

This document alone will provide a lot of useful information about the company and may be enough to approve them to supply in the short term.

A vendor audit is not always necessary if a vendor proves over time to be a good supplier or if the vendor questionnaire gives a positive result. It is recommended, however, that the following vendors should be audited in all cases:

1. Vendors who are shown by the response given on the vendor questionnaire to have inadequacies.

2. Vendors whose product or service has shown an unacceptable high level of non-conformance to requirements.

3. Vendors or sub-contractors of critical parts or services.

Most vendors will not object to being assessed if they value your business.

A vendor audit should be systematic and comprehensive. A checklist or prompt document may be used to assist the auditor in covering all areas effectively. The auditor should be accompanied at all times by a member of the vendor's staff. In this way the vendor is given every opportunity to explain or justify any non compliances identified by the auditor. The results of the audit should be tabulated on a checklist to enable a classification to be made.

VENDOR RATING

Vendor rating should not be confused with vendor assessment. The latter is used to assess the quality system of the vendor by the means previously discussed whereas vendor rating is used to monitor the performance of the vendor in relation to the quality of each delivery or at the completion of each contract.

The criteria used in rating the vendor is based on quality of the service being provided. The term "quality" in this case can be defined as:

- Conformance to specification

- Packaging

- Documentation

- Delivery.

The term "delivery" normally refers to the number of days late (or early) as against an agreed delivery date. This is particularly important if the supplier is operating a "just-in-time" system. If not, it is usual to allow a plus or minus two day tolerance on the agreed date before the vendor is deemed to have acquired a non-compliance.

INDEX